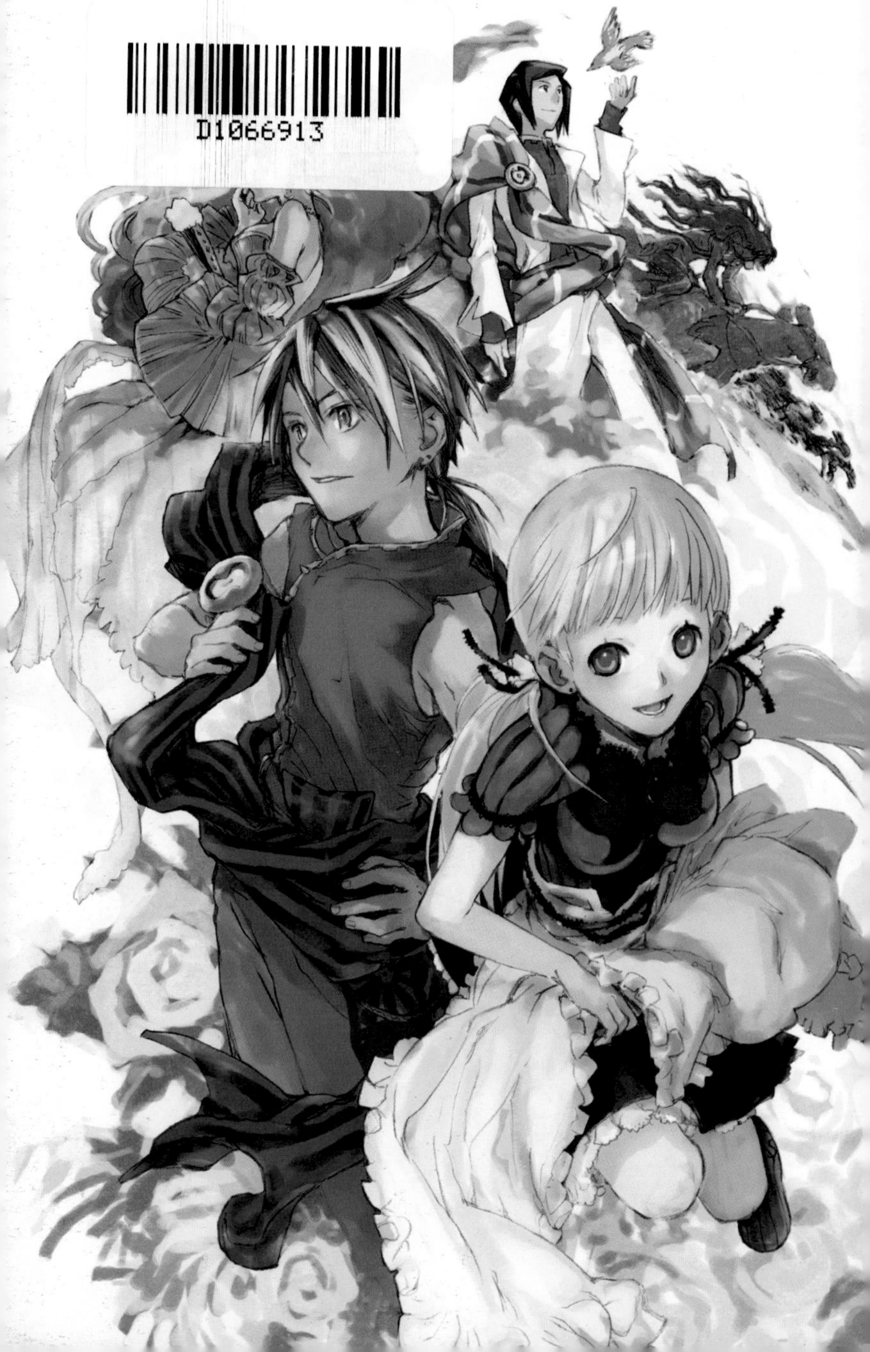

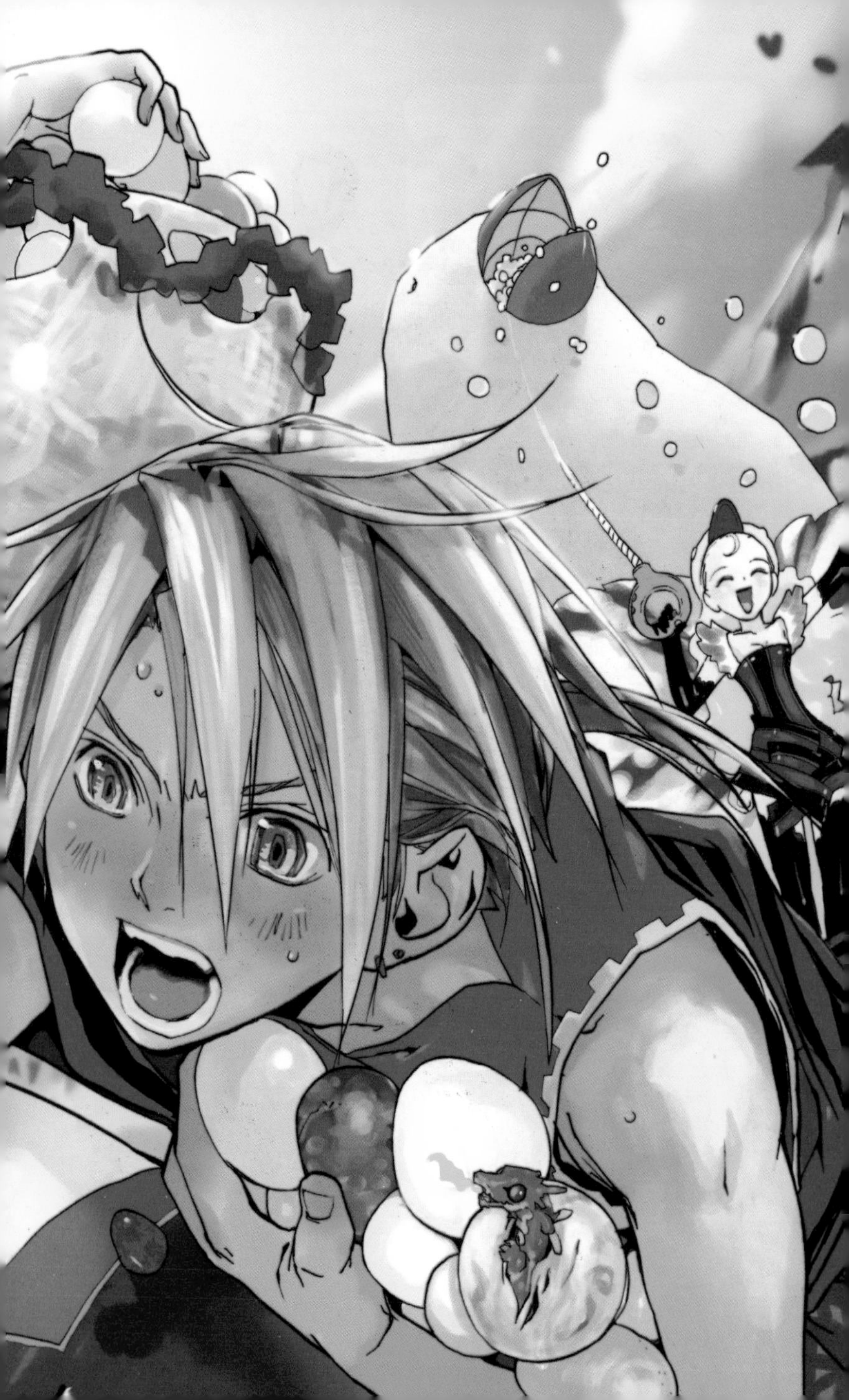

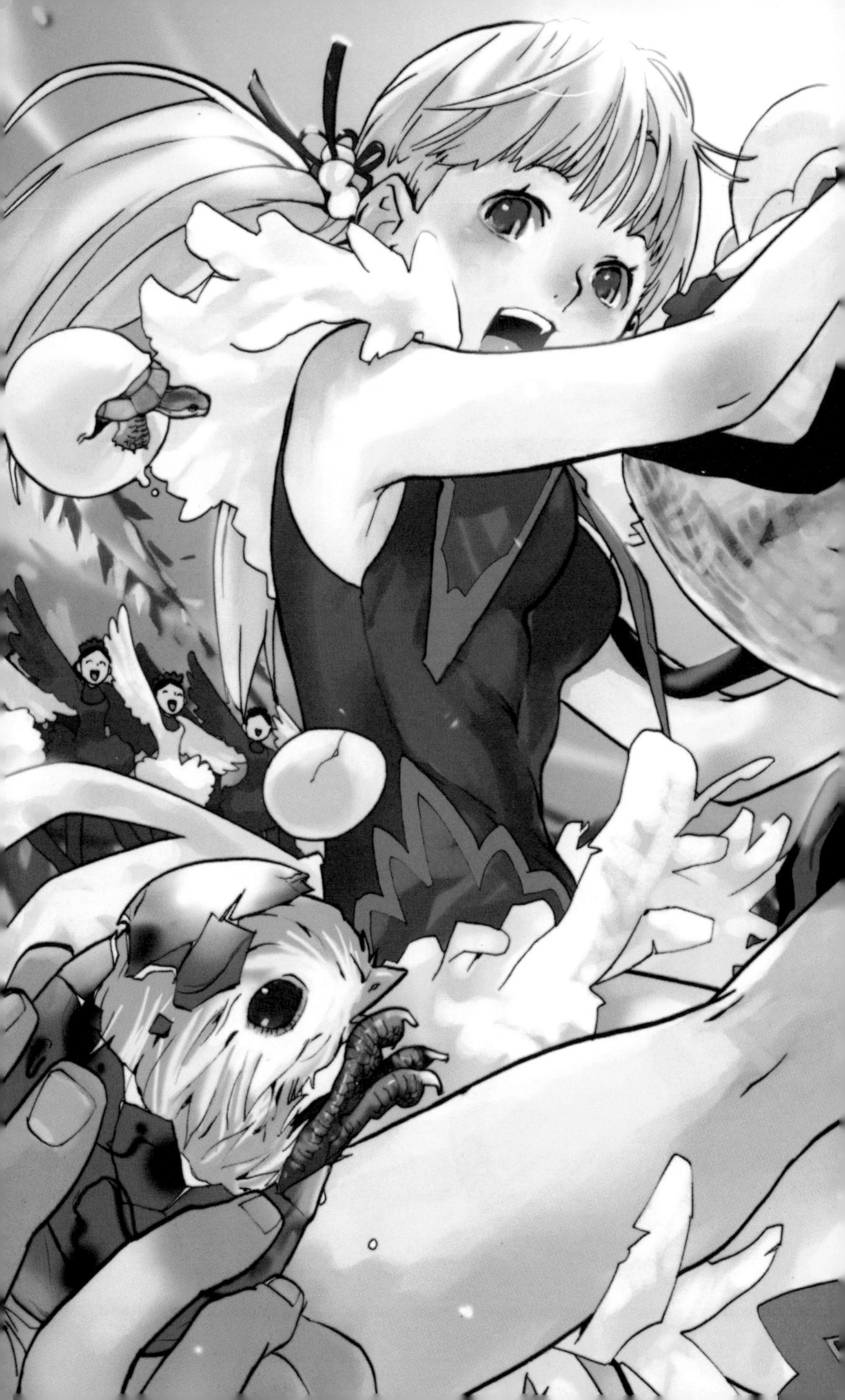

1 CONTENTS

1520

十五二十

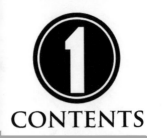

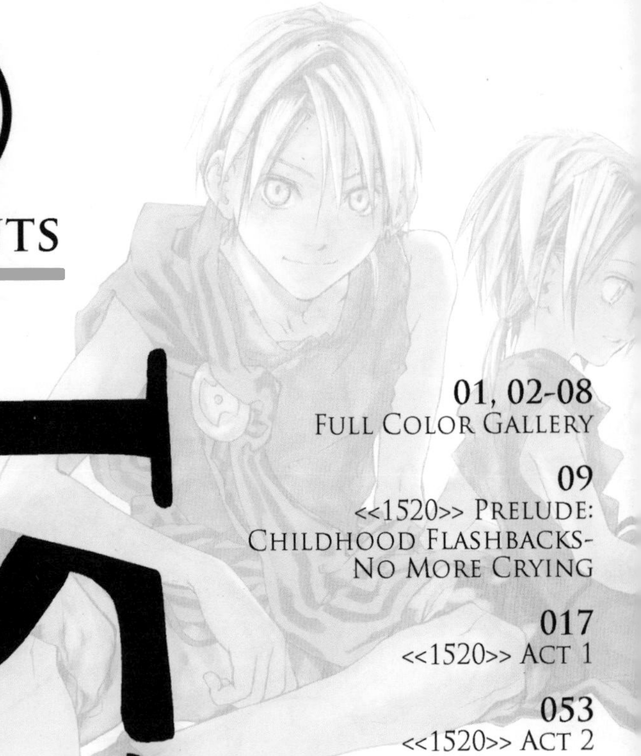

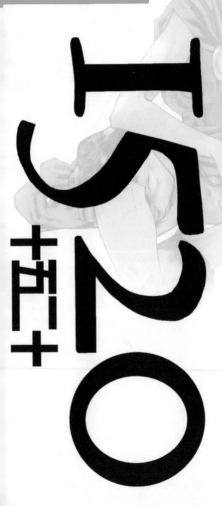

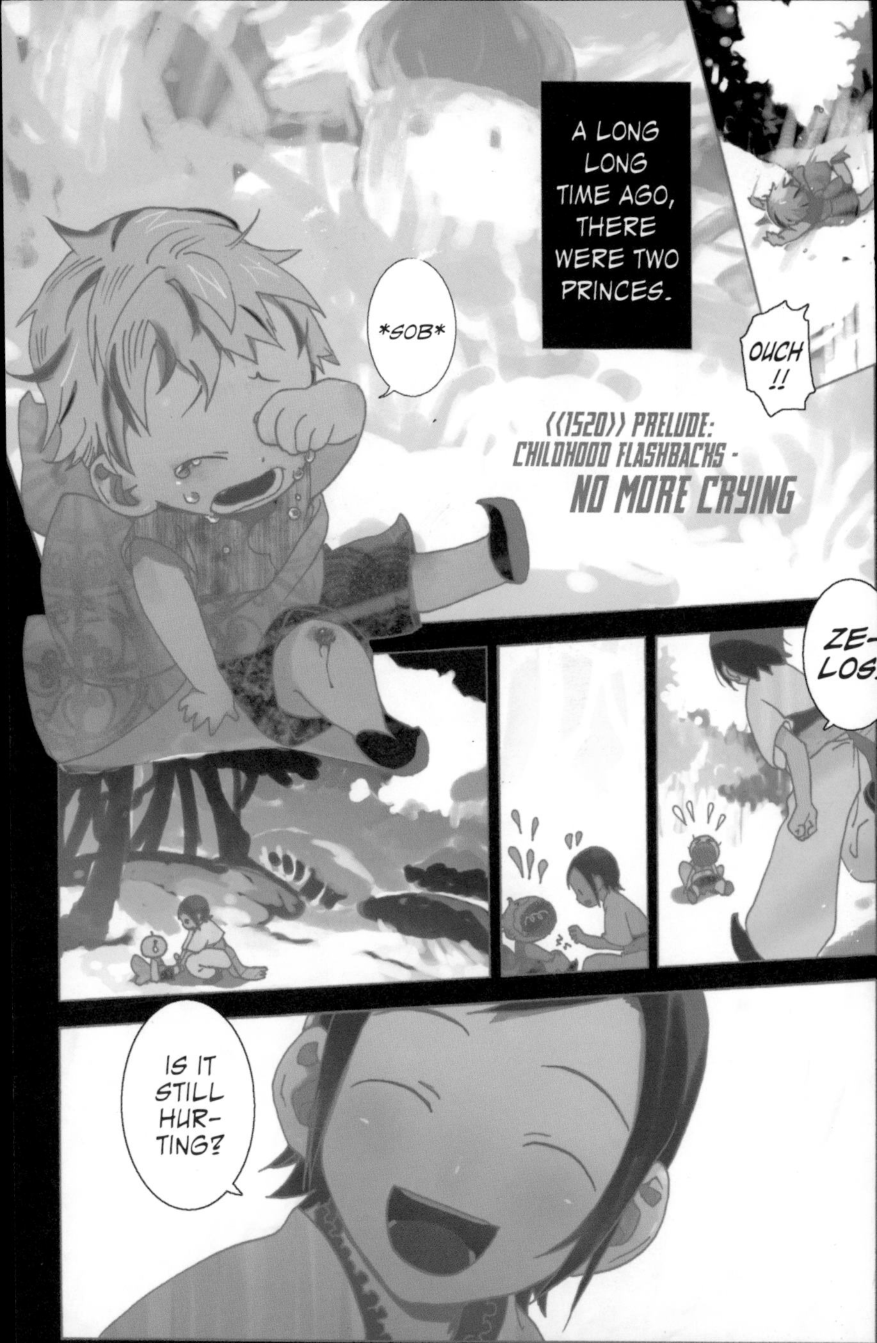
OUCH !!
A LONG LONG TIME AGO, THERE WERE TWO PRINCES.
SOB
((1520)) PRELUDE: CHILDHOOD FLASHBACKS -
NO MORE CRYING
ZE-LOS
IS IT STILL HUR-TING?

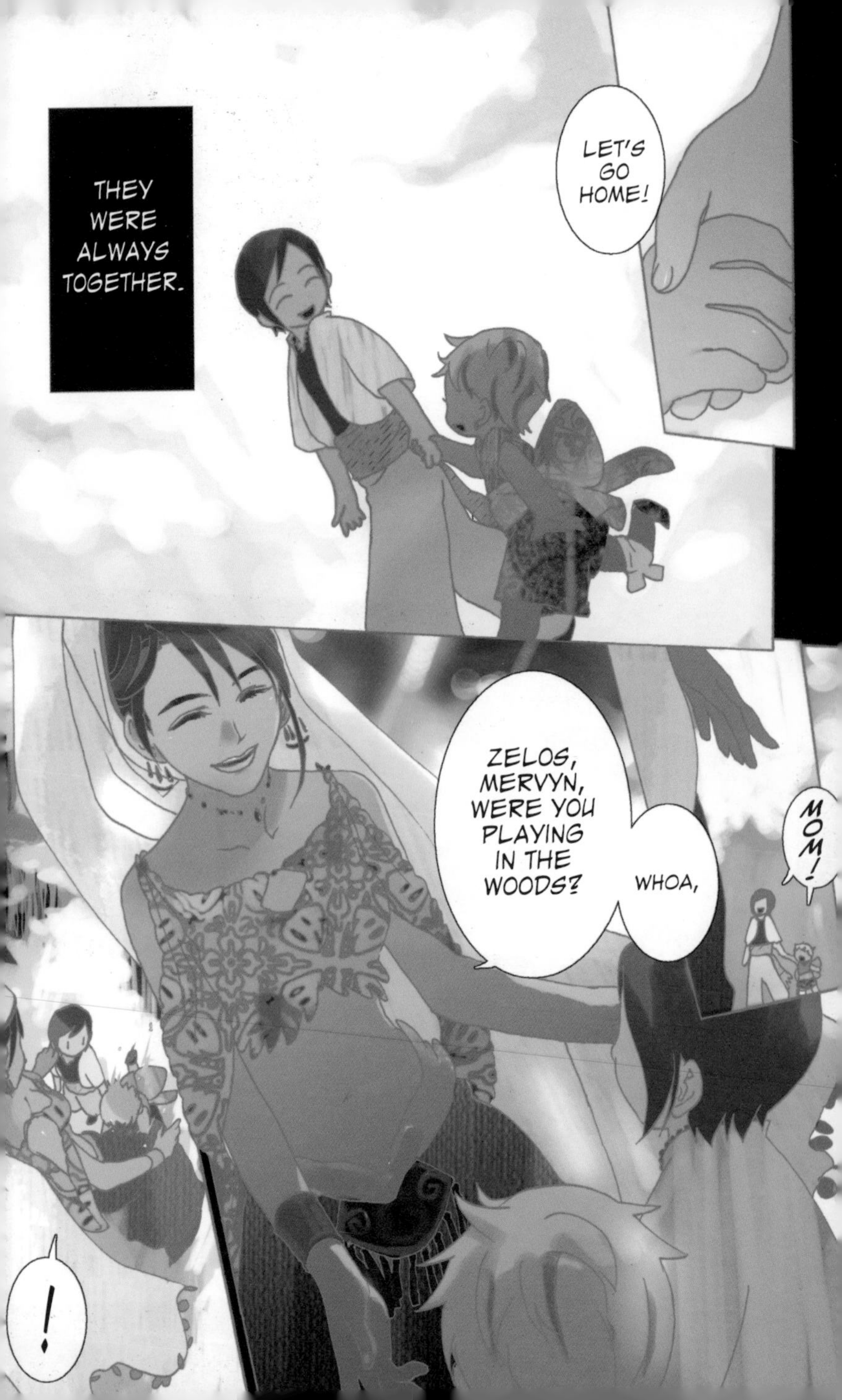
LET'S GO HOME!
THEY WERE ALWAYS TOGETHER.
MOM!
WHOA,
ZELOS, MERVYN, WERE YOU PLAYING IN THE WOODS?
!

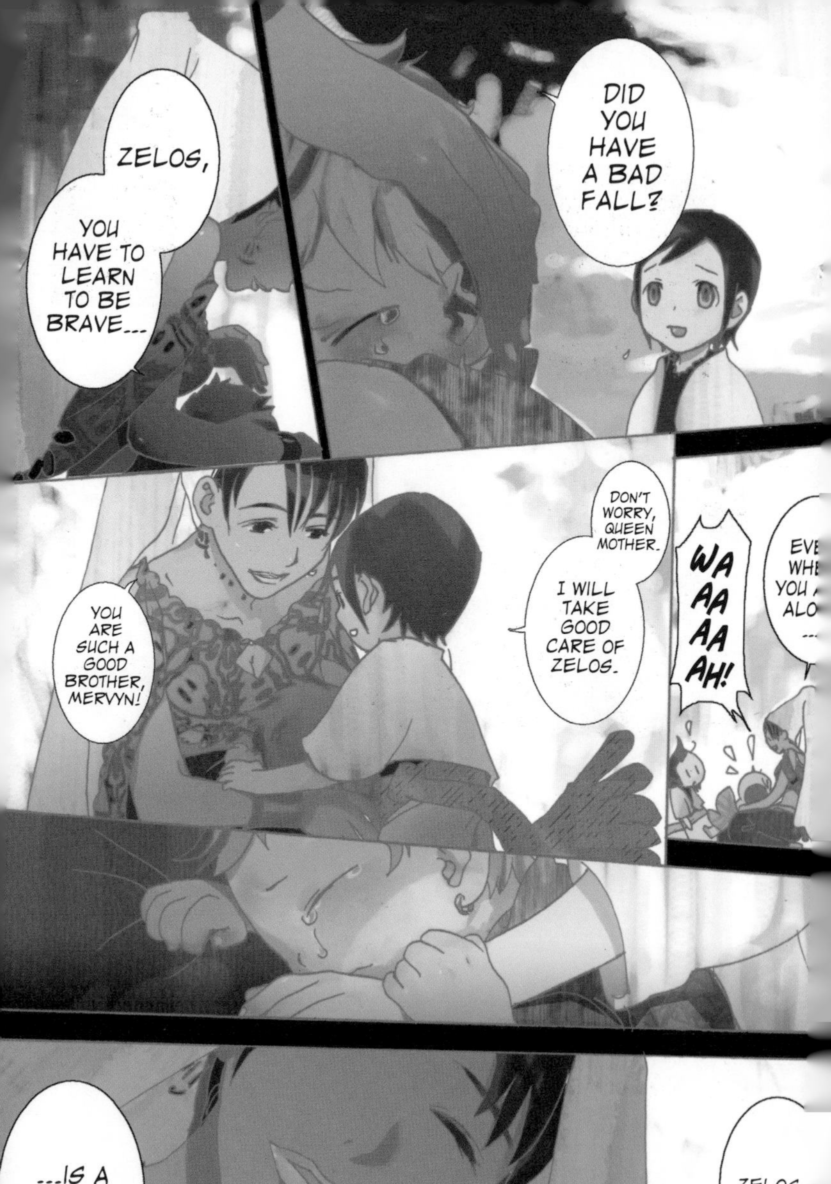
DID YOU HAVE A BAD FALL?
ZELOS,
YOU HAVE TO LEARN TO BE BRAVE...
WAAAAAAAH!
DON'T WORRY, QUEEN MOTHER.
I WILL TAKE GOOD CARE OF ZELOS.
YOU ARE SUCH A GOOD BROTHER, MERVYN!
ZELOS.
...IS A CRYING BABY!

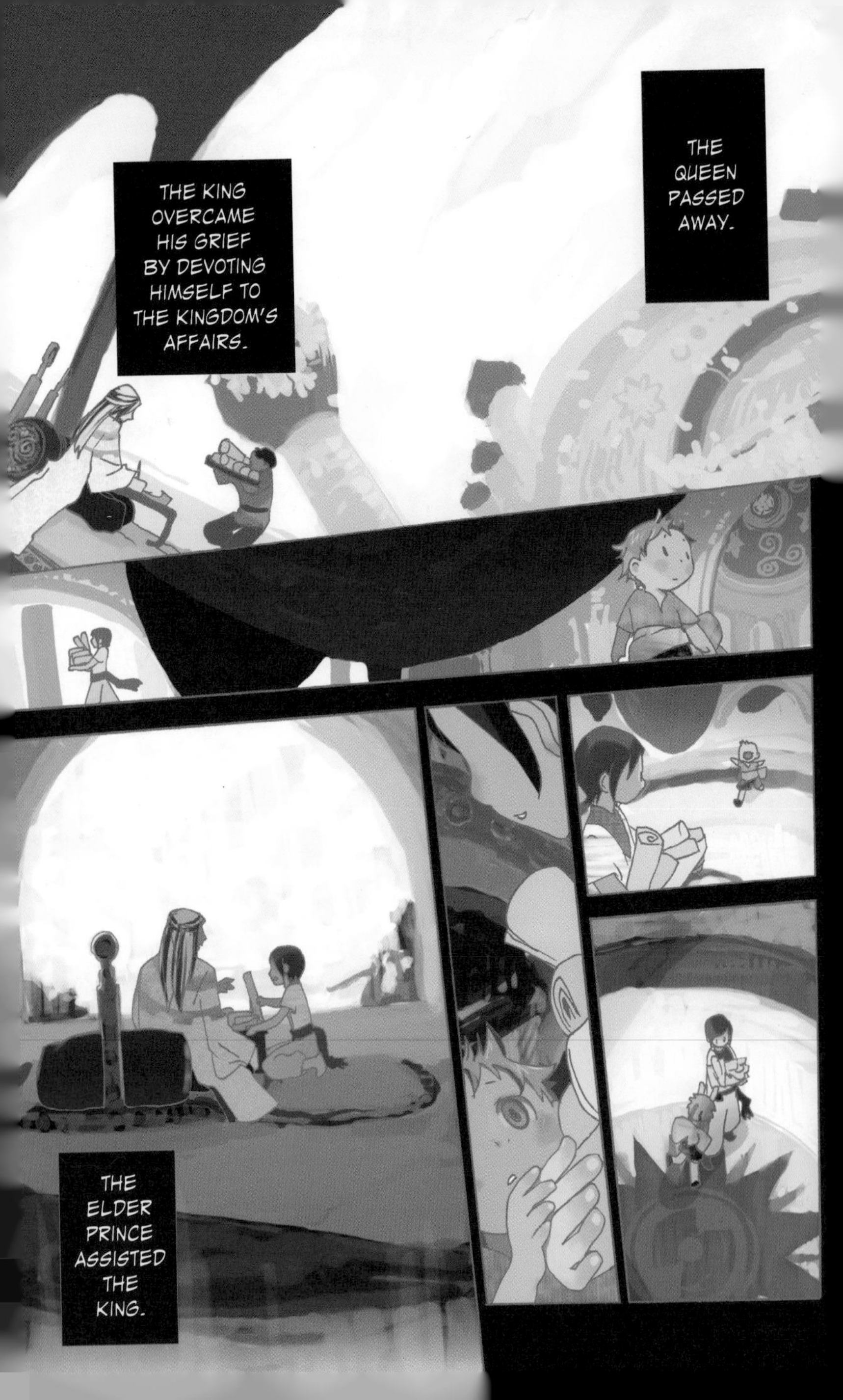
THE QUEEN PASSED AWAY.
THE KING OVERCAME HIS GRIEF BY DEVOTING HIMSELF TO THE KINGDOM'S AFFAIRS.
THE ELDER PRINCE ASSISTED THE KING.

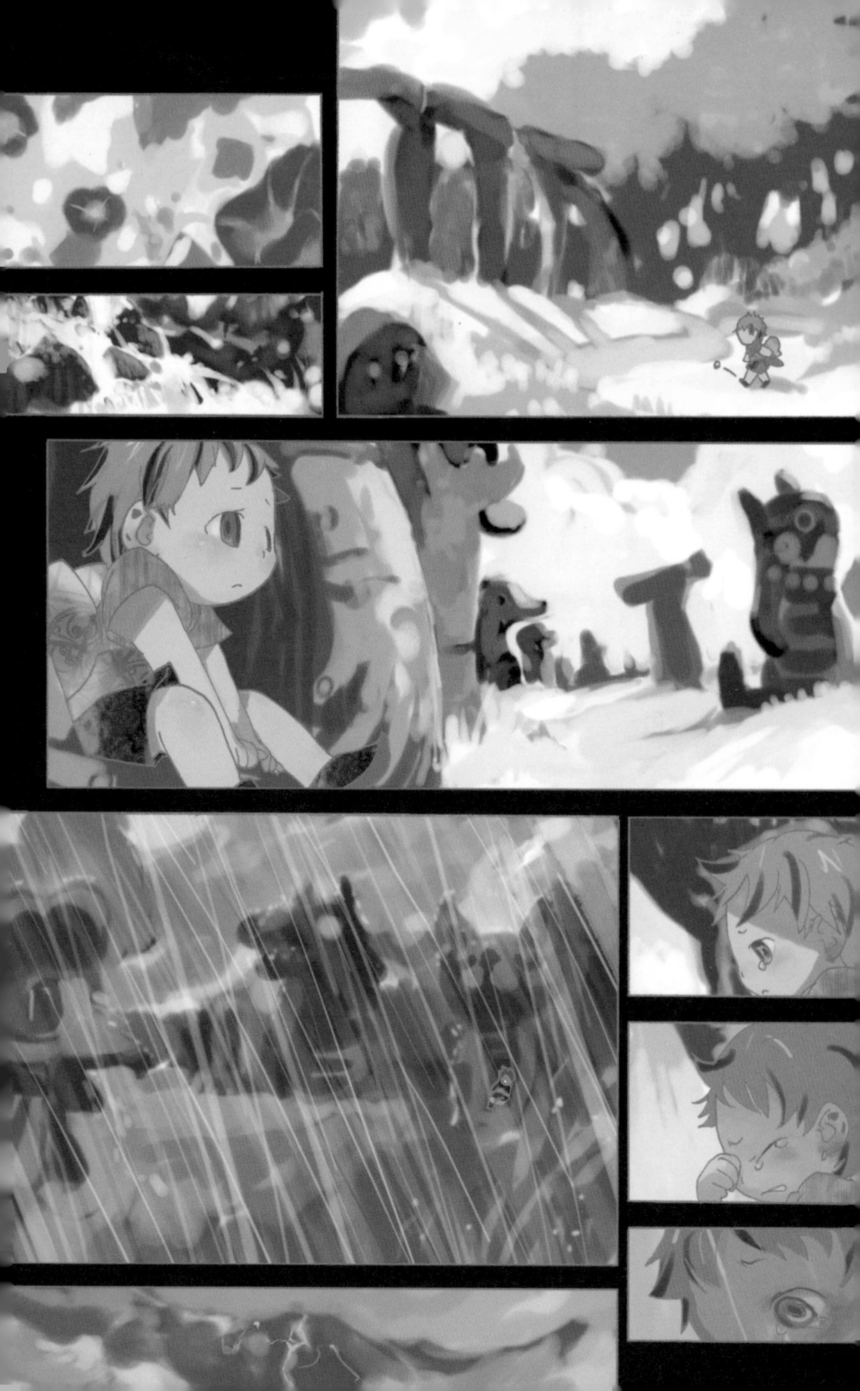

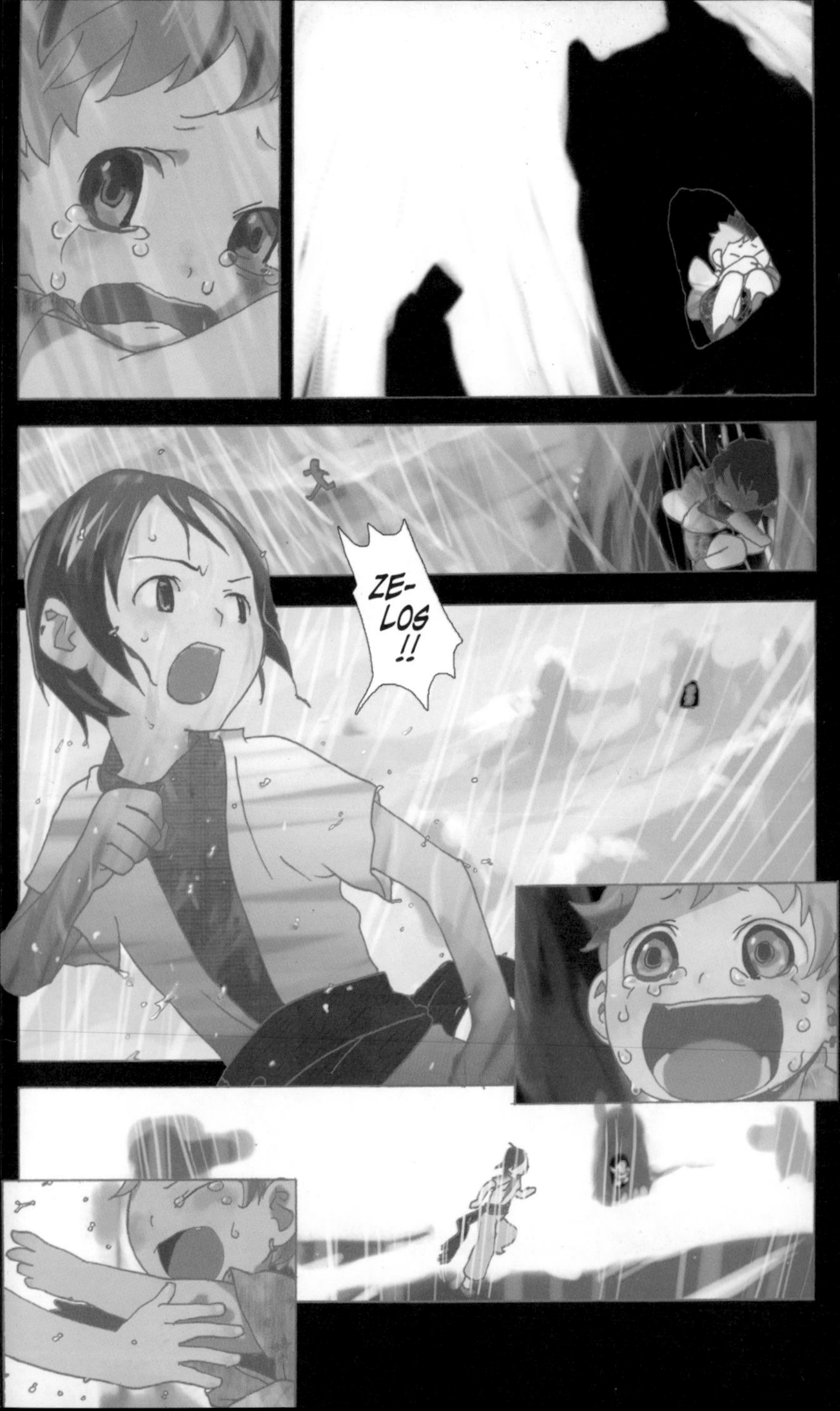
ZE-LOS!!

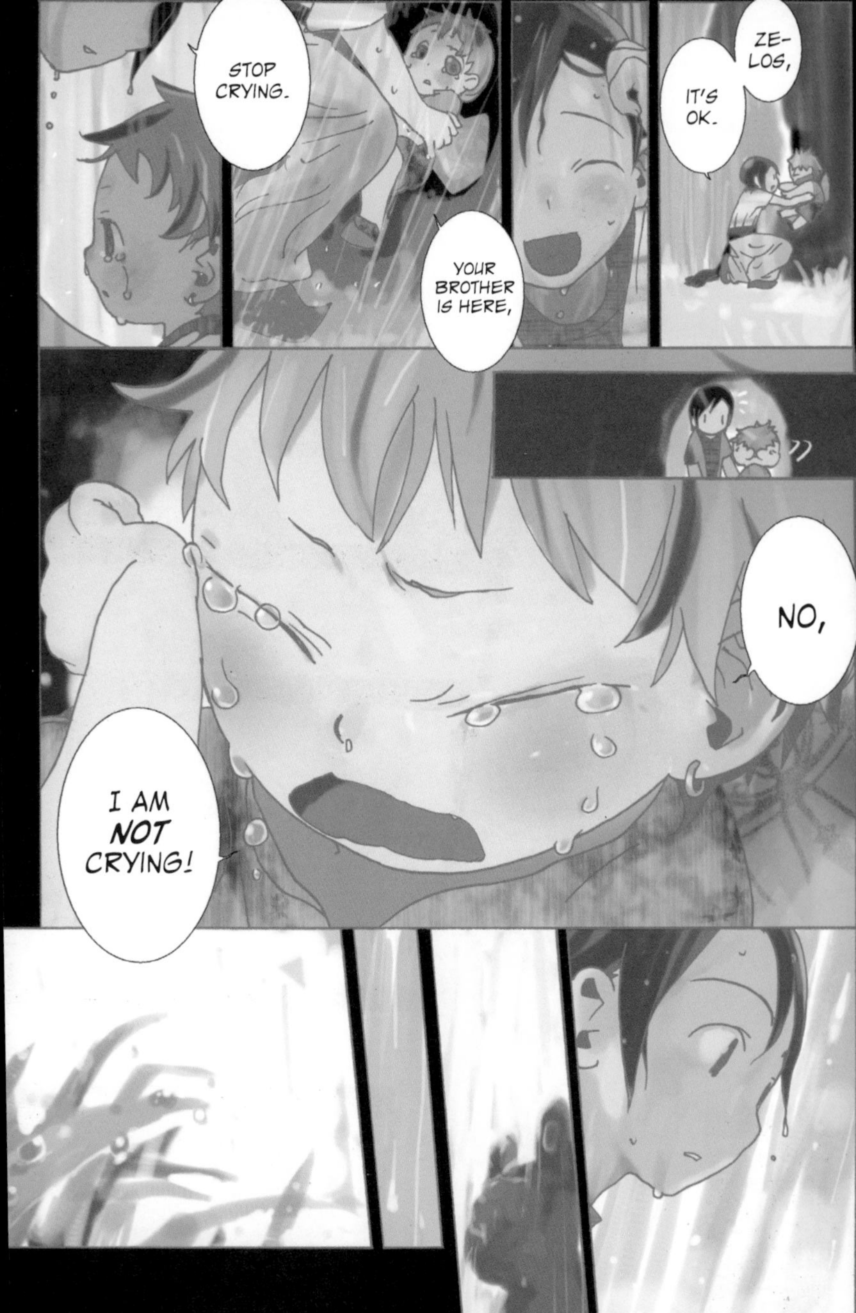
ZE-
LOS,
IT'S
OK.
YOUR
BROTHER
IS HERE,
STOP
CRYING.
NO,
I AM
NOT
CRYING!

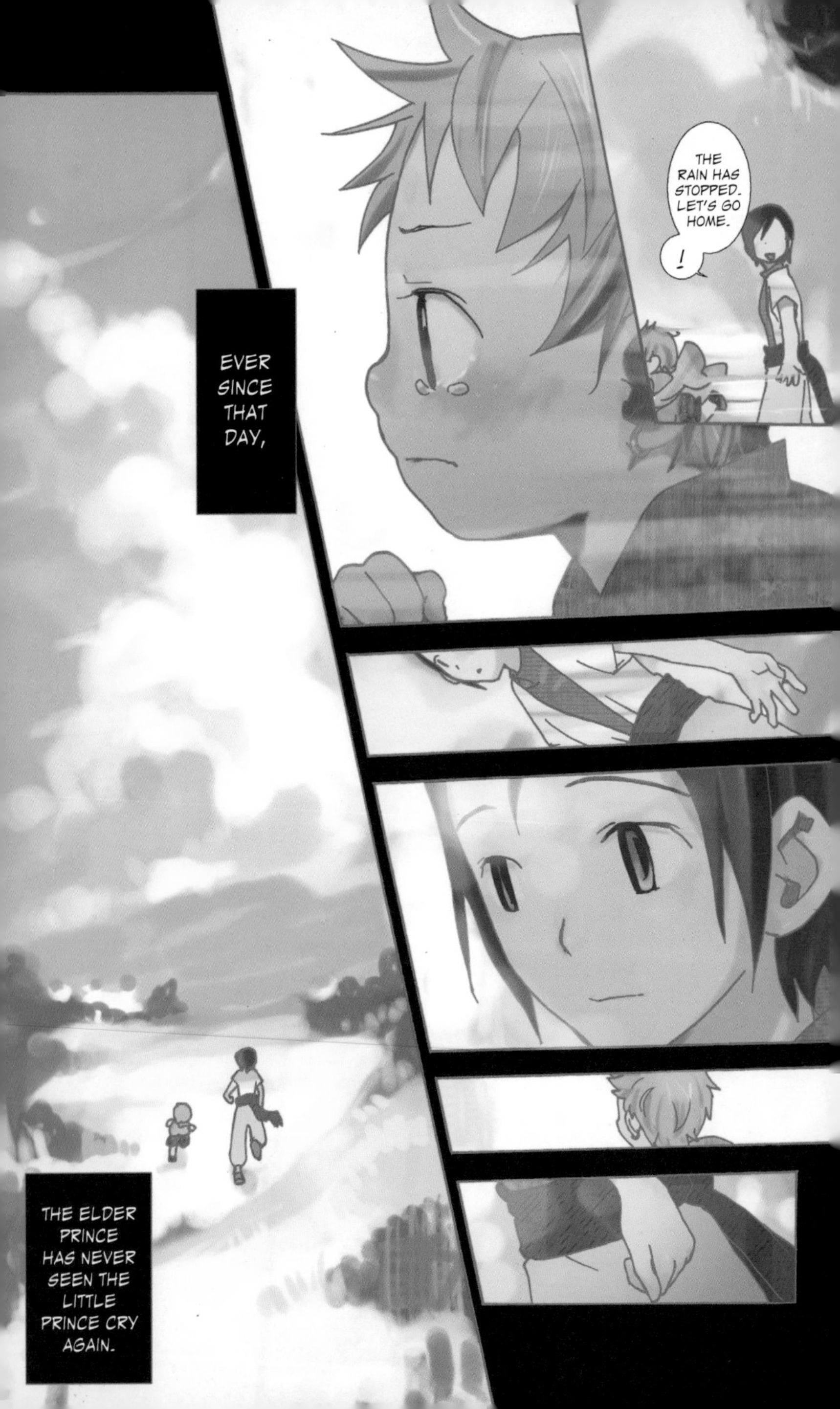
THE RAIN HAS STOPPED. LET'S GO HOME.
!
EVER SINCE THAT DAY,
THE ELDER PRINCE HAS NEVER SEEN THE LITTLE PRINCE CRY AGAIN.

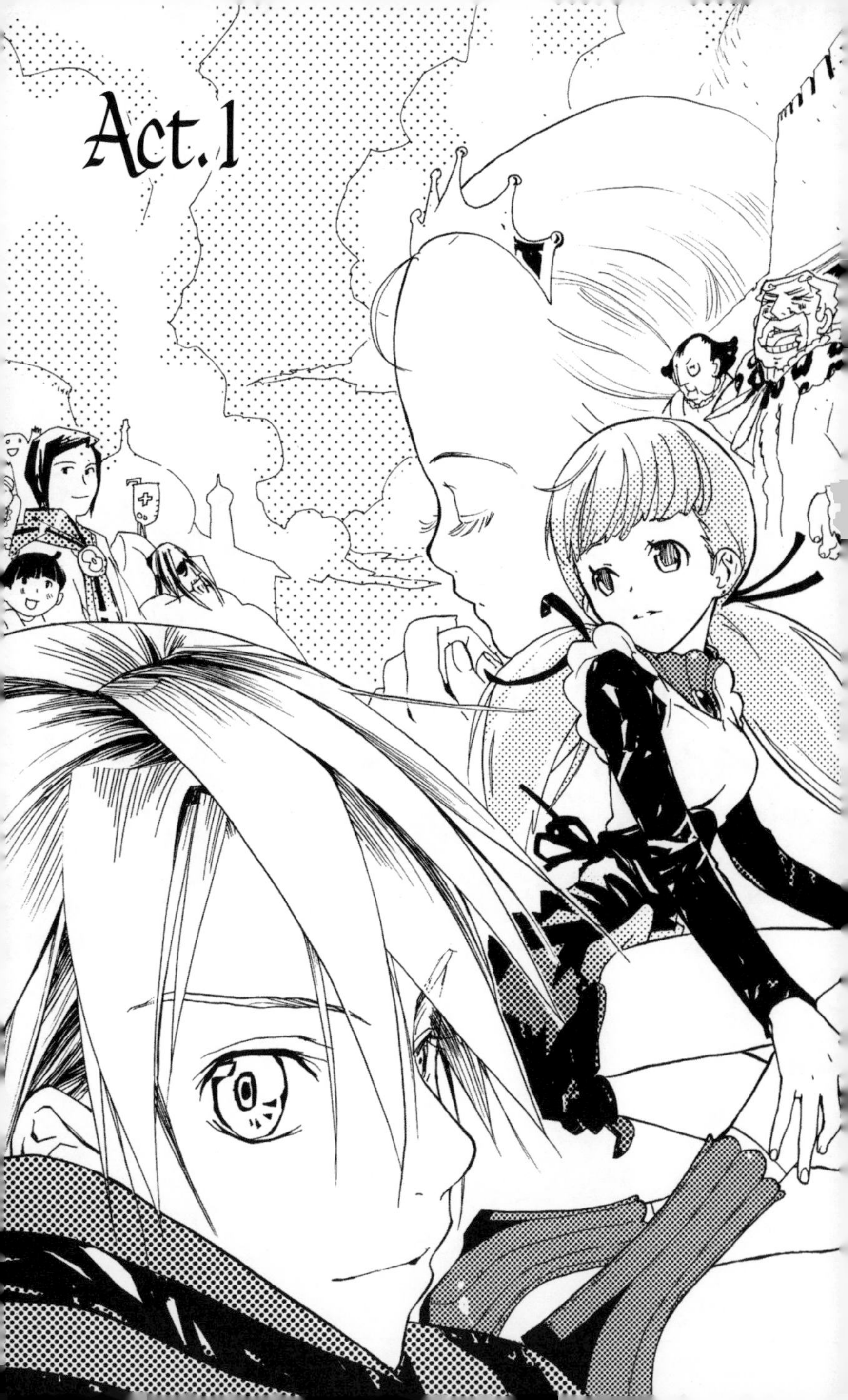
Act.1

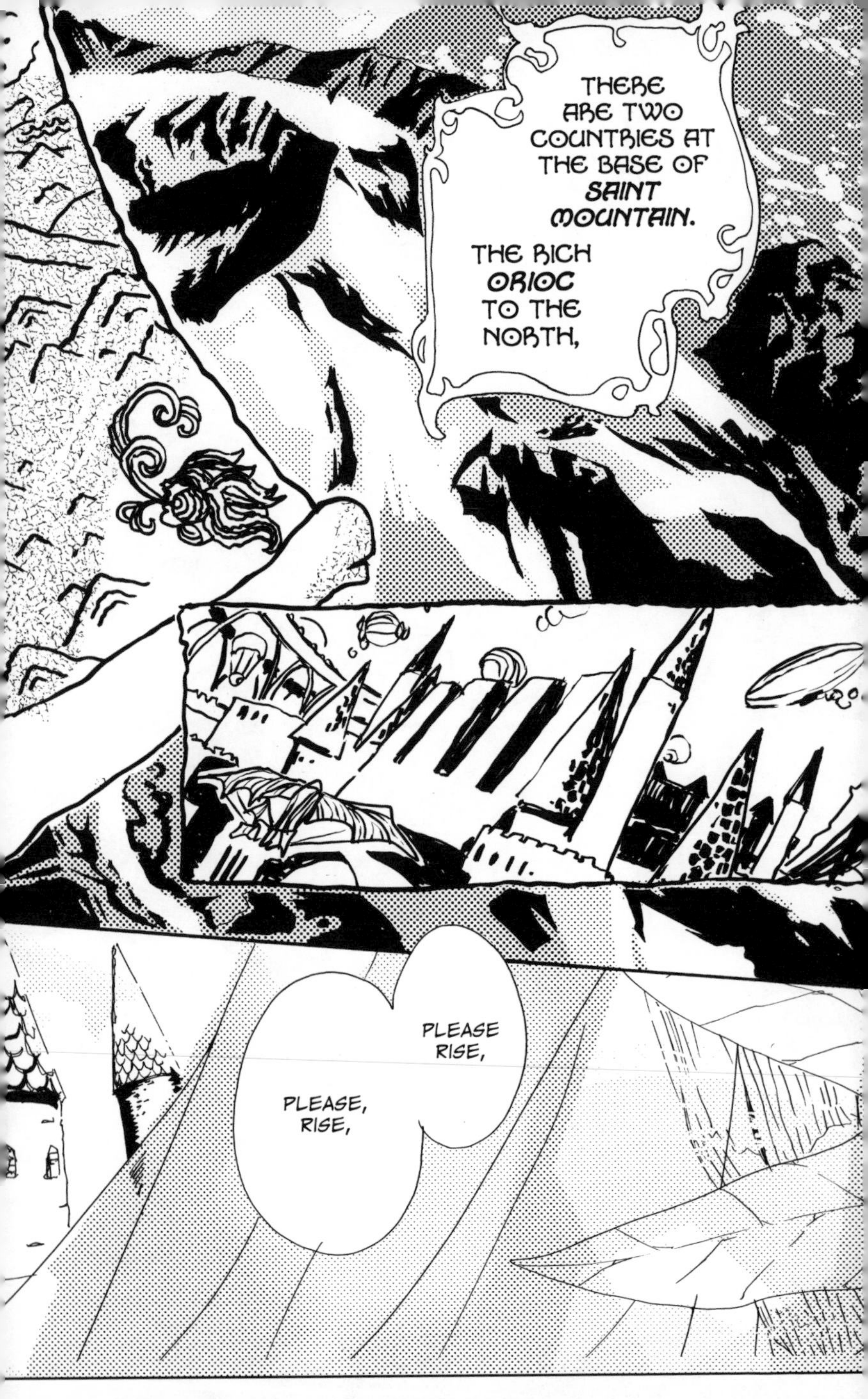
THERE ARE TWO COUNTRIES AT THE BASE OF SAINT MOUNTAIN.
THE RICH ORIOC TO THE NORTH,
PLEASE RISE,
PLEASE, RISE,

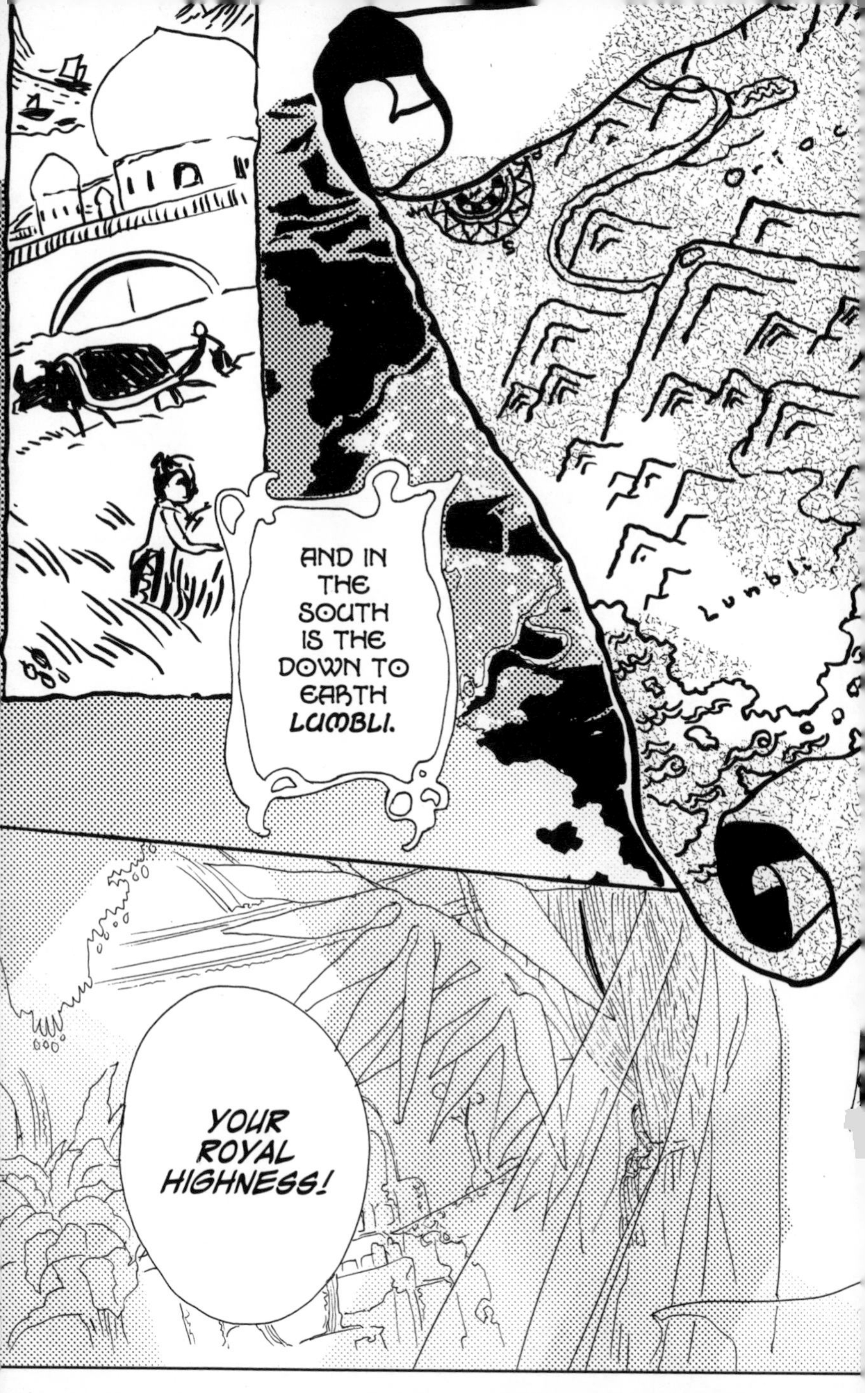
AND IN THE SOUTH IS THE DOWN TO EARTH LUMBLI.
YOUR ROYAL HIGHNESS!

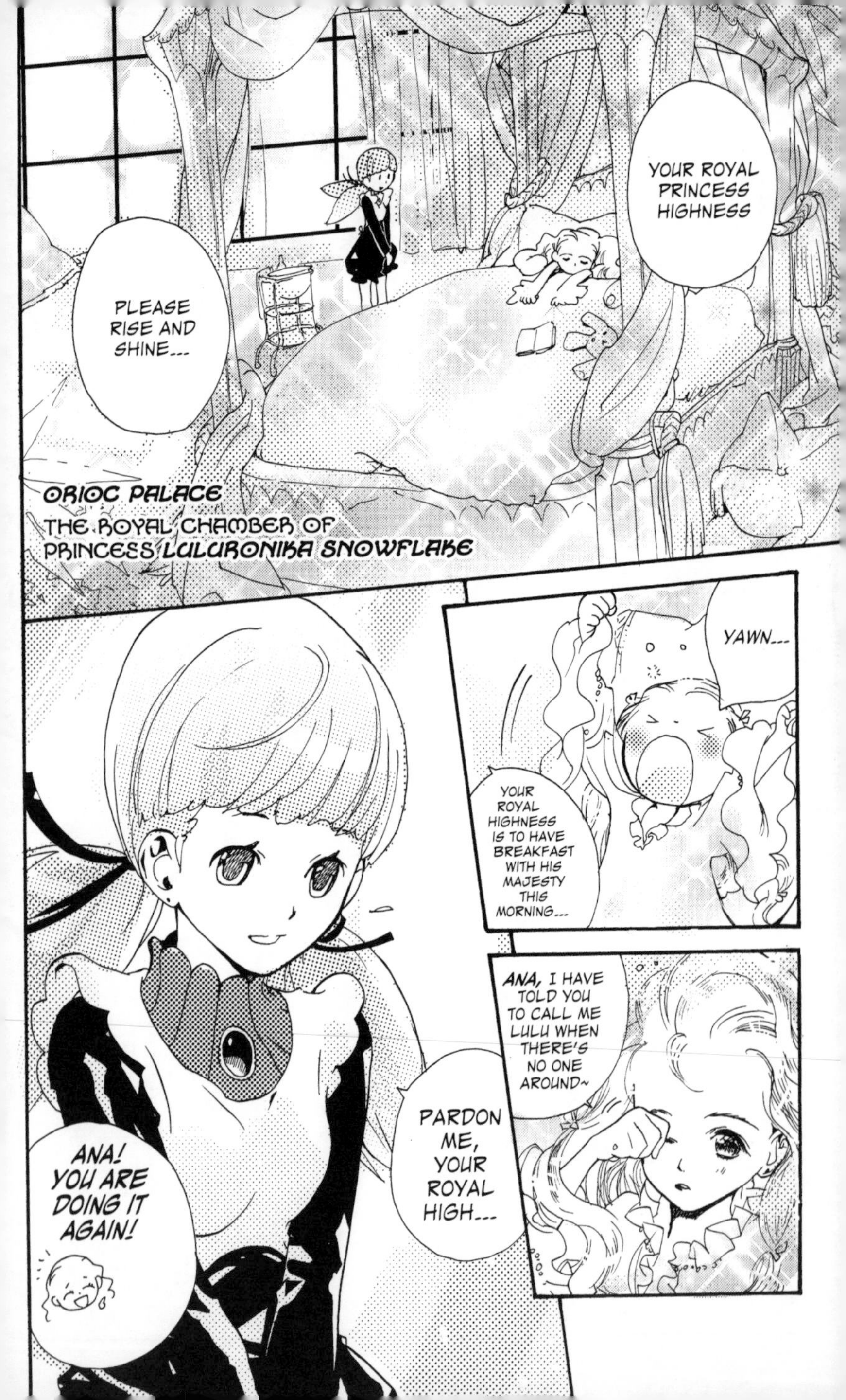
YOUR ROYAL PRINCESS HIGHNESS
PLEASE RISE AND SHINE...
ORIOC PALACE
THE ROYAL CHAMBER OF PRINCESS LULURONIKA SNOWFLAKE
YAWN...
YOUR ROYAL HIGHNESS IS TO HAVE BREAKFAST WITH HIS MAJESTY THIS MORNING...
ANA, I HAVE TOLD YOU TO CALL ME LULU WHEN THERE'S NO ONE AROUND~
PARDON ME, YOUR ROYAL HIGH...
ANA! YOU ARE DOING IT AGAIN!

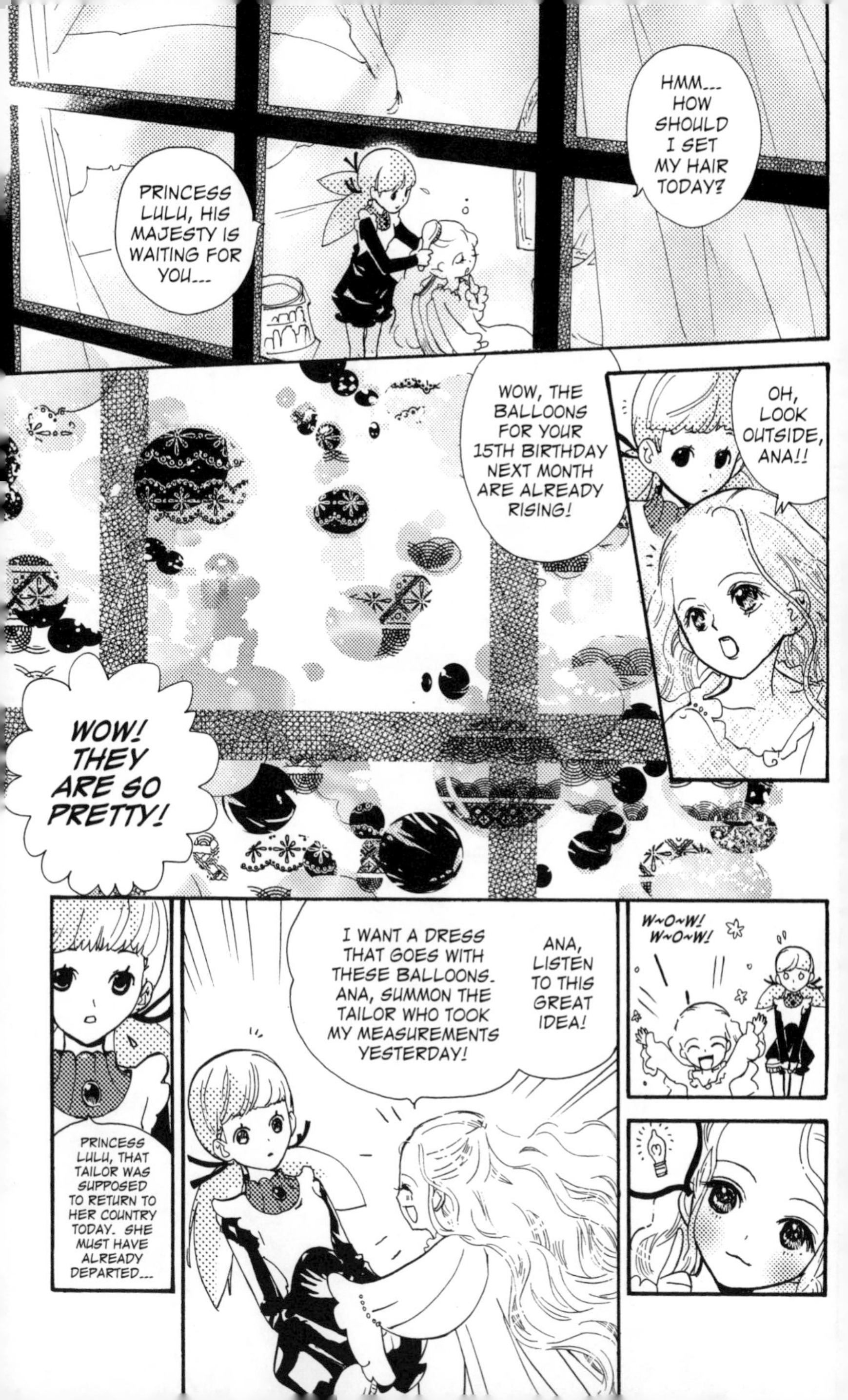
HMM... HOW SHOULD I SET MY HAIR TODAY?
PRINCESS LULU, HIS MAJESTY IS WAITING FOR YOU...
OH, LOOK OUTSIDE, ANA!!
WOW, THE BALLOONS FOR YOUR 15TH BIRTHDAY NEXT MONTH ARE ALREADY RISING!
WOW! THEY ARE SO PRETTY!
W~O~W! W~O~W!
ANA, LISTEN TO THIS GREAT IDEA!
I WANT A DRESS THAT GOES WITH THESE BALLOONS. ANA, SUMMON THE TAILOR WHO TOOK MY MEASUREMENTS YESTERDAY!
PRINCESS LULU, THAT TAILOR WAS SUPPOSED TO RETURN TO HER COUNTRY TODAY. SHE MUST HAVE ALREADY DEPARTED...

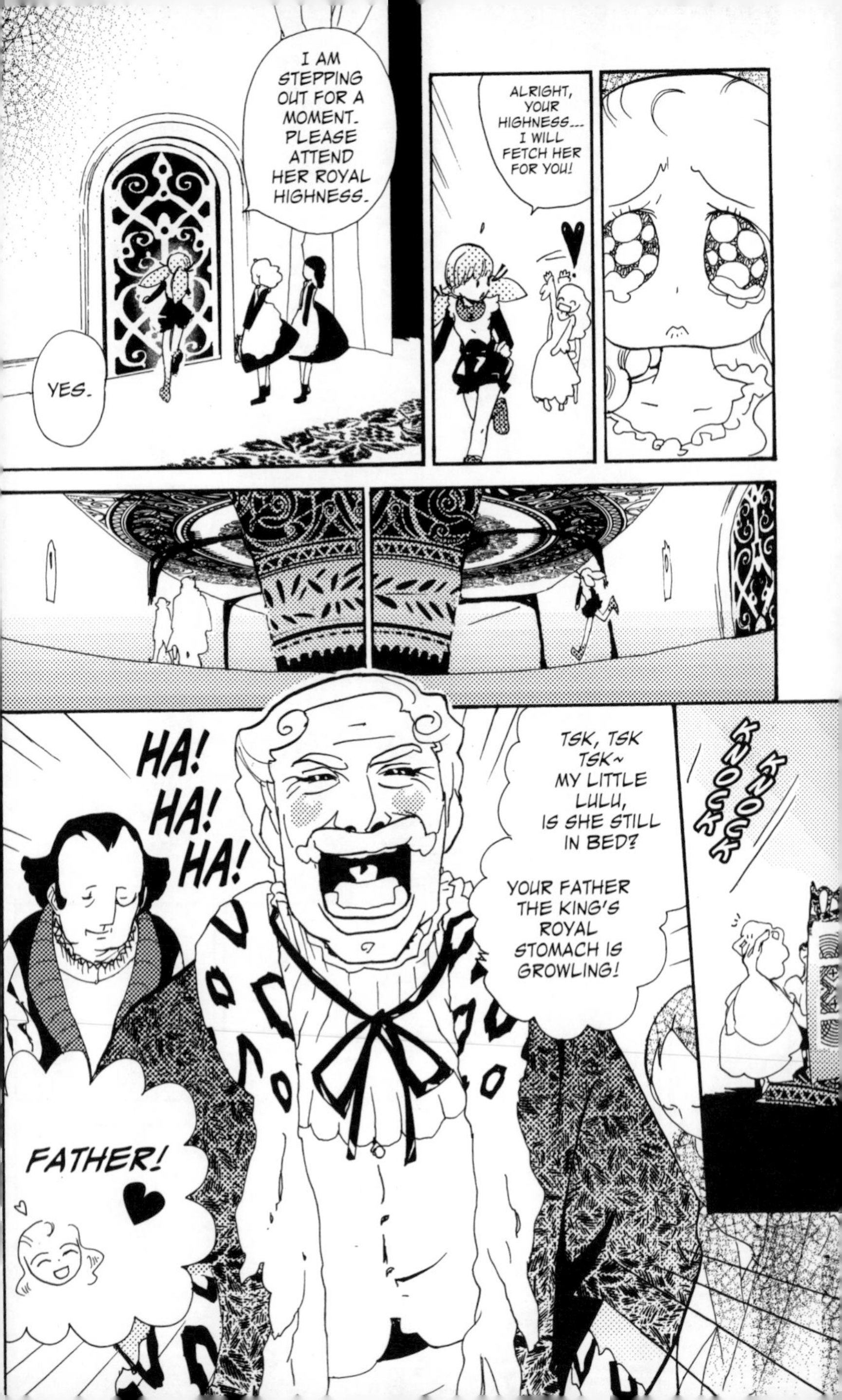
ALRIGHT, YOUR HIGHNESS... I WILL FETCH HER FOR YOU!
I AM STEPPING OUT FOR A MOMENT. PLEASE ATTEND HER ROYAL HIGHNESS.
YES.
KNOCK KNOCK
TSK, TSK TSK~ MY LITTLE LULU, IS SHE STILL IN BED?
YOUR FATHER THE KING'S ROYAL STOMACH IS GROWLING!
HA! HA! HA!
FATHER!

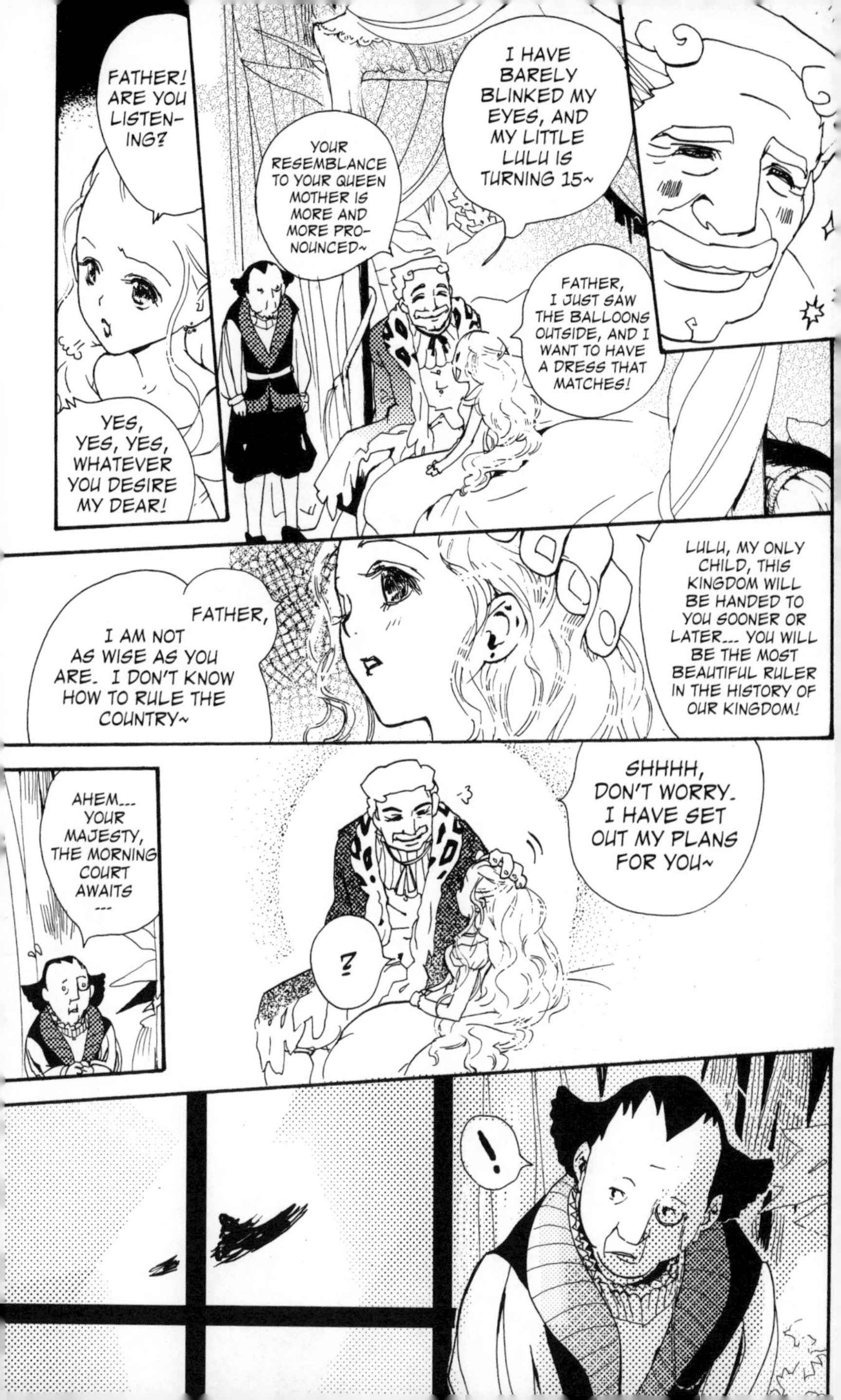
I HAVE BARELY BLINKED MY EYES, AND MY LITTLE LULU IS TURNING 15~
YOUR RESEMBLANCE TO YOUR QUEEN MOTHER IS MORE AND MORE PRO-NOUNCED~
FATHER, I JUST SAW THE BALLOONS OUTSIDE, AND I WANT TO HAVE A DRESS THAT MATCHES!
FATHER! ARE YOU LISTEN-ING?
YES, YES, YES, WHATEVER YOU DESIRE MY DEAR!
LULU, MY ONLY CHILD, THIS KINGDOM WILL BE HANDED TO YOU SOONER OR LATER... YOU WILL BE THE MOST BEAUTIFUL RULER IN THE HISTORY OF OUR KINGDOM!
FATHER, I AM NOT AS WISE AS YOU ARE. I DON'T KNOW HOW TO RULE THE COUNTRY~
SHHHH, DON'T WORRY. I HAVE SET OUT MY PLANS FOR YOU~
?
AHEM... YOUR MAJESTY, THE MORNING COURT AWAITS ...
!

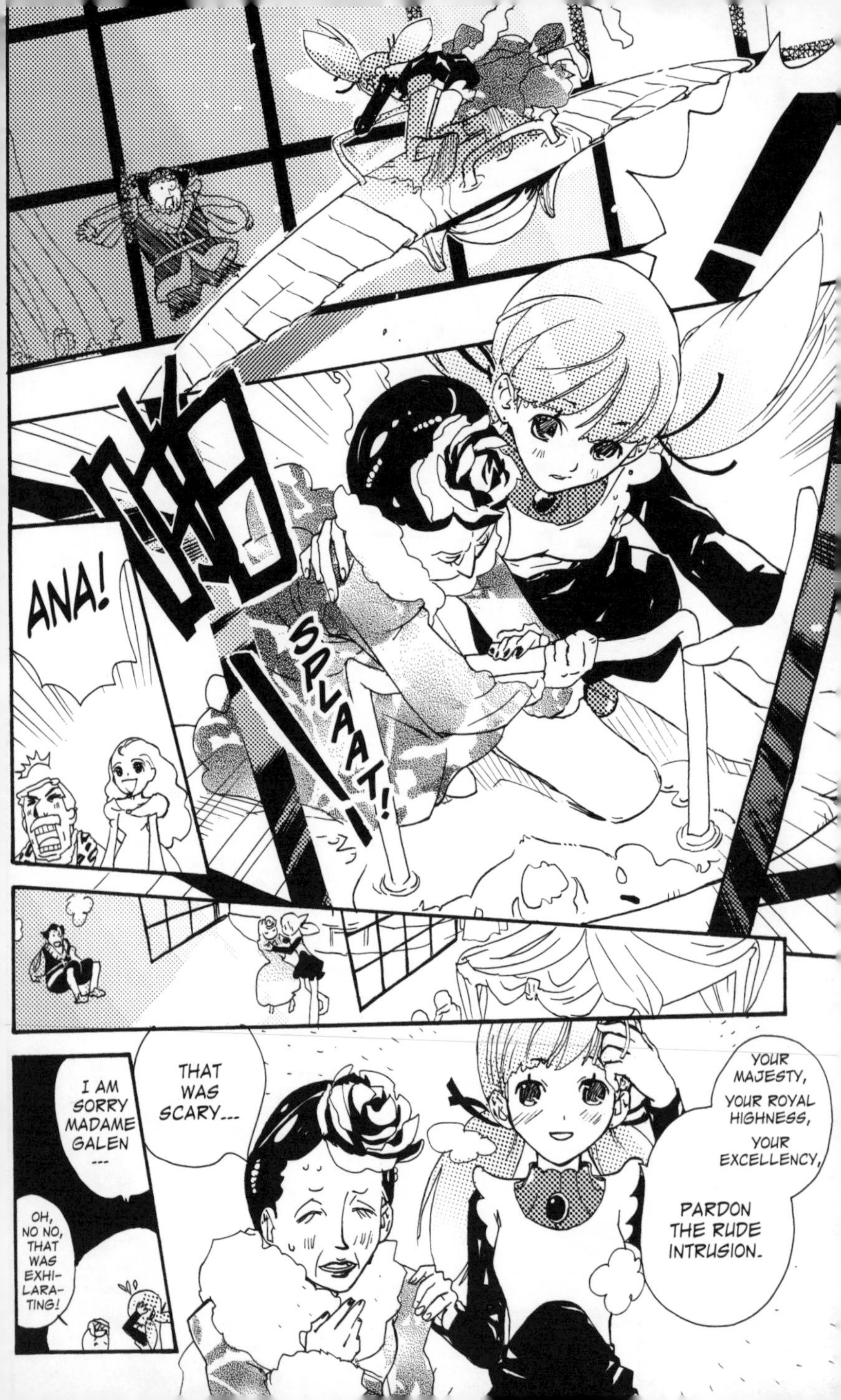
SPLAAAT!!
ANA!
YOUR MAJESTY, YOUR ROYAL HIGHNESS, YOUR EXCELLENCY,
PARDON THE RUDE INTRUSION.
THAT WAS SCARY...
I AM SORRY MADAME GALEN ---
OH, NO NO, THAT WAS EXHILARATING!

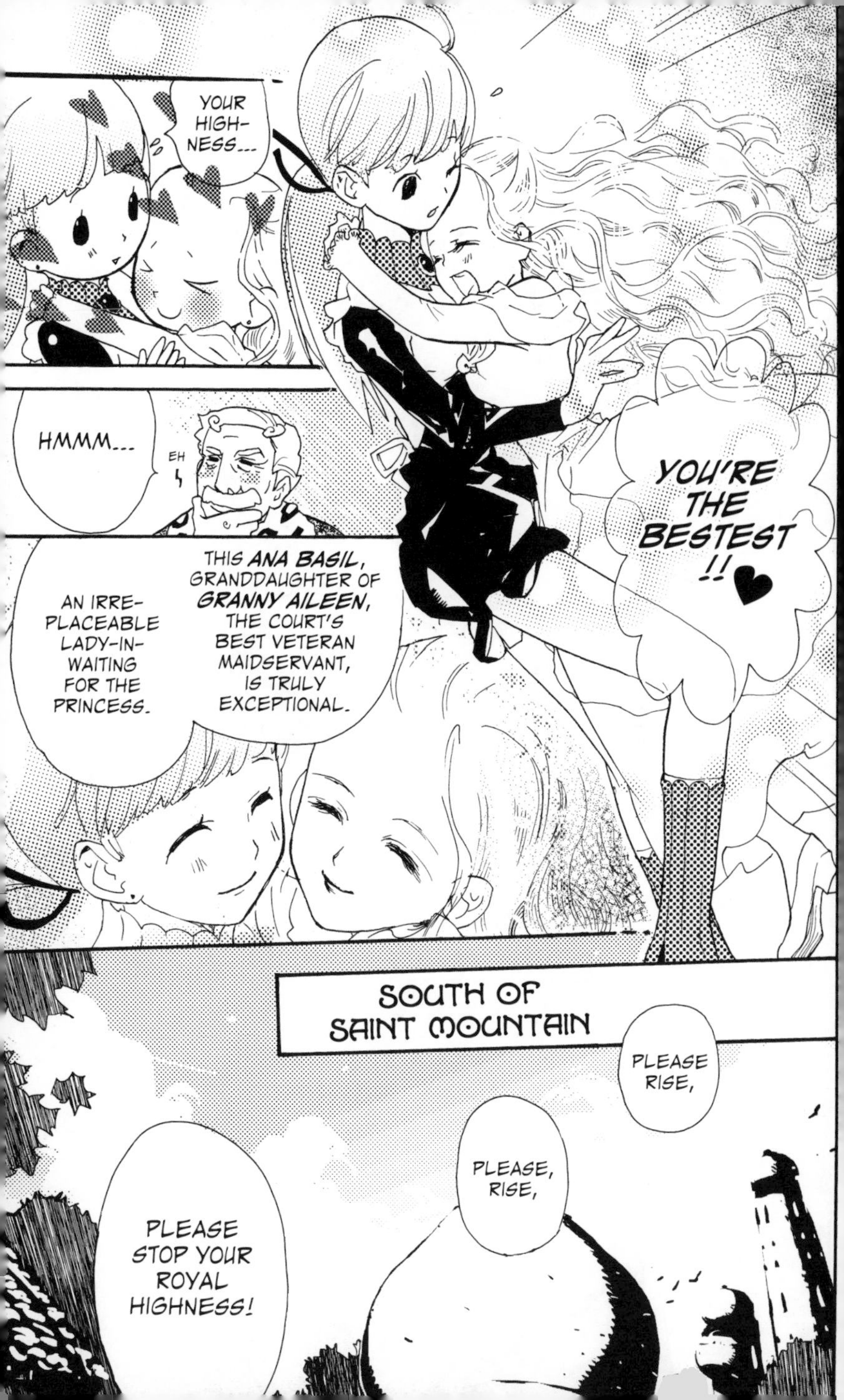
YOU'RE THE BESTEST!! ♥
YOUR HIGHNESS...
HMMM...
EH
THIS ANA BASIL, GRANDDAUGHTER OF GRANNY AILEEN, THE COURT'S BEST VETERAN MAIDSERVANT, IS TRULY EXCEPTIONAL.
AN IRREPLACEABLE LADY-IN-WAITING FOR THE PRINCESS.
SOUTH OF SAINT MOUNTAIN
PLEASE RISE,
PLEASE, RISE,
PLEASE STOP YOUR ROYAL HIGHNESS!

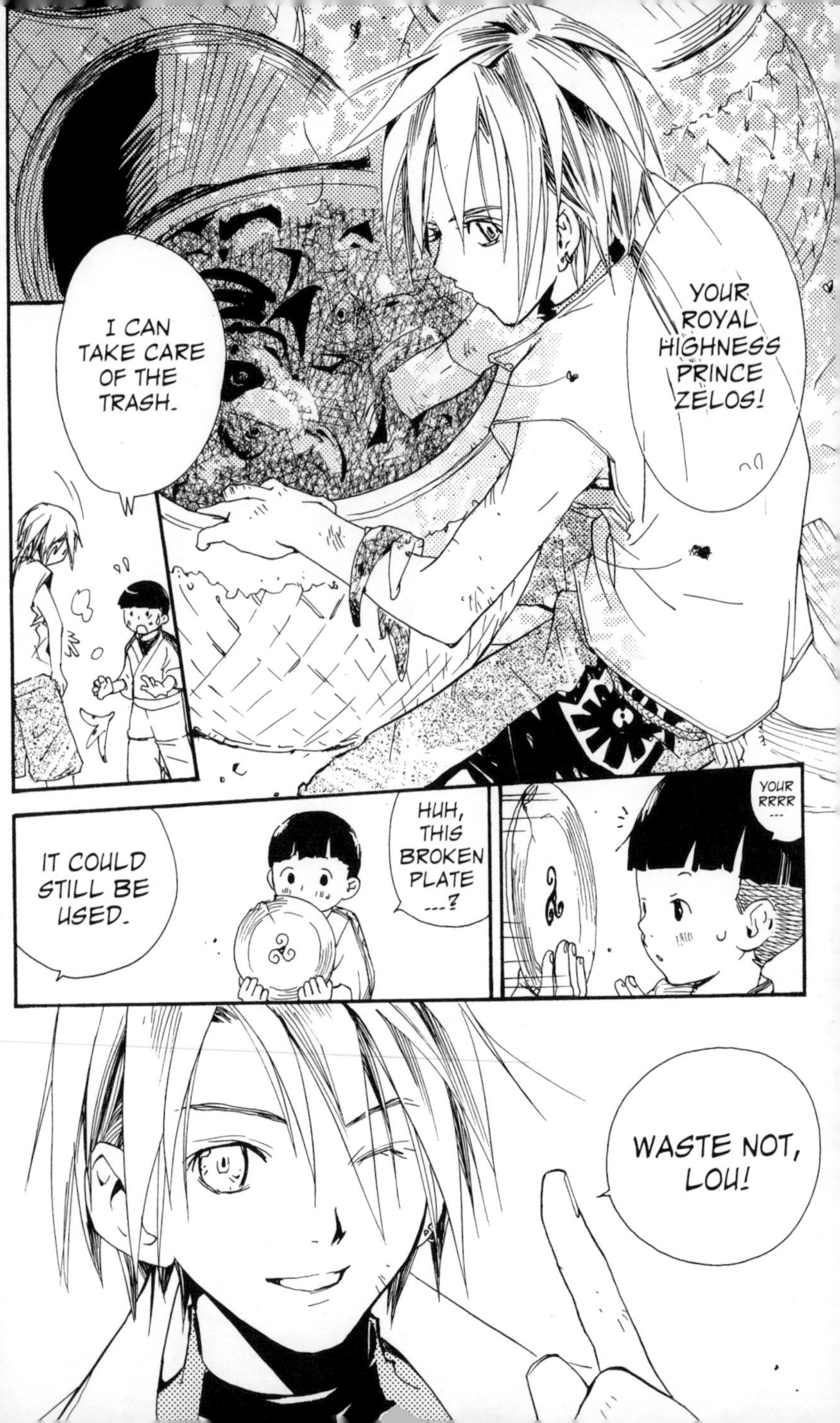

YOUR ROYAL HIGHNESS PRINCE ZELOS!
I CAN TAKE CARE OF THE TRASH.
YOUR RRRR ---
HUH, THIS BROKEN PLATE ---?
IT COULD STILL BE USED.
WASTE NOT, LOU!

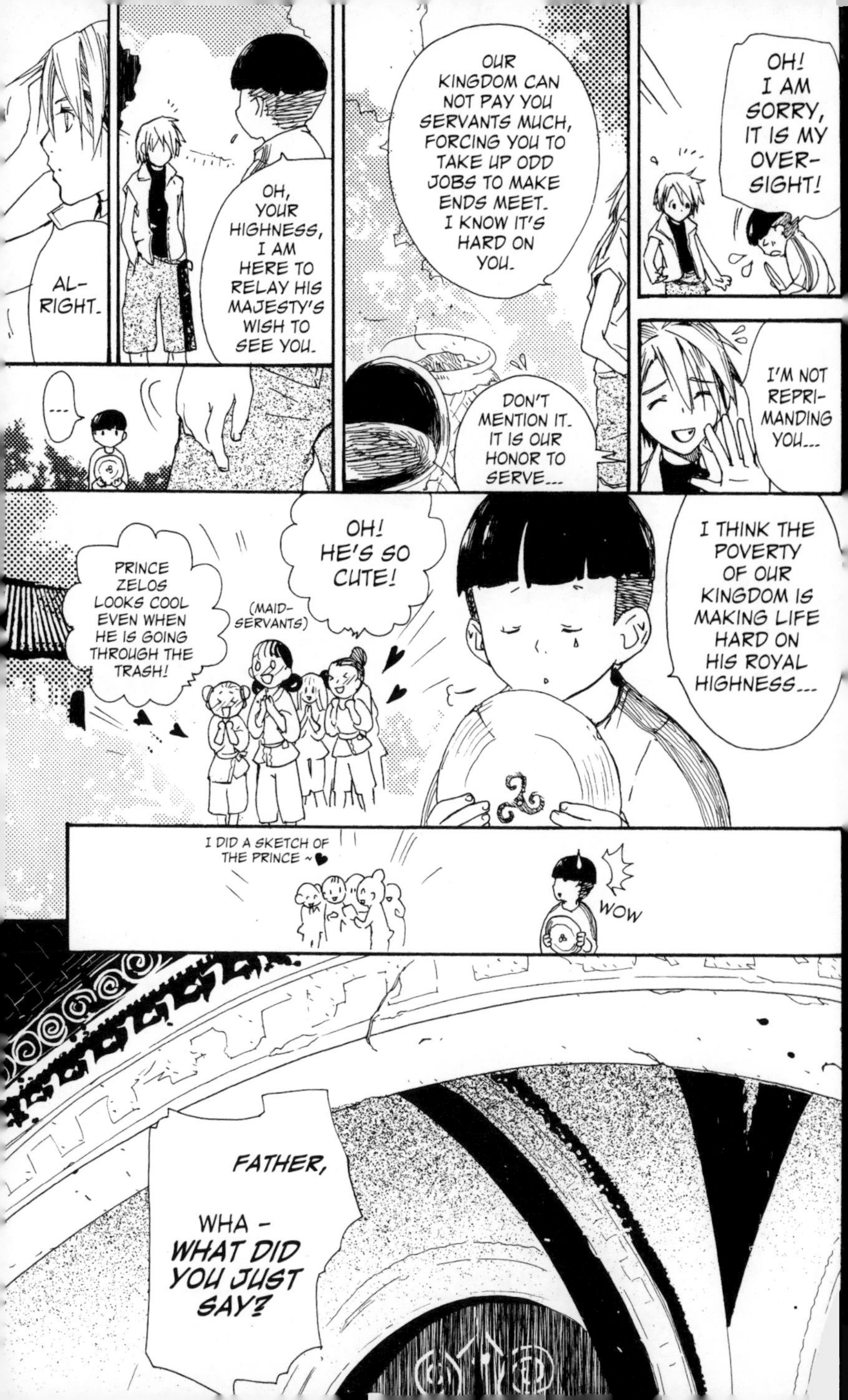
OH! I AM SORRY, IT IS MY OVER-SIGHT!
I'M NOT REPRI-MANDING YOU...
OUR KINGDOM CAN NOT PAY YOU SERVANTS MUCH, FORCING YOU TO TAKE UP ODD JOBS TO MAKE ENDS MEET. I KNOW IT'S HARD ON YOU.
DON'T MENTION IT. IT IS OUR HONOR TO SERVE...
OH, YOUR HIGHNESS, I AM HERE TO RELAY HIS MAJESTY'S WISH TO SEE YOU.
AL-RIGHT.
...
I THINK THE POVERTY OF OUR KINGDOM IS MAKING LIFE HARD ON HIS ROYAL HIGHNESS...
OH! HE'S SO CUTE!
(MAID-SERVANTS)
PRINCE ZELOS LOOKS COOL EVEN WHEN HE IS GOING THROUGH THE TRASH!
WOW
I DID A SKETCH OF THE PRINCE ~♥
FATHER,
WHA - WHAT DID YOU JUST SAY?

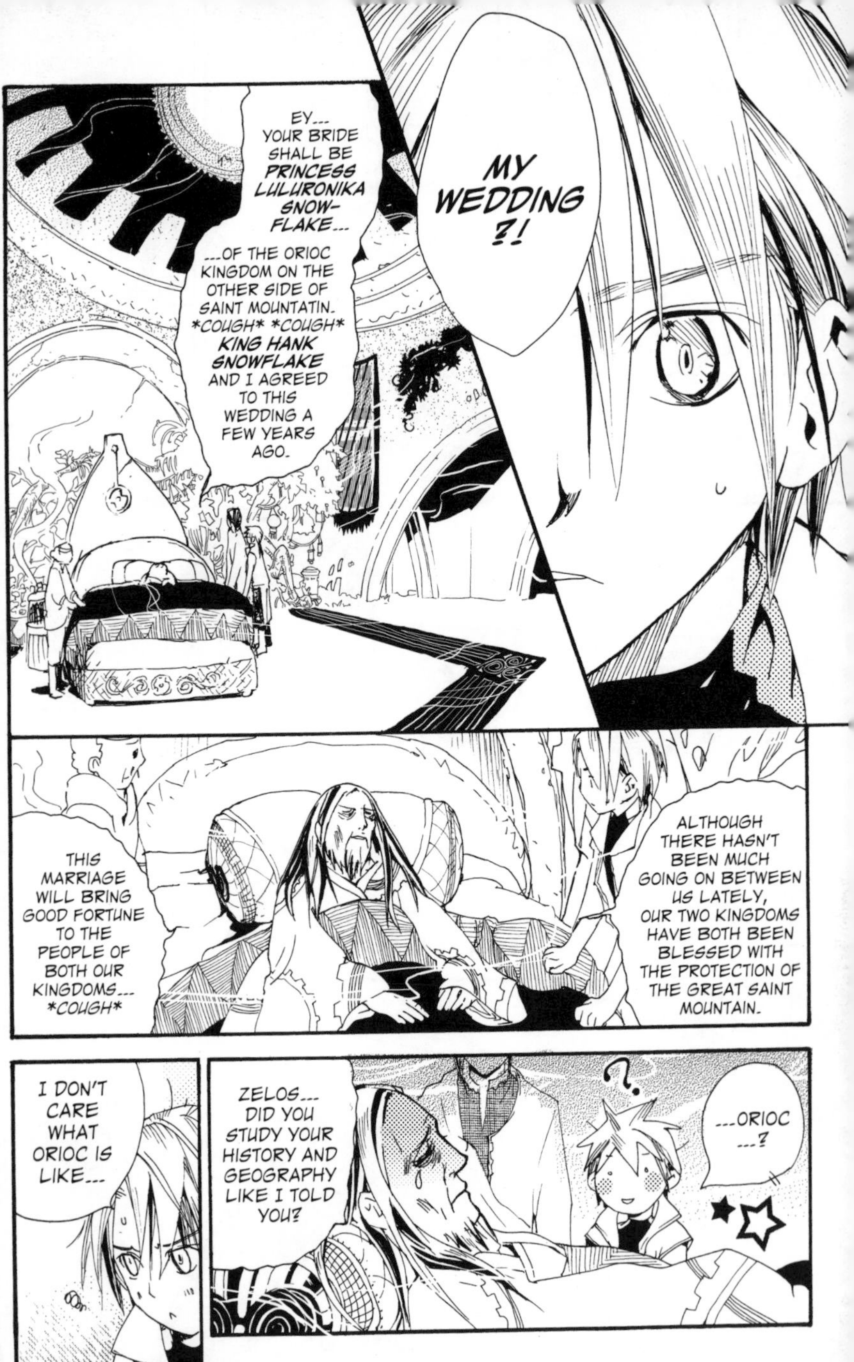
MY WEDDING ?!
EY... YOUR BRIDE SHALL BE **PRINCESS LULURONIKA SNOWFLAKE**...
...OF THE ORIOC KINGDOM ON THE OTHER SIDE OF SAINT MOUNTATIN. *COUGH* *COUGH* **KING HANK SNOWFLAKE** AND I AGREED TO THIS WEDDING A FEW YEARS AGO.
ALTHOUGH THERE HASN'T BEEN MUCH GOING ON BETWEEN US LATELY, OUR TWO KINGDOMS HAVE BOTH BEEN BLESSED WITH THE PROTECTION OF THE GREAT SAINT MOUNTAIN.
THIS MARRIAGE WILL BRING GOOD FORTUNE TO THE PEOPLE OF BOTH OUR KINGDOMS... *COUGH*
...ORIOC ...?
ZELOS... DID YOU STUDY YOUR HISTORY AND GEOGRAPHY LIKE I TOLD YOU?
I DON'T CARE WHAT ORIOC IS LIKE...

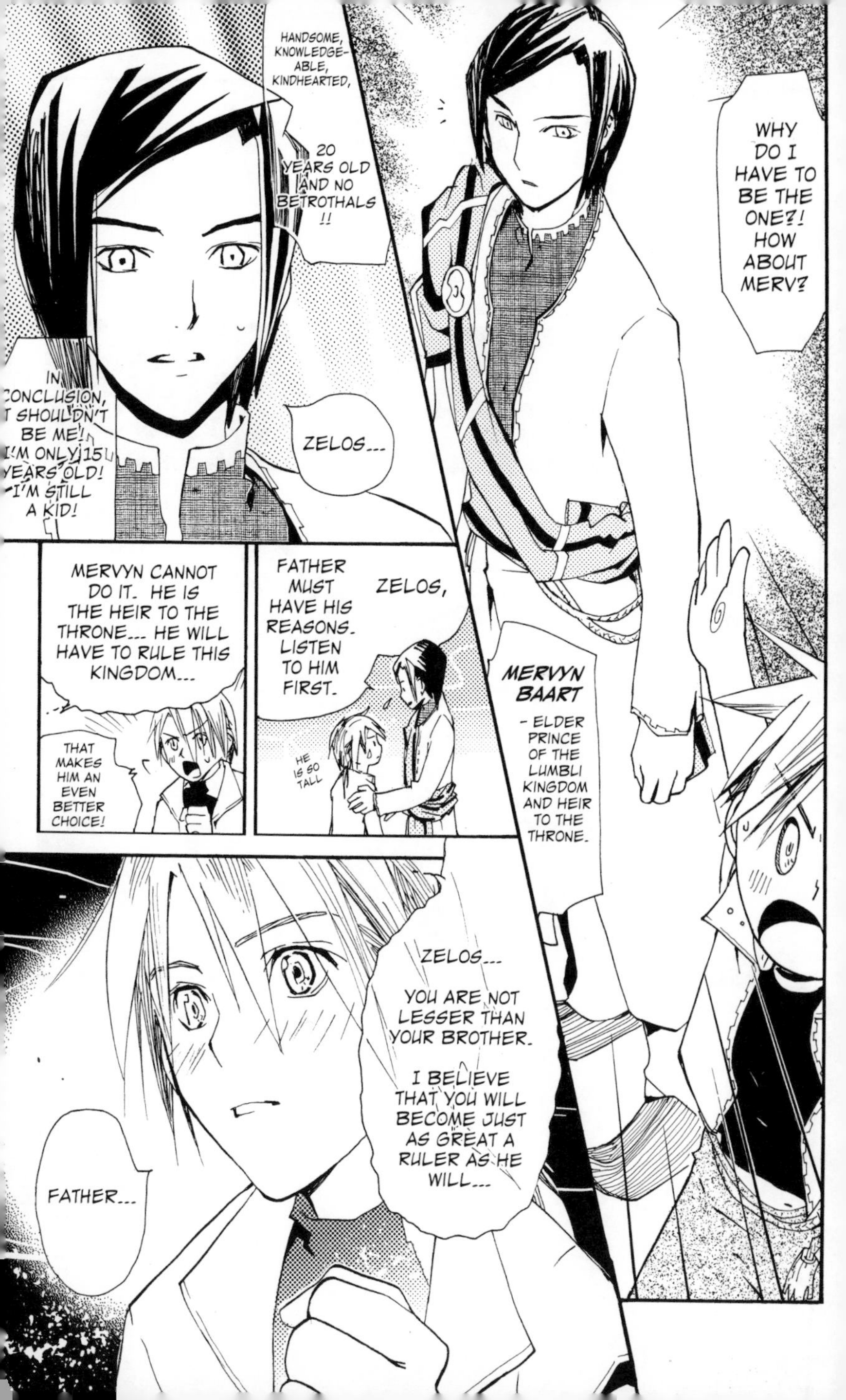
WHY DO I HAVE TO BE THE ONE?! HOW ABOUT MERV?
MERVYN BAART - ELDER PRINCE OF THE LUMBLI KINGDOM AND HEIR TO THE THRONE.
HANDSOME, KNOWLEDGE-ABLE, KINDHEARTED,
20 YEARS OLD AND NO BETROTHALS !!
IN CONCLUSION, IT SHOULDN'T BE ME! I'M ONLY 15 YEARS OLD! I'M STILL A KID!
ZELOS...
ZELOS,
FATHER MUST HAVE HIS REASONS. LISTEN TO HIM FIRST.
HE IS SO TALL
MERVYN CANNOT DO IT. HE IS THE HEIR TO THE THRONE... HE WILL HAVE TO RULE THIS KINGDOM...
THAT MAKES HIM AN EVEN BETTER CHOICE!
ZELOS...
YOU ARE NOT LESSER THAN YOUR BROTHER.
I BELIEVE THAT YOU WILL BECOME JUST AS GREAT A RULER AS HE WILL...
FATHER...

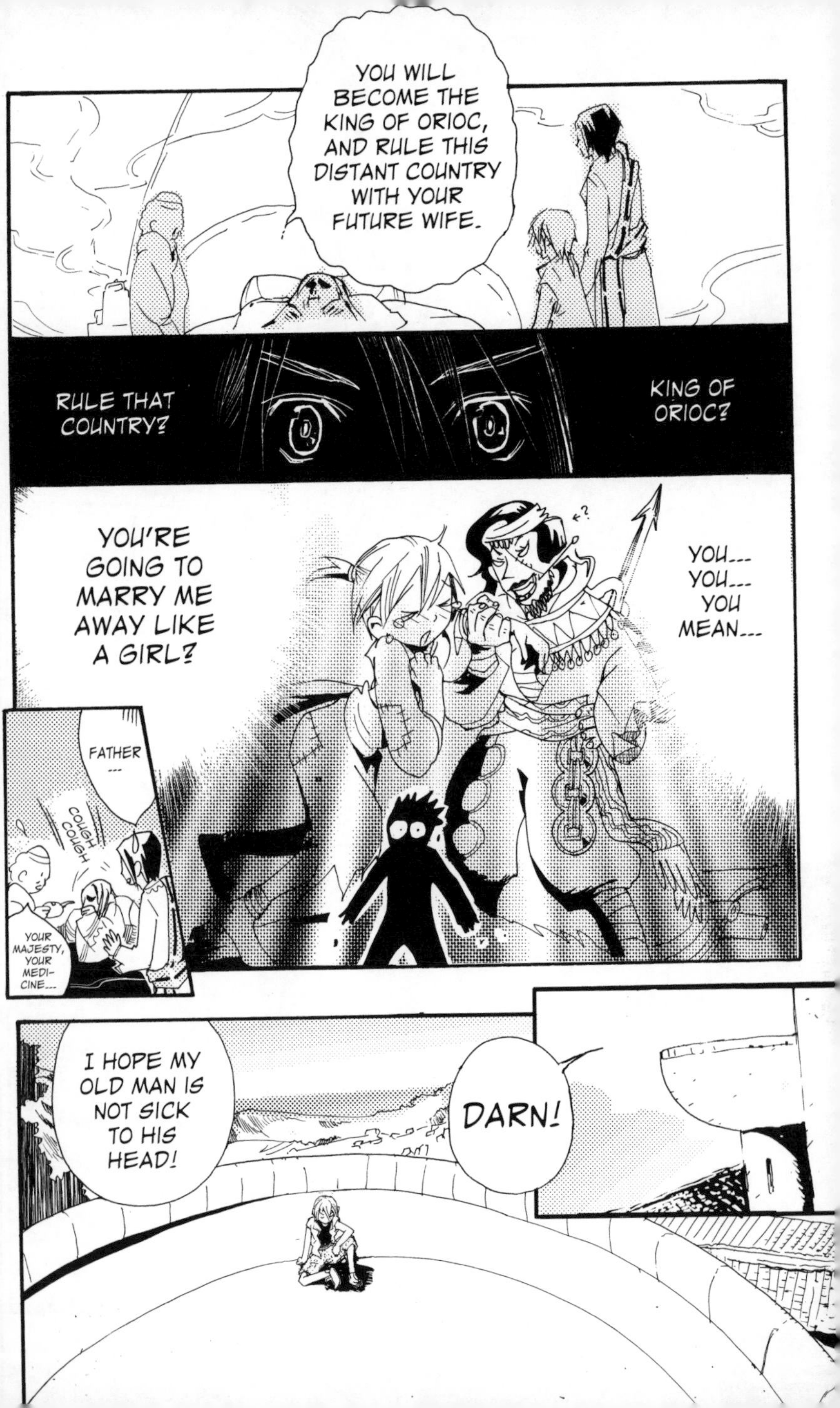
YOU WILL BECOME THE KING OF ORIOC, AND RULE THIS DISTANT COUNTRY WITH YOUR FUTURE WIFE.
KING OF ORIOC?
RULE THAT COUNTRY?
YOU... YOU... YOU MEAN...
YOU'RE GOING TO MARRY ME AWAY LIKE A GIRL?
FATHER ---
COUGH COUGH
YOUR MAJESTY, YOUR MEDICINE...
DARN!
I HOPE MY OLD MAN IS NOT SICK TO HIS HEAD!

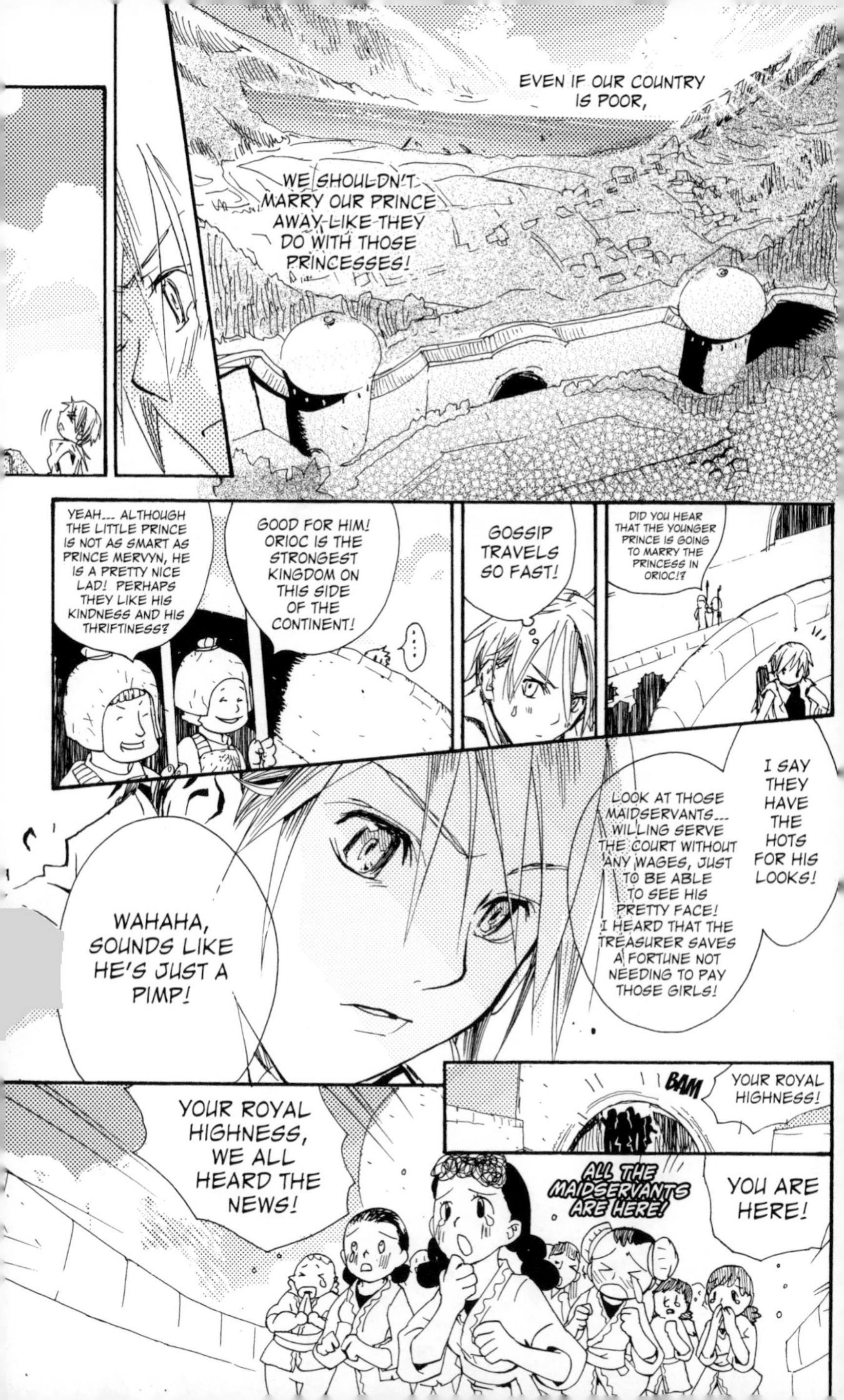
EVEN IF OUR COUNTRY IS POOR,
WE SHOULDN'T MARRY OUR PRINCE AWAY LIKE THEY DO WITH THOSE PRINCESSES!
DID YOU HEAR THAT THE YOUNGER PRINCE IS GOING TO MARRY THE PRINCESS IN ORIOC!?
GOSSIP TRAVELS SO FAST!
GOOD FOR HIM! ORIOC IS THE STRONGEST KINGDOM ON THIS SIDE OF THE CONTINENT!
....
YEAH... ALTHOUGH THE LITTLE PRINCE IS NOT AS SMART AS PRINCE MERVYN, HE IS A PRETTY NICE LAD! PERHAPS THEY LIKE HIS KINDNESS AND HIS THRIFTINESS?
I SAY THEY HAVE THE HOTS FOR HIS LOOKS!
LOOK AT THOSE MAIDSERVANTS... WILLING SERVE THE COURT WITHOUT ANY WAGES, JUST TO BE ABLE TO SEE HIS PRETTY FACE! I HEARD THAT THE TREASURER SAVES A FORTUNE NOT NEEDING TO PAY THOSE GIRLS!
WAHAHA, SOUNDS LIKE HE'S JUST A PIMP!
BAM
YOUR ROYAL HIGHNESS!
YOU ARE HERE!
ALL THE MAIDSERVANTS ARE HERE!
YOUR ROYAL HIGHNESS, WE ALL HEARD THE NEWS!

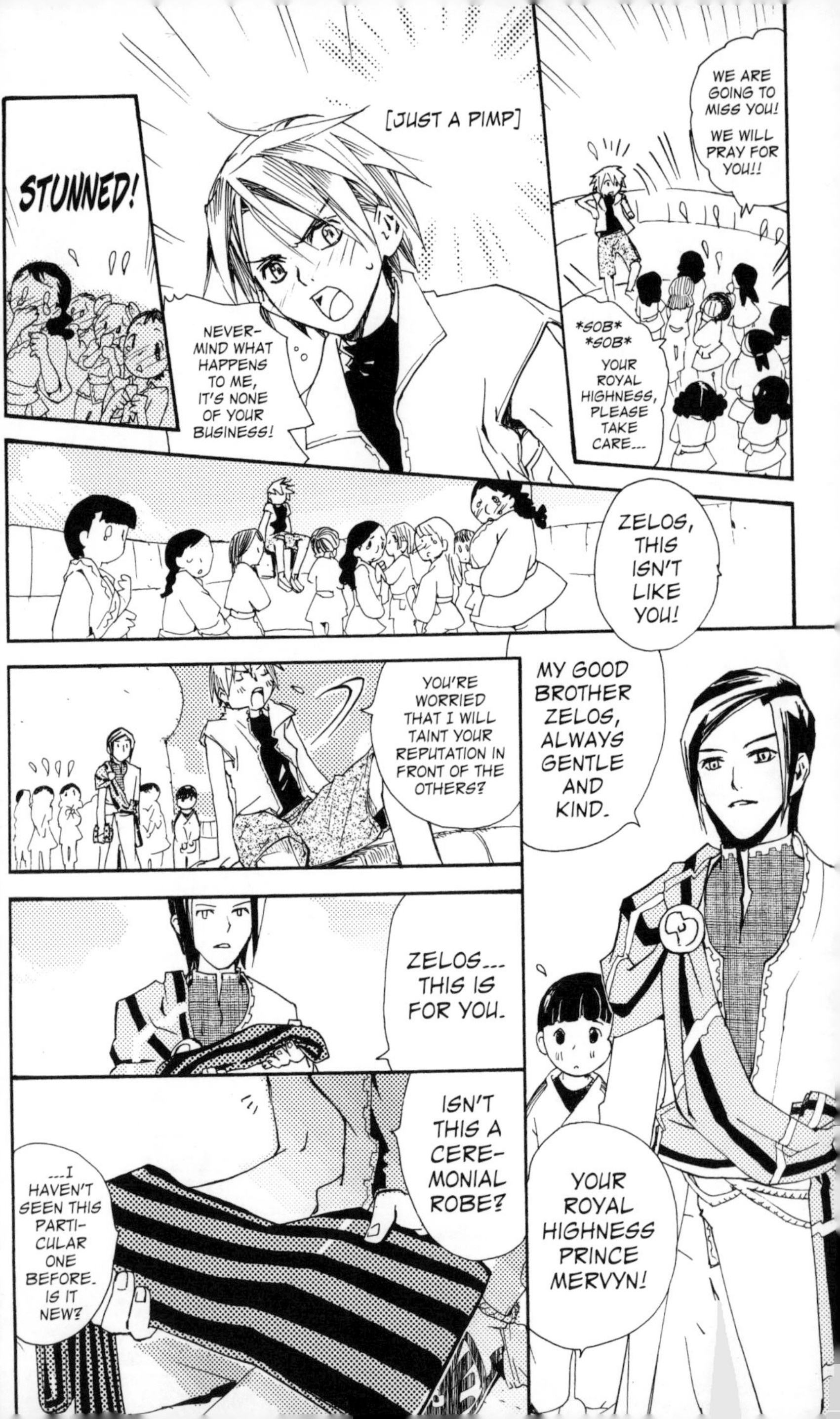
WE ARE GOING TO MISS YOU! WE WILL PRAY FOR YOU!!
SOB *SOB*
YOUR ROYAL HIGHNESS, PLEASE TAKE CARE...
[JUST A PIMP]
NEVER-MIND WHAT HAPPENS TO ME, IT'S NONE OF YOUR BUSINESS!
STUNNED!
ZELOS, THIS ISN'T LIKE YOU!
MY GOOD BROTHER ZELOS, ALWAYS GENTLE AND KIND.
YOUR ROYAL HIGHNESS PRINCE MERVYN!
YOU'RE WORRIED THAT I WILL TAINT YOUR REPUTATION IN FRONT OF THE OTHERS?
ZELOS... THIS IS FOR YOU.
ISN'T THIS A CEREMONIAL ROBE?
...I HAVEN'T SEEN THIS PARTICULAR ONE BEFORE. IS IT NEW?

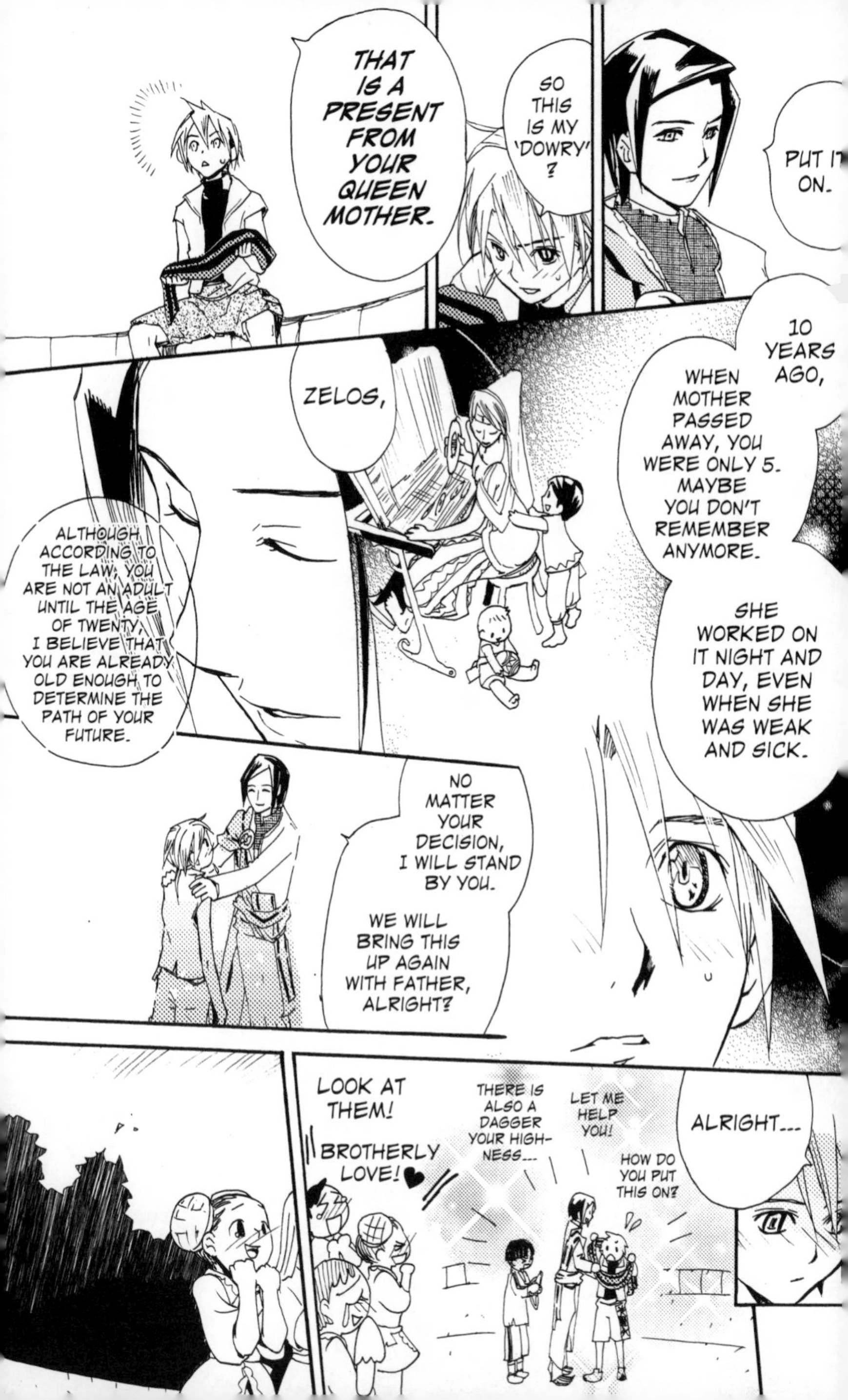
PUT IT ON.
SO THIS IS MY 'DOWRY'?
THAT IS A PRESENT FROM YOUR QUEEN MOTHER.
10 YEARS AGO, WHEN MOTHER PASSED AWAY, YOU WERE ONLY 5. MAYBE YOU DON'T REMEMBER ANYMORE.
SHE WORKED ON IT NIGHT AND DAY, EVEN WHEN SHE WAS WEAK AND SICK.
ZELOS,
ALTHOUGH ACCORDING TO THE LAW, YOU ARE NOT AN ADULT UNTIL THE AGE OF TWENTY, I BELIEVE THAT YOU ARE ALREADY OLD ENOUGH TO DETERMINE THE PATH OF YOUR FUTURE.
NO MATTER YOUR DECISION, I WILL STAND BY YOU.
WE WILL BRING THIS UP AGAIN WITH FATHER, ALRIGHT?
ALRIGHT...
LET ME HELP YOU!
HOW DO YOU PUT THIS ON?
THERE IS ALSO A DAGGER YOUR HIGH-NESS...
LOOK AT THEM!
BROTHERLY LOVE!♥

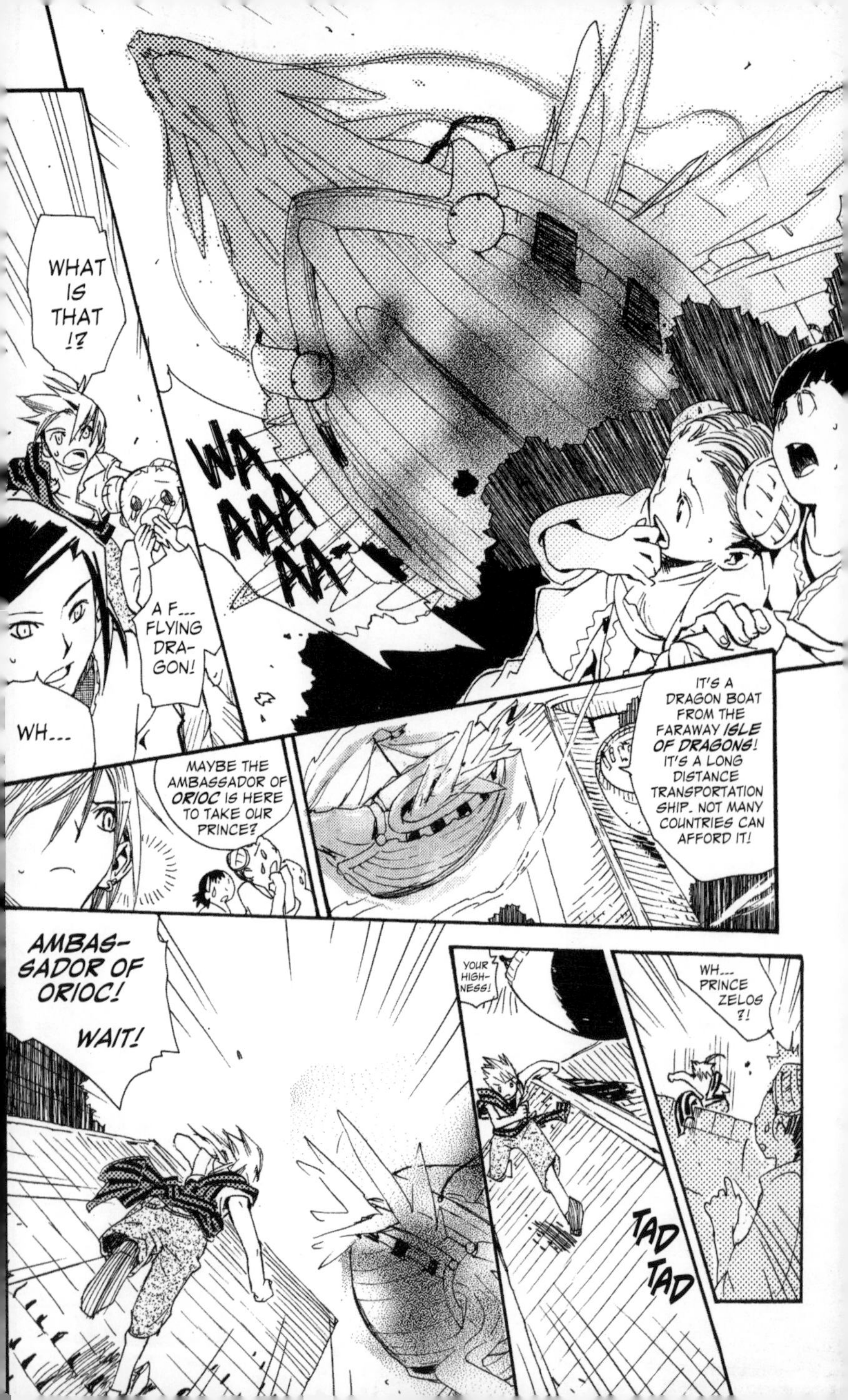
WAAAAAAA-
WHAT IS THAT !?
A F... FLYING DRAGON!
WH...
IT'S A DRAGON BOAT FROM THE FARAWAY ISLE OF DRAGONS! IT'S A LONG DISTANCE TRANSPORTATION SHIP. NOT MANY COUNTRIES CAN AFFORD IT!
MAYBE THE AMBASSADOR OF ORIOC IS HERE TO TAKE OUR PRINCE?
WH... PRINCE ZELOS ?!
YOUR HIGHNESS!
TAD TAD
AMBASSADOR OF ORIOC!
WAIT!

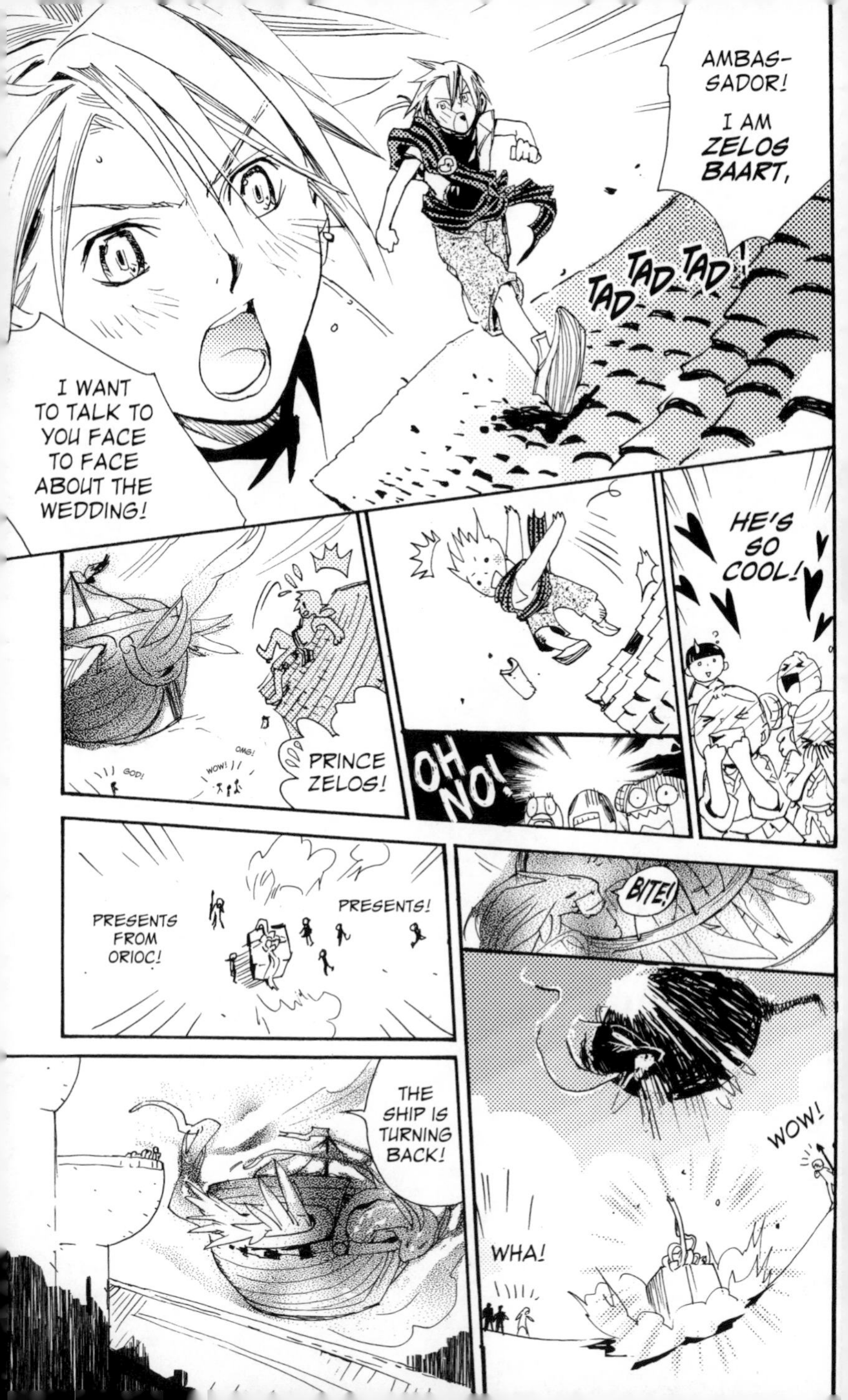

AMBAS-SADOR!
I AM ZELOS BAART,
TAD TAD TAD TAD!
I WANT TO TALK TO YOU FACE TO FACE ABOUT THE WEDDING!
HE'S SO COOL!
OH NO!
PRINCE ZELOS!
OMG!
WOW!
GOD!
BITE!
WOW!
WHA!
PRESENTS!
PRESENTS FROM ORIOC!
THE SHIP IS TURNING BACK!

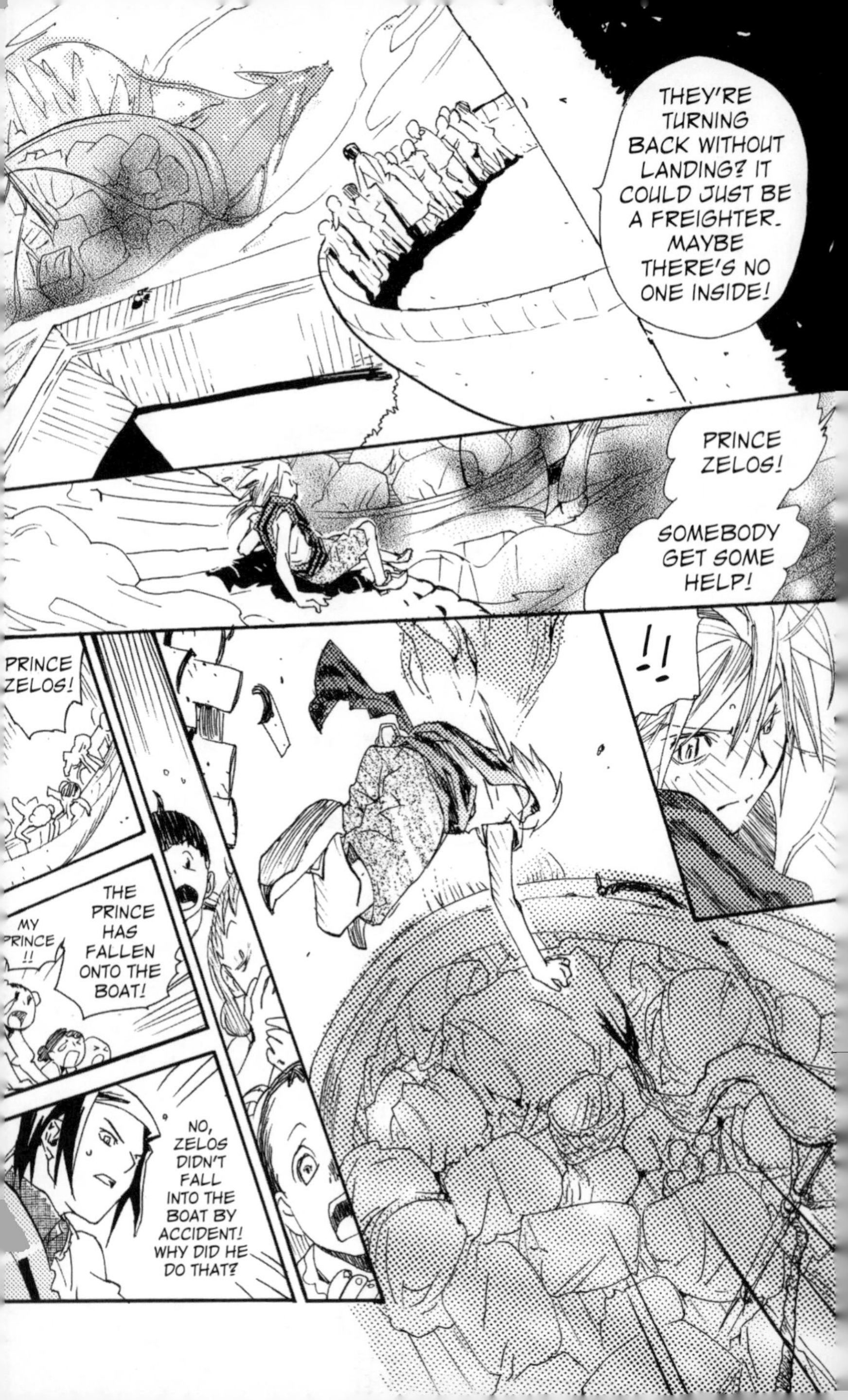
THEY'RE TURNING BACK WITHOUT LANDING? IT COULD JUST BE A FREIGHTER. MAYBE THERE'S NO ONE INSIDE!
PRINCE ZELOS!
SOMEBODY GET SOME HELP!
!!
PRINCE ZELOS!
THE PRINCE HAS FALLEN ONTO THE BOAT!
MY PRINCE!!
NO, ZELOS DIDN'T FALL INTO THE BOAT BY ACCIDENT! WHY DID HE DO THAT?

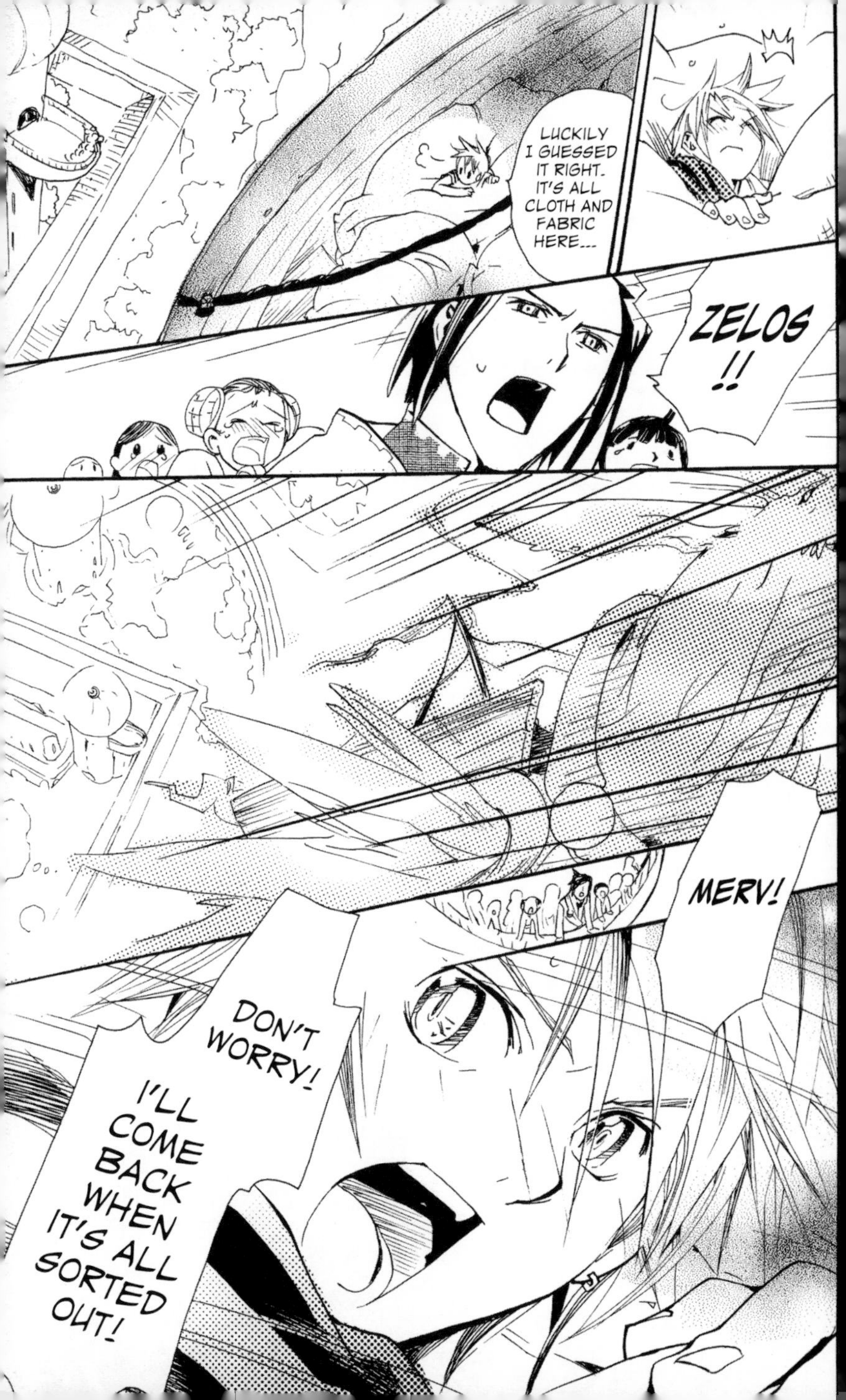
LUCKILY I GUESSED IT RIGHT. IT'S ALL CLOTH AND FABRIC HERE...
ZELOS!!
MERV!
DON'T WORRY!
I'LL COME BACK WHEN IT'S ALL SORTED OUT!

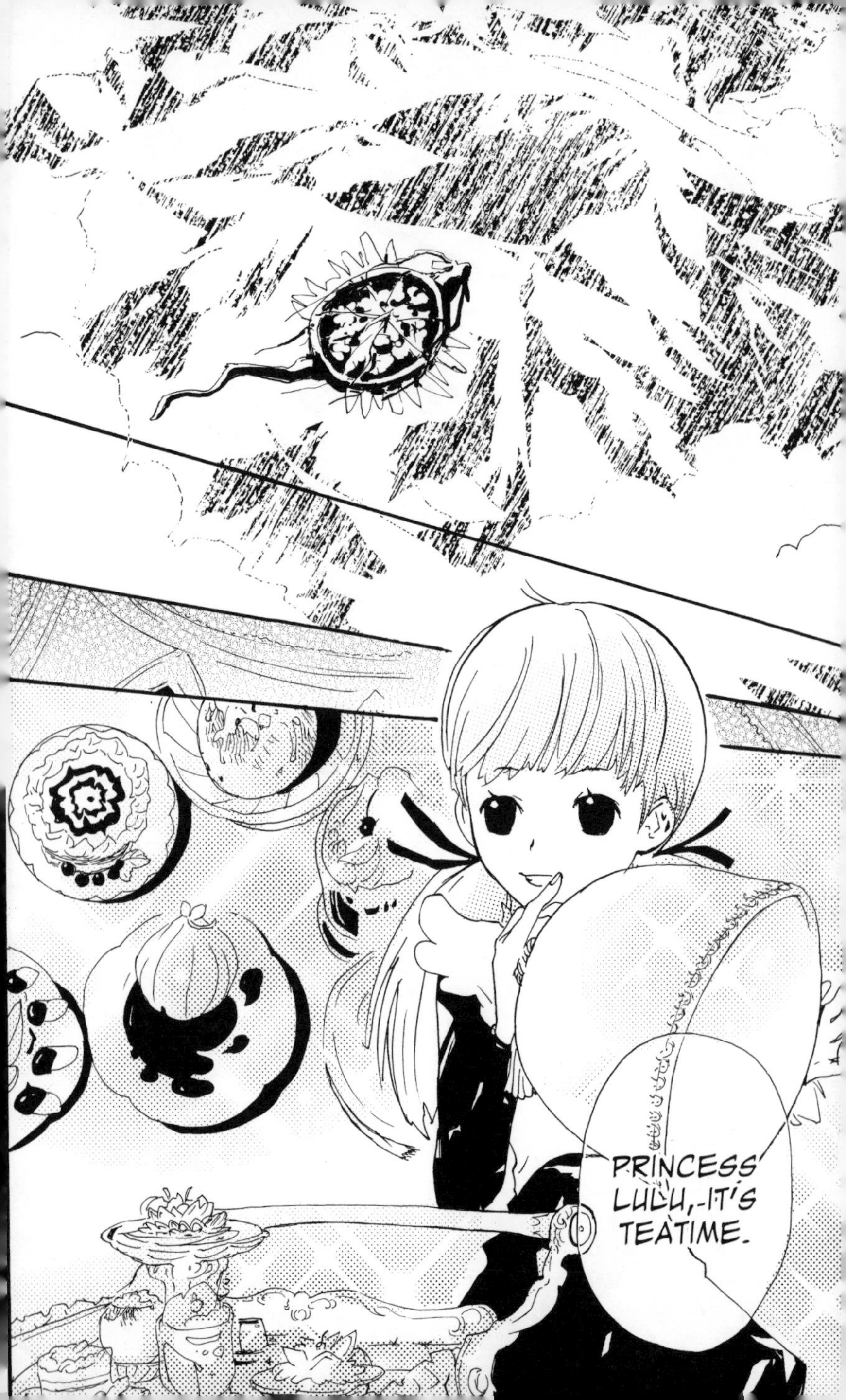
PRINCESS LULU, IT'S TEATIME.

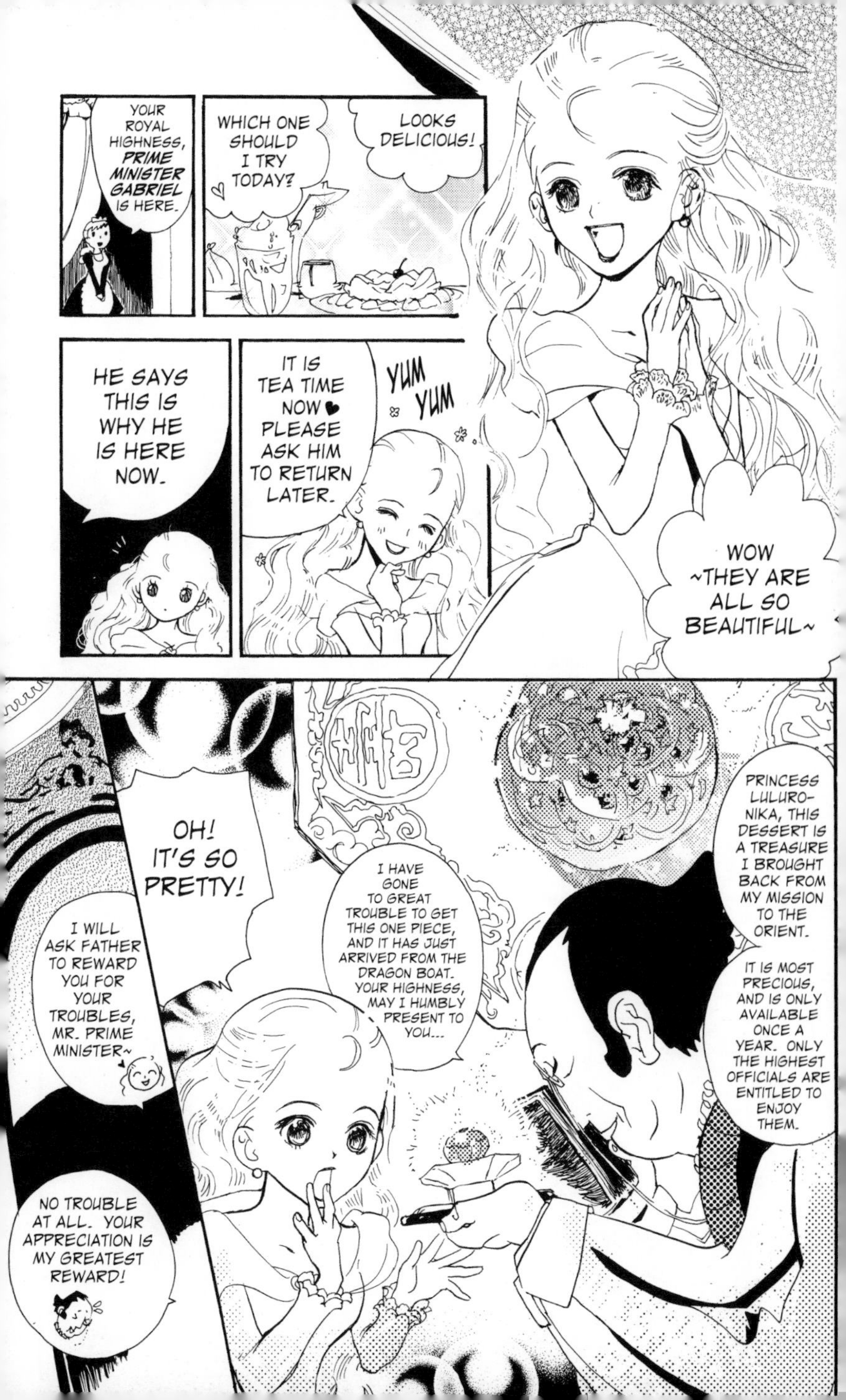
WOW ~THEY ARE ALL SO BEAUTIFUL~
LOOKS DELICIOUS!
WHICH ONE SHOULD I TRY TODAY?
YOUR ROYAL HIGHNESS, PRIME MINISTER GABRIEL IS HERE.
YUM YUM
IT IS TEA TIME NOW♥ PLEASE ASK HIM TO RETURN LATER.
HE SAYS THIS IS WHY HE IS HERE NOW.
PRINCESS LULURONIKA, THIS DESSERT IS A TREASURE I BROUGHT BACK FROM MY MISSION TO THE ORIENT.
IT IS MOST PRECIOUS, AND IS ONLY AVAILABLE ONCE A YEAR. ONLY THE HIGHEST OFFICIALS ARE ENTITLED TO ENJOY THEM.
I HAVE GONE TO GREAT TROUBLE TO GET THIS ONE PIECE, AND IT HAS JUST ARRIVED FROM THE DRAGON BOAT. YOUR HIGHNESS, MAY I HUMBLY PRESENT TO YOU...
OH! IT'S SO PRETTY!
I WILL ASK FATHER TO REWARD YOU FOR YOUR TROUBLES, MR. PRIME MINISTER~
NO TROUBLE AT ALL. YOUR APPRECIATION IS MY GREATEST REWARD!

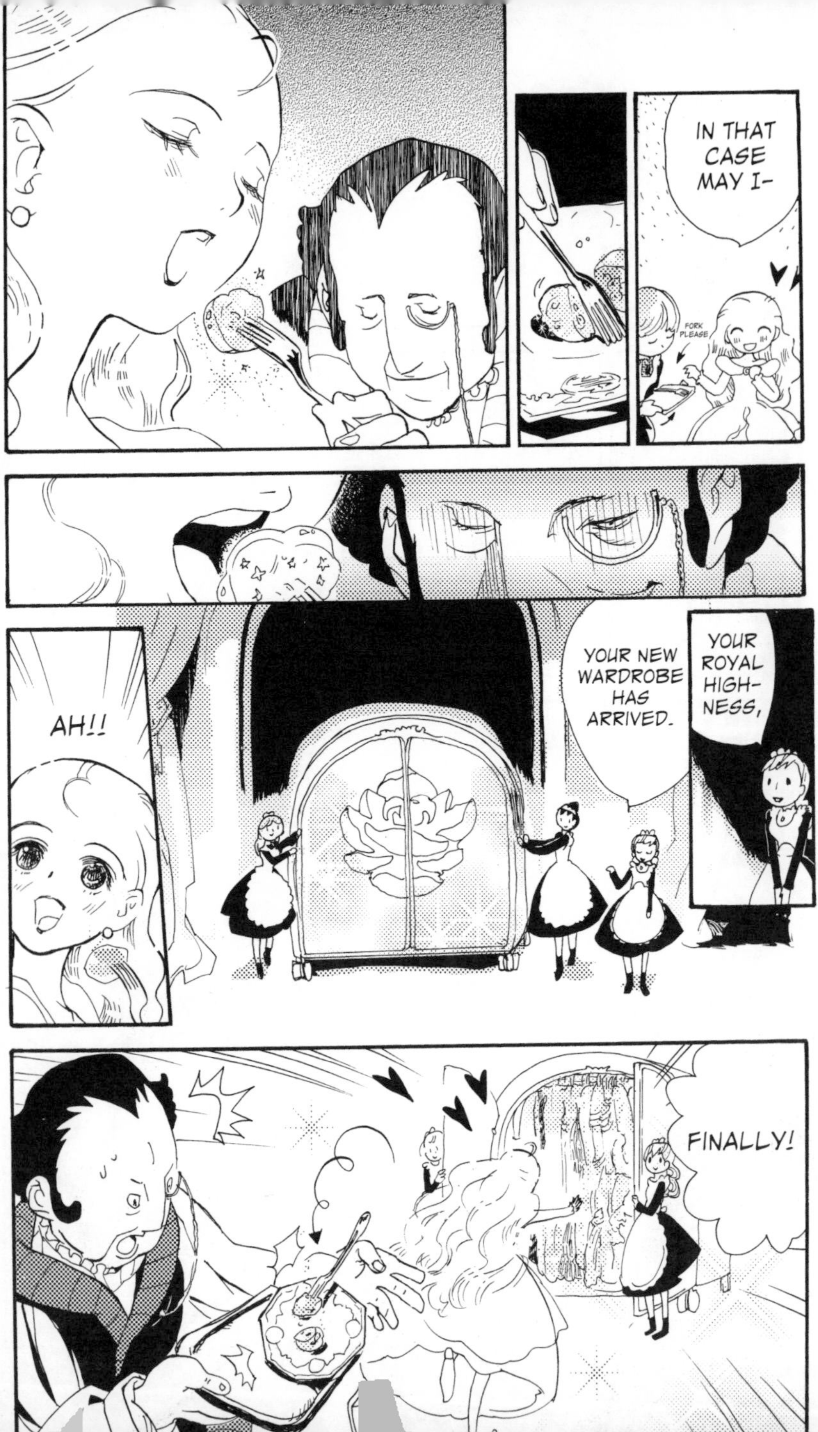
IN THAT CASE MAY I-
FORK PLEASE
YOUR ROYAL HIGH-NESS,
YOUR NEW WARDROBE HAS ARRIVED.
AH!!
FINALLY!

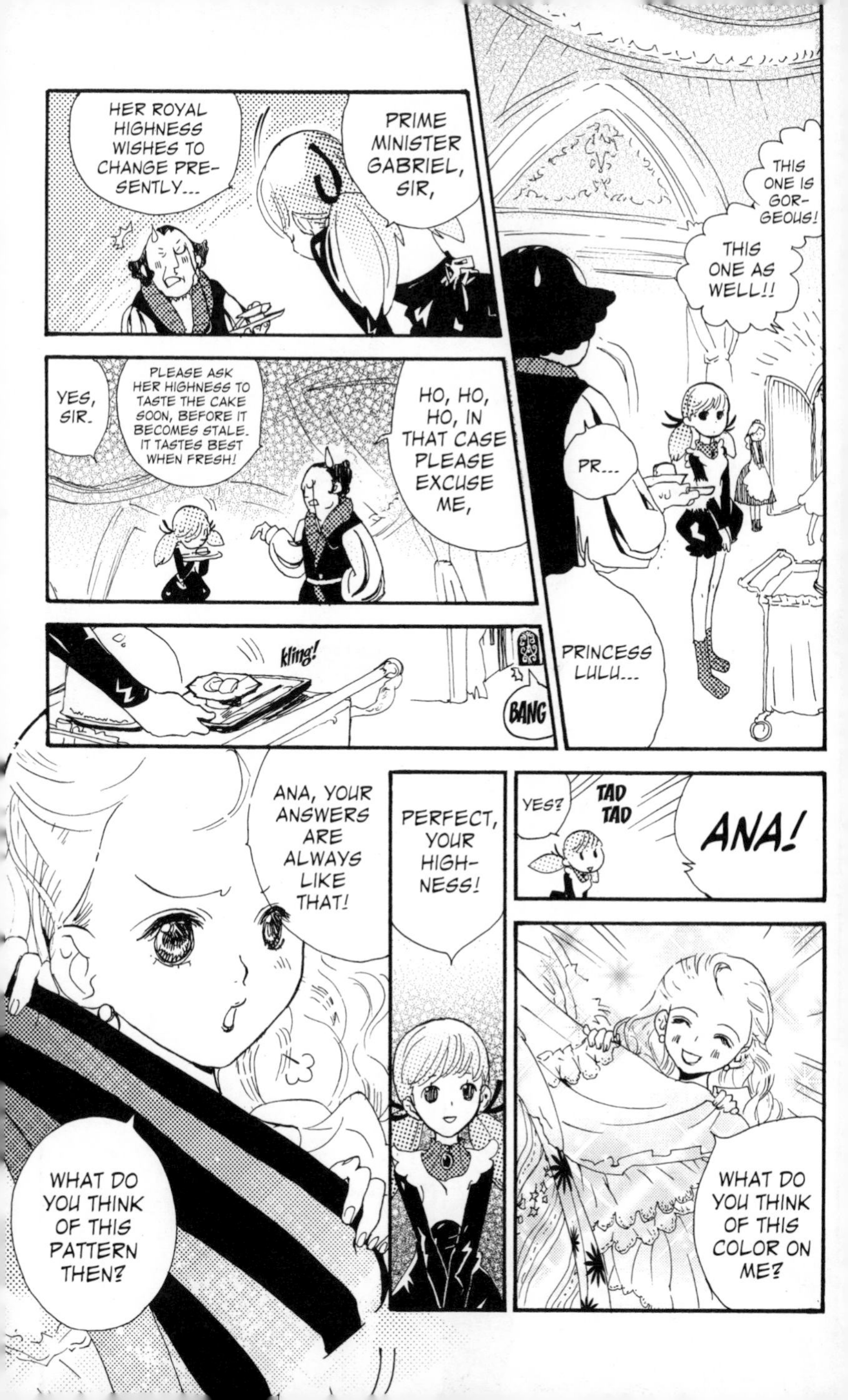
THIS ONE IS GORGEOUS!
THIS ONE AS WELL!!
PR...
PRINCESS LULU...
PRIME MINISTER GABRIEL, SIR,
HER ROYAL HIGHNESS WISHES TO CHANGE PRESENTLY...
HO, HO, HO, IN THAT CASE PLEASE EXCUSE ME,
PLEASE ASK HER HIGHNESS TO TASTE THE CAKE SOON, BEFORE IT BECOMES STALE. IT TASTES BEST WHEN FRESH!
YES, SIR.
kling!
BANG
ANA!
TAD TAD
YES?
WHAT DO YOU THINK OF THIS COLOR ON ME?
PERFECT, YOUR HIGHNESS!
ANA, YOUR ANSWERS ARE ALWAYS LIKE THAT!
WHAT DO YOU THINK OF THIS PATTERN THEN?

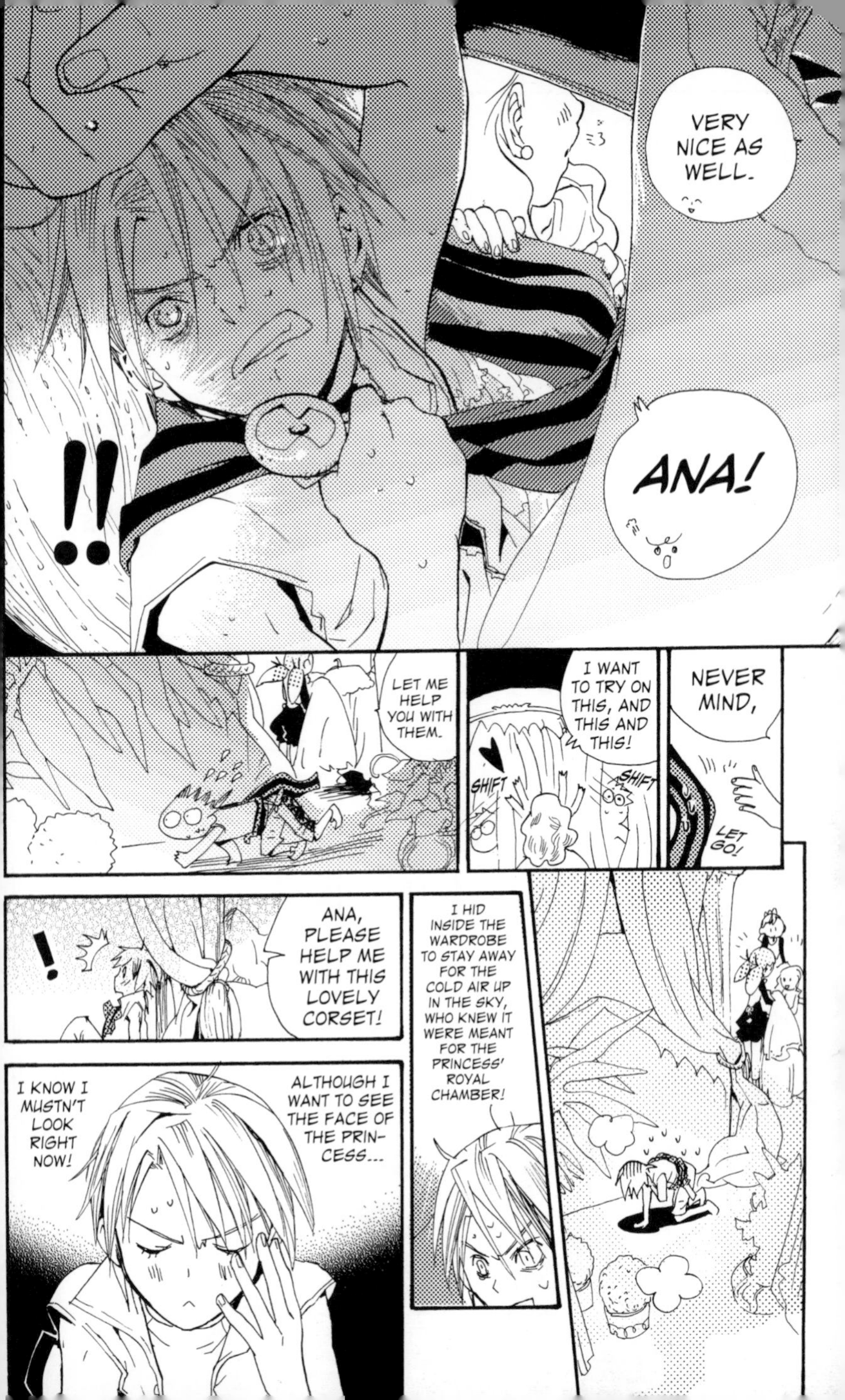
VERY NICE AS WELL.
ANA!
!!
NEVER MIND,
LET GO!
I WANT TO TRY ON THIS, AND THIS AND THIS!
SHIFT
SHIFT
LET ME HELP YOU WITH THEM.
I HID INSIDE THE WARDROBE TO STAY AWAY FOR THE COLD AIR UP IN THE SKY, WHO KNEW IT WERE MEANT FOR THE PRINCESS' ROYAL CHAMBER!
ANA, PLEASE HELP ME WITH THIS LOVELY CORSET!
!
ALTHOUGH I WANT TO SEE THE FACE OF THE PRIN-CESS...
I KNOW I MUSTN'T LOOK RIGHT NOW!

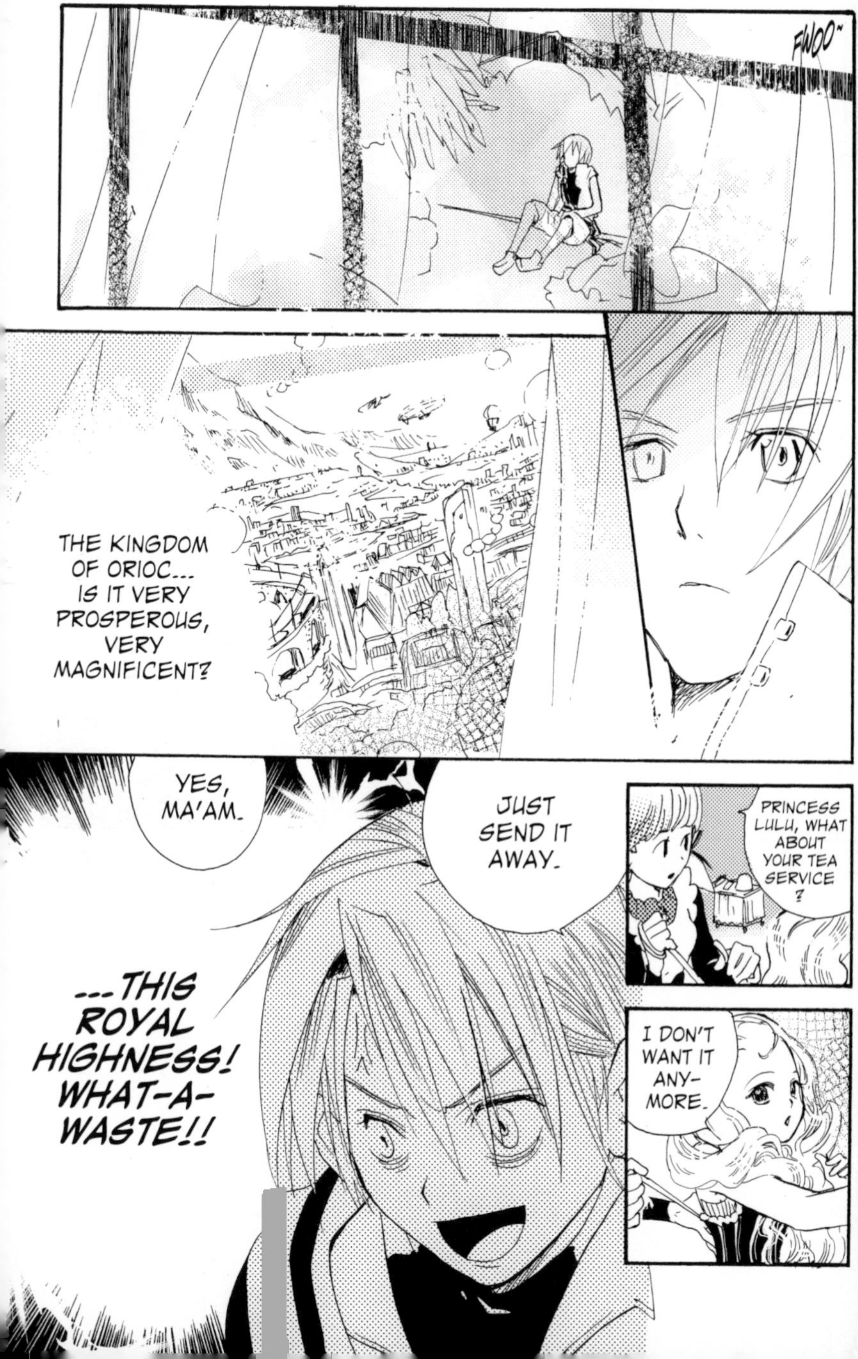
FWOO~
THE KINGDOM OF ORIOC... IS IT VERY PROSPEROUS, VERY MAGNIFICENT?
PRINCESS LULU, WHAT ABOUT YOUR TEA SERVICE?
I DON'T WANT IT ANYMORE.
JUST SEND IT AWAY.
YES, MA'AM.
...THIS ROYAL HIGHNESS! WHAT-A-WASTE!!

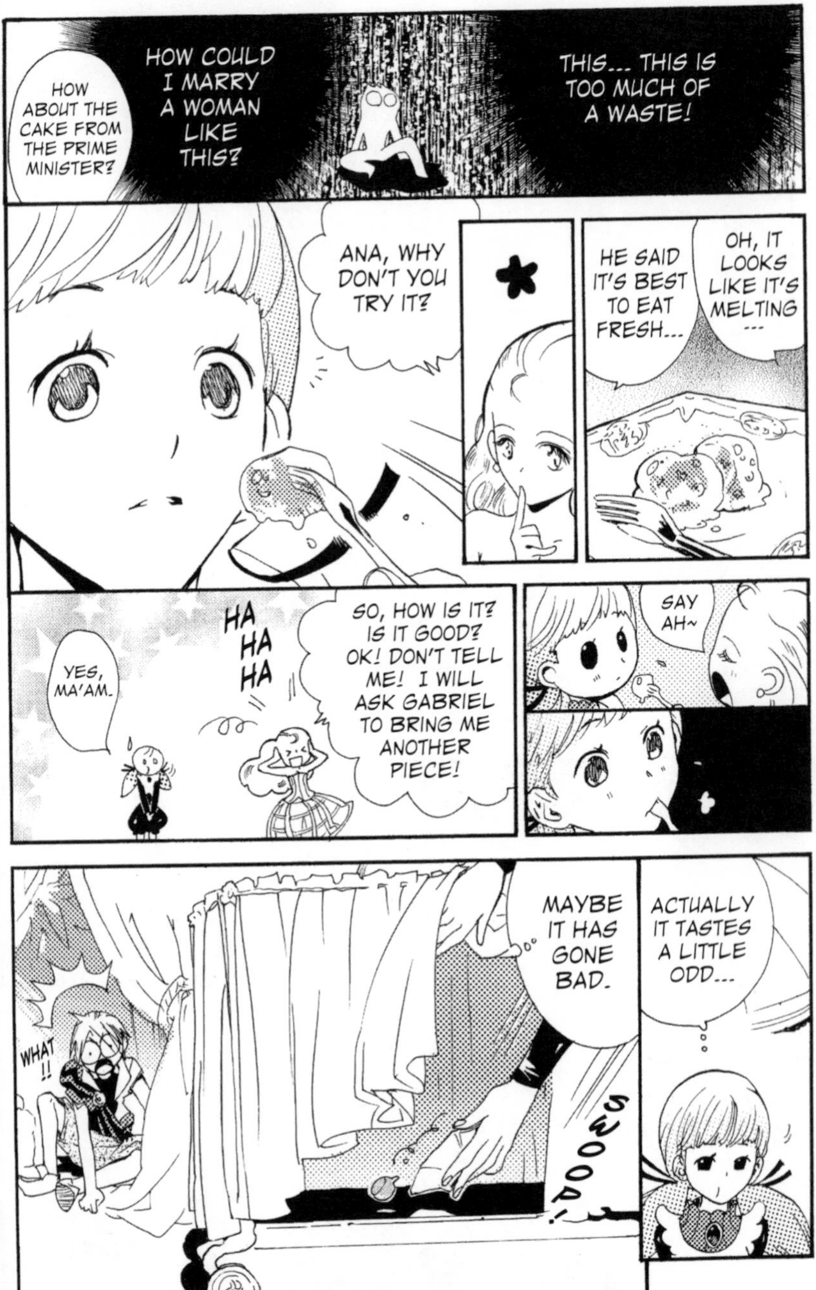
THIS... THIS IS TOO MUCH OF A WASTE!
HOW COULD I MARRY A WOMAN LIKE THIS?
HOW ABOUT THE CAKE FROM THE PRIME MINISTER?
OH, IT LOOKS LIKE IT'S MELTING...
HE SAID IT'S BEST TO EAT FRESH...
ANA, WHY DON'T YOU TRY IT?
SAY AH~
SO, HOW IS IT? IS IT GOOD? OK! DON'T TELL ME! I WILL ASK GABRIEL TO BRING ME ANOTHER PIECE!
HA HA HA
YES, MA'AM.
ACTUALLY IT TASTES A LITTLE ODD...
MAYBE IT HAS GONE BAD.
SWOOP!
WHAT !!

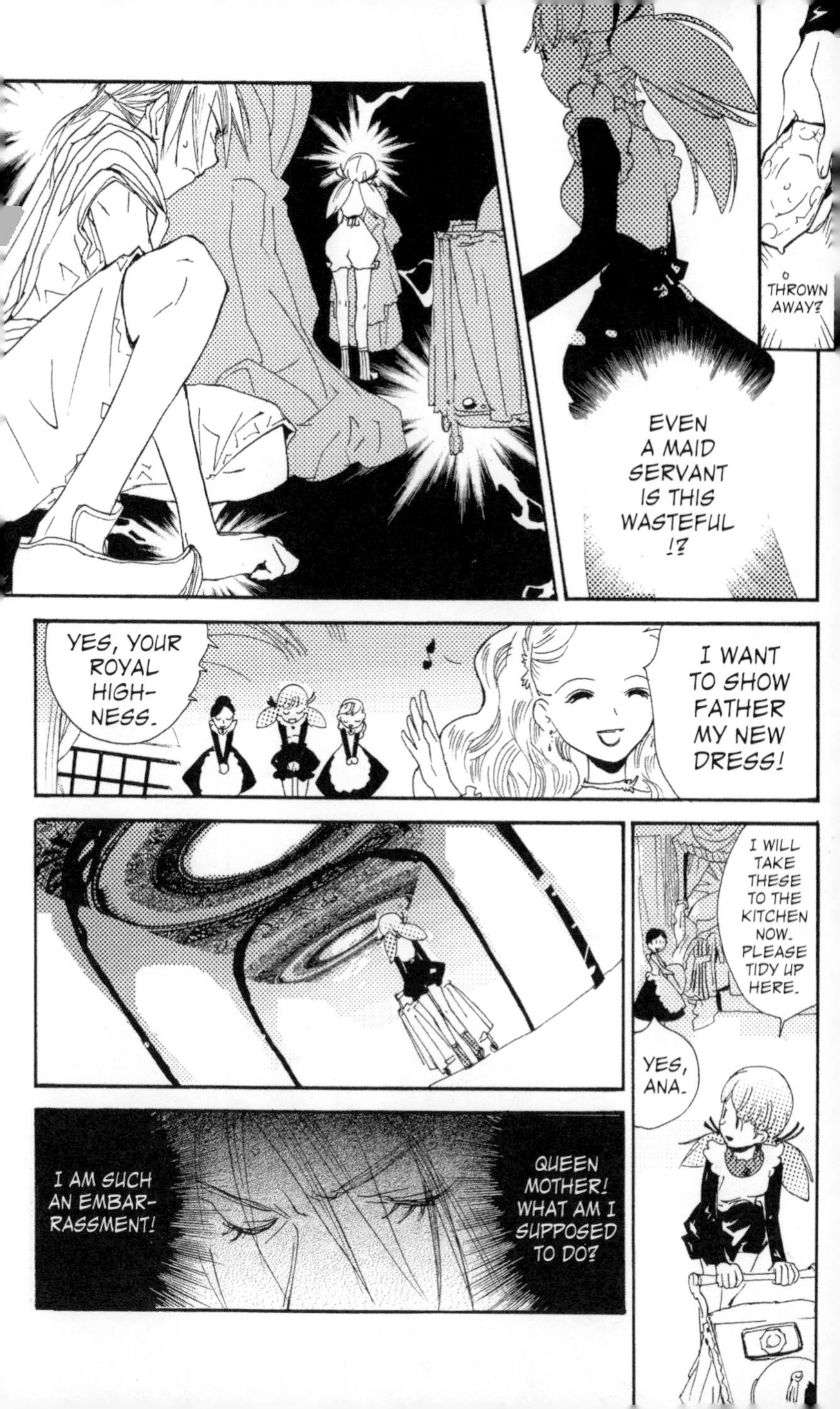
THROWN AWAY?
EVEN A MAID SERVANT IS THIS WASTEFUL !?
I WANT TO SHOW FATHER MY NEW DRESS!
YES, YOUR ROYAL HIGH-NESS.
I WILL TAKE THESE TO THE KITCHEN NOW. PLEASE TIDY UP HERE.
YES, ANA.
QUEEN MOTHER! WHAT AM I SUPPOSED TO DO?
I AM SUCH AN EMBAR-RASSMENT!

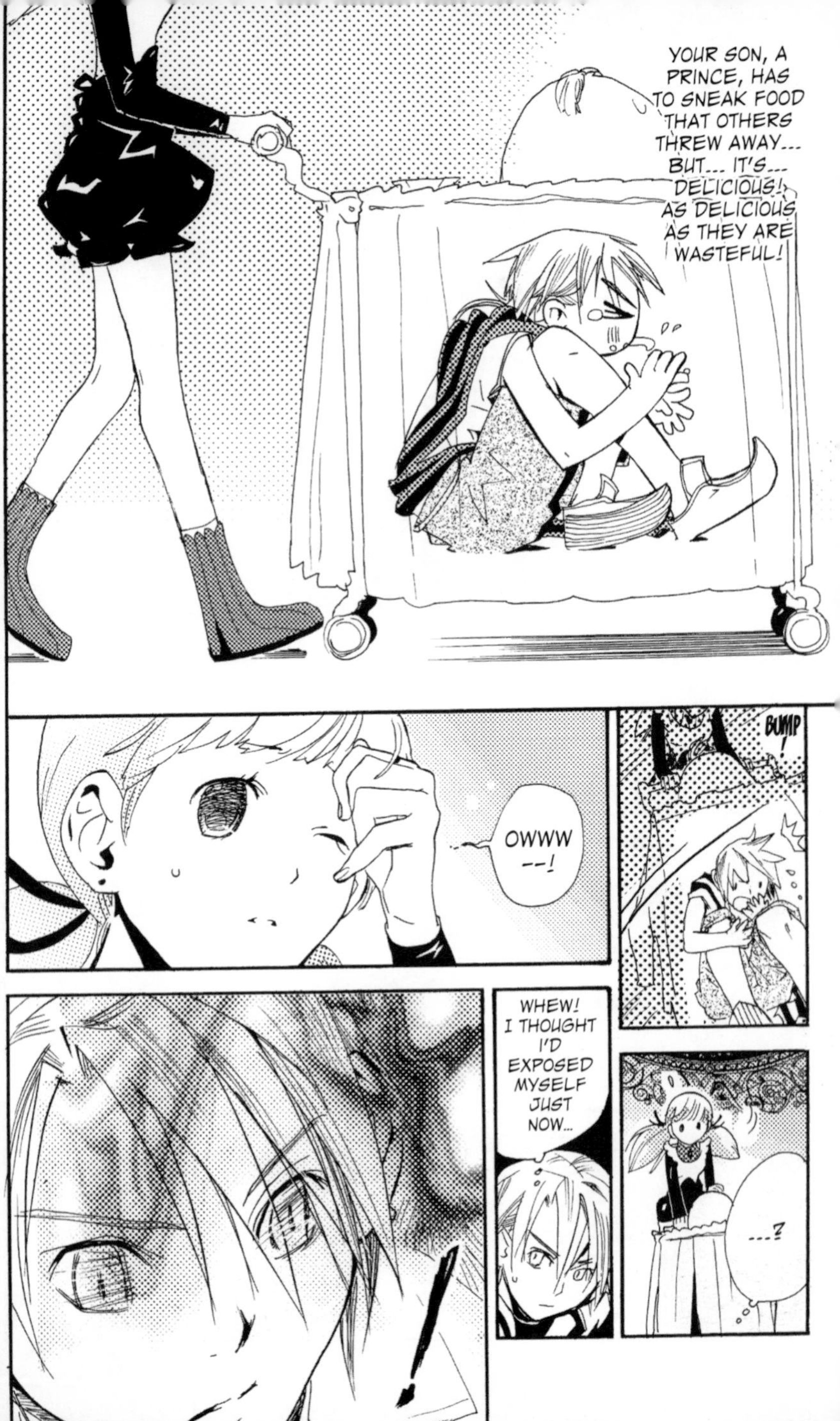
YOUR SON, A PRINCE, HAS TO SNEAK FOOD THAT OTHERS THREW AWAY... BUT... IT'S... DELICIOUS! AS DELICIOUS AS THEY ARE WASTEFUL!
BUMP!
OWWW--!
...?
WHEW! I THOUGHT I'D EXPOSED MYSELF JUST NOW...

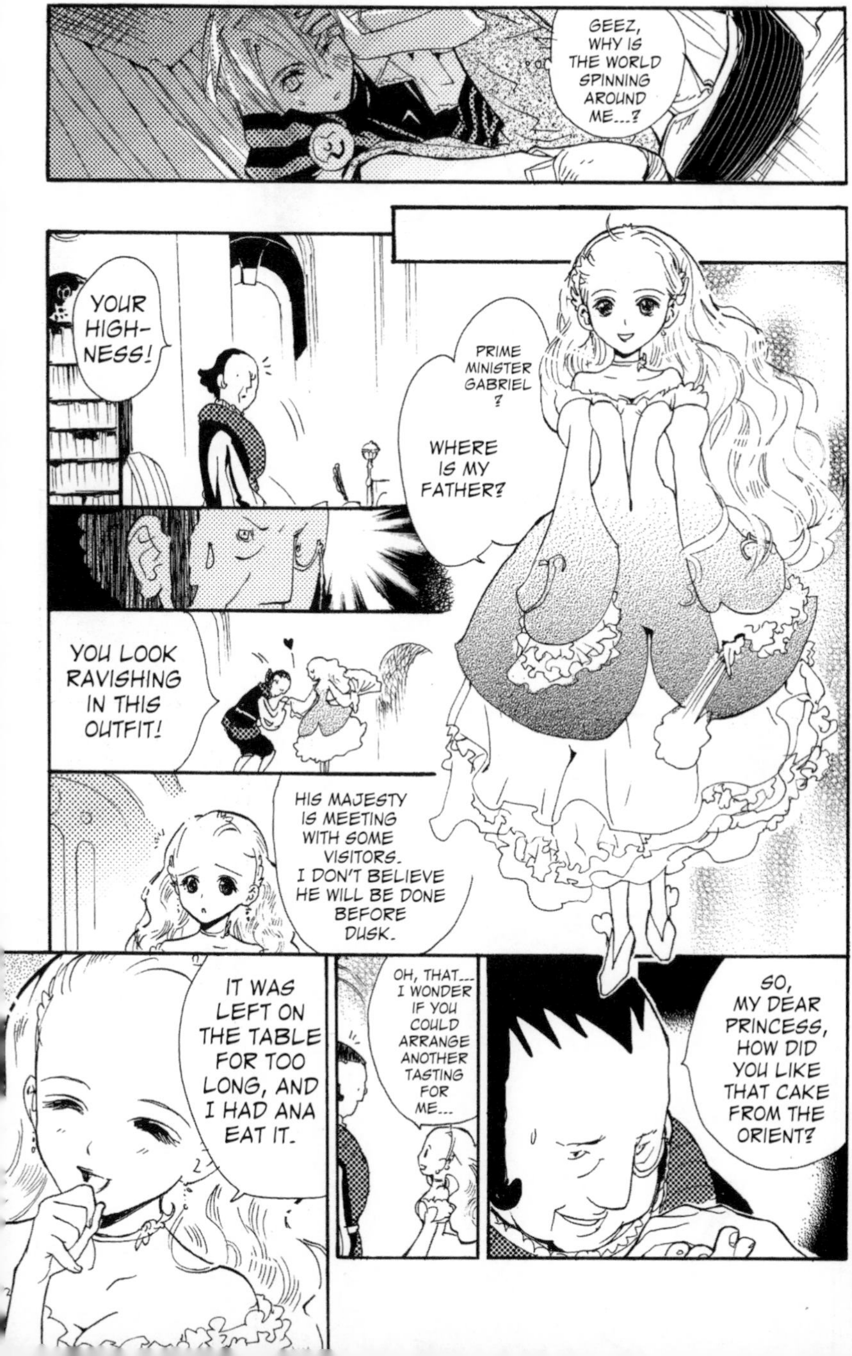
GEEZ, WHY IS THE WORLD SPINNING AROUND ME...?
PRIME MINISTER GABRIEL?
WHERE IS MY FATHER?
YOUR HIGHNESS!
YOU LOOK RAVISHING IN THIS OUTFIT!
HIS MAJESTY IS MEETING WITH SOME VISITORS. I DON'T BELIEVE HE WILL BE DONE BEFORE DUSK.
SO, MY DEAR PRINCESS, HOW DID YOU LIKE THAT CAKE FROM THE ORIENT?
OH, THAT... I WONDER IF YOU COULD ARRANGE ANOTHER TASTING FOR ME...
IT WAS LEFT ON THE TABLE FOR TOO LONG, AND I HAD ANA EAT IT.

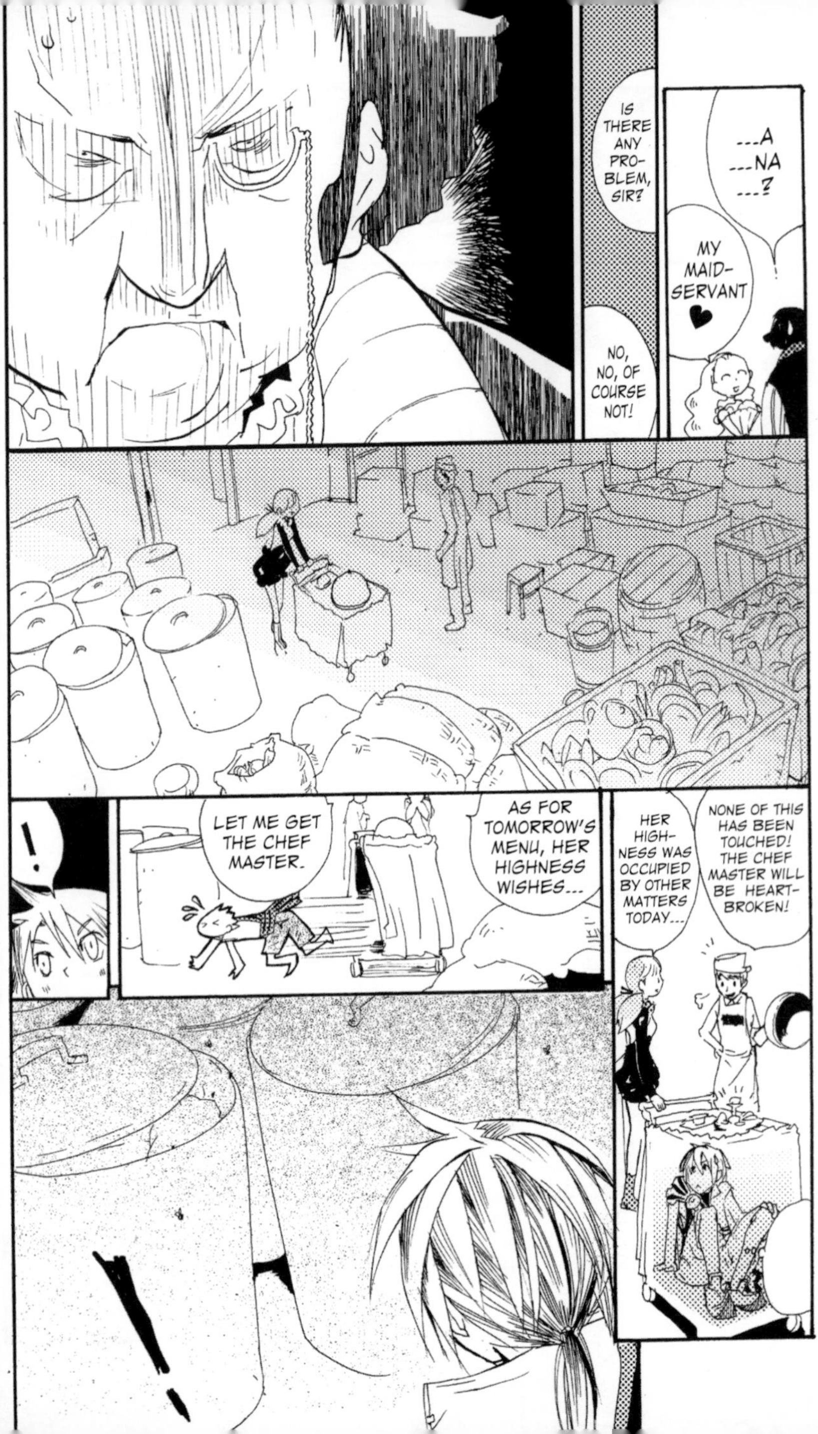

...A
...NA
...?
MY MAID-SERVANT ♥
IS THERE ANY PRO-BLEM, SIR?
NO, NO, OF COURSE NOT!
NONE OF THIS HAS BEEN TOUCHED! THE CHEF MASTER WILL BE HEART-BROKEN!
HER HIGH-NESS WAS OCCUPIED BY OTHER MATTERS TODAY...
AS FOR TOMORROW'S MENU, HER HIGHNESS WISHES...
LET ME GET THE CHEF MASTER.
!

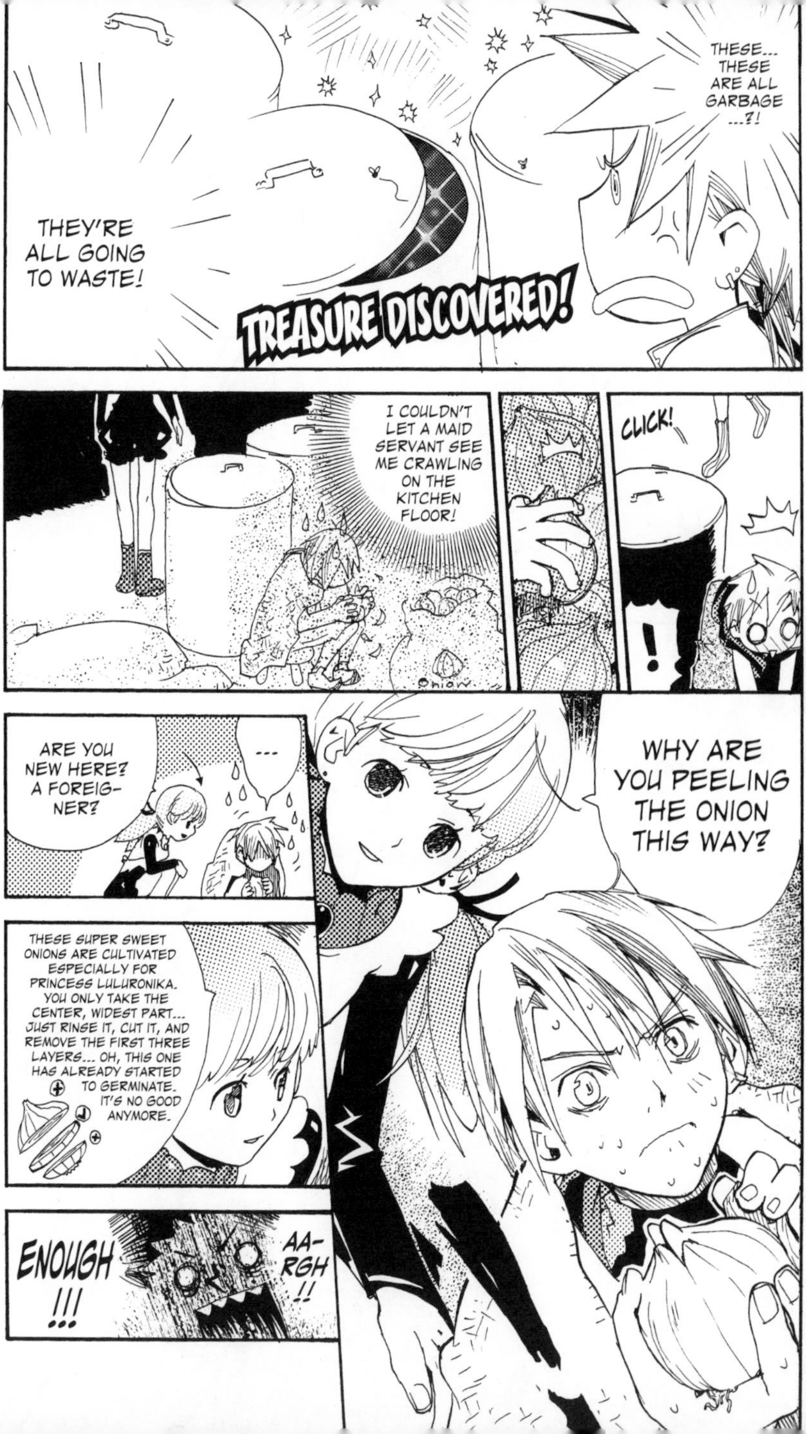
THESE... THESE ARE ALL GARBAGE...?!
THEY'RE ALL GOING TO WASTE!
TREASURE DISCOVERED!
CLICK!
!
I COULDN'T LET A MAID SERVANT SEE ME CRAWLING ON THE KITCHEN FLOOR!
Onion
WHY ARE YOU PEELING THE ONION THIS WAY?

ARE YOU NEW HERE? A FOREIG-NER?
THESE SUPER SWEET ONIONS ARE CULTIVATED ESPECIALLY FOR PRINCESS LULURONIKA. YOU ONLY TAKE THE CENTER, WIDEST PART... JUST RINSE IT, CUT IT, AND REMOVE THE FIRST THREE LAYERS... OH, THIS ONE HAS ALREADY STARTED TO GERMINATE. IT'S NO GOOD ANYMORE.
AA-RGH!!
ENOUGH!!!...

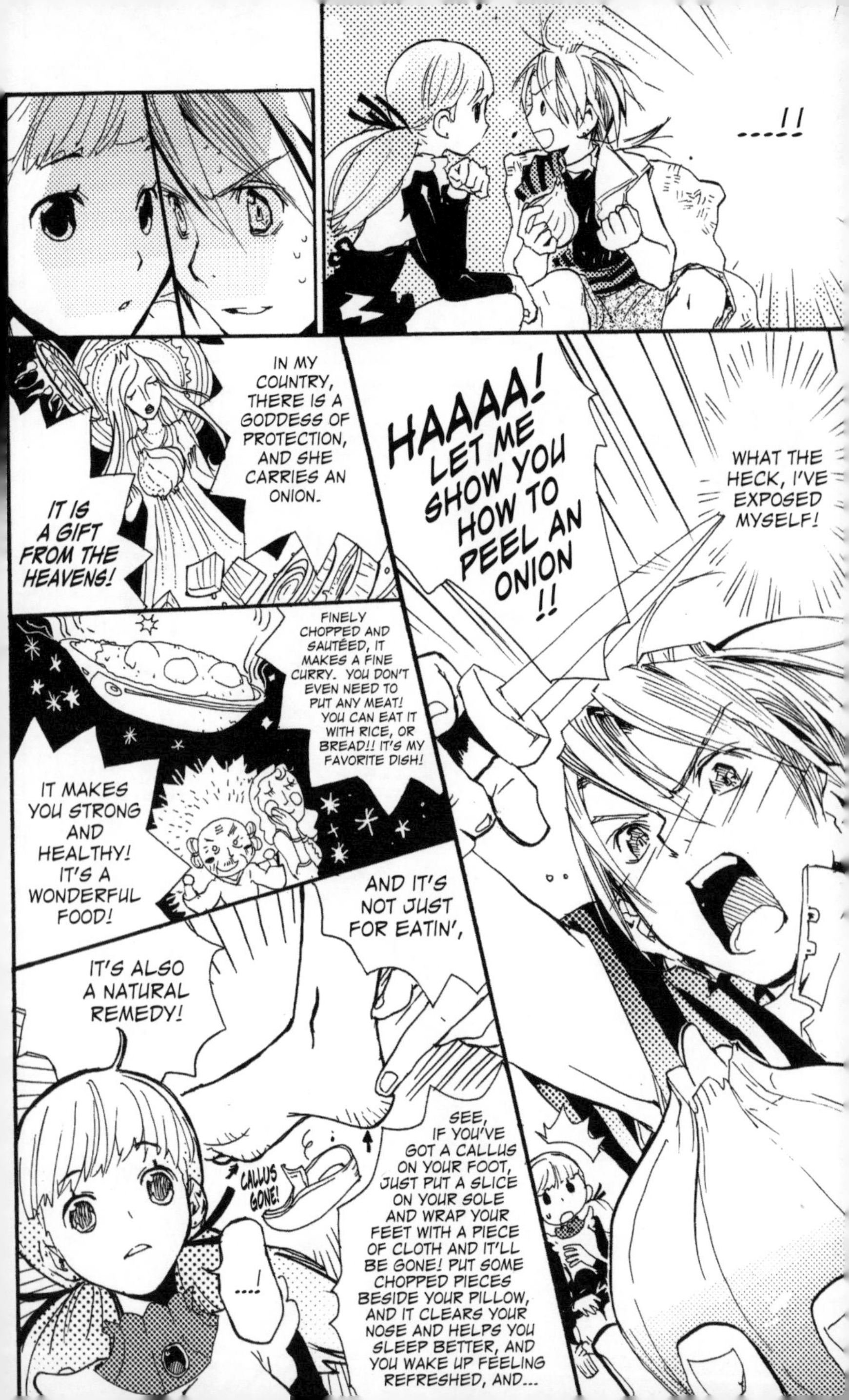
...!!
HAAAA! LET ME SHOW YOU HOW TO PEEL AN ONION!!
WHAT THE HECK, I'VE EXPOSED MYSELF!
IN MY COUNTRY, THERE IS A GODDESS OF PROTECTION, AND SHE CARRIES AN ONION.
IT IS A GIFT FROM THE HEAVENS!
FINELY CHOPPED AND SAUTÉED, IT MAKES A FINE CURRY. YOU DON'T EVEN NEED TO PUT ANY MEAT! YOU CAN EAT IT WITH RICE, OR BREAD!! IT'S MY FAVORITE DISH!
IT MAKES YOU STRONG AND HEALTHY! IT'S A WONDERFUL FOOD!
AND IT'S NOT JUST FOR EATIN',
IT'S ALSO A NATURAL REMEDY!
SEE, IF YOU'VE GOT A CALLUS ON YOUR FOOT, JUST PUT A SLICE ON YOUR SOLE AND WRAP YOUR FEET WITH A PIECE OF CLOTH AND IT'LL BE GONE! PUT SOME CHOPPED PIECES BESIDE YOUR PILLOW, AND IT CLEARS YOUR NOSE AND HELPS YOU SLEEP BETTER, AND YOU WAKE UP FEELING REFRESHED, AND...
CALLUS GONE!
...!

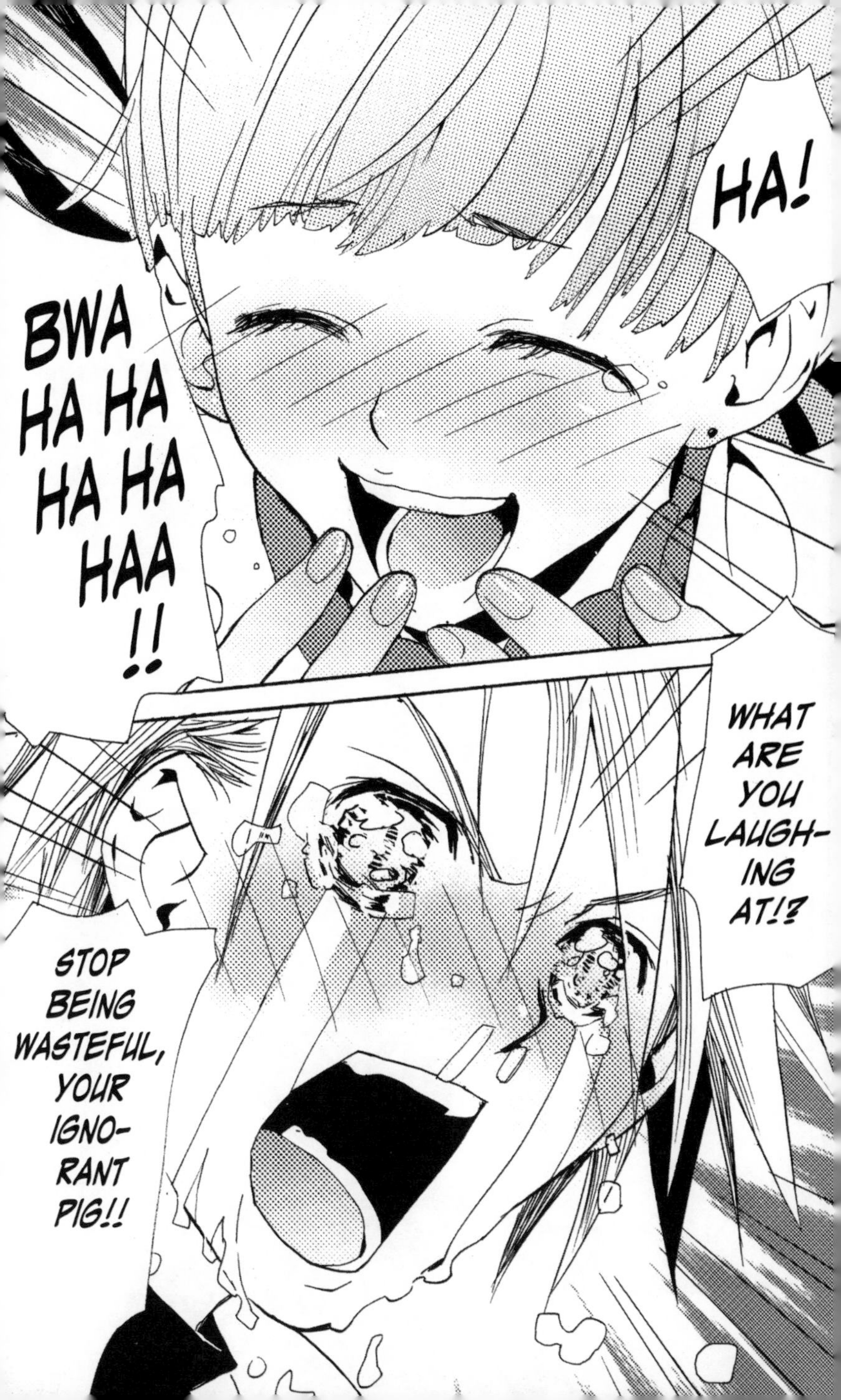
HA!
BWA HA HA HA HA HAA!!
WHAT ARE YOU LAUGHING AT!?
STOP BEING WASTEFUL, YOUR IGNORANT PIG!!

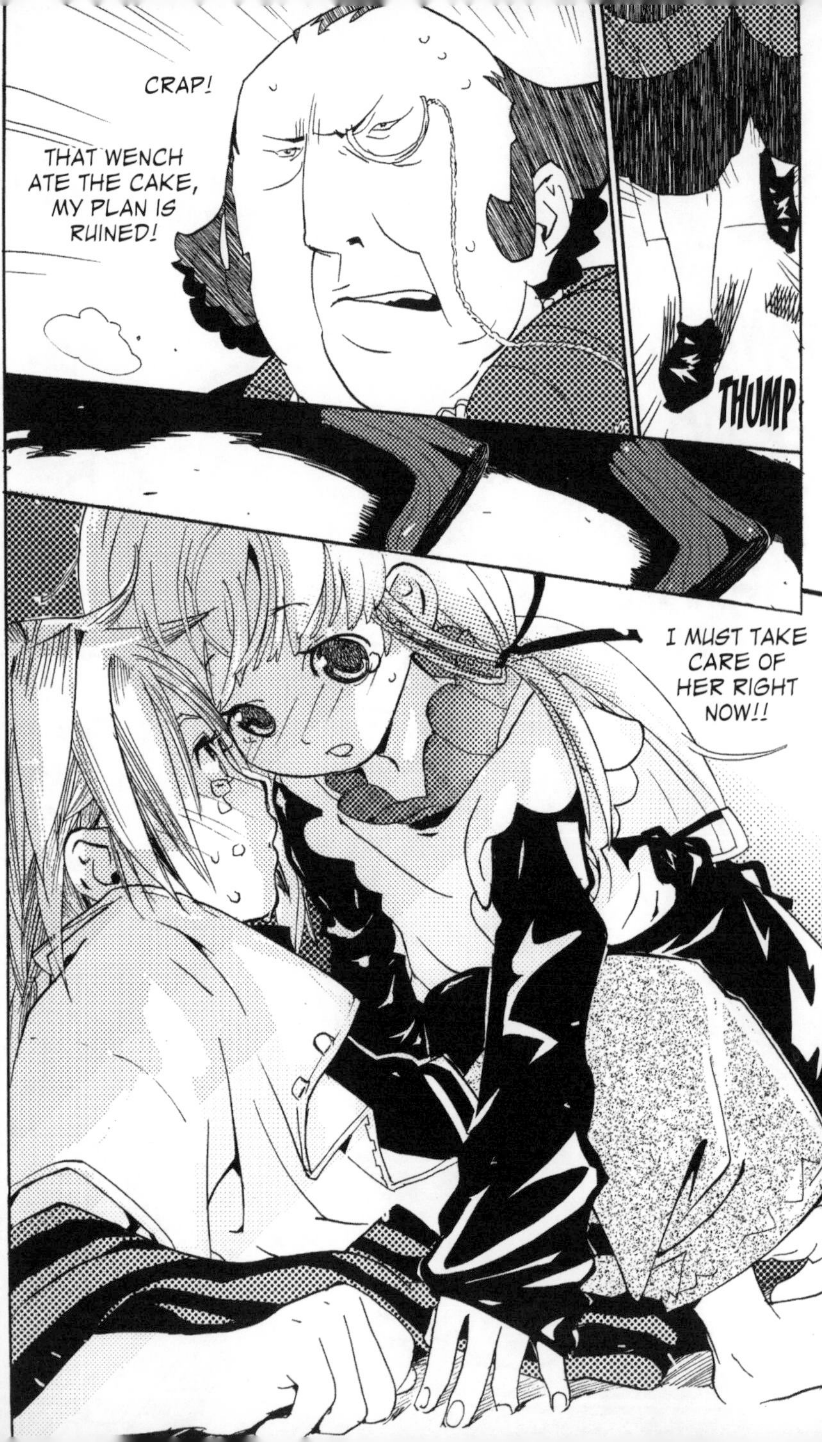
THUMP
CRAP!
THAT WENCH ATE THE CAKE, MY PLAN IS RUINED!
I MUST TAKE CARE OF HER RIGHT NOW!!

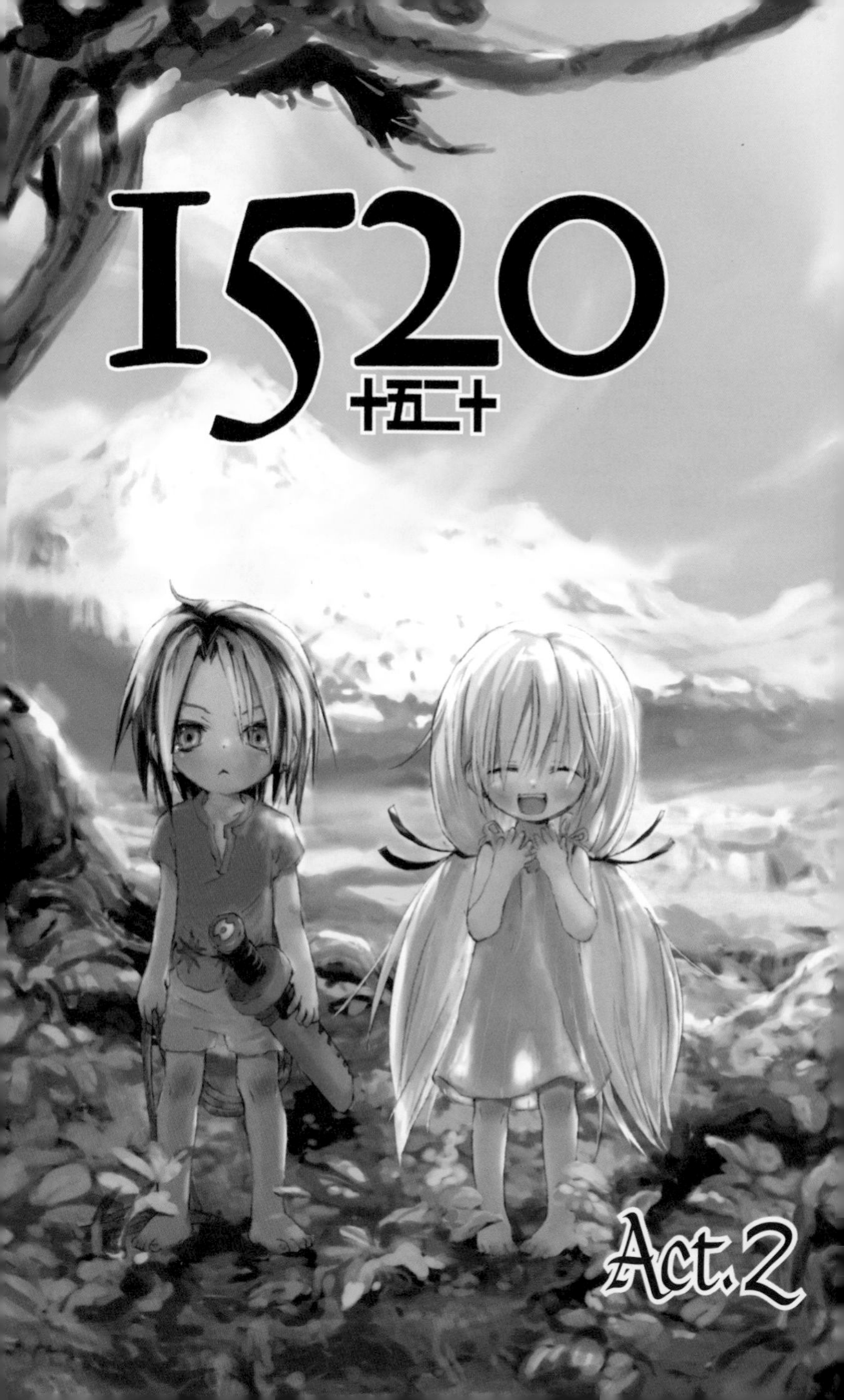
1520
十五二十
Act.2

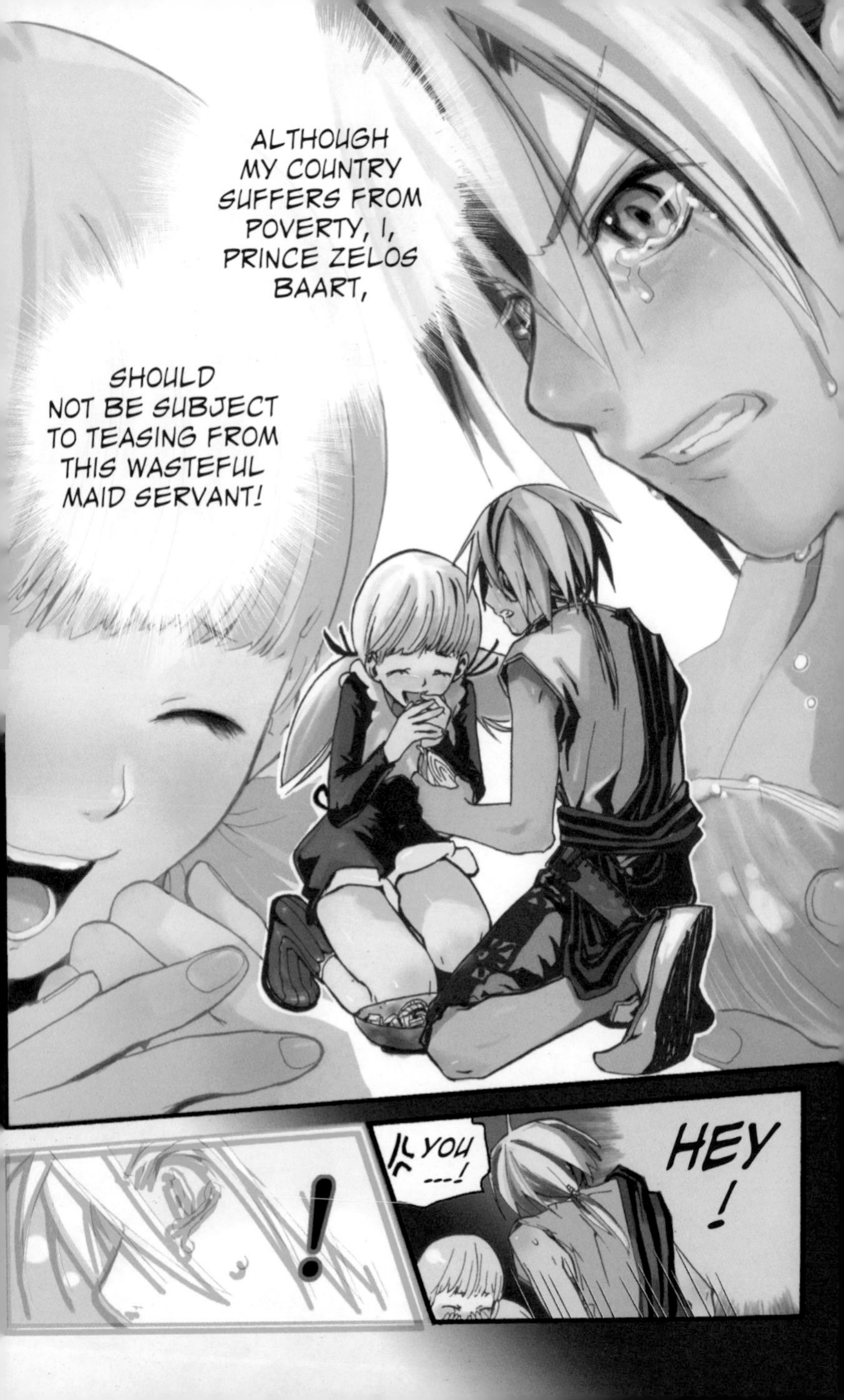
ALTHOUGH MY COUNTRY SUFFERS FROM POVERTY, I, PRINCE ZELOS BAART,
SHOULD NOT BE SUBJECT TO TEASING FROM THIS WASTEFUL MAID SERVANT!
HEY!
YOU ---!
!

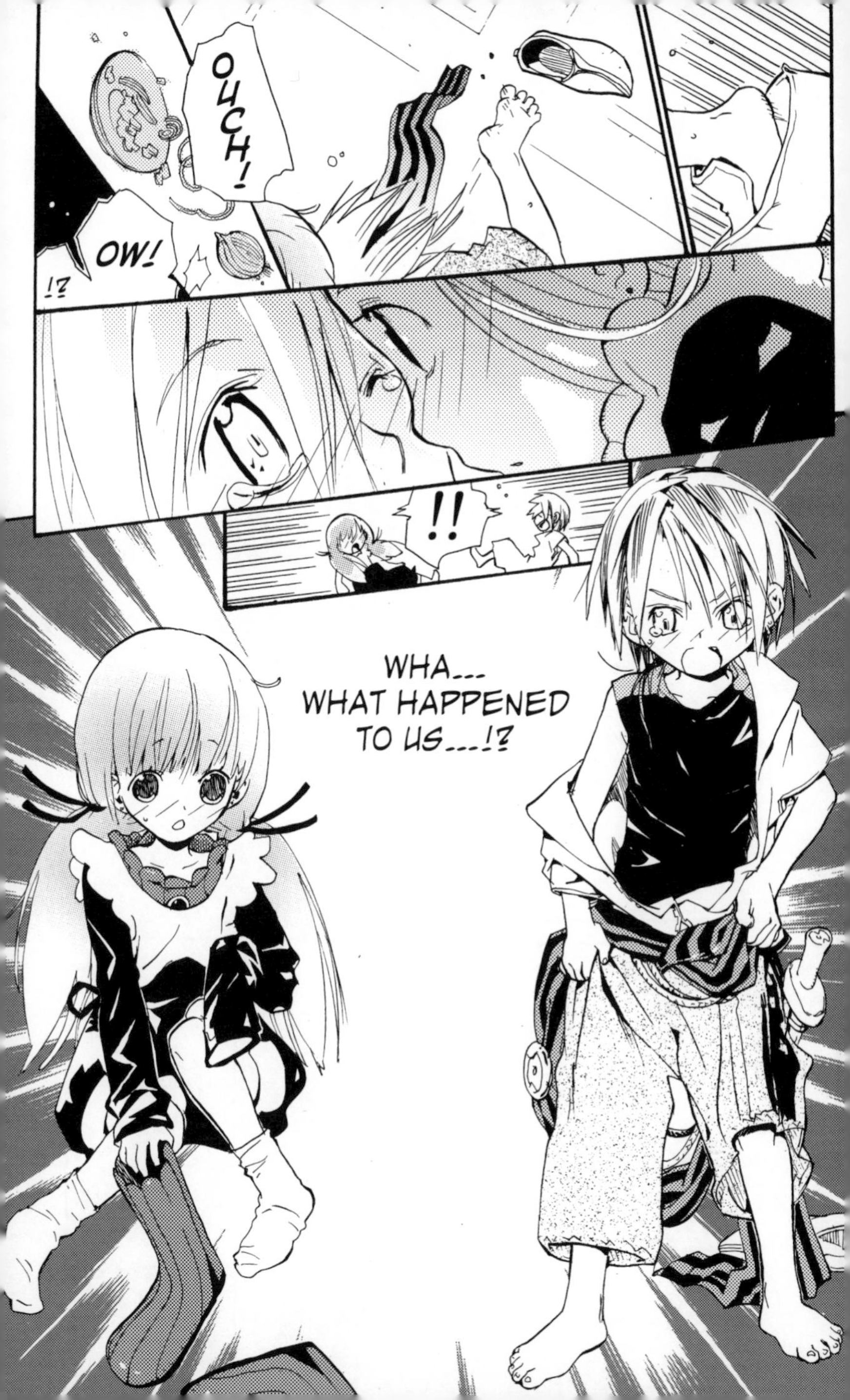
OUCH!
OW!
!?
!!
WHA...
WHAT HAPPENED
TO US...!?

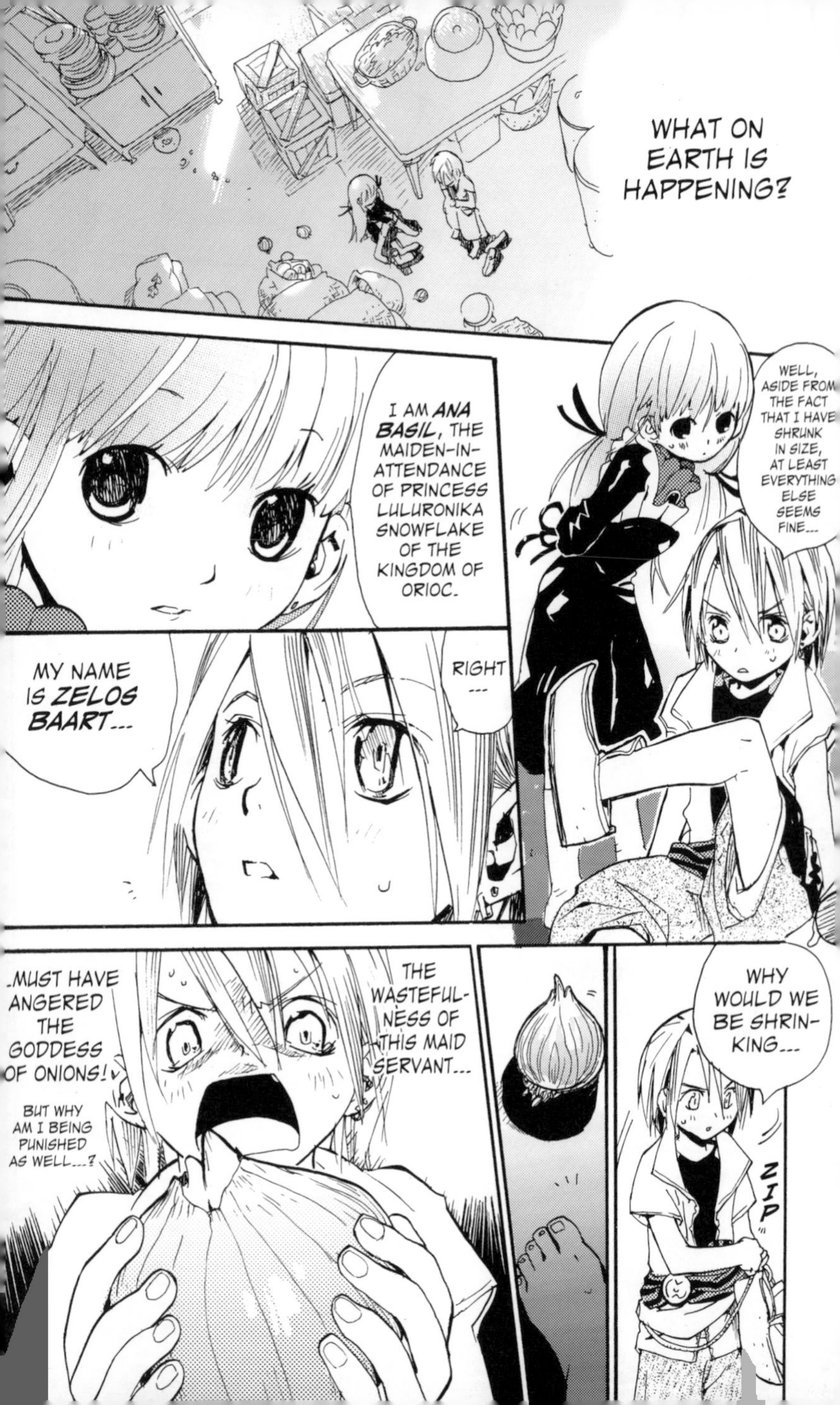
WHAT ON EARTH IS HAPPENING?
WELL, ASIDE FROM THE FACT THAT I HAVE SHRUNK IN SIZE, AT LEAST EVERYTHING ELSE SEEMS FINE...
I AM ANA BASIL, THE MAIDEN-IN-ATTENDANCE OF PRINCESS LULURONIKA SNOWFLAKE OF THE KINGDOM OF ORIOC.
RIGHT...
MY NAME IS ZELOS BAART...
WHY WOULD WE BE SHRIN-KING...
ZIP
THE WASTEFUL-NESS OF THIS MAID SERVANT...
..MUST HAVE ANGERED THE GODDESS OF ONIONS!
BUT WHY AM I BEING PUNISHED AS WELL...?

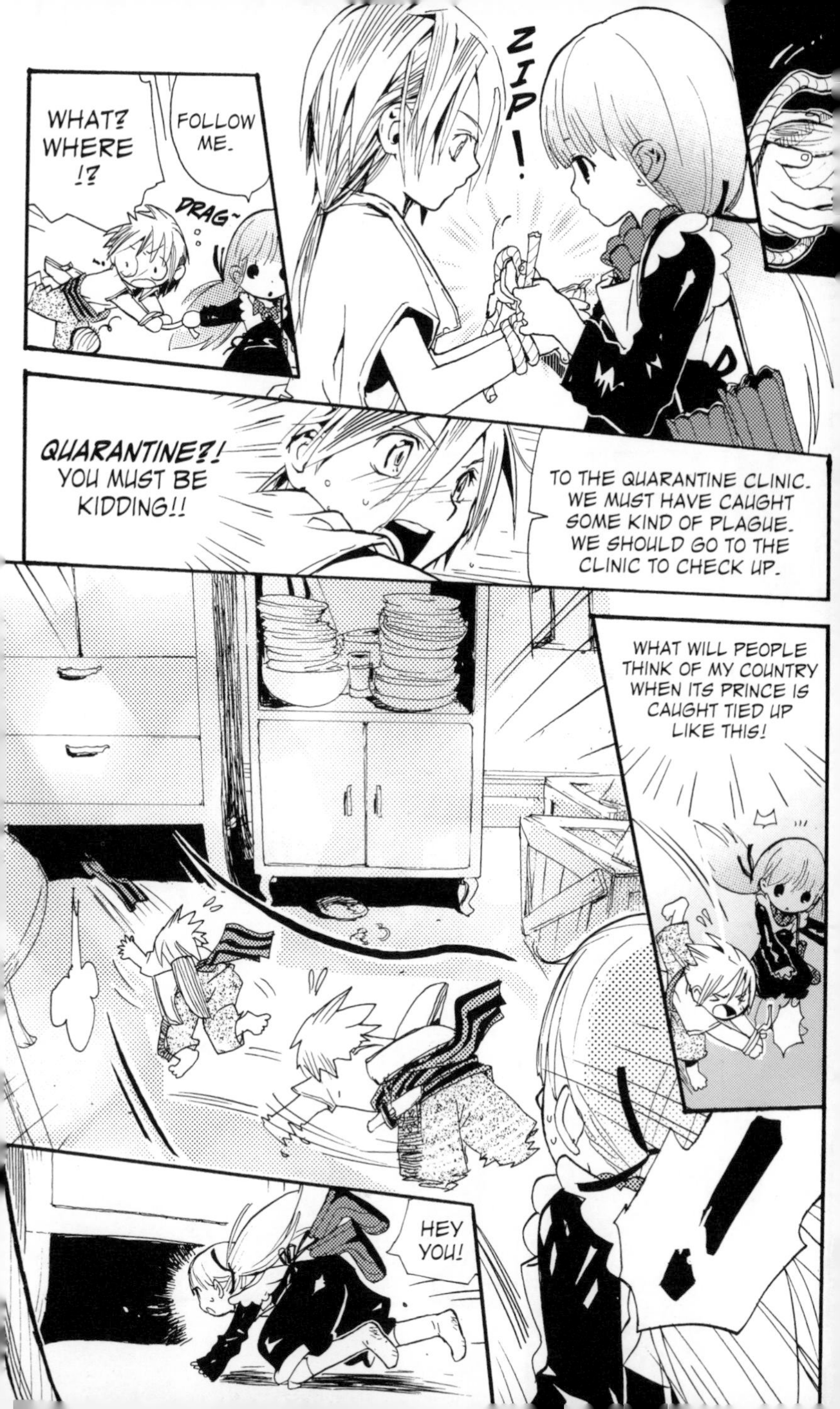
ZIP!
FOLLOW ME.
WHAT? WHERE !?
DRAG~
TO THE QUARANTINE CLINIC. WE MUST HAVE CAUGHT SOME KIND OF PLAGUE. WE SHOULD GO TO THE CLINIC TO CHECK UP.
QUARANTINE?! YOU MUST BE KIDDING!!
WHAT WILL PEOPLE THINK OF MY COUNTRY WHEN ITS PRINCE IS CAUGHT TIED UP LIKE THIS!
HEY YOU!

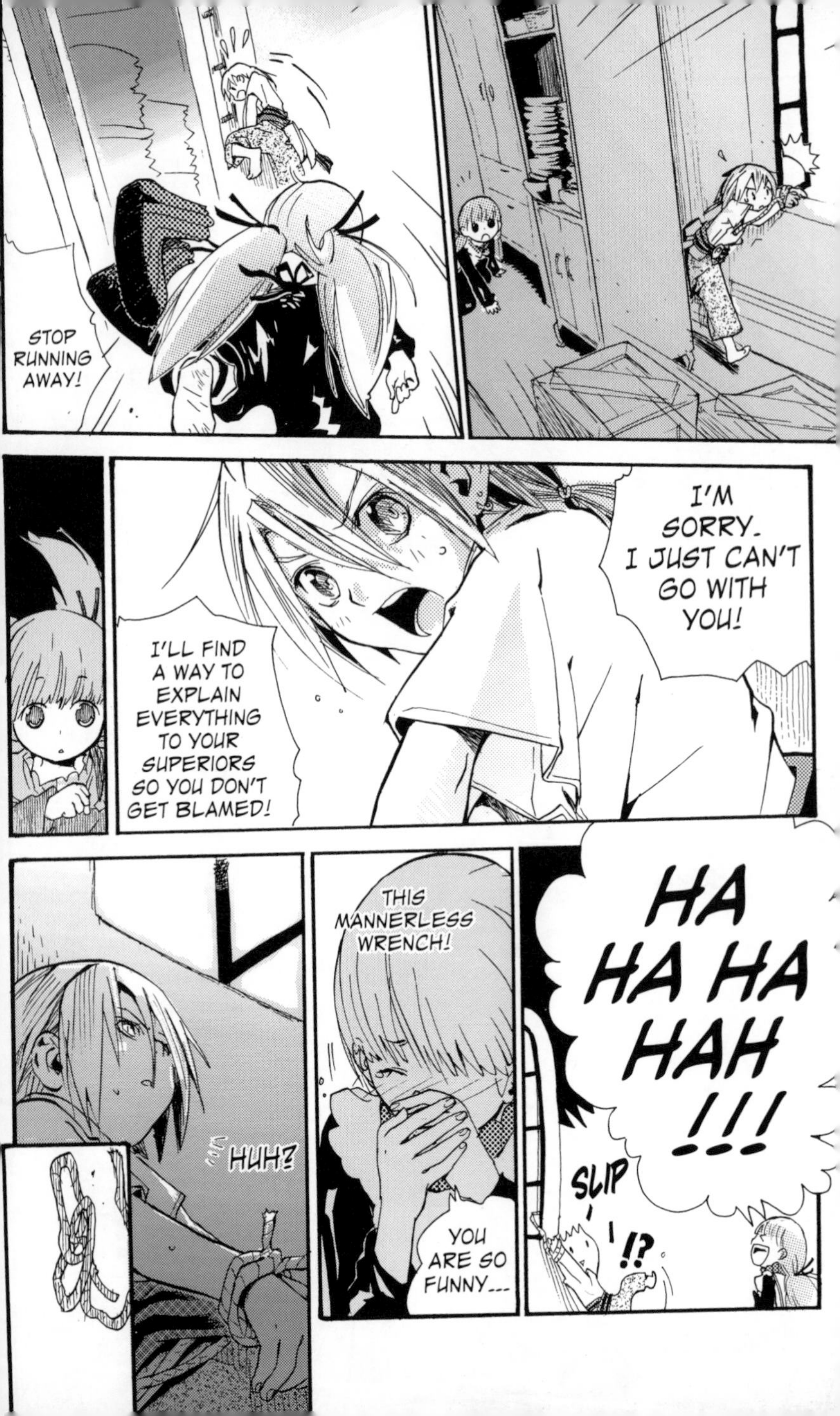

STOP RUNNING AWAY!
I'M SORRY. I JUST CAN'T GO WITH YOU!
I'LL FIND A WAY TO EXPLAIN EVERYTHING TO YOUR SUPERIORS SO YOU DON'T GET BLAMED!
HA HA HA HA HAH !!!
SLIP
!?
THIS MANNERLESS WRENCH!
YOU ARE SO FUNNY...
HUH?

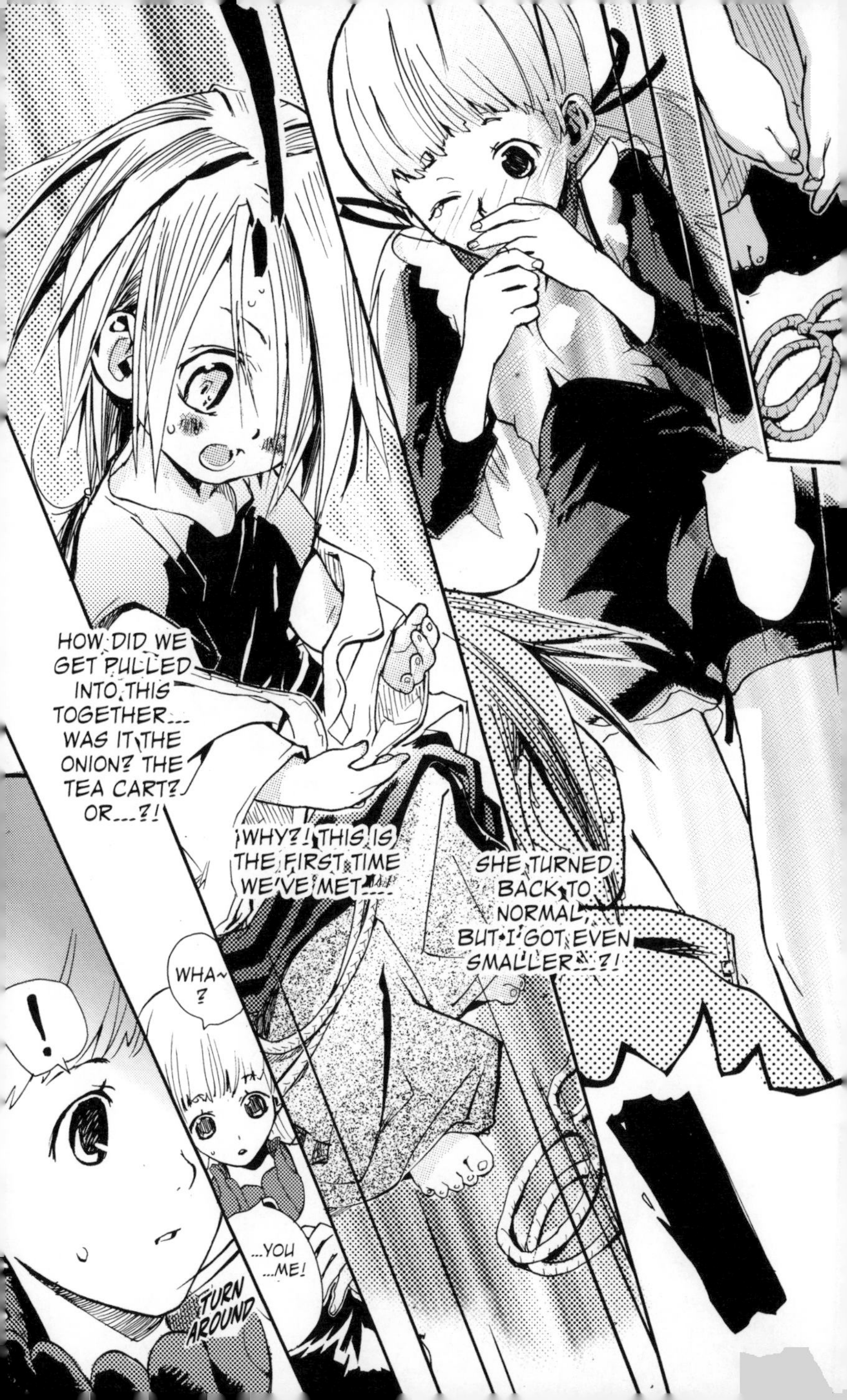
SHE TURNED BACK TO NORMAL, BUT I GOT EVEN SMALLER...?!
WHY?! THIS IS THE FIRST TIME WE'VE MET...
HOW DID WE GET PULLED INTO THIS TOGETHER... WAS IT THE ONION? THE TEA CART? OR...?!
WHA~?
!
...YOU ...ME!
TURN AROUND

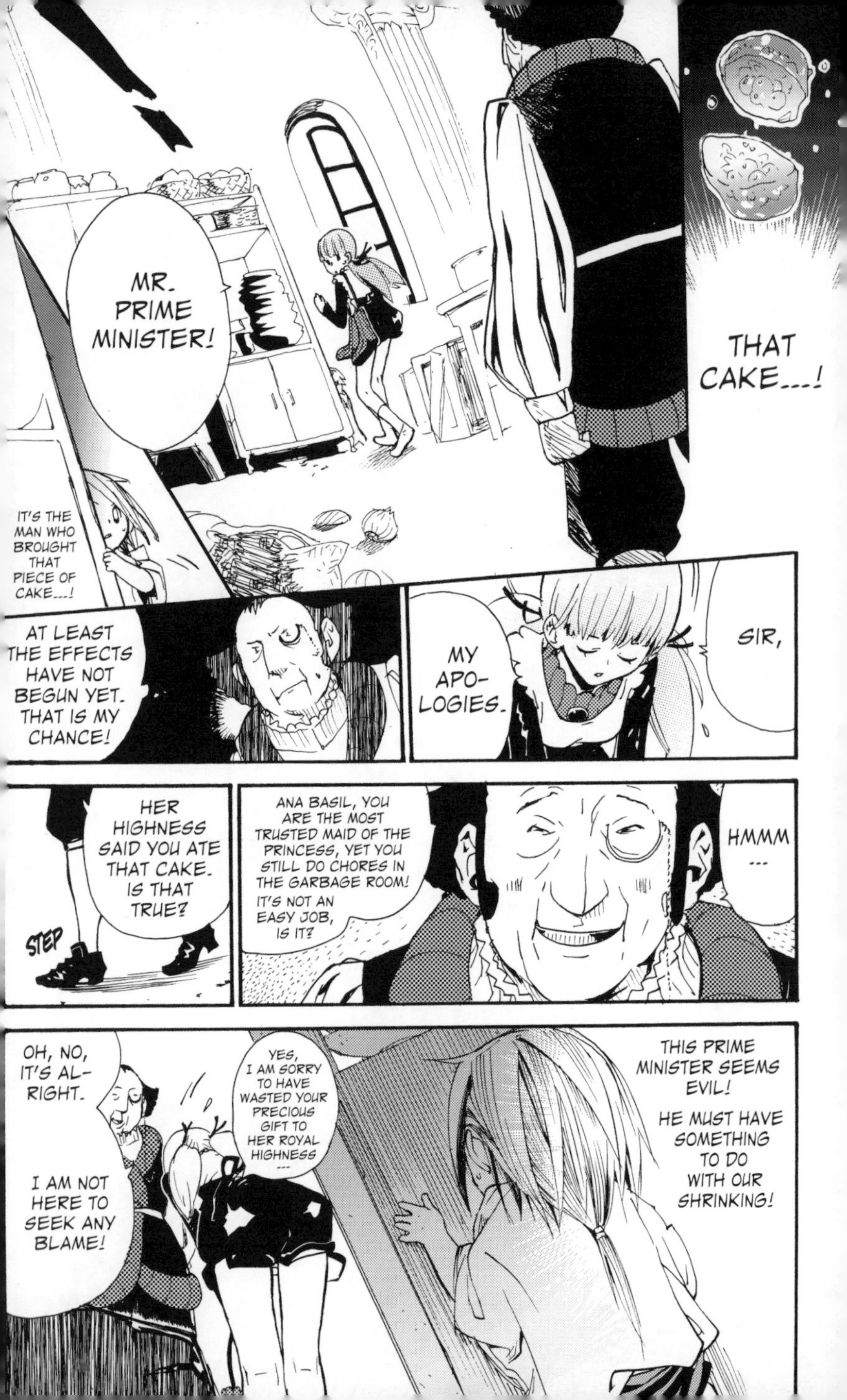
THAT CAKE...!
MR. PRIME MINISTER!
IT'S THE MAN WHO BROUGHT THAT PIECE OF CAKE...!
SIR,
MY APOLOGIES.
AT LEAST THE EFFECTS HAVE NOT BEGUN YET. THAT IS MY CHANCE!
HMMM...
ANA BASIL, YOU ARE THE MOST TRUSTED MAID OF THE PRINCESS, YET YOU STILL DO CHORES IN THE GARBAGE ROOM!
IT'S NOT AN EASY JOB, IS IT?
HER HIGHNESS SAID YOU ATE THAT CAKE. IS THAT TRUE?
STEP
THIS PRIME MINISTER SEEMS EVIL!
HE MUST HAVE SOMETHING TO DO WITH OUR SHRINKING!
YES, I AM SORRY TO HAVE WASTED YOUR PRECIOUS GIFT TO HER ROYAL HIGHNESS...
OH, NO, IT'S ALRIGHT.
I AM NOT HERE TO SEEK ANY BLAME!

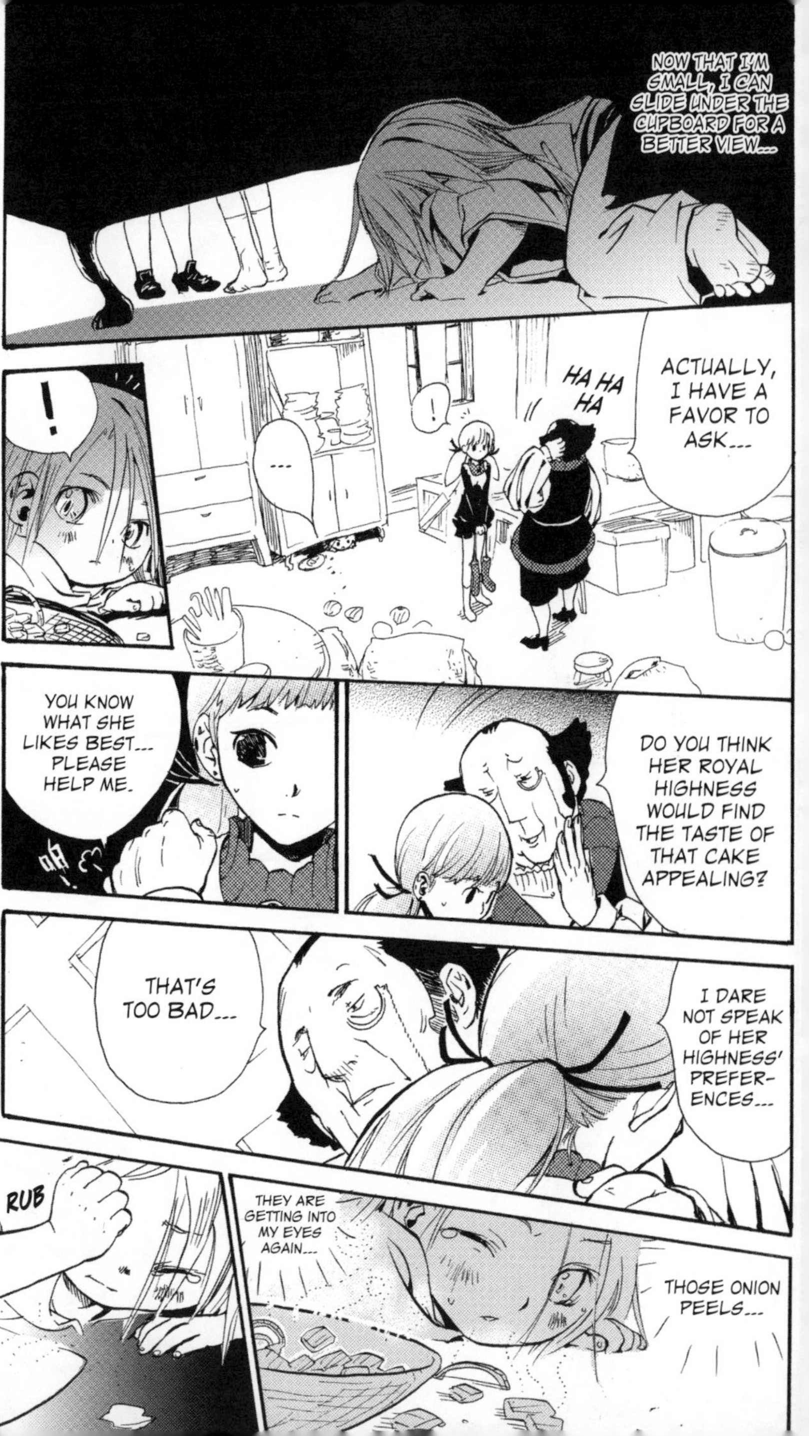
NOW THAT I'M SMALL, I CAN SLIDE UNDER THE CUPBOARD FOR A BETTER VIEW...
ACTUALLY, I HAVE A FAVOR TO ASK...
HA HA HA
!
...
!
DO YOU THINK HER ROYAL HIGHNESS WOULD FIND THE TASTE OF THAT CAKE APPEALING?
YOU KNOW WHAT SHE LIKES BEST... PLEASE HELP ME.
I DARE NOT SPEAK OF HER HIGHNESS' PREFERENCES...
THAT'S TOO BAD...
THOSE ONION PEELS...
THEY ARE GETTING INTO MY EYES AGAIN...
RUB

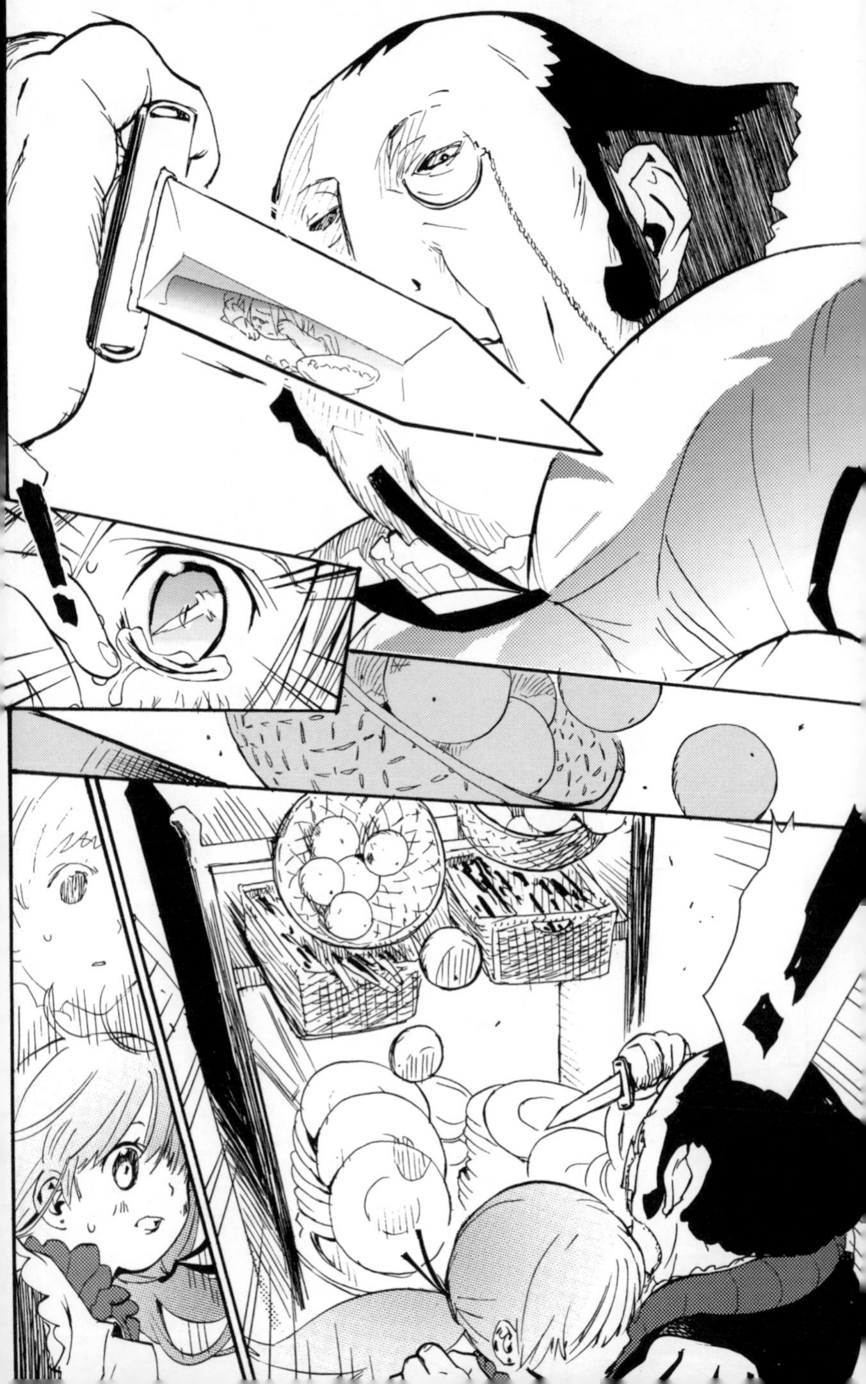

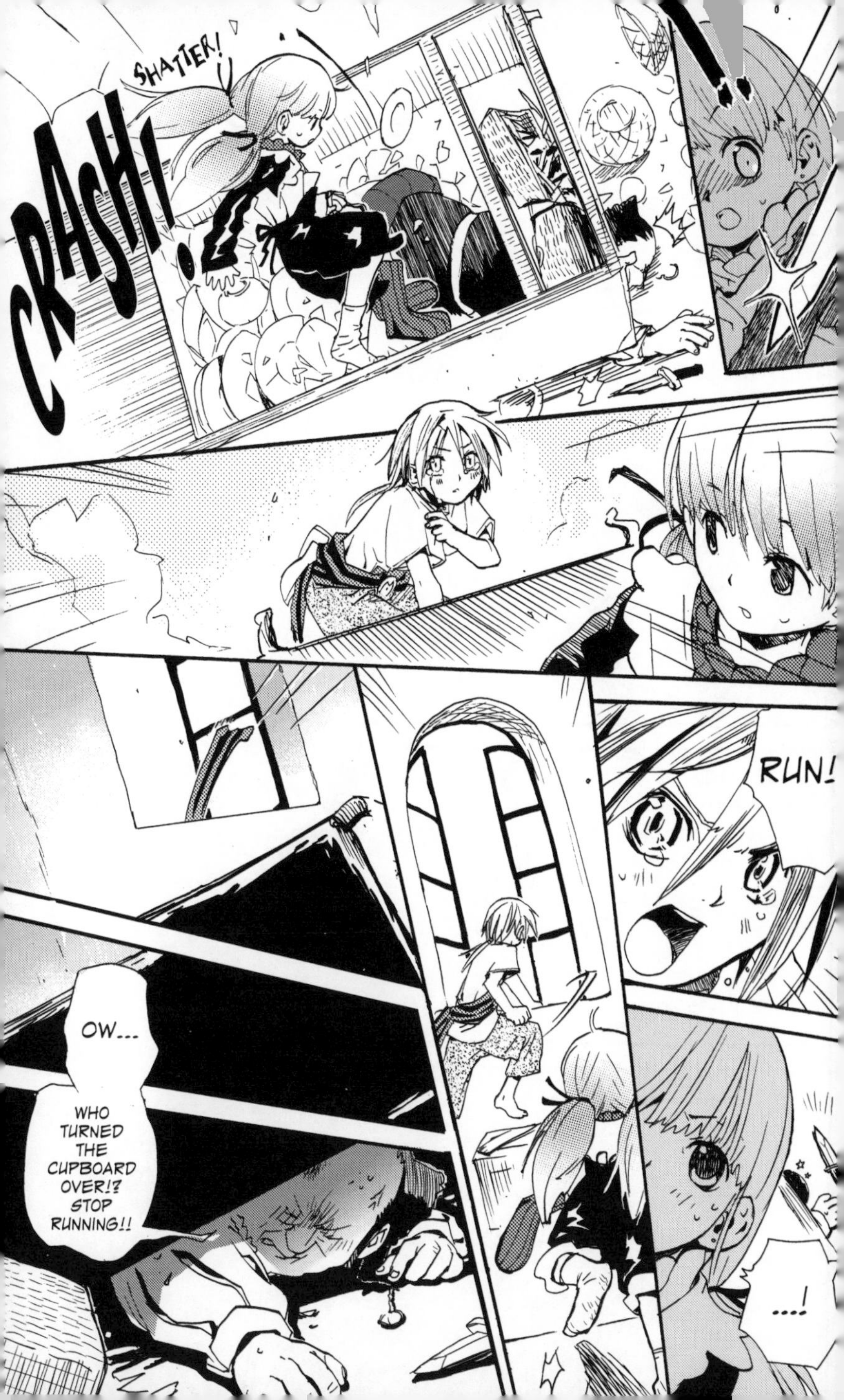
!!
SHATTER!
CRASH!
RUN!
....!
OW...
WHO TURNED THE CUPBOARD OVER!? STOP RUNNING!!

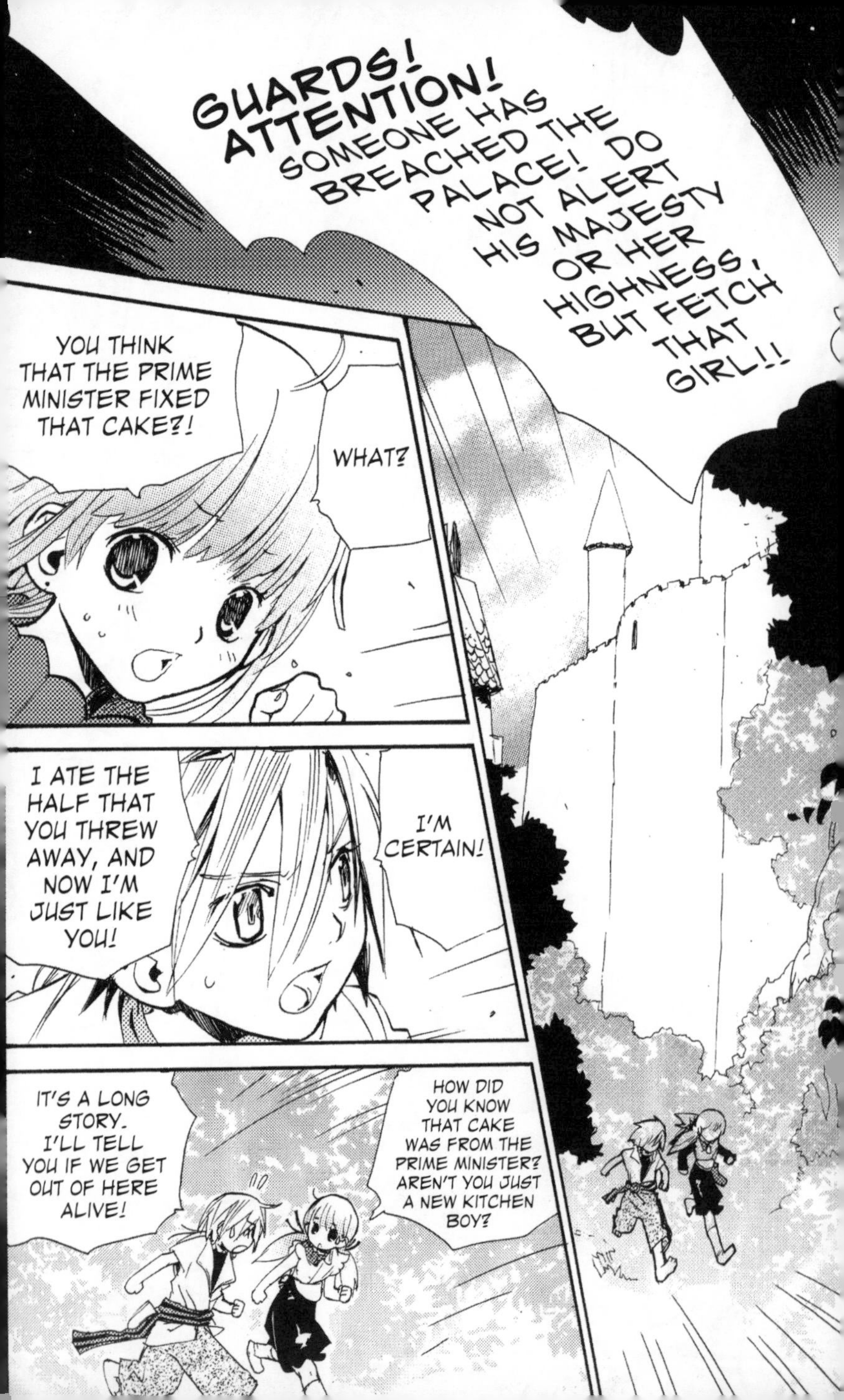
GUARDS! ATTENTION! SOMEONE HAS BREACHED THE PALACE! DO NOT ALERT HIS MAJESTY OR HER HIGHNESS, BUT FETCH THAT GIRL!!
WHAT?
YOU THINK THAT THE PRIME MINISTER FIXED THAT CAKE?!
I'M CERTAIN!
I ATE THE HALF THAT YOU THREW AWAY, AND NOW I'M JUST LIKE YOU!
HOW DID YOU KNOW THAT CAKE WAS FROM THE PRIME MINISTER? AREN'T YOU JUST A NEW KITCHEN BOY?
IT'S A LONG STORY. I'LL TELL YOU IF WE GET OUT OF HERE ALIVE!

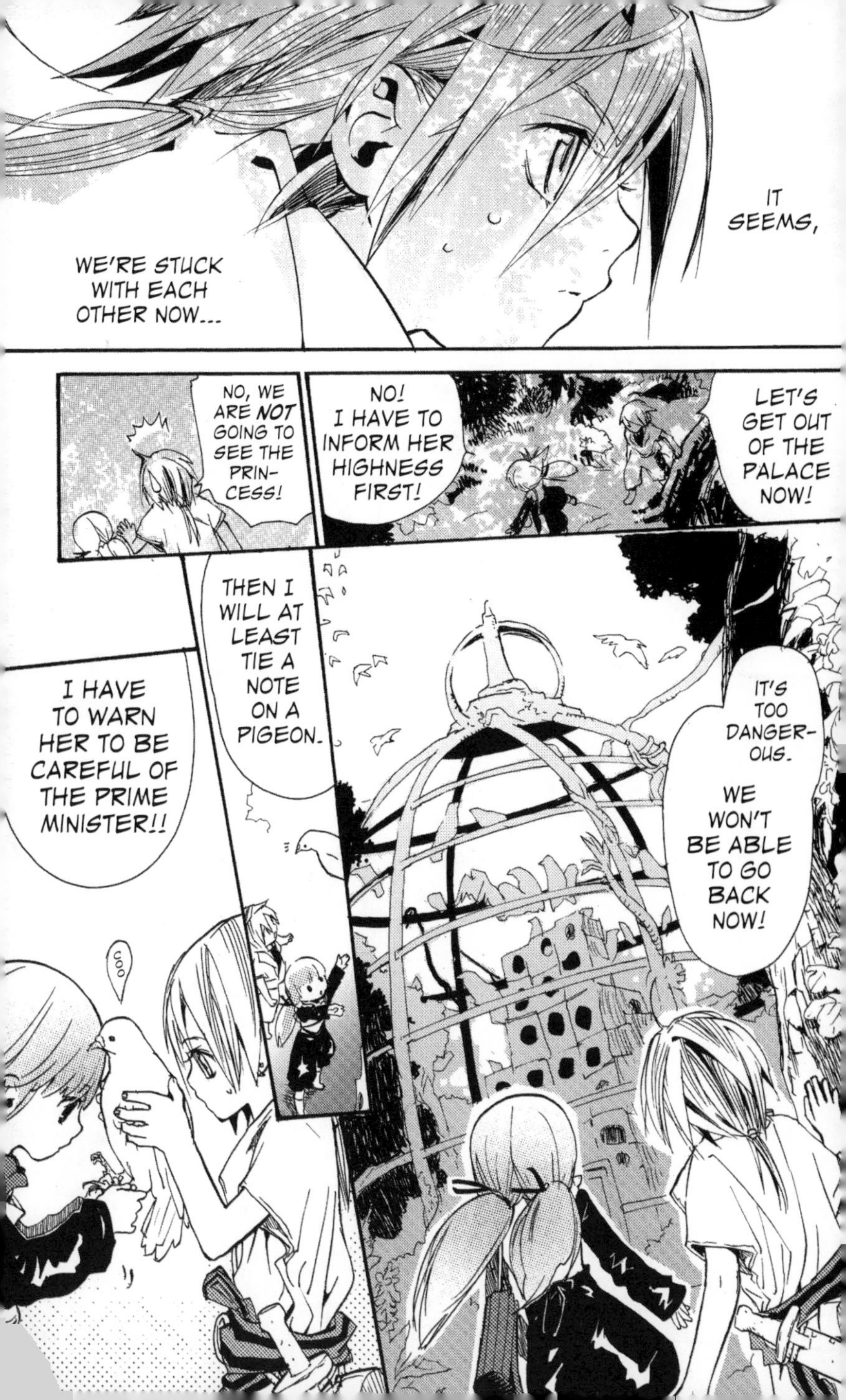
IT SEEMS,
WE'RE STUCK WITH EACH OTHER NOW...
LET'S GET OUT OF THE PALACE NOW!
NO! I HAVE TO INFORM HER HIGHNESS FIRST!
NO, WE ARE *NOT* GOING TO SEE THE PRINCESS!
IT'S TOO DANGEROUS.
WE WON'T BE ABLE TO GO BACK NOW!
I HAVE TO WARN HER TO BE CAREFUL OF THE PRIME MINISTER!!
THEN I WILL AT LEAST TIE A NOTE ON A PIGEON.
COO

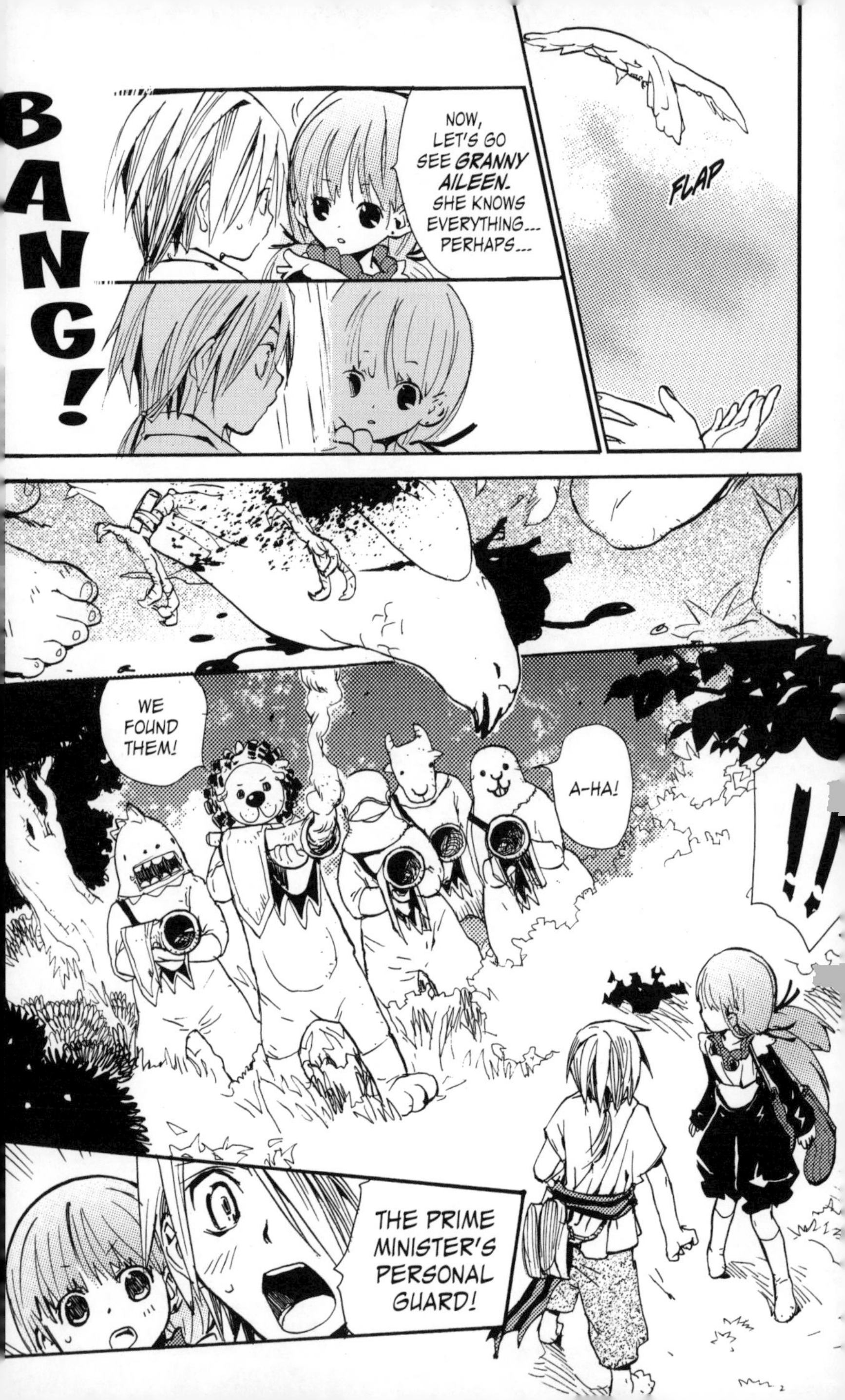
FLAP
NOW, LET'S GO SEE GRANNY AILEEN. SHE KNOWS EVERYTHING... PERHAPS...
BANG!
!!
A-HA!
WE FOUND THEM!
THE PRIME MINISTER'S PERSONAL GUARD!

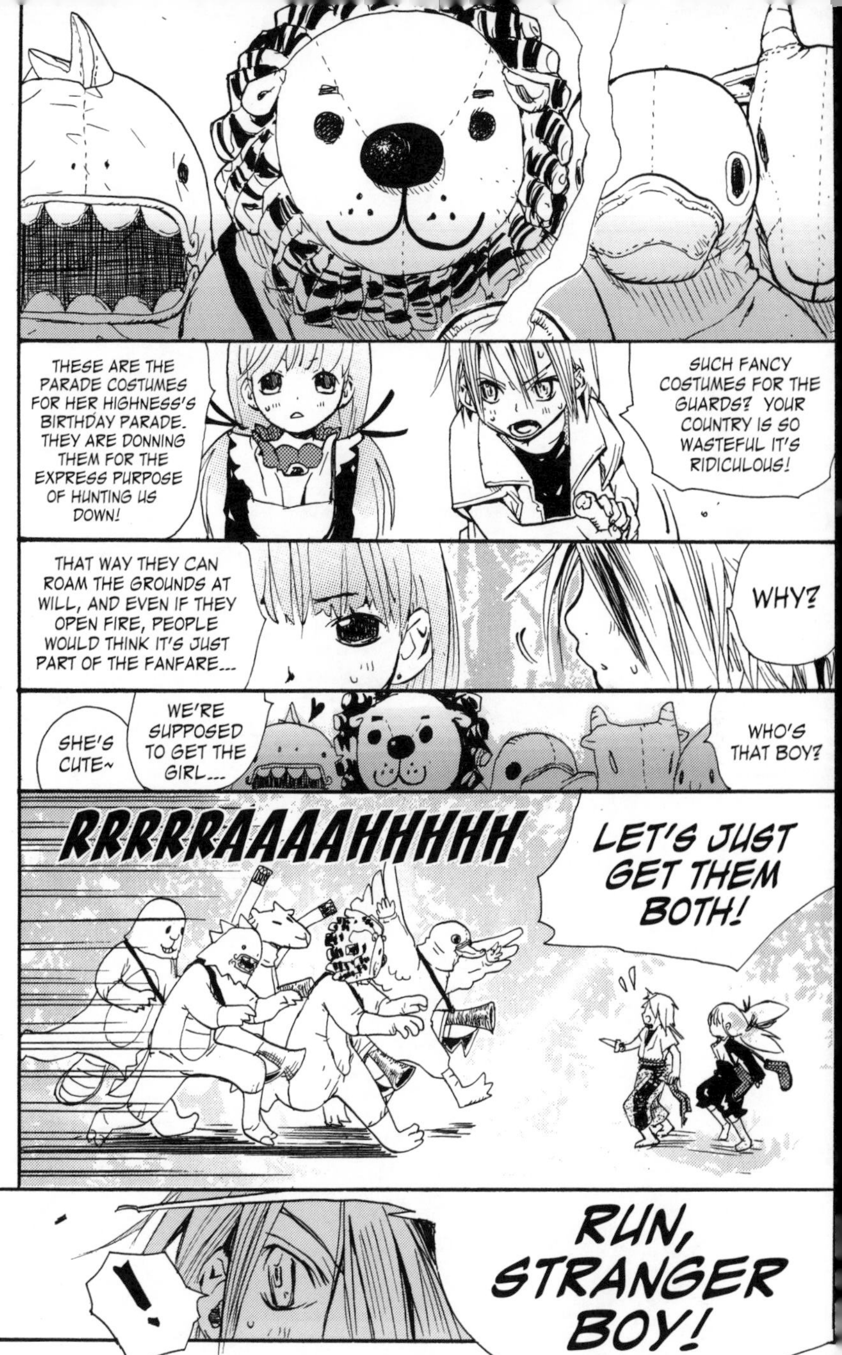
SUCH FANCY COSTUMES FOR THE GUARDS? YOUR COUNTRY IS SO WASTEFUL IT'S RIDICULOUS!
THESE ARE THE PARADE COSTUMES FOR HER HIGHNESS'S BIRTHDAY PARADE. THEY ARE DONNING THEM FOR THE EXPRESS PURPOSE OF HUNTING US DOWN!
WHY?
THAT WAY THEY CAN ROAM THE GROUNDS AT WILL, AND EVEN IF THEY OPEN FIRE, PEOPLE WOULD THINK IT'S JUST PART OF THE FANFARE...
WHO'S THAT BOY?
WE'RE SUPPOSED TO GET THE GIRL...
SHE'S CUTE~
LET'S JUST GET THEM BOTH!
RRRRRAAAAHHHHHH
RUN, STRANGER BOY!
!

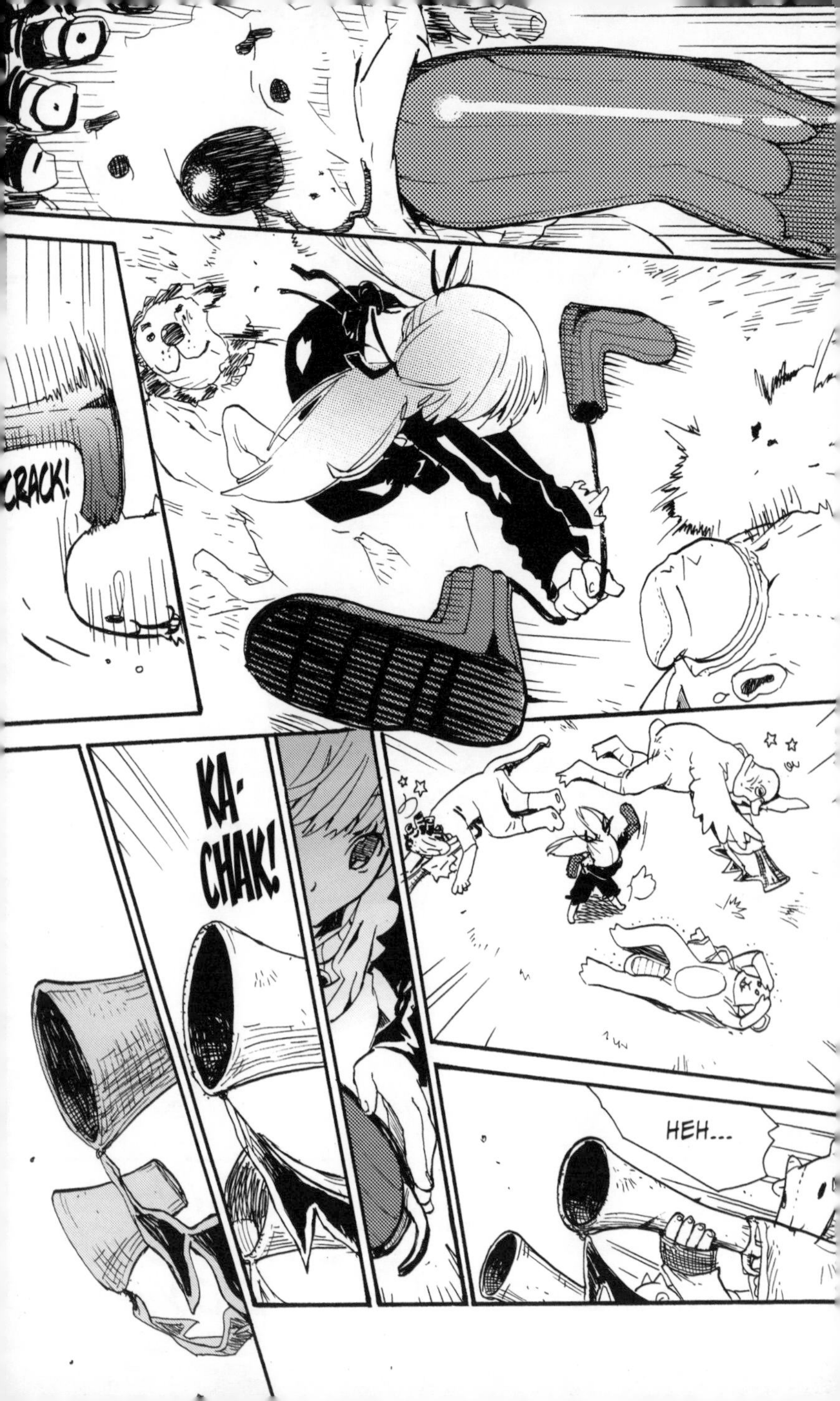
CRACK!
KA-CHAK!
HEH...

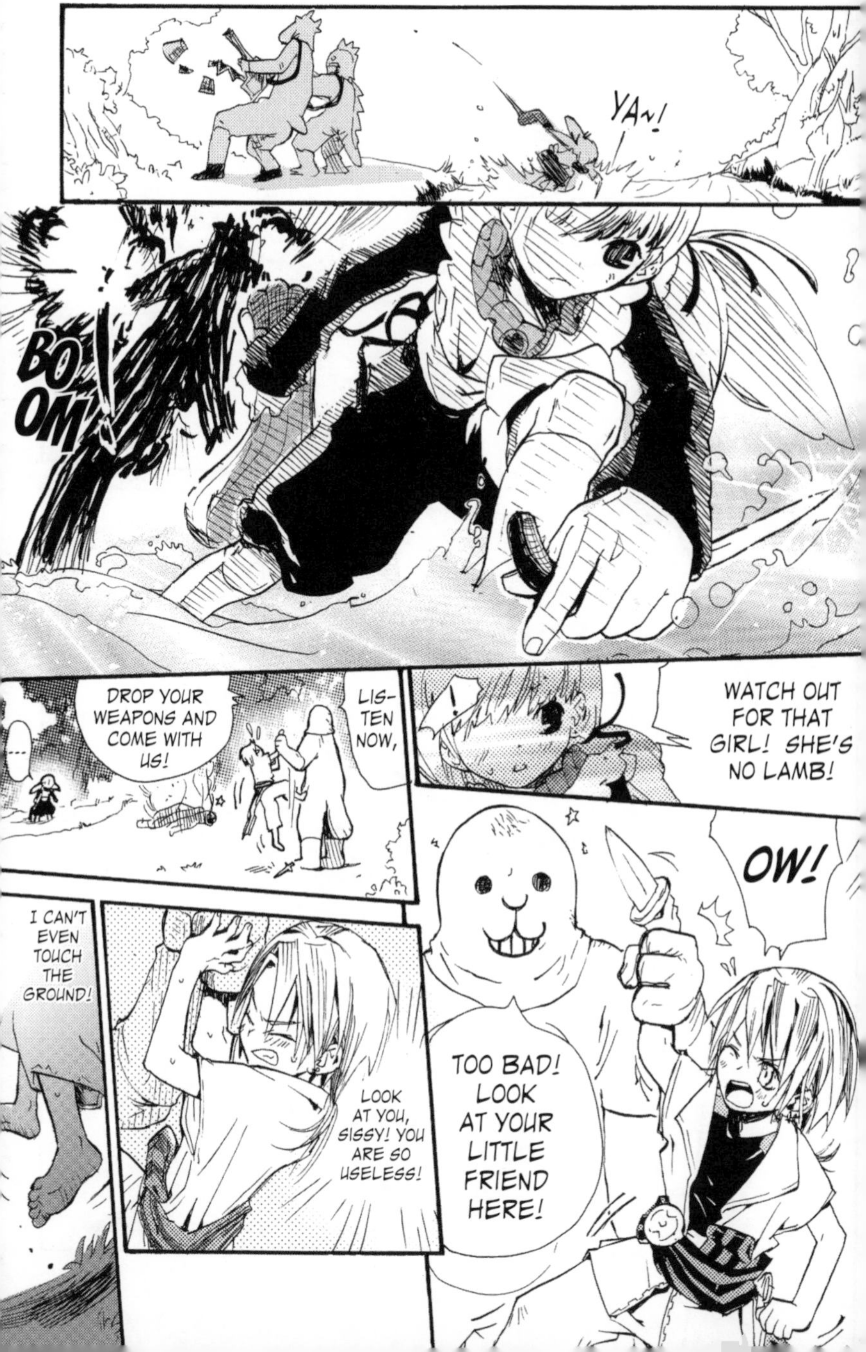
YA~!
BOOM!
WATCH OUT FOR THAT GIRL! SHE'S NO LAMB!
!
LIS-TEN NOW,
DROP YOUR WEAPONS AND COME WITH US!
...
OW!
TOO BAD! LOOK AT YOUR LITTLE FRIEND HERE!
LOOK AT YOU, SISSY! YOU ARE SO USELESS!
I CAN'T EVEN TOUCH THE GROUND!

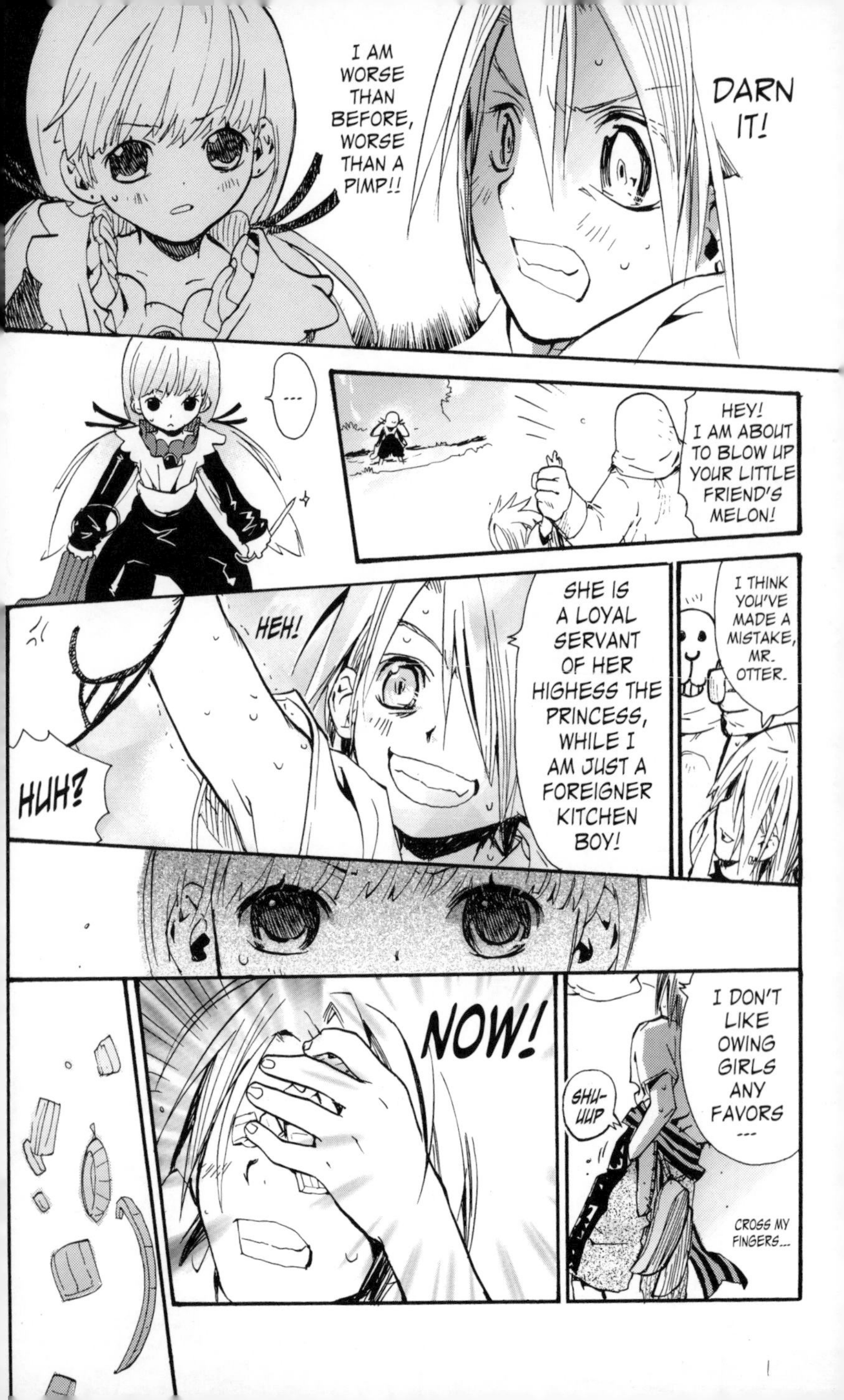
DARN IT!
I AM WORSE THAN BEFORE, WORSE THAN A PIMP!!
HEY! I AM ABOUT TO BLOW UP YOUR LITTLE FRIEND'S MELON!

I THINK YOU'VE MADE A MISTAKE, MR. OTTER.
SHE IS A LOYAL SERVANT OF HER HIGHESS THE PRINCESS, WHILE I AM JUST A FOREIGNER KITCHEN BOY!
HEH!
HUH?
I DON'T LIKE OWING GIRLS ANY FAVORS ---
SHU-UUP
CROSS MY FINGERS...
NOW!

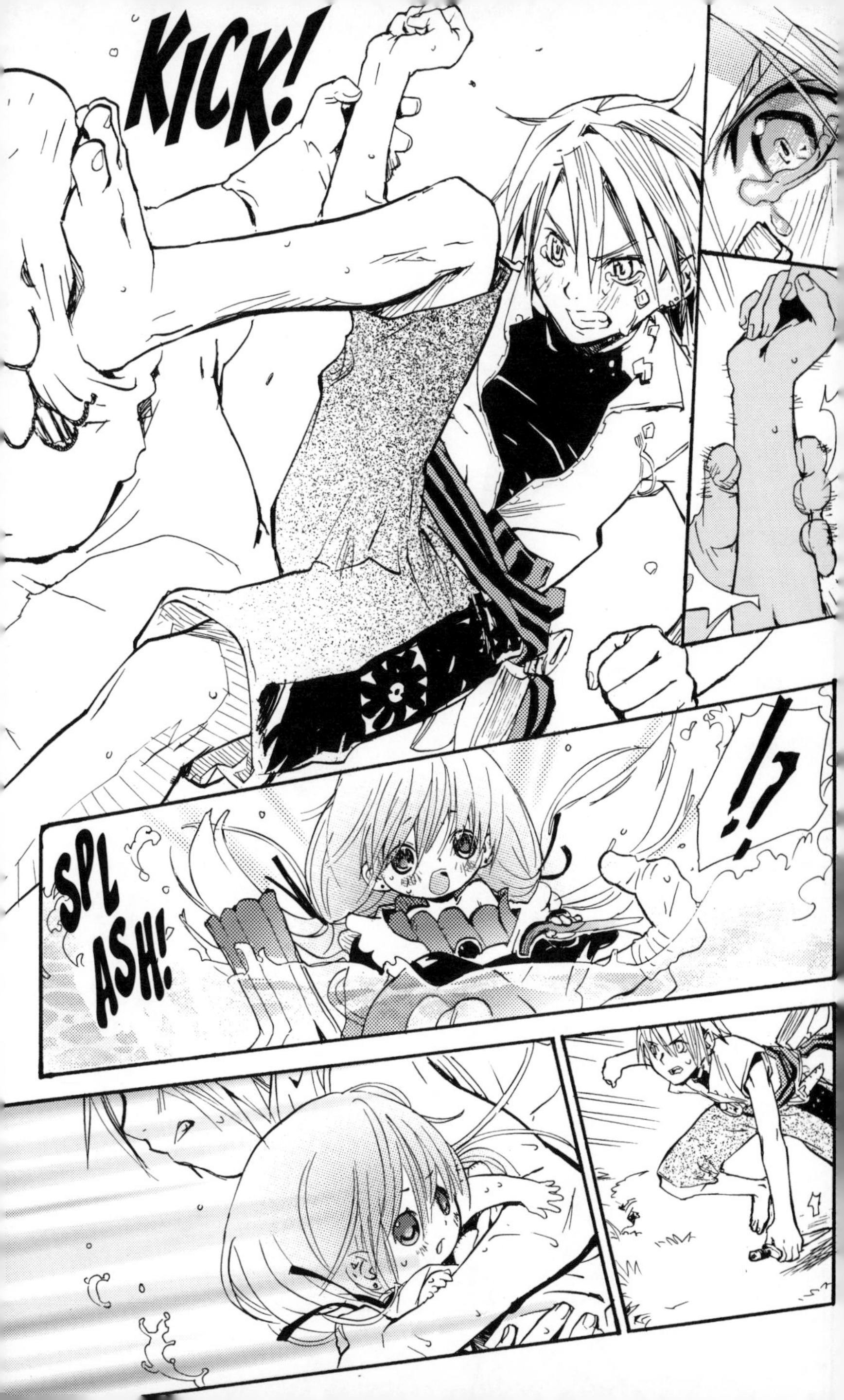
KICK!
!?
SPL ASH!

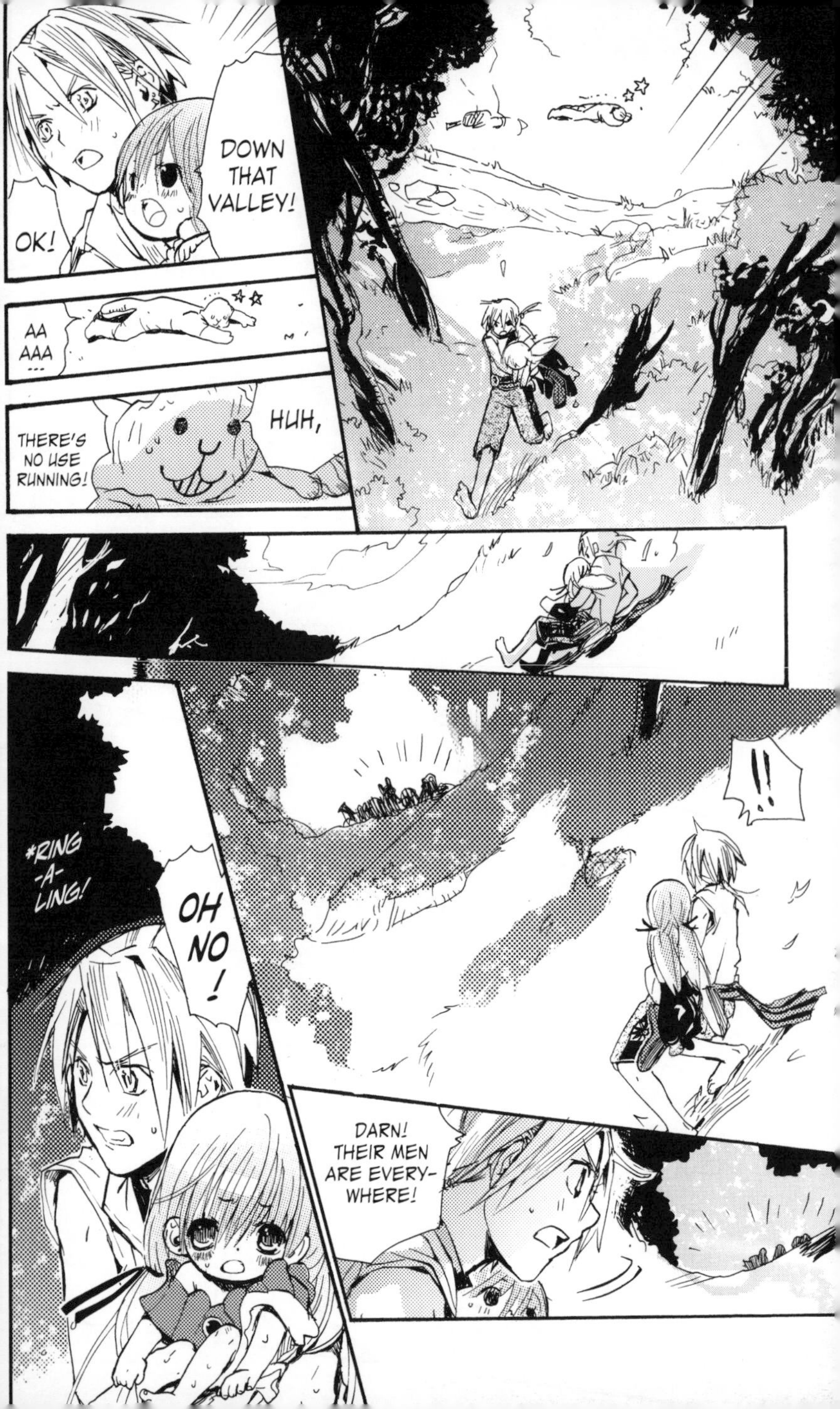
DOWN THAT VALLEY!
OK!
AA AAA ...
HUH,
THERE'S NO USE RUNNING!
!!
DARN! THEIR MEN ARE EVERY-WHERE!
OH NO!
*RING -A- LING!

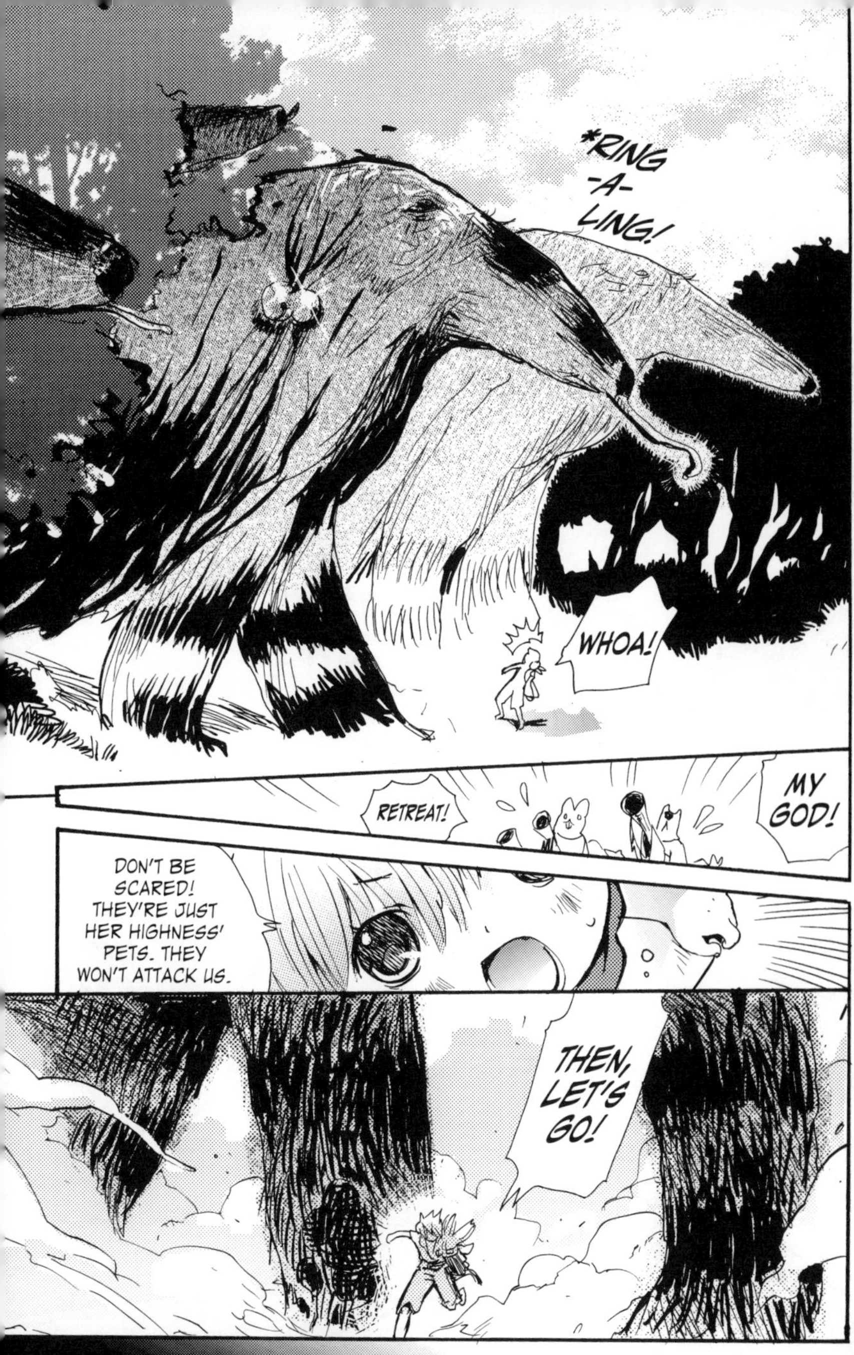
*RING-A-LING!
WHOA!
MY GOD!
RETREAT!
DON'T BE SCARED! THEY'RE JUST HER HIGHNESS' PETS. THEY WON'T ATTACK US.
THEN, LET'S GO!

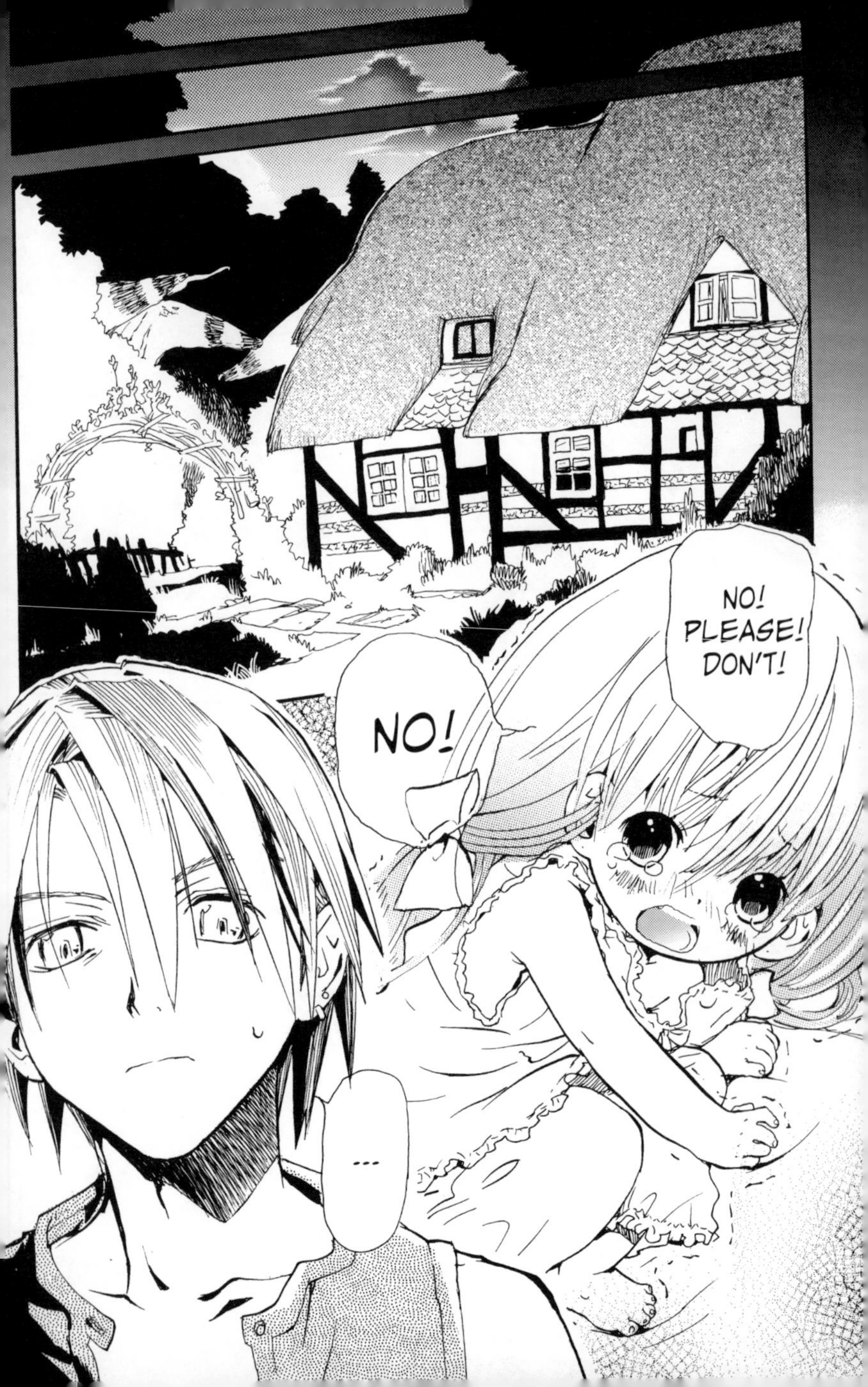
NO! PLEASE! DON'T!
NO!
...

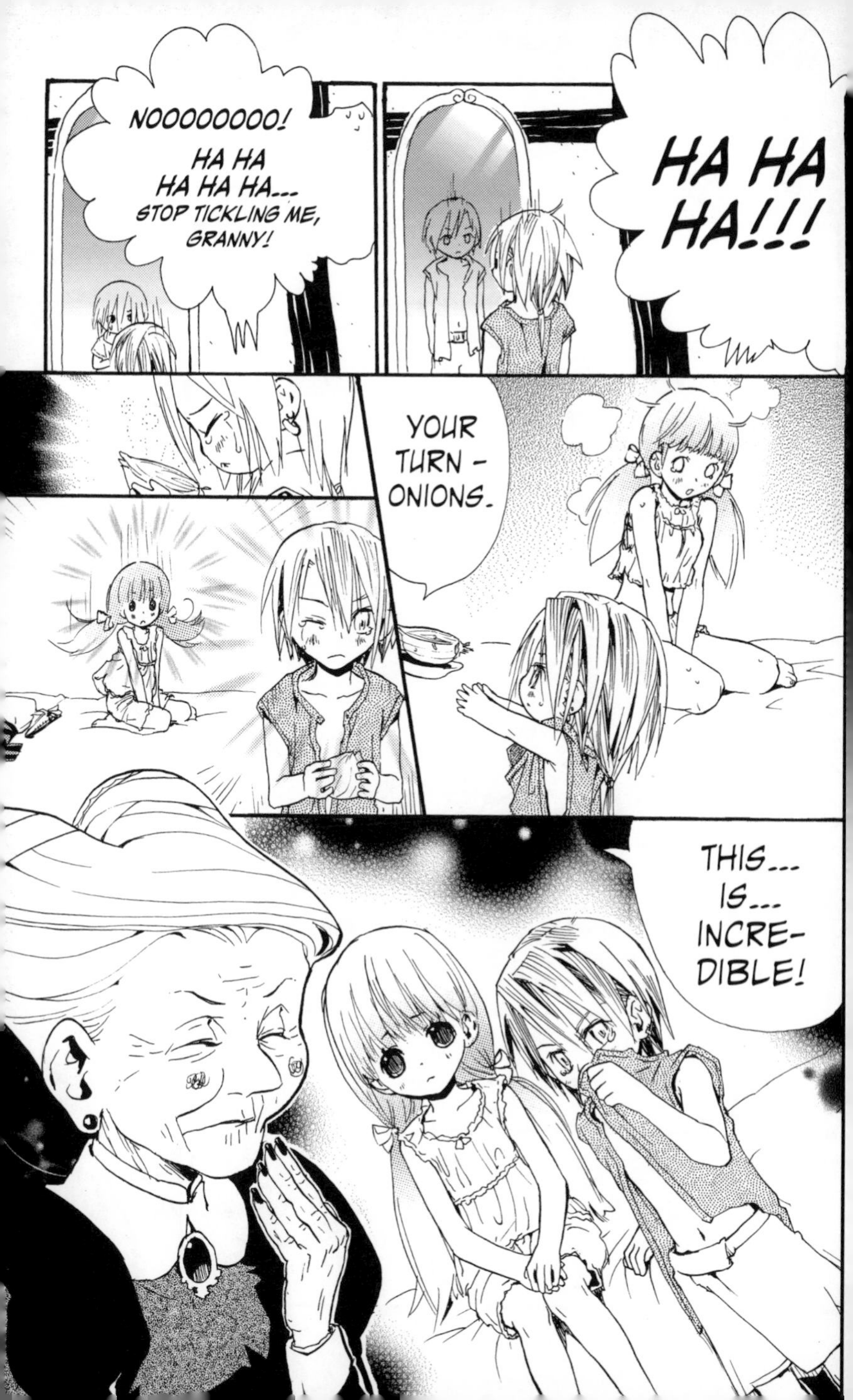
HA HA HA!!!
NOOOOOOOO! HA HA HA HA HA... STOP TICKLING ME, GRANNY!
YOUR TURN - ONIONS.
THIS... IS... INCRE-DIBLE!

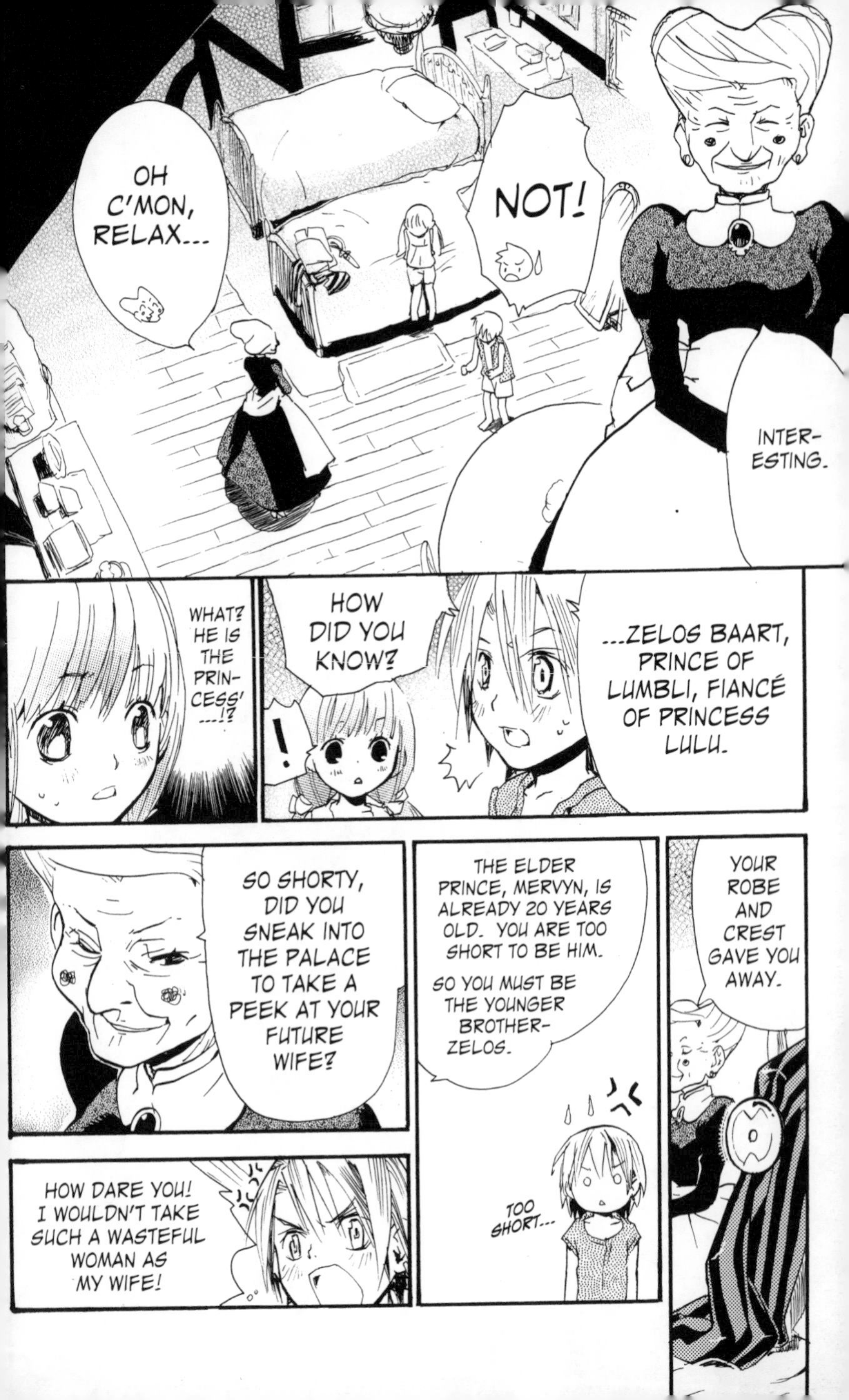
NOT!
OH C'MON, RELAX...
INTER-ESTING.
...ZELOS BAART, PRINCE OF LUMBLI, FIANCÉ OF PRINCESS LULU.
HOW DID YOU KNOW?
WHAT? HE IS THE PRIN-CESS' ...!?
YOUR ROBE AND CREST GAVE YOU AWAY.
THE ELDER PRINCE, MERVYN, IS ALREADY 20 YEARS OLD. YOU ARE TOO SHORT TO BE HIM.
SO YOU MUST BE THE YOUNGER BROTHER-ZELOS.
TOO SHORT...
SO SHORTY, DID YOU SNEAK INTO THE PALACE TO TAKE A PEEK AT YOUR FUTURE WIFE?
HOW DARE YOU! I WOULDN'T TAKE SUCH A WASTEFUL WOMAN AS MY WIFE!

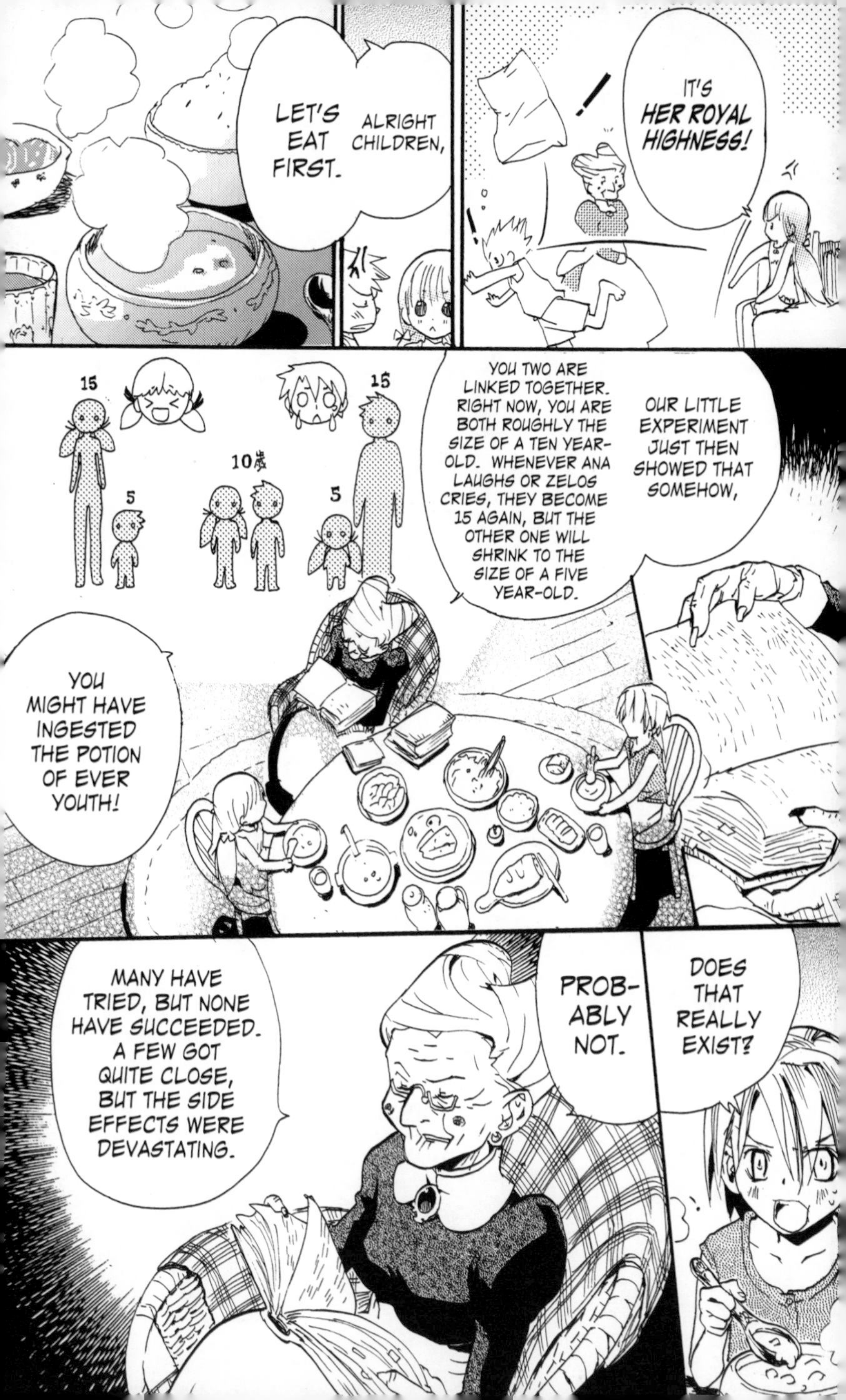

IT'S HER ROYAL HIGHNESS!
ALRIGHT CHILDREN,
LET'S EAT FIRST.
OUR LITTLE EXPERIMENT JUST THEN SHOWED THAT SOMEHOW,
YOU TWO ARE LINKED TOGETHER. RIGHT NOW, YOU ARE BOTH ROUGHLY THE SIZE OF A TEN YEAR-OLD. WHENEVER ANA LAUGHS OR ZELOS CRIES, THEY BECOME 15 AGAIN, BUT THE OTHER ONE WILL SHRINK TO THE SIZE OF A FIVE YEAR-OLD.
15
5
10歳
15
5
YOU MIGHT HAVE INGESTED THE POTION OF EVER YOUTH!
DOES THAT REALLY EXIST?
PROB-ABLY NOT.
MANY HAVE TRIED, BUT NONE HAVE SUCCEEDED. A FEW GOT QUITE CLOSE, BUT THE SIDE EFFECTS WERE DEVASTATING.

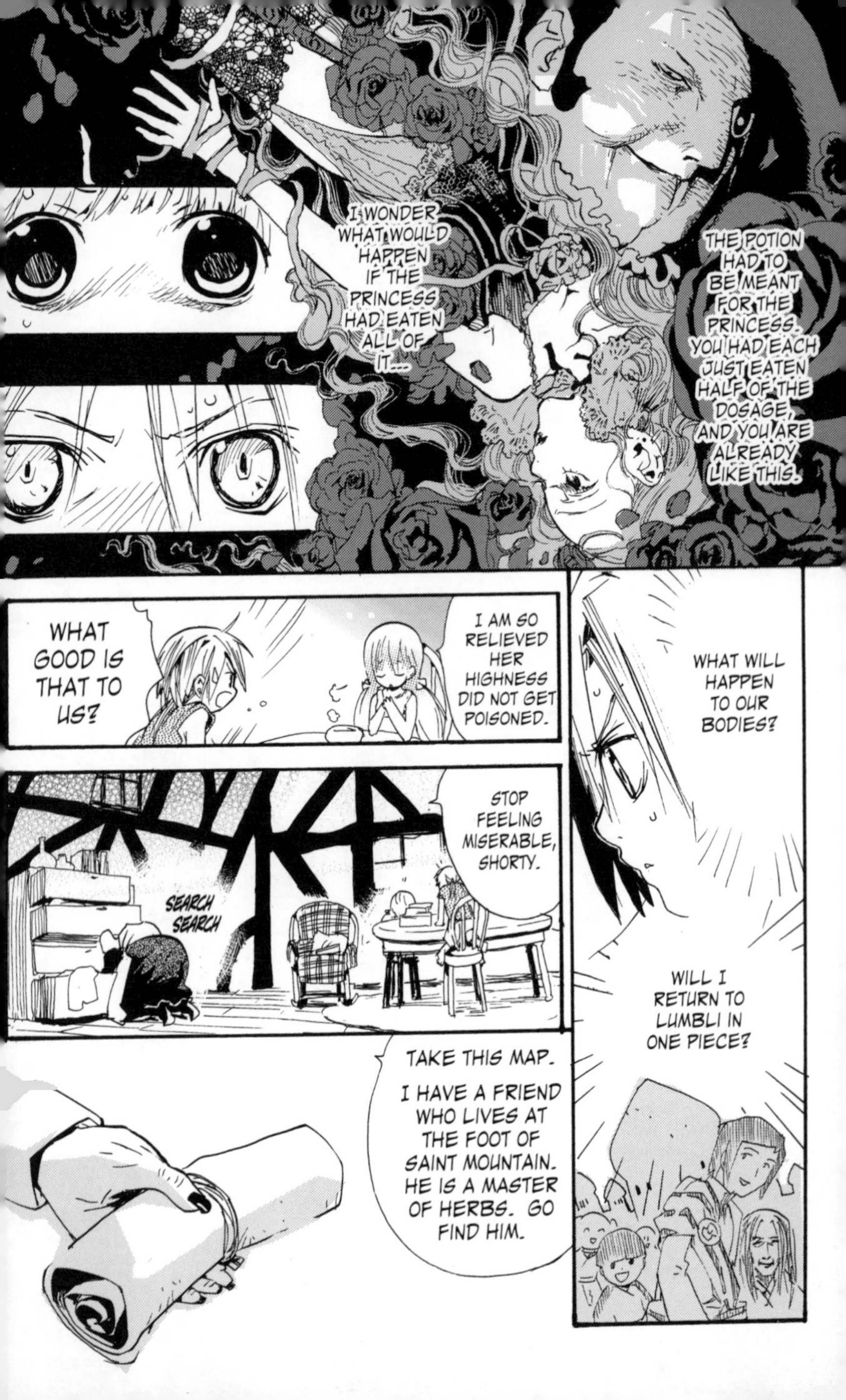
THE POTION HAD TO BE MEANT FOR THE PRINCESS. YOU HAD EACH JUST EATEN HALF OF THE DOSAGE, AND YOU ARE ALREADY LIKE THIS.
I WONDER WHAT WOULD HAPPEN IF THE PRINCESS HAD EATEN ALL OF IT...
WHAT WILL HAPPEN TO OUR BODIES?
WILL I RETURN TO LUMBLI IN ONE PIECE?
I AM SO RELIEVED HER HIGHNESS DID NOT GET POISONED.
WHAT GOOD IS THAT TO US?
STOP FEELING MISERABLE, SHORTY.
SEARCH SEARCH
TAKE THIS MAP.
I HAVE A FRIEND WHO LIVES AT THE FOOT OF SAINT MOUNTAIN. HE IS A MASTER OF HERBS. GO FIND HIM.

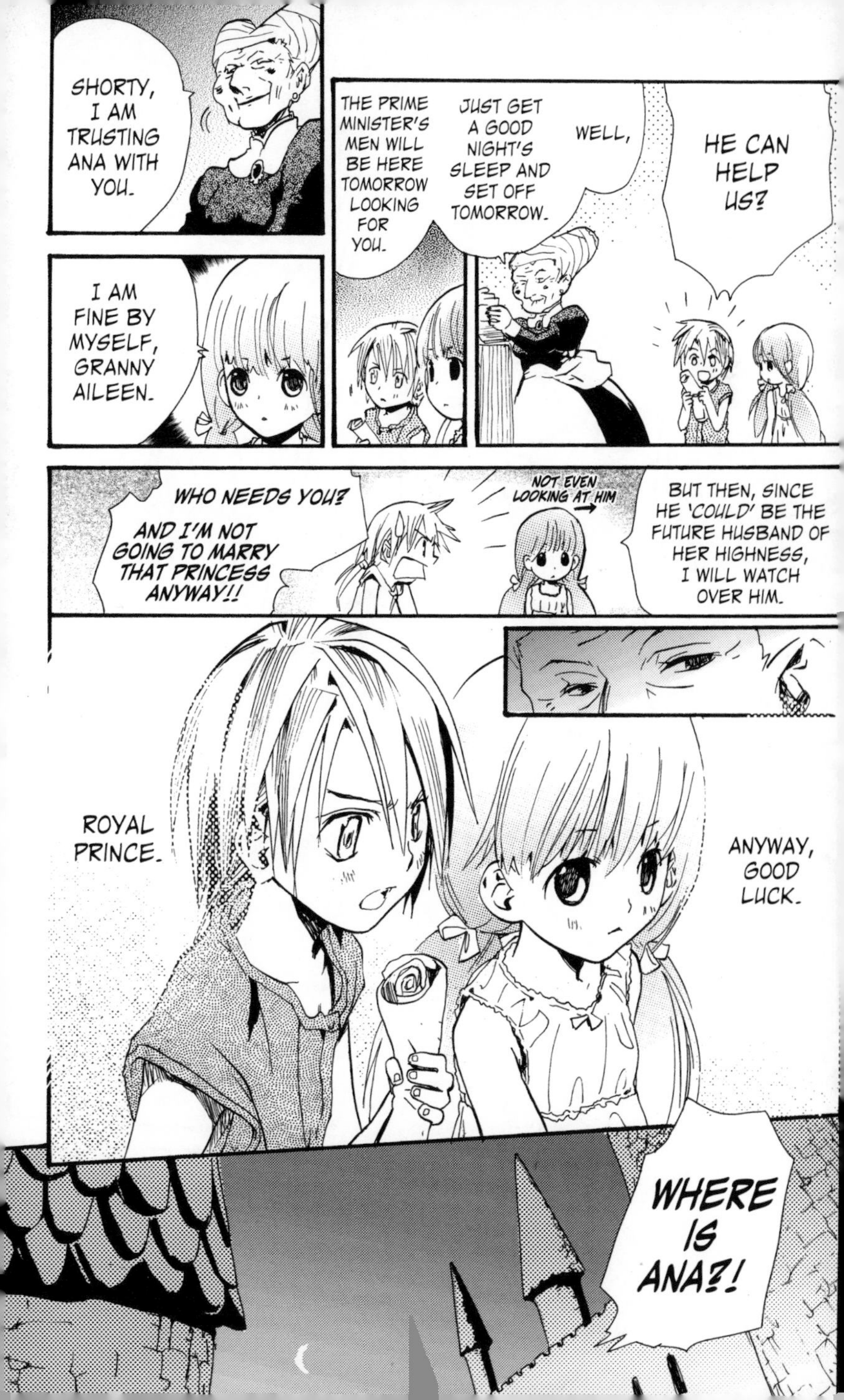
HE CAN HELP US?
WELL,
JUST GET A GOOD NIGHT'S SLEEP AND SET OFF TOMORROW.
THE PRIME MINISTER'S MEN WILL BE HERE TOMORROW LOOKING FOR YOU.
SHORTY, I AM TRUSTING ANA WITH YOU.
I AM FINE BY MYSELF, GRANNY AILEEN.
BUT THEN, SINCE HE 'COULD' BE THE FUTURE HUSBAND OF HER HIGHNESS, I WILL WATCH OVER HIM.
NOT EVEN LOOKING AT HIM
WHO NEEDS YOU?
AND I'M NOT GOING TO MARRY THAT PRINCESS ANYWAY!!
ANYWAY, GOOD LUCK.
ROYAL PRINCE.
WHERE IS ANA?!

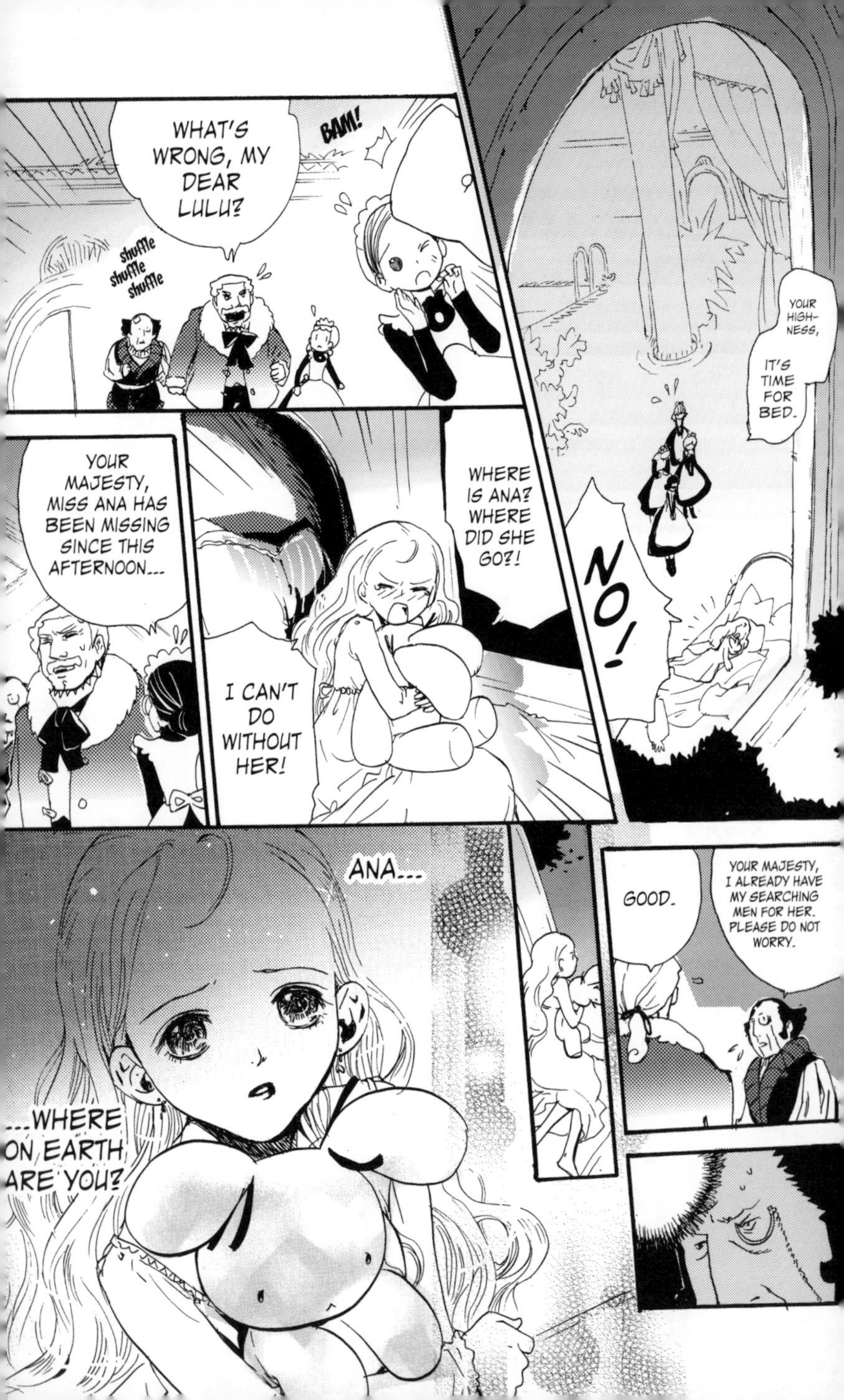
YOUR HIGHNESS,
IT'S TIME FOR BED.
NO!
BAM!
WHAT'S WRONG, MY DEAR LULU?
shuffle shuffle shuffle
WHERE IS ANA? WHERE DID SHE GO?!
I CAN'T DO WITHOUT HER!
YOUR MAJESTY, MISS ANA HAS BEEN MISSING SINCE THIS AFTERNOON...
YOUR MAJESTY, I ALREADY HAVE MY SEARCHING MEN FOR HER. PLEASE DO NOT WORRY.
GOOD.
ANA...
...WHERE ON EARTH ARE YOU?

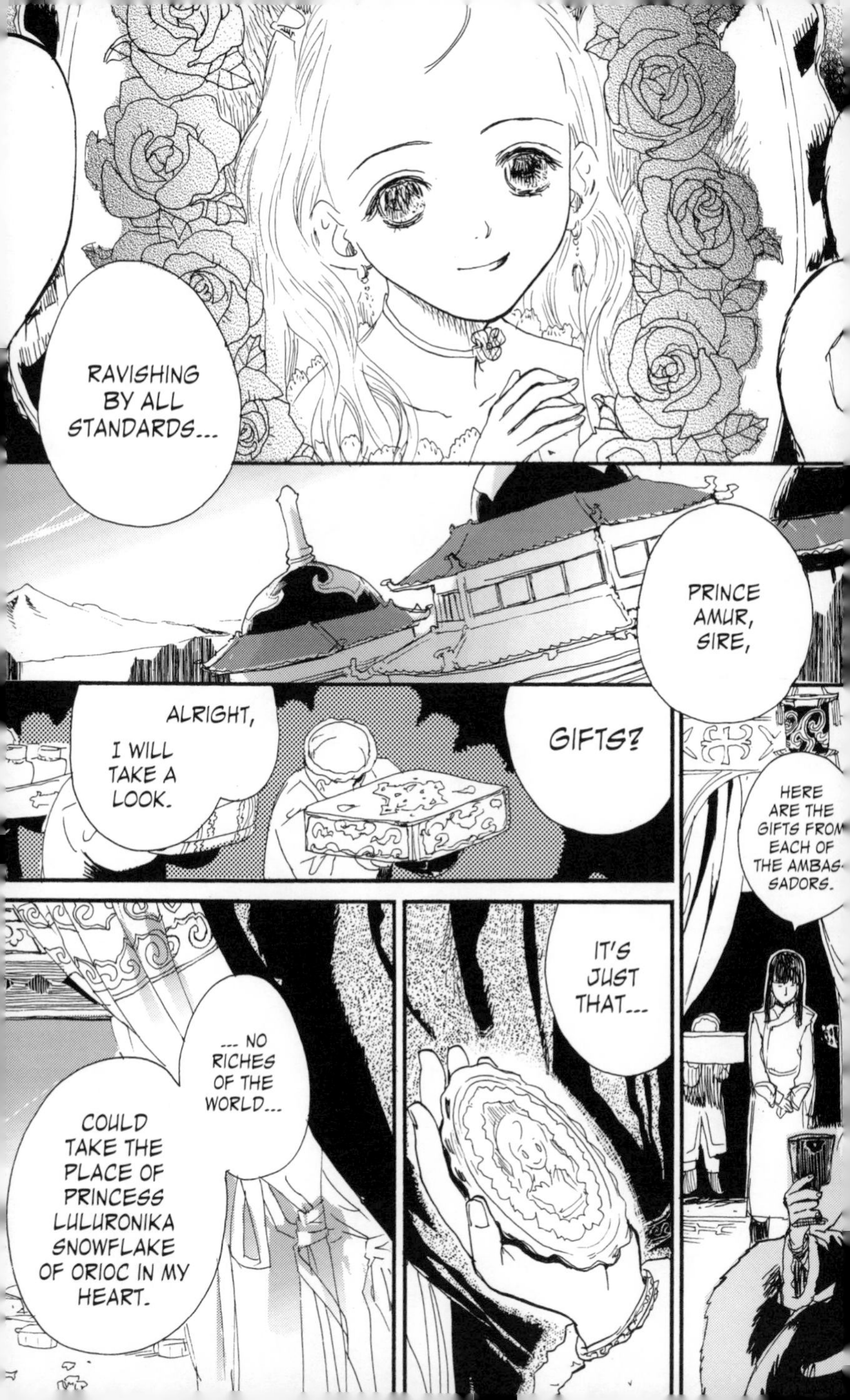
RAVISHING BY ALL STANDARDS...
PRINCE AMUR, SIRE,
HERE ARE THE GIFTS FROM EACH OF THE AMBAS-SADORS.
GIFTS?
ALRIGHT,
I WILL TAKE A LOOK.
IT'S JUST THAT...
... NO RICHES OF THE WORLD...
COULD TAKE THE PLACE OF PRINCESS LULURONIKA SNOWFLAKE OF ORIOC IN MY HEART.

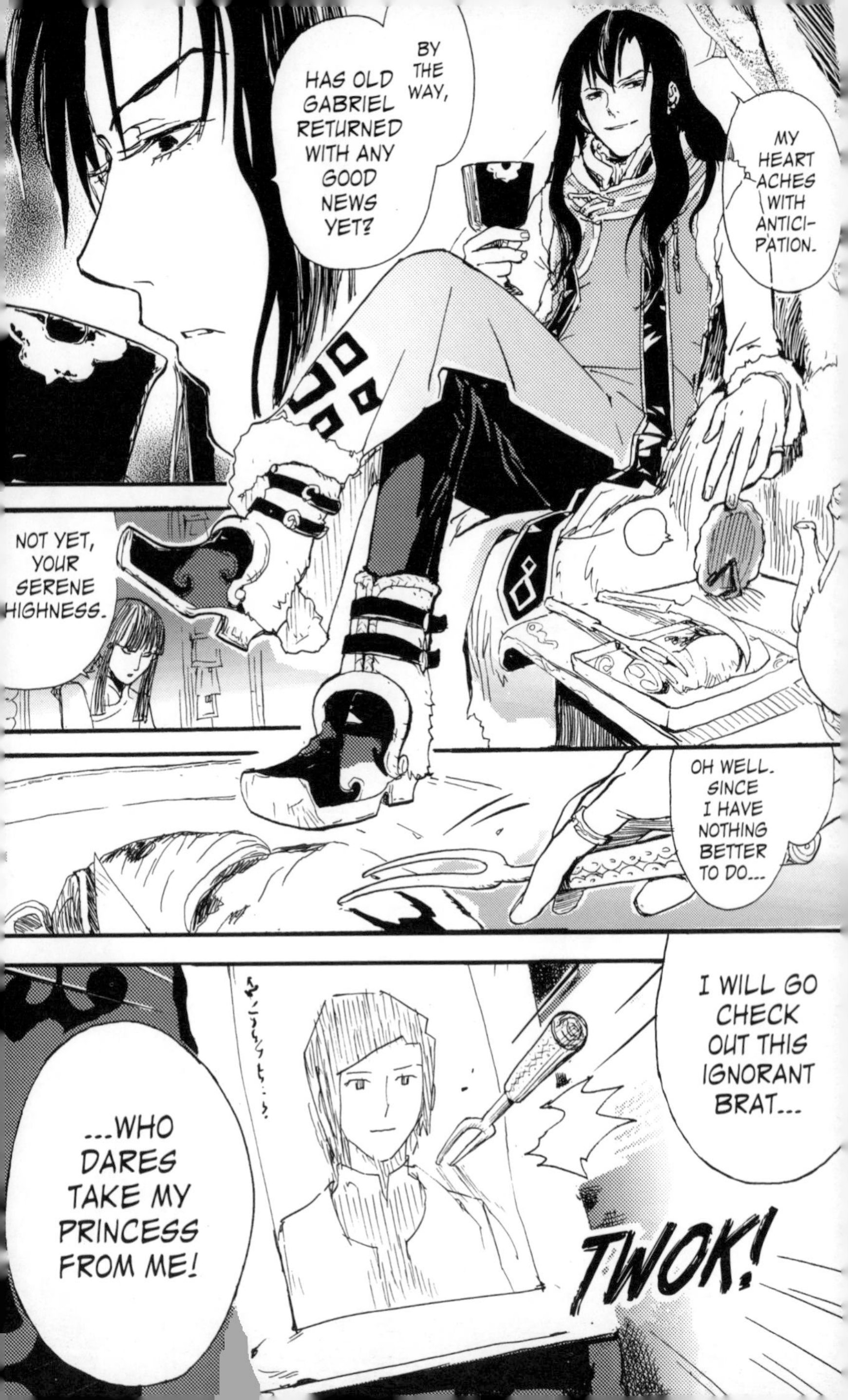
BY THE WAY, HAS OLD GABRIEL RETURNED WITH ANY GOOD NEWS YET?
MY HEART ACHES WITH ANTICIPATION.
NOT YET, YOUR SERENE HIGHNESS.
OH WELL. SINCE I HAVE NOTHING BETTER TO DO...
I WILL GO CHECK OUT THIS IGNORANT BRAT...
...WHO DARES TAKE MY PRINCESS FROM ME!
TWOK!

Act.3

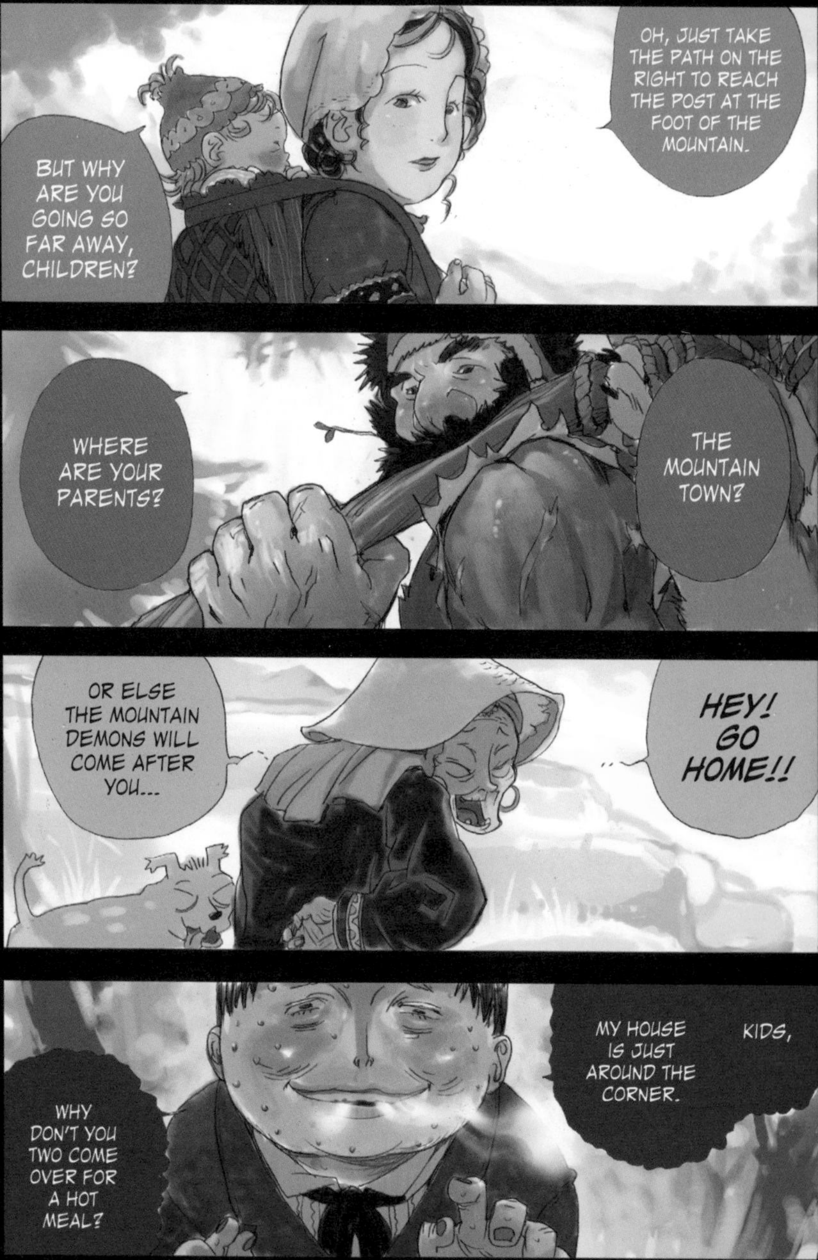
OH, JUST TAKE THE PATH ON THE RIGHT TO REACH THE POST AT THE FOOT OF THE MOUNTAIN.
BUT WHY ARE YOU GOING SO FAR AWAY, CHILDREN?
THE MOUNTAIN TOWN?
WHERE ARE YOUR PARENTS?
HEY! GO HOME!!
OR ELSE THE MOUNTAIN DEMONS WILL COME AFTER YOU...
KIDS,
MY HOUSE IS JUST AROUND THE CORNER.
WHY DON'T YOU TWO COME OVER FOR A HOT MEAL?

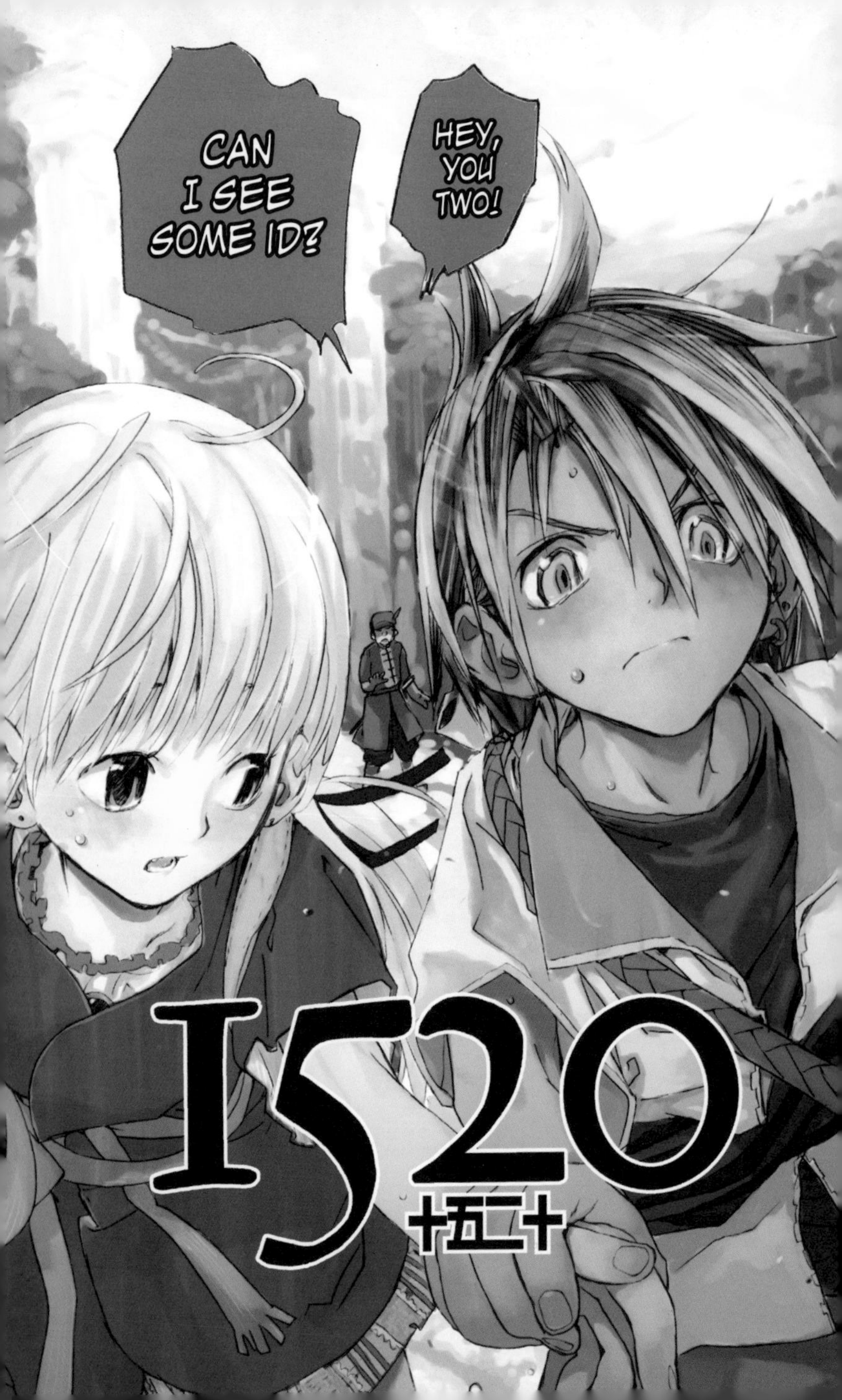
HEY, YOU TWO!
CAN I SEE SOME ID?
1520
十五二十

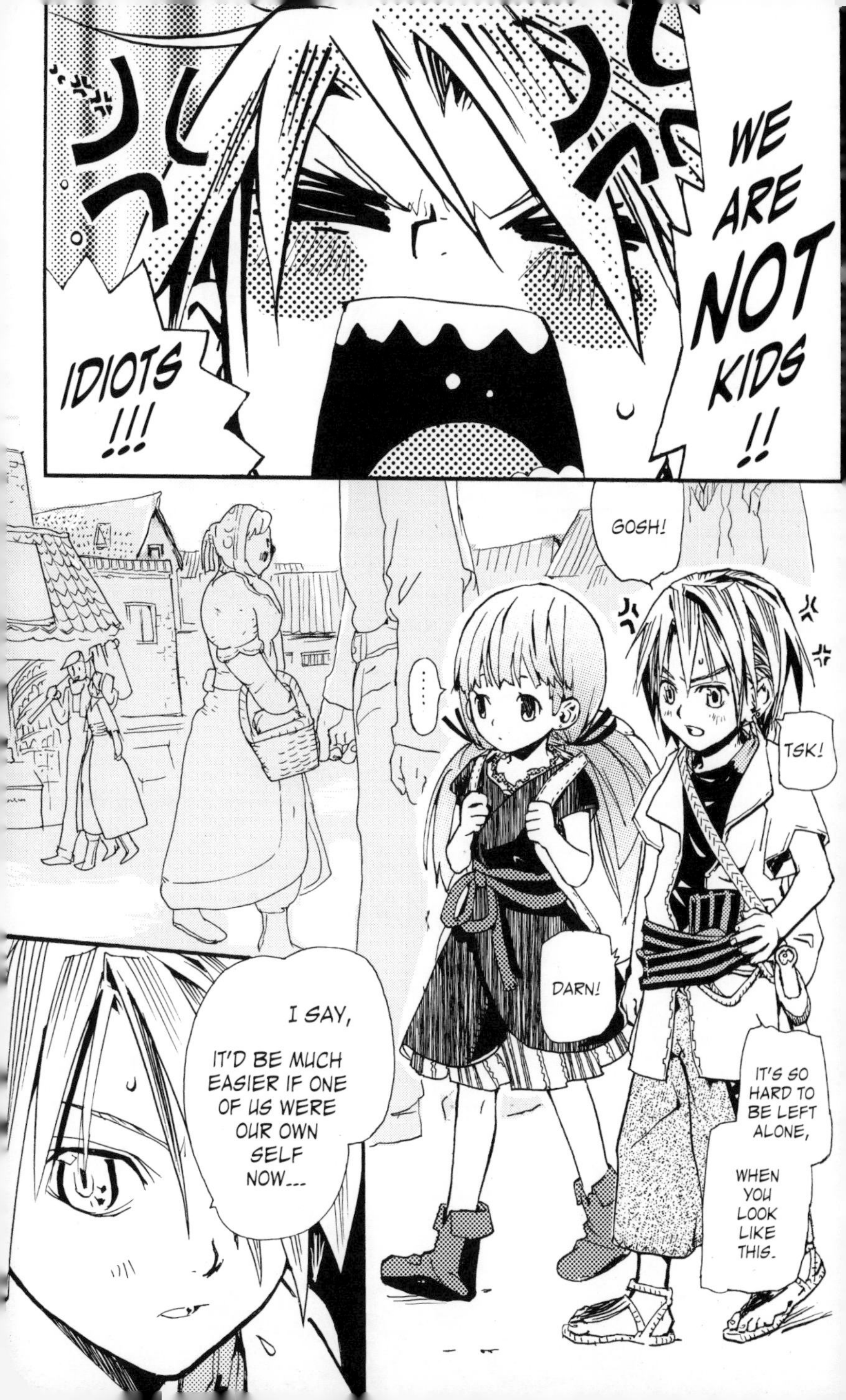
WE ARE NOT KIDS !!
IDIOTS !!!
GOSH!
TSK!
......
DARN!
IT'S SO HARD TO BE LEFT ALONE,
WHEN YOU LOOK LIKE THIS.
I SAY,
IT'D BE MUCH EASIER IF ONE OF US WERE OUR OWN SELF NOW...

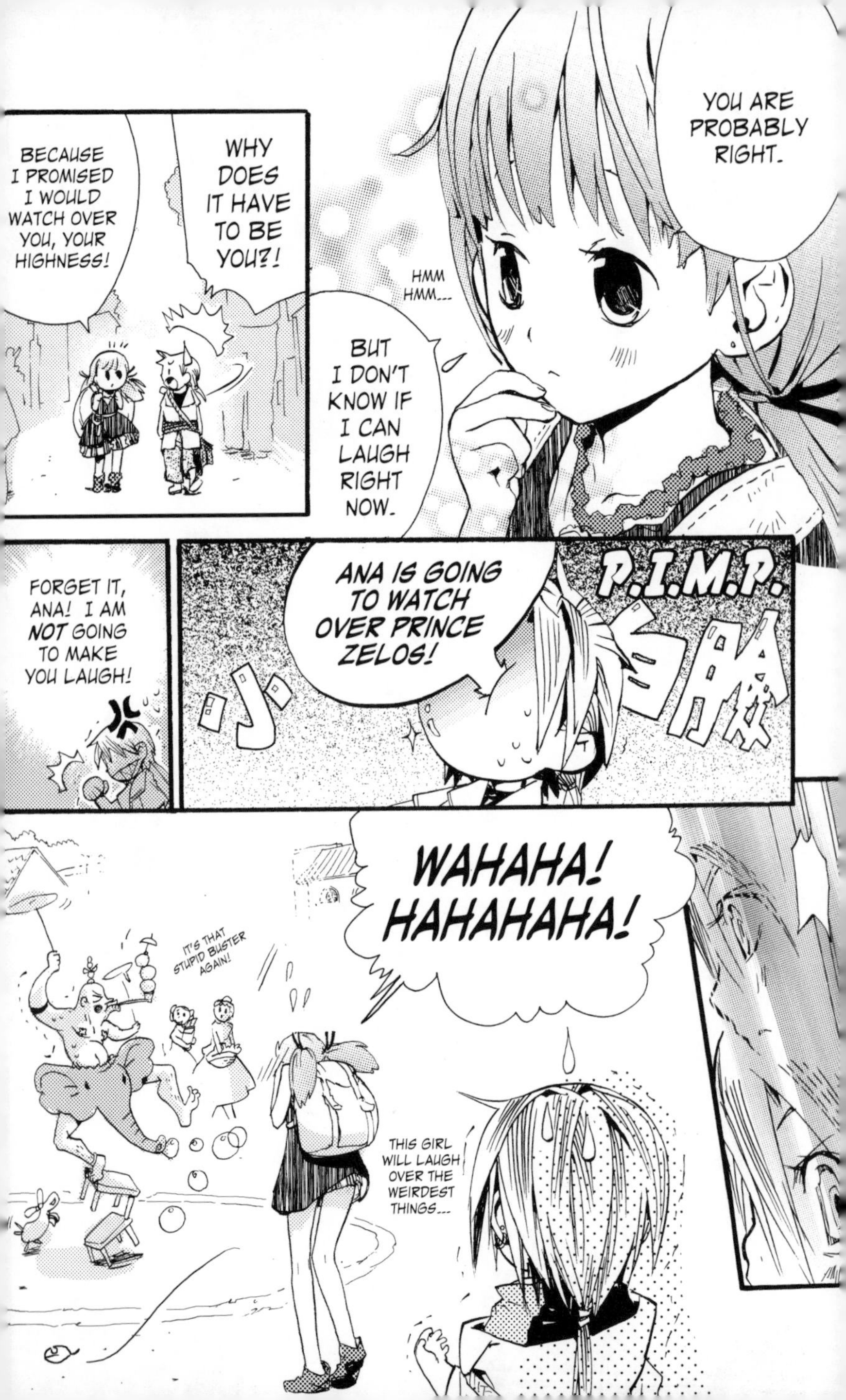
YOU ARE PROBABLY RIGHT.
HMM HMM...
BUT I DON'T KNOW IF I CAN LAUGH RIGHT NOW.
WHY DOES IT HAVE TO BE YOU?!
BECAUSE I PROMISED I WOULD WATCH OVER YOU, YOUR HIGHNESS!
P.I.M.P.
ANA IS GOING TO WATCH OVER PRINCE ZELOS!
FORGET IT, ANA! I AM NOT GOING TO MAKE YOU LAUGH!
WAHAHA! HAHAHAHA!
IT'S THAT STUPID BUSTER AGAIN!
THIS GIRL WILL LAUGH OVER THE WEIRDEST THINGS...

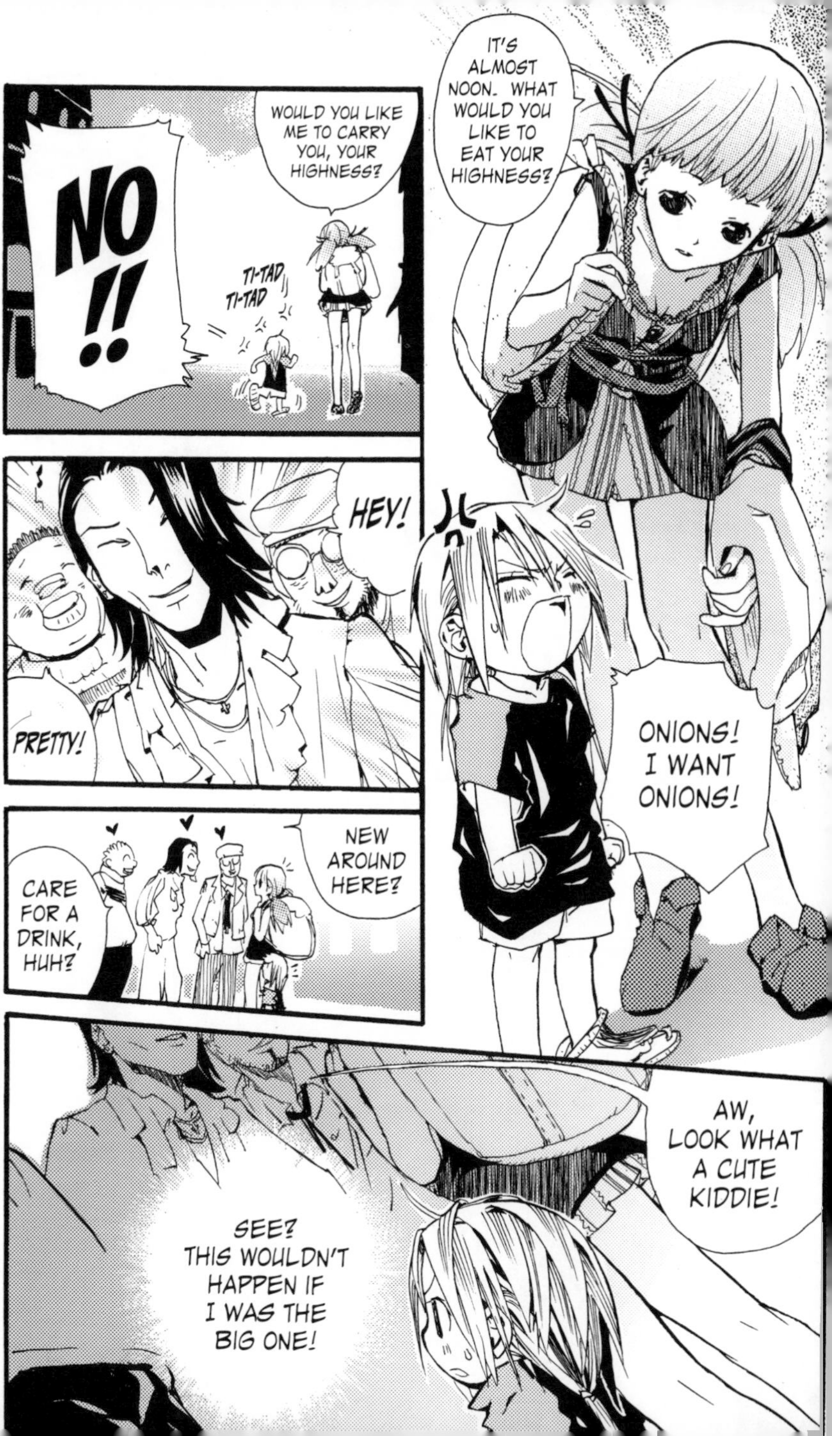
IT'S ALMOST NOON. WHAT WOULD YOU LIKE TO EAT YOUR HIGHNESS?
ONIONS! I WANT ONIONS!
WOULD YOU LIKE ME TO CARRY YOU, YOUR HIGHNESS?
TI-TAD TI-TAD
NO!!
HEY!
PRETTY!
NEW AROUND HERE?
CARE FOR A DRINK, HUH?
AW, LOOK WHAT A CUTE KIDDIE!
SEE? THIS WOULDN'T HAPPEN IF I WAS THE BIG ONE!

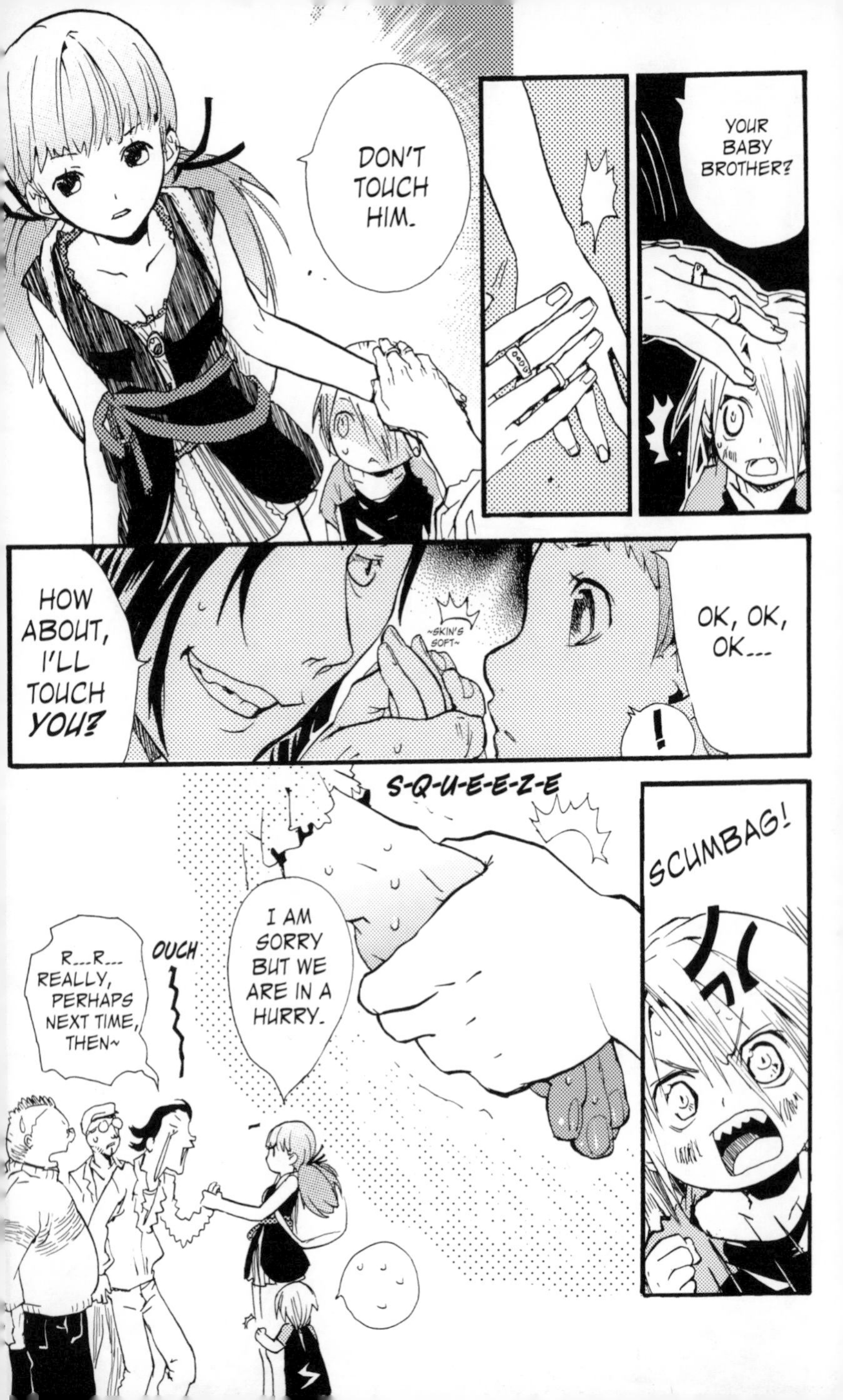
YOUR BABY BROTHER?
DON'T TOUCH HIM.
OK, OK, OK...
!
~SKIN'S SOFT~
HOW ABOUT, I'LL TOUCH YOU?
SCUMBAG!
S-Q-U-E-E-Z-E
I AM SORRY BUT WE ARE IN A HURRY.
OUCH
R... R... REALLY, PERHAPS NEXT TIME, THEN~

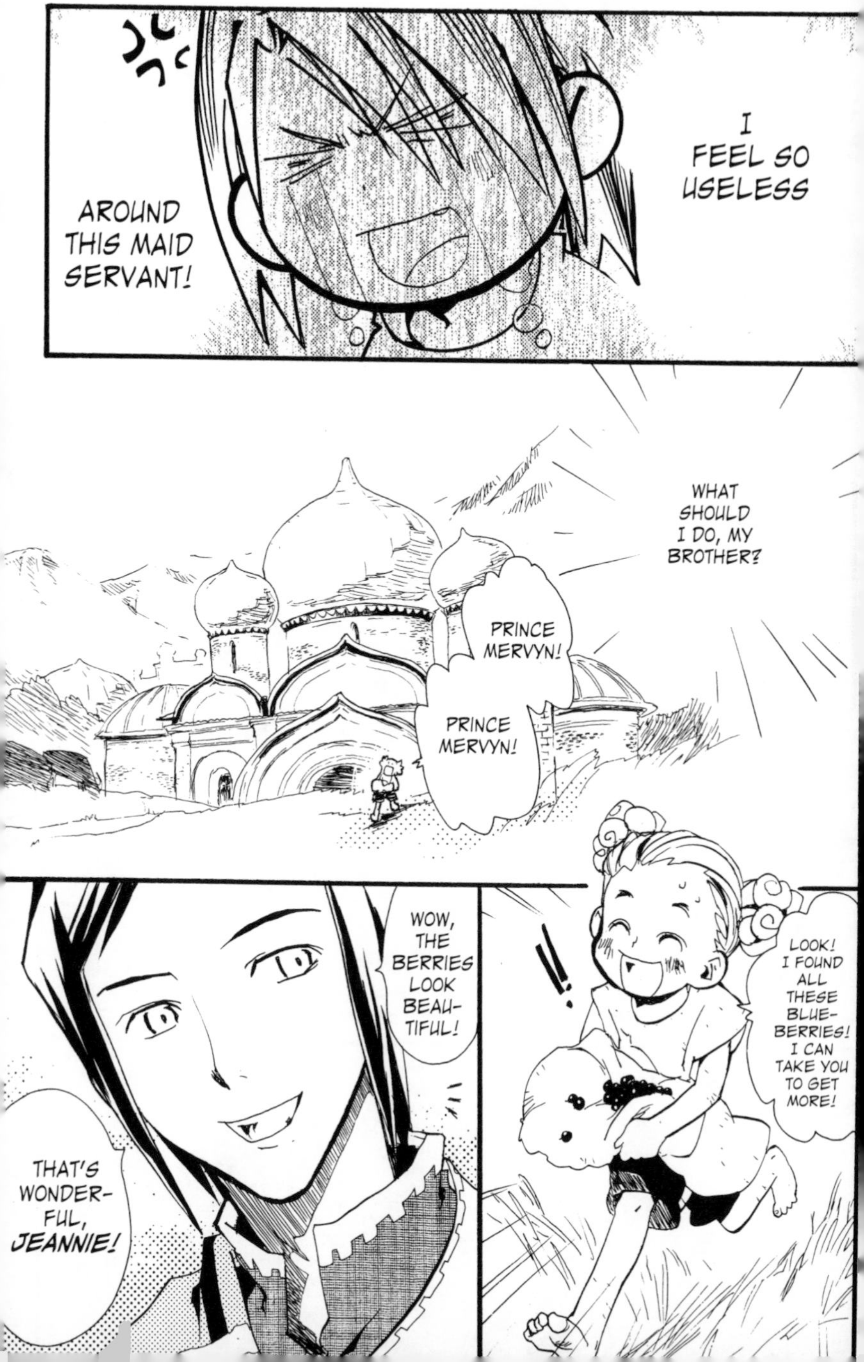

I FEEL SO USELESS
AROUND THIS MAID SERVANT!
WHAT SHOULD I DO, MY BROTHER?
PRINCE MERVYN!
PRINCE MERVYN!
LOOK! I FOUND ALL THESE BLUE-BERRIES! I CAN TAKE YOU TO GET MORE!
!!
WOW, THE BERRIES LOOK BEAU-TIFUL!
THAT'S WONDER-FUL, JEANNIE!

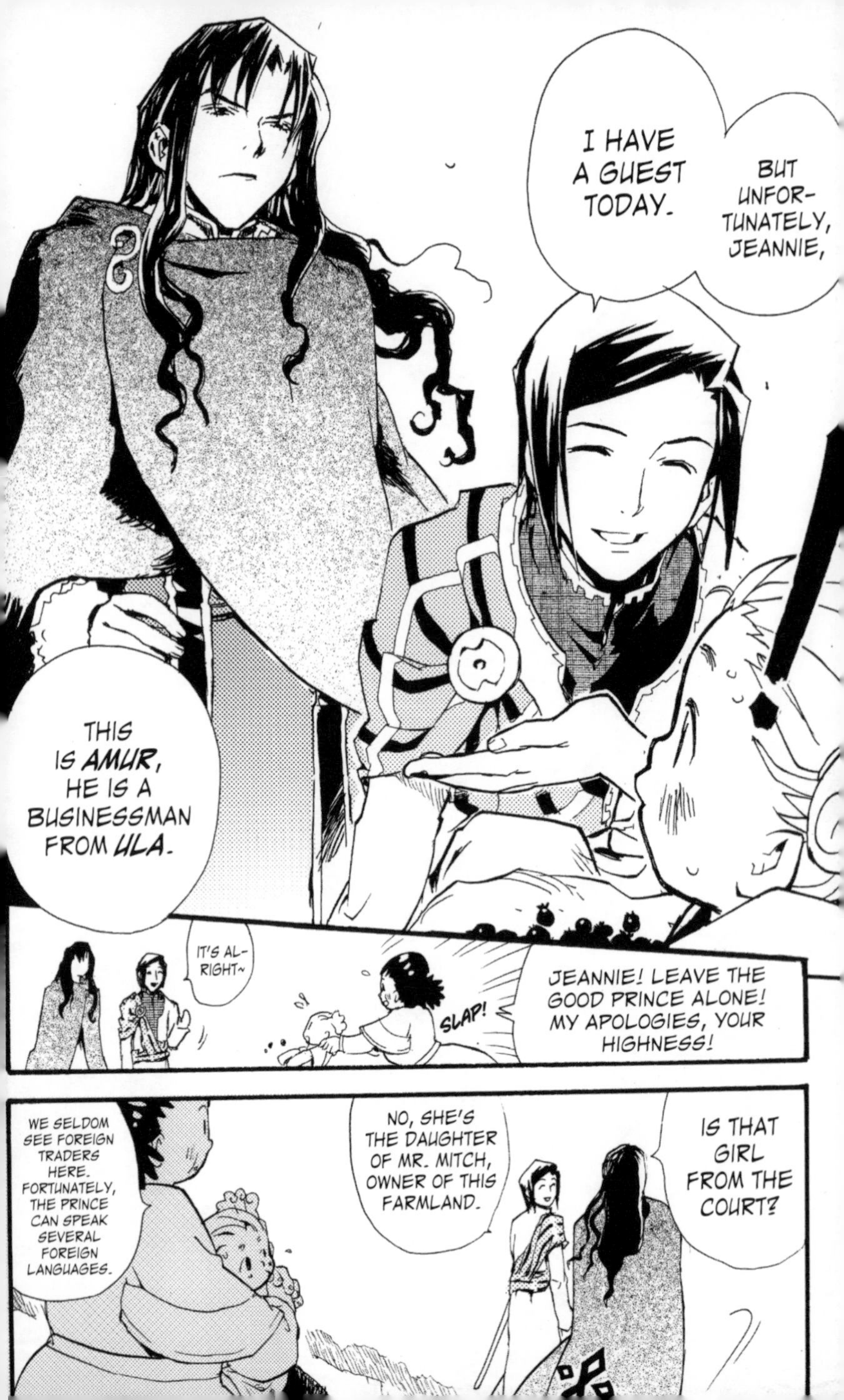
BUT UNFOR-TUNATELY, JEANNIE,
I HAVE A GUEST TODAY.
THIS IS AMUR, HE IS A BUSINESSMAN FROM ULA.
JEANNIE! LEAVE THE GOOD PRINCE ALONE! MY APOLOGIES, YOUR HIGHNESS!
SLAP!
IT'S AL-RIGHT~
IS THAT GIRL FROM THE COURT?
NO, SHE'S THE DAUGHTER OF MR. MITCH, OWNER OF THIS FARMLAND.
WE SELDOM SEE FOREIGN TRADERS HERE. FORTUNATELY, THE PRINCE CAN SPEAK SEVERAL FOREIGN LANGUAGES.

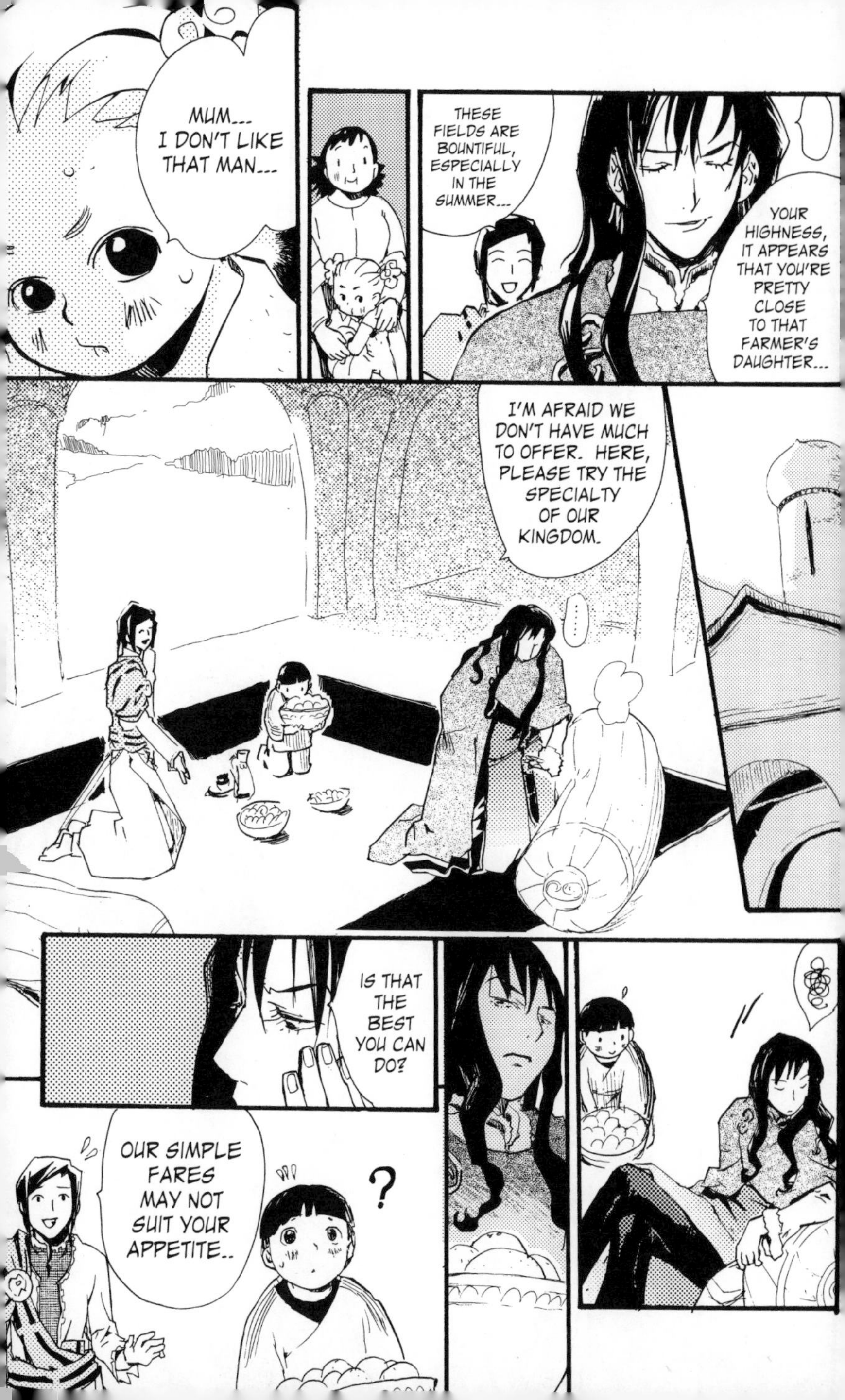
THESE FIELDS ARE BOUNTIFUL, ESPECIALLY IN THE SUMMER...
YOUR HIGHNESS, IT APPEARS THAT YOU'RE PRETTY CLOSE TO THAT FARMER'S DAUGHTER...
MUM... I DON'T LIKE THAT MAN...
I'M AFRAID WE DON'T HAVE MUCH TO OFFER. HERE, PLEASE TRY THE SPECIALTY OF OUR KINGDOM.
......
IS THAT THE BEST YOU CAN DO?
?
OUR SIMPLE FARES MAY NOT SUIT YOUR APPETITE..

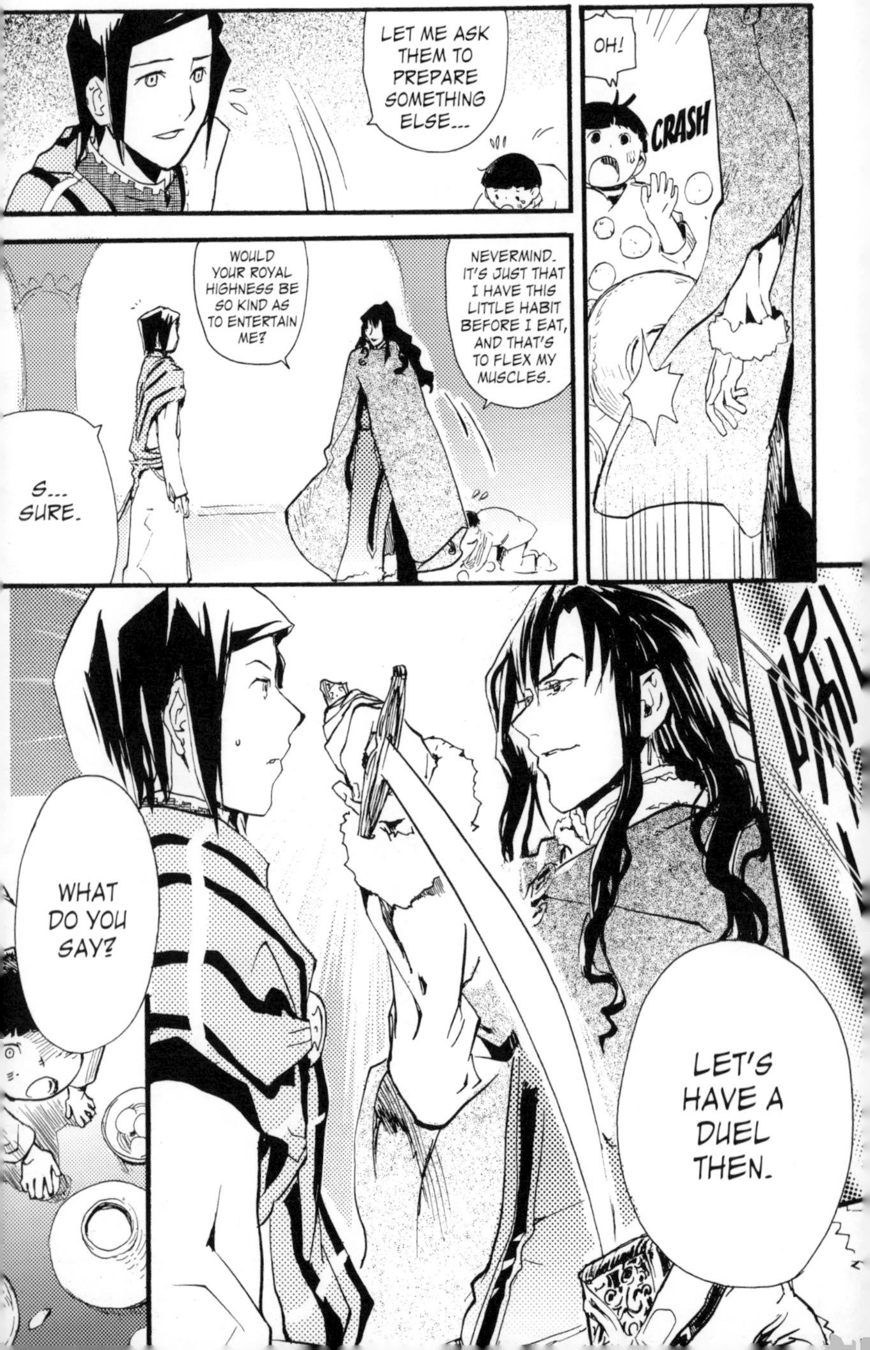
OH!
CRASH
LET ME ASK THEM TO PREPARE SOMETHING ELSE...
NEVERMIND. IT'S JUST THAT I HAVE THIS LITTLE HABIT BEFORE I EAT, AND THAT'S TO FLEX MY MUSCLES.
WOULD YOUR ROYAL HIGHNESS BE SO KIND AS TO ENTERTAIN ME?
S... SURE.
LET'S HAVE A DUEL THEN.
WHAT DO YOU SAY?

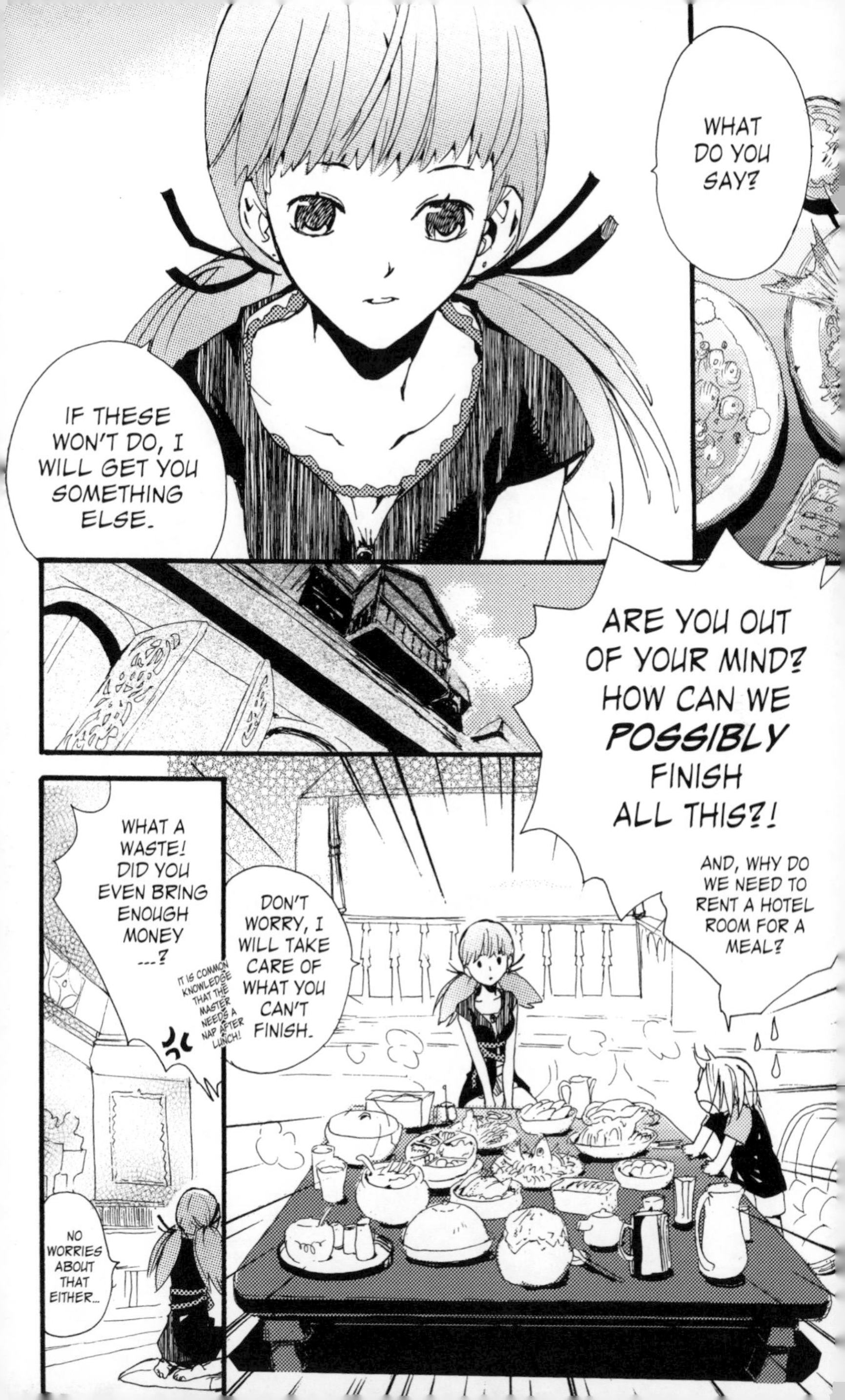
WHAT DO YOU SAY?
IF THESE WON'T DO, I WILL GET YOU SOMETHING ELSE.
ARE YOU OUT OF YOUR MIND? HOW CAN WE *POSSIBLY* FINISH ALL THIS?!
AND, WHY DO WE NEED TO RENT A HOTEL ROOM FOR A MEAL?
DON'T WORRY, I WILL TAKE CARE OF WHAT YOU CAN'T FINISH.
IT IS COMMON KNOWLEDGE THAT THE MASTER NEEDS A NAP AFTER LUNCH!
WHAT A WASTE! DID YOU EVEN BRING ENOUGH MONEY ...?
NO WORRIES ABOUT THAT EITHER...

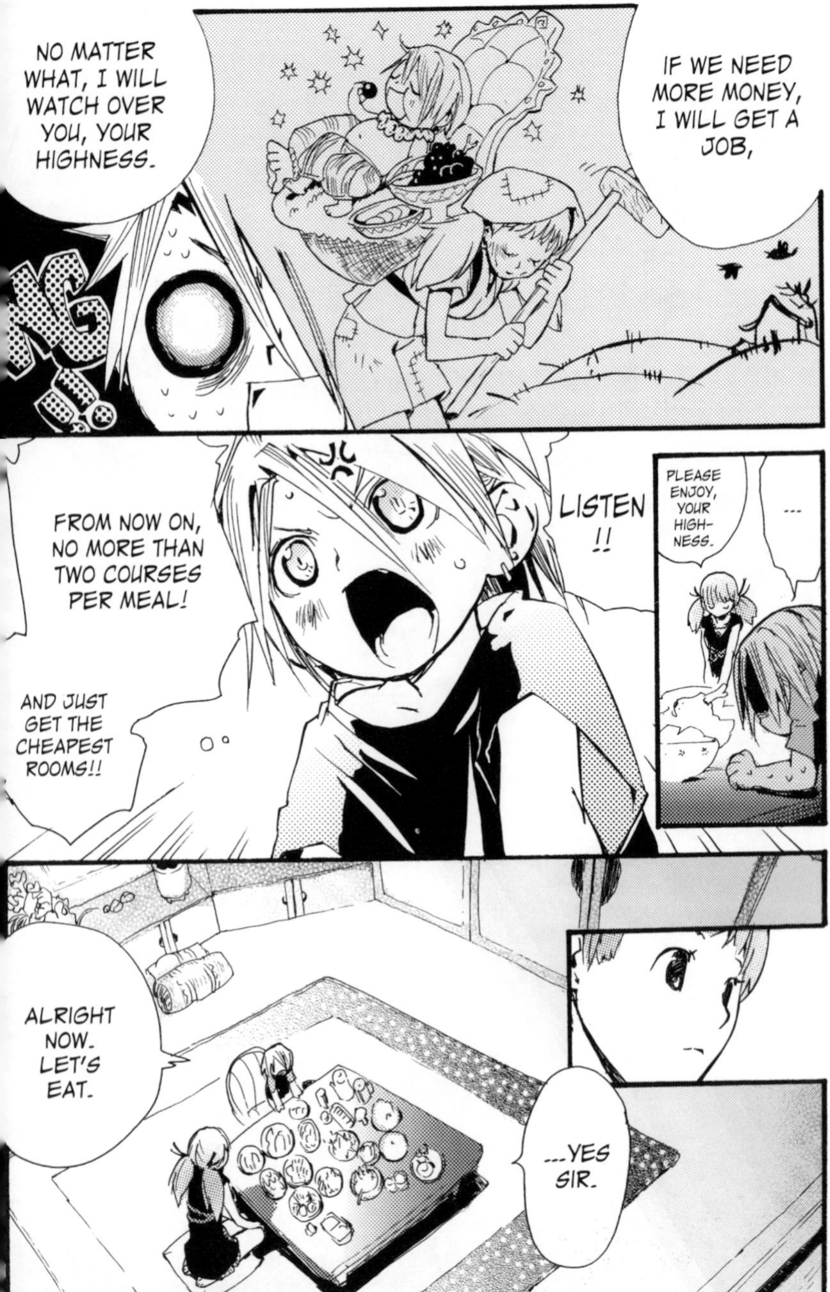
IF WE NEED MORE MONEY, I WILL GET A JOB,
NO MATTER WHAT, I WILL WATCH OVER YOU, YOUR HIGHNESS.
PLEASE ENJOY, YOUR HIGH-NESS.
...
LISTEN!!
FROM NOW ON, NO MORE THAN TWO COURSES PER MEAL!
AND JUST GET THE CHEAPEST ROOMS!!
...YES SIR.
ALRIGHT NOW. LET'S EAT.

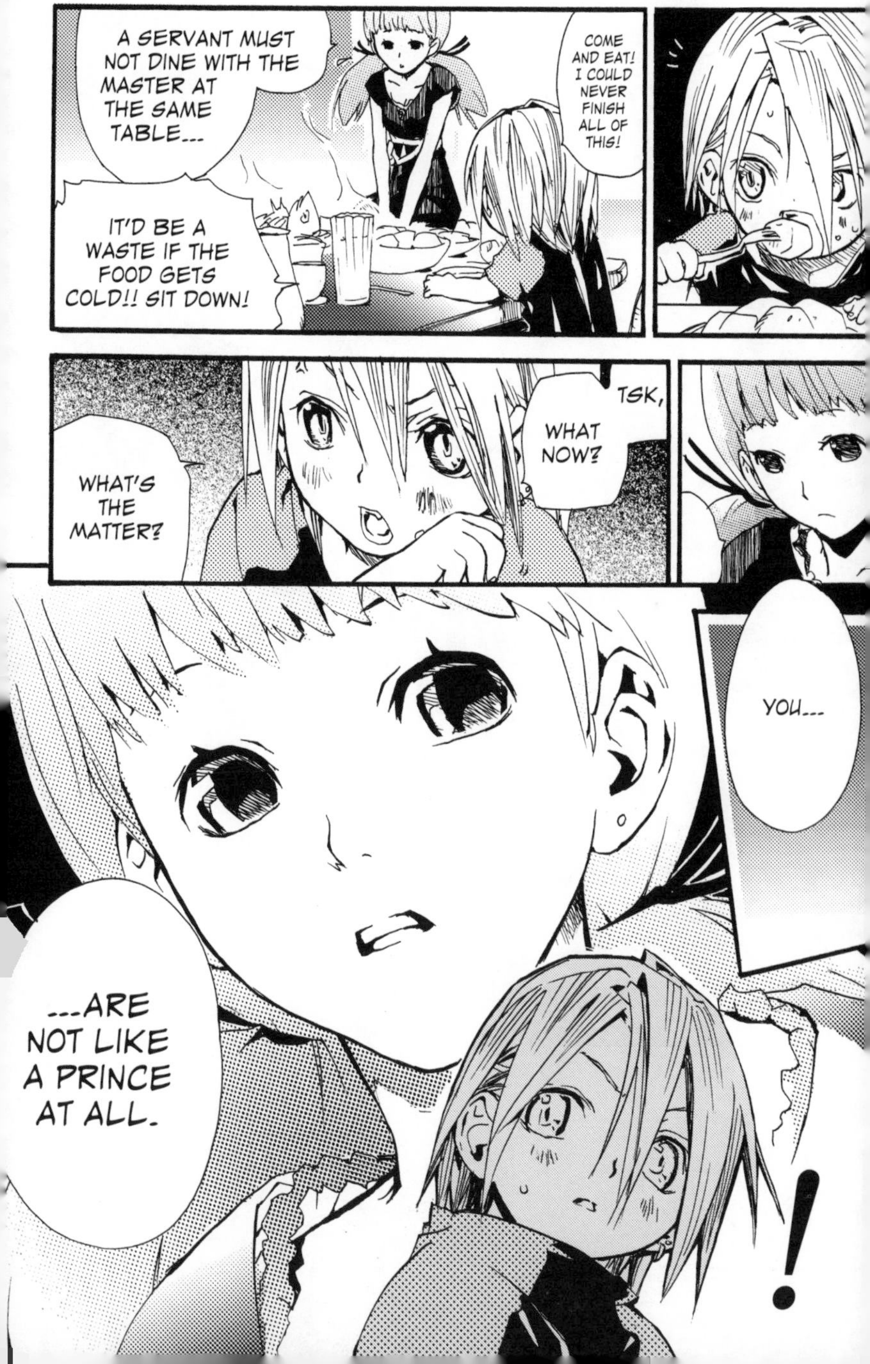
COME AND EAT! I COULD NEVER FINISH ALL OF THIS!
A SERVANT MUST NOT DINE WITH THE MASTER AT THE SAME TABLE...
IT'D BE A WASTE IF THE FOOD GETS COLD!! SIT DOWN!
TSK,
WHAT NOW?
WHAT'S THE MATTER?
YOU...
...ARE NOT LIKE A PRINCE AT ALL.
!

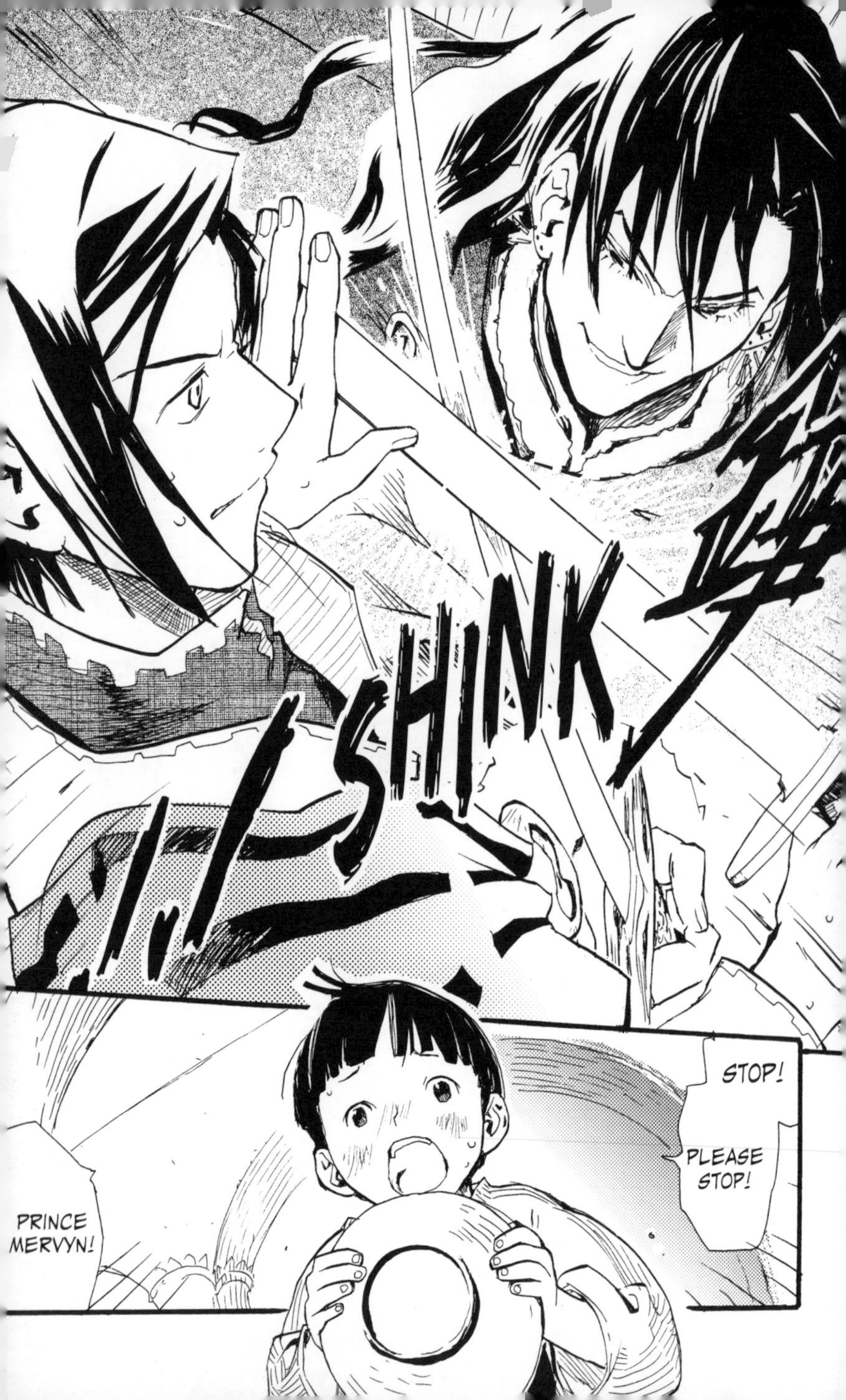
SHINK
STOP!
PLEASE STOP!
PRINCE MERVYN!

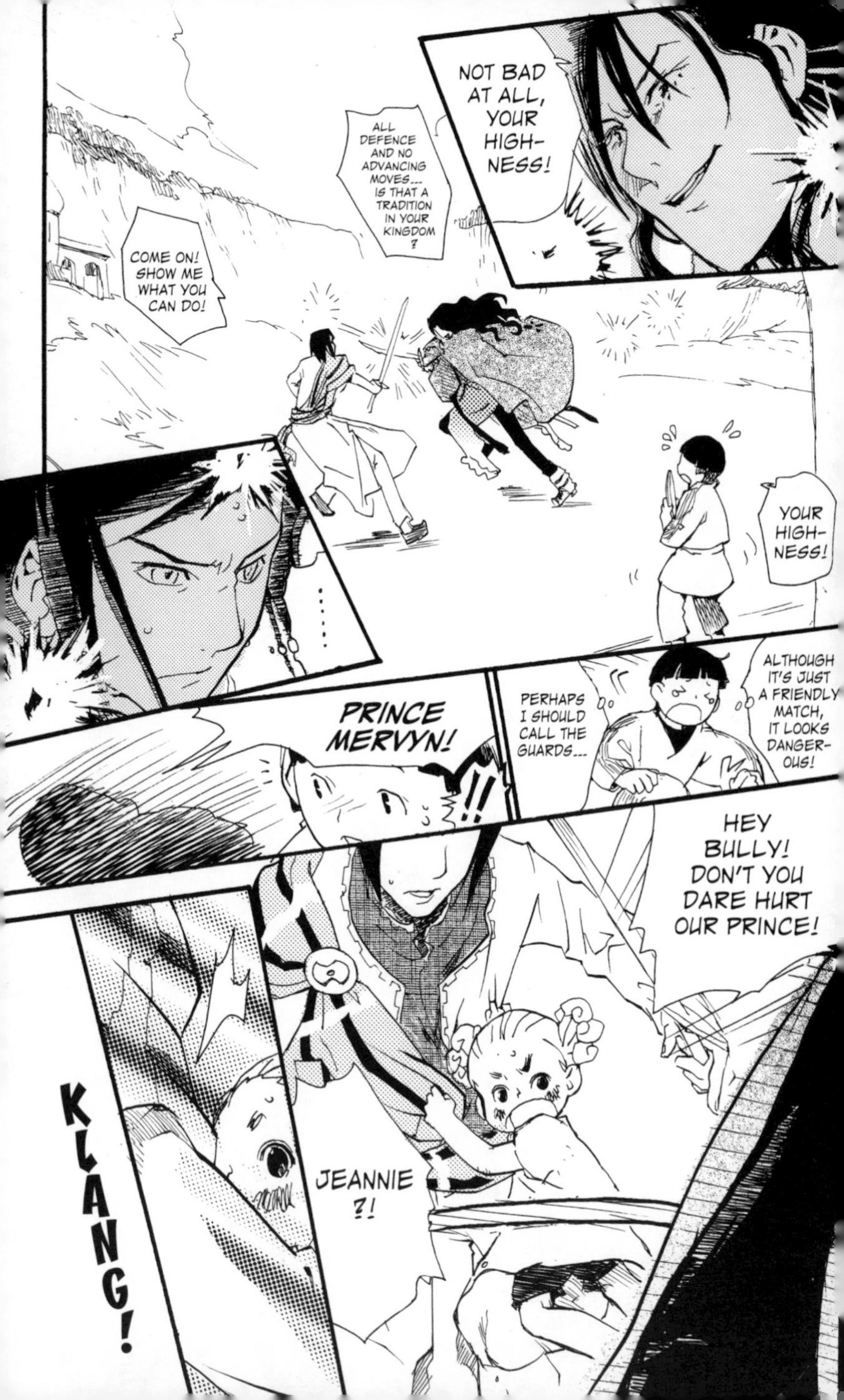

NOT BAD AT ALL, YOUR HIGH-NESS!
ALL DEFENCE AND NO ADVANCING MOVES... IS THAT A TRADITION IN YOUR KINGDOM ?
COME ON! SHOW ME WHAT YOU CAN DO!
YOUR HIGH-NESS!
......
ALTHOUGH IT'S JUST A FRIENDLY MATCH, IT LOOKS DANGER-OUS!
PERHAPS I SHOULD CALL THE GUARDS...
PRINCE MERVYN!
!!
HEY BULLY! DON'T YOU DARE HURT OUR PRINCE!
JEANNIE ?!
KLANG!

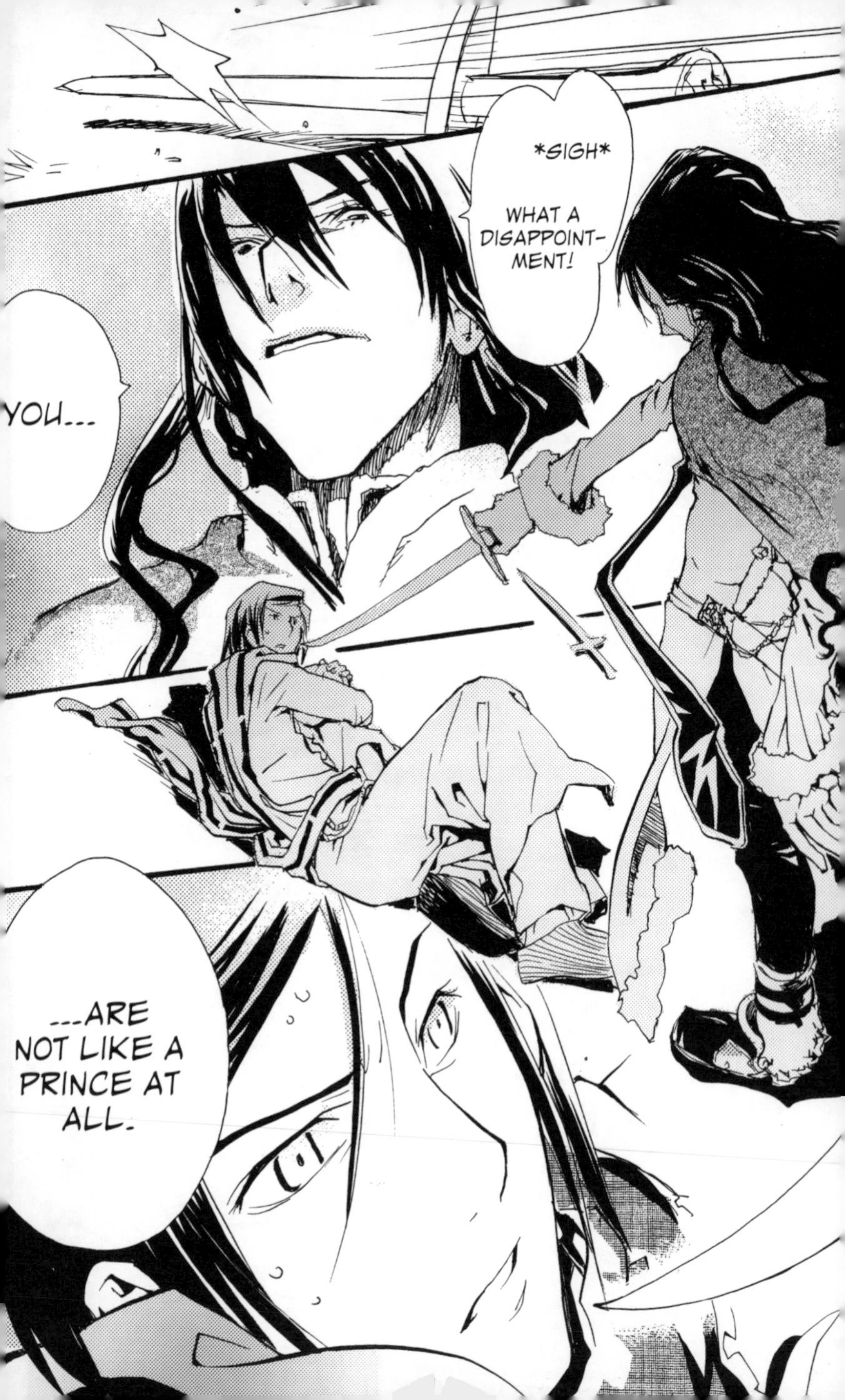
SIGH
WHAT A DISAPPOINT-MENT!
YOU...
...ARE NOT LIKE A PRINCE AT ALL.

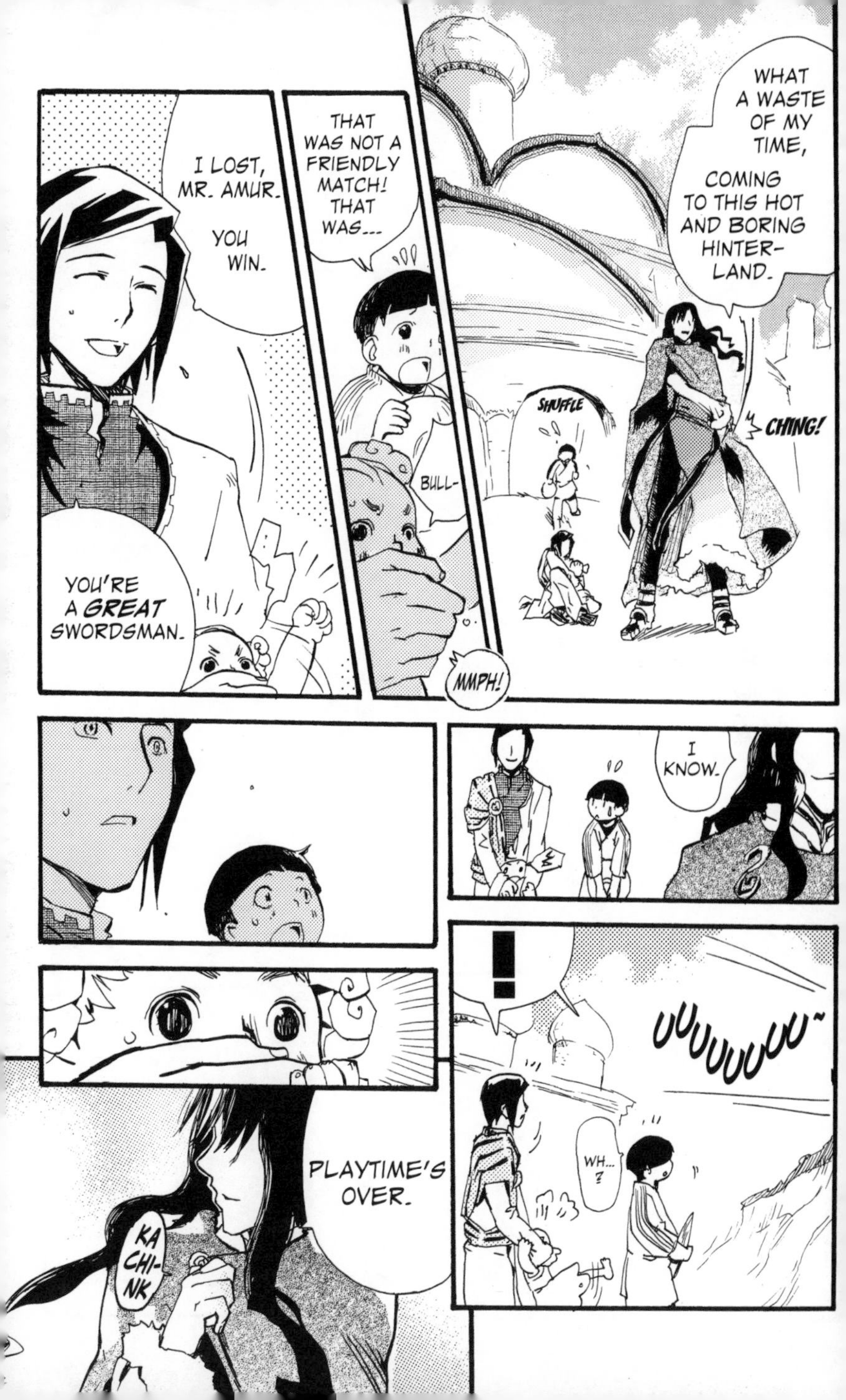
WHAT A WASTE OF MY TIME,
COMING TO THIS HOT AND BORING HINTER-LAND.
SHUFFLE
CHING!
THAT WAS NOT A FRIENDLY MATCH! THAT WAS...
BULL-
MMPH!
I LOST, MR. AMUR.
YOU WIN.
YOU'RE A GREAT SWORDSMAN.
I KNOW.
!
UUUUUUUU~
WH...?
PLAYTIME'S OVER.
KA CHI-NK

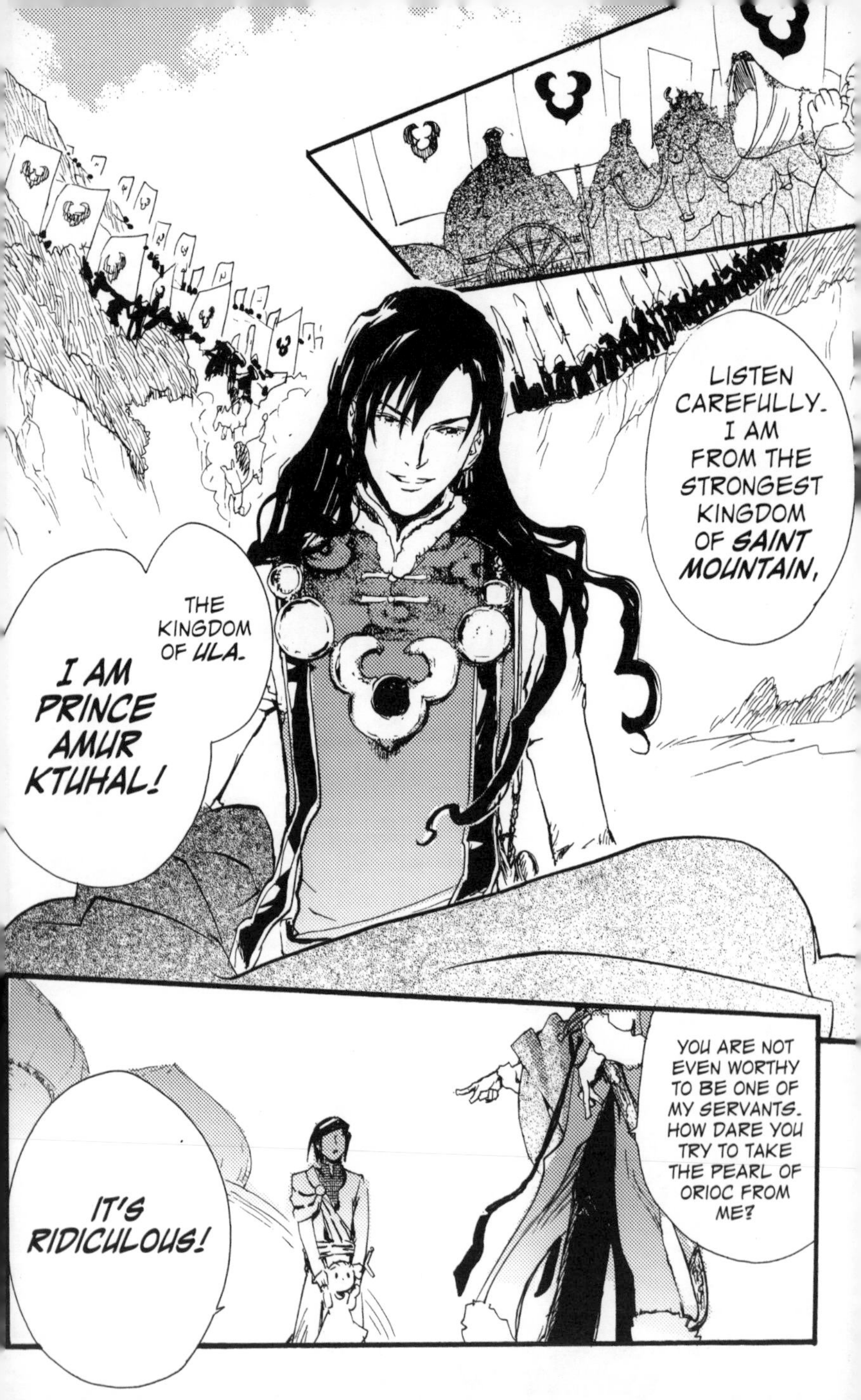
LISTEN CAREFULLY. I AM FROM THE STRONGEST KINGDOM OF SAINT MOUNTAIN,
THE KINGDOM OF ULA.
I AM PRINCE AMUR KTUHAL!
YOU ARE NOT EVEN WORTHY TO BE ONE OF MY SERVANTS. HOW DARE YOU TRY TO TAKE THE PEARL OF ORIOC FROM ME?
IT'S RIDICULOUS!

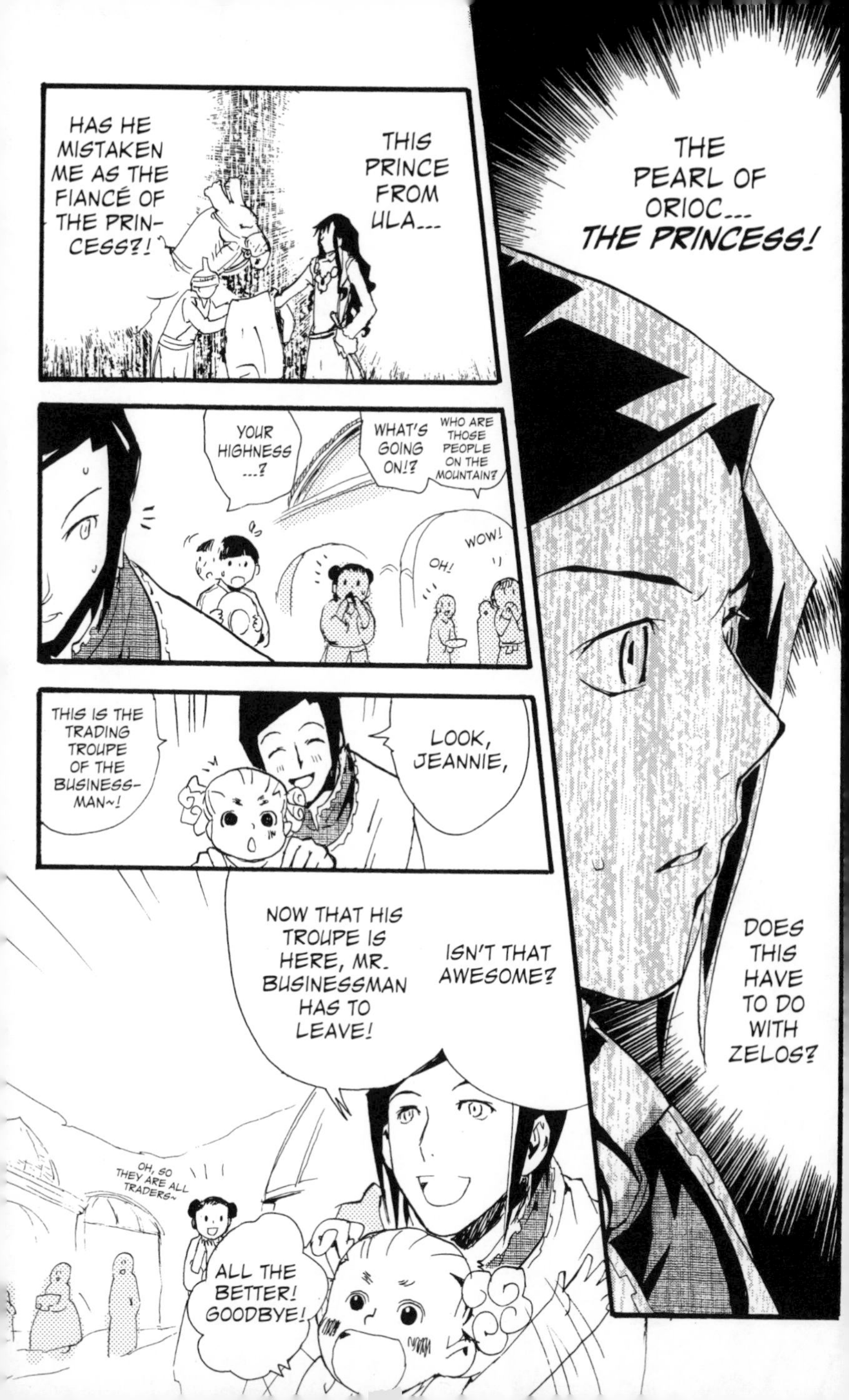
THE PEARL OF ORIOC... THE PRINCESS!
DOES THIS HAVE TO DO WITH ZELOS?
THIS PRINCE FROM ULA...
HAS HE MISTAKEN ME AS THE FIANCÉ OF THE PRIN-CESS?!
WHO ARE THOSE PEOPLE ON THE MOUNTAIN?
WHAT'S GOING ON!?
YOUR HIGHNESS ...?
WOW!
OH!
LOOK, JEANNIE,
THIS IS THE TRADING TROUPE OF THE BUSINESS-MAN~!
ISN'T THAT AWESOME?
NOW THAT HIS TROUPE IS HERE, MR. BUSINESSMAN HAS TO LEAVE!
OH, SO THEY ARE ALL TRADERS~
ALL THE BETTER! GOODBYE!

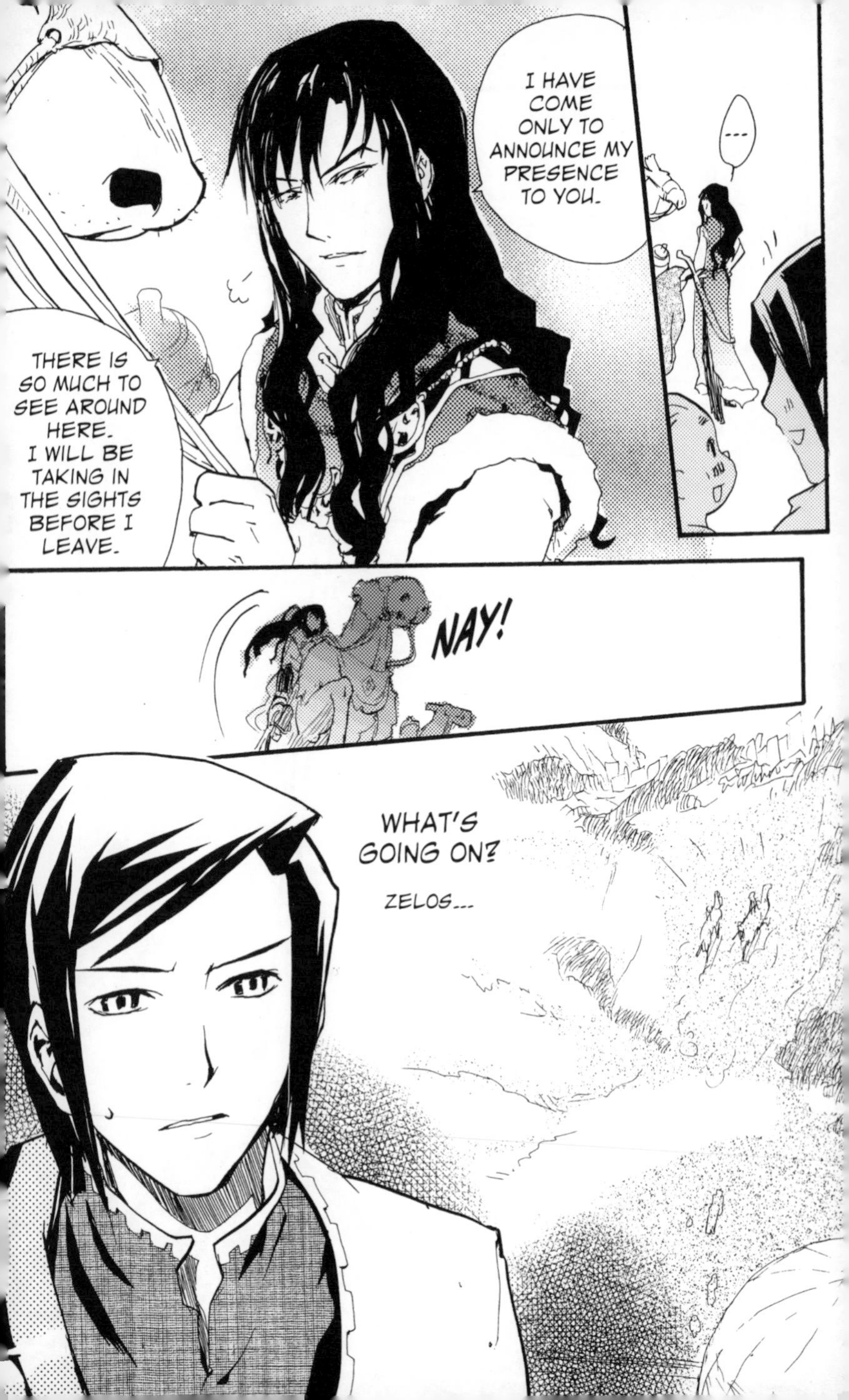
...
I HAVE COME ONLY TO ANNOUNCE MY PRESENCE TO YOU.
THERE IS SO MUCH TO SEE AROUND HERE. I WILL BE TAKING IN THE SIGHTS BEFORE I LEAVE.
NAY!
WHAT'S GOING ON?
ZELOS...

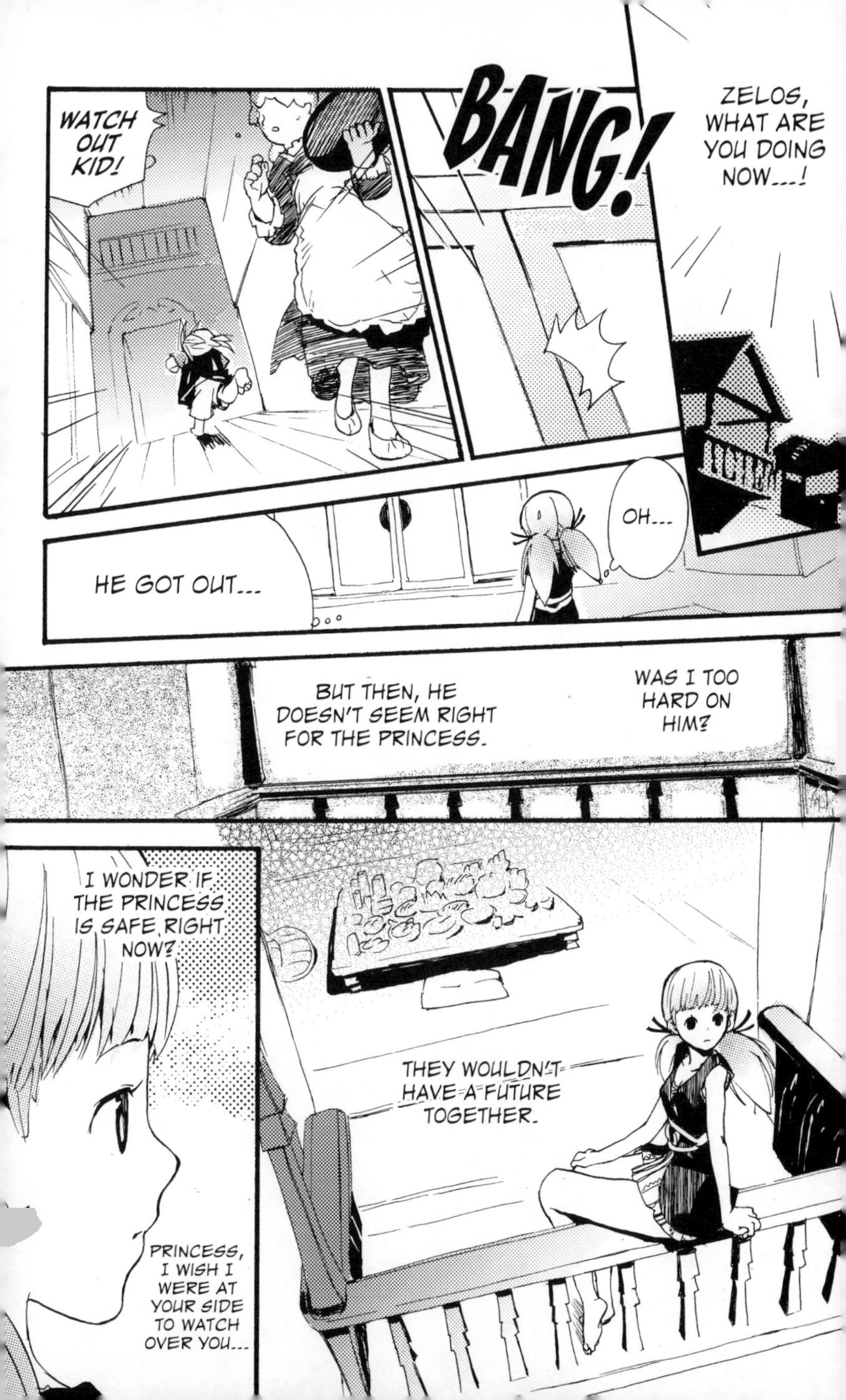
ZELOS, WHAT ARE YOU DOING NOW...!
BANG!
WATCH OUT KID!
OH...
HE GOT OUT...
WAS I TOO HARD ON HIM?
BUT THEN, HE DOESN'T SEEM RIGHT FOR THE PRINCESS.
THEY WOULDN'T HAVE A FUTURE TOGETHER.
I WONDER IF THE PRINCESS IS SAFE RIGHT NOW?
PRINCESS, I WISH I WERE AT YOUR SIDE TO WATCH OVER YOU...

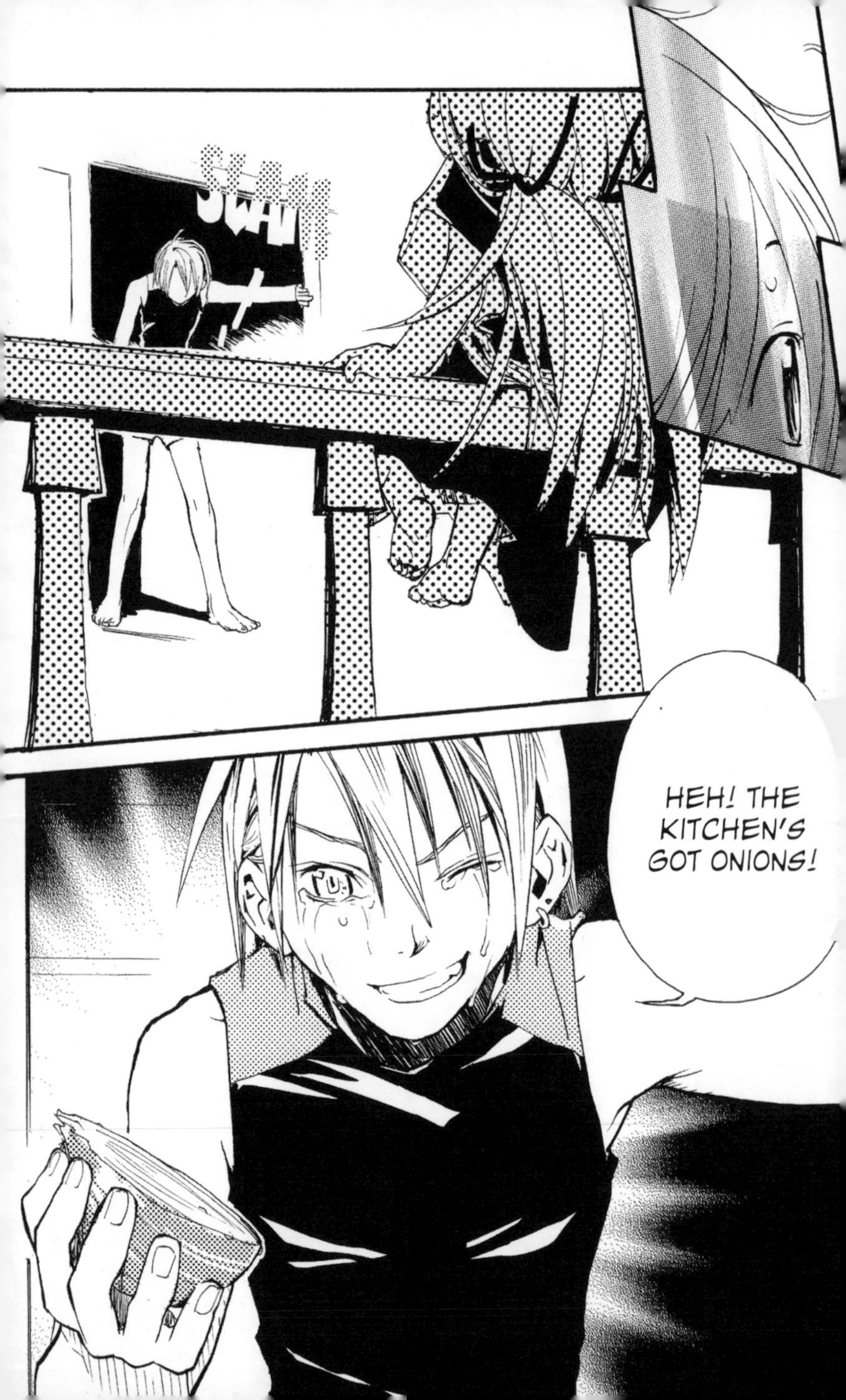
HEH! THE KITCHEN'S GOT ONIONS!

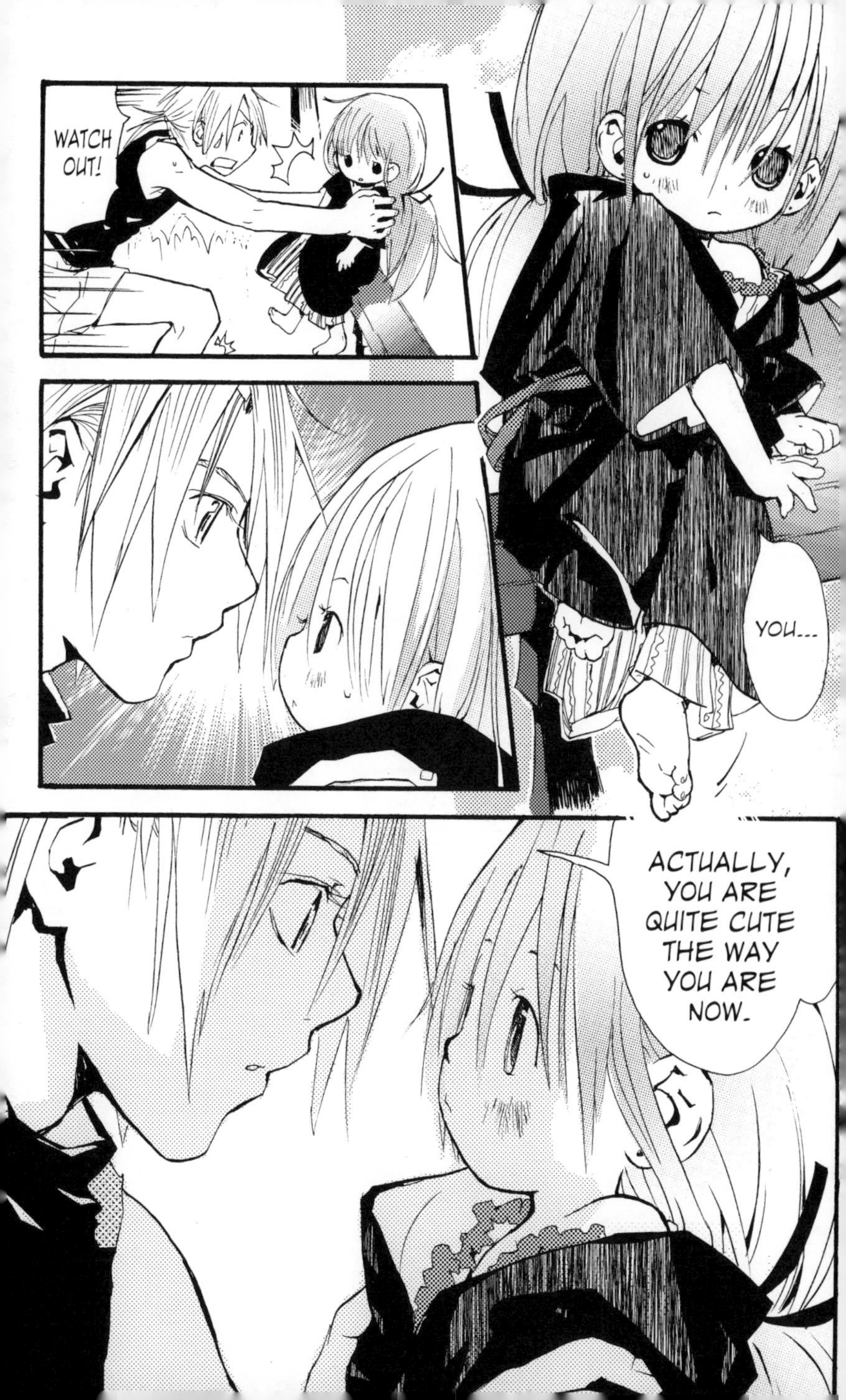
YOU...
WATCH OUT!
ACTUALLY, YOU ARE QUITE CUTE THE WAY YOU ARE NOW.

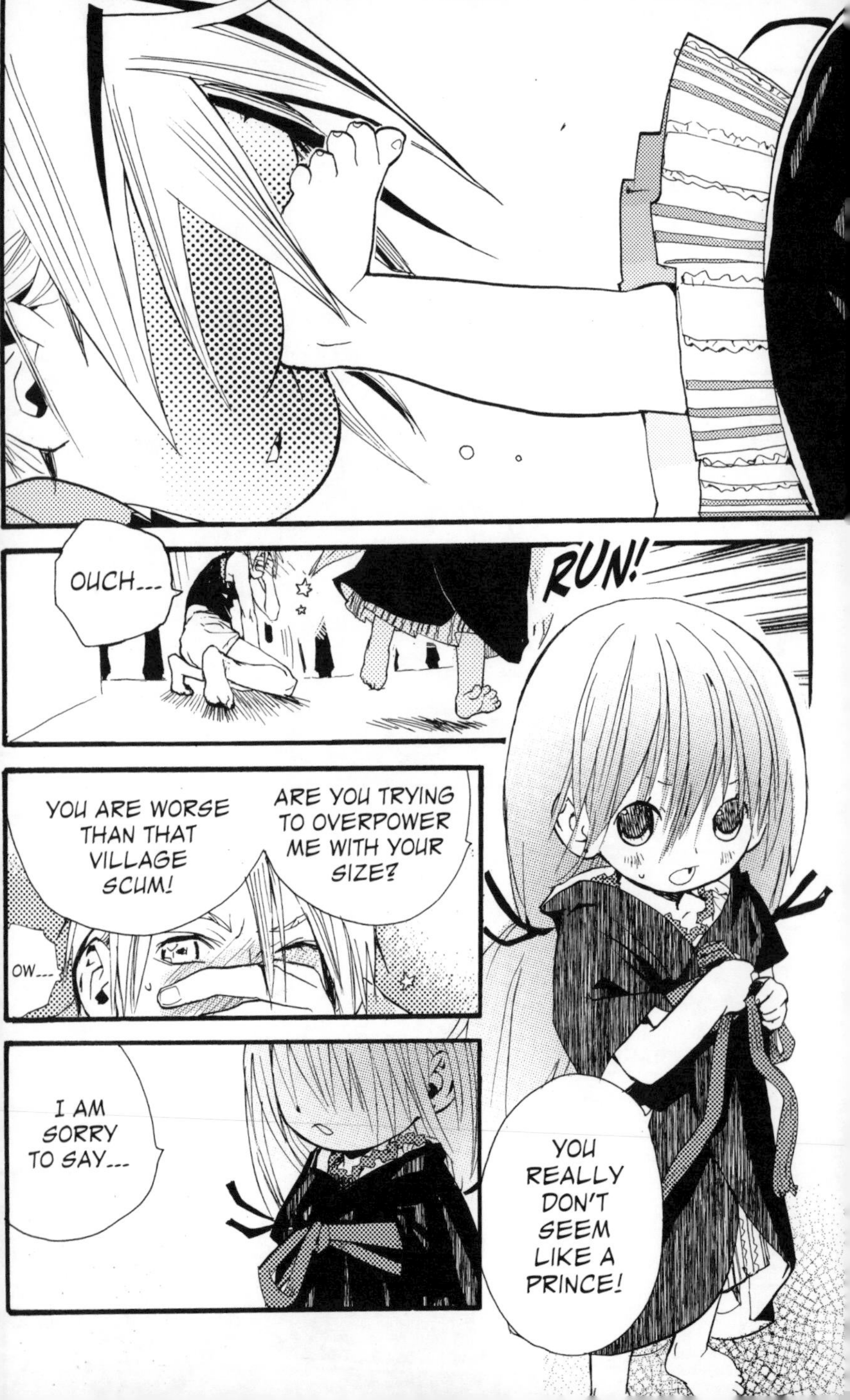
RUN!
OUCH...
ARE YOU TRYING TO OVERPOWER ME WITH YOUR SIZE?
YOU ARE WORSE THAN THAT VILLAGE SCUM!
OW...
I AM SORRY TO SAY...
YOU REALLY DON'T SEEM LIKE A PRINCE!

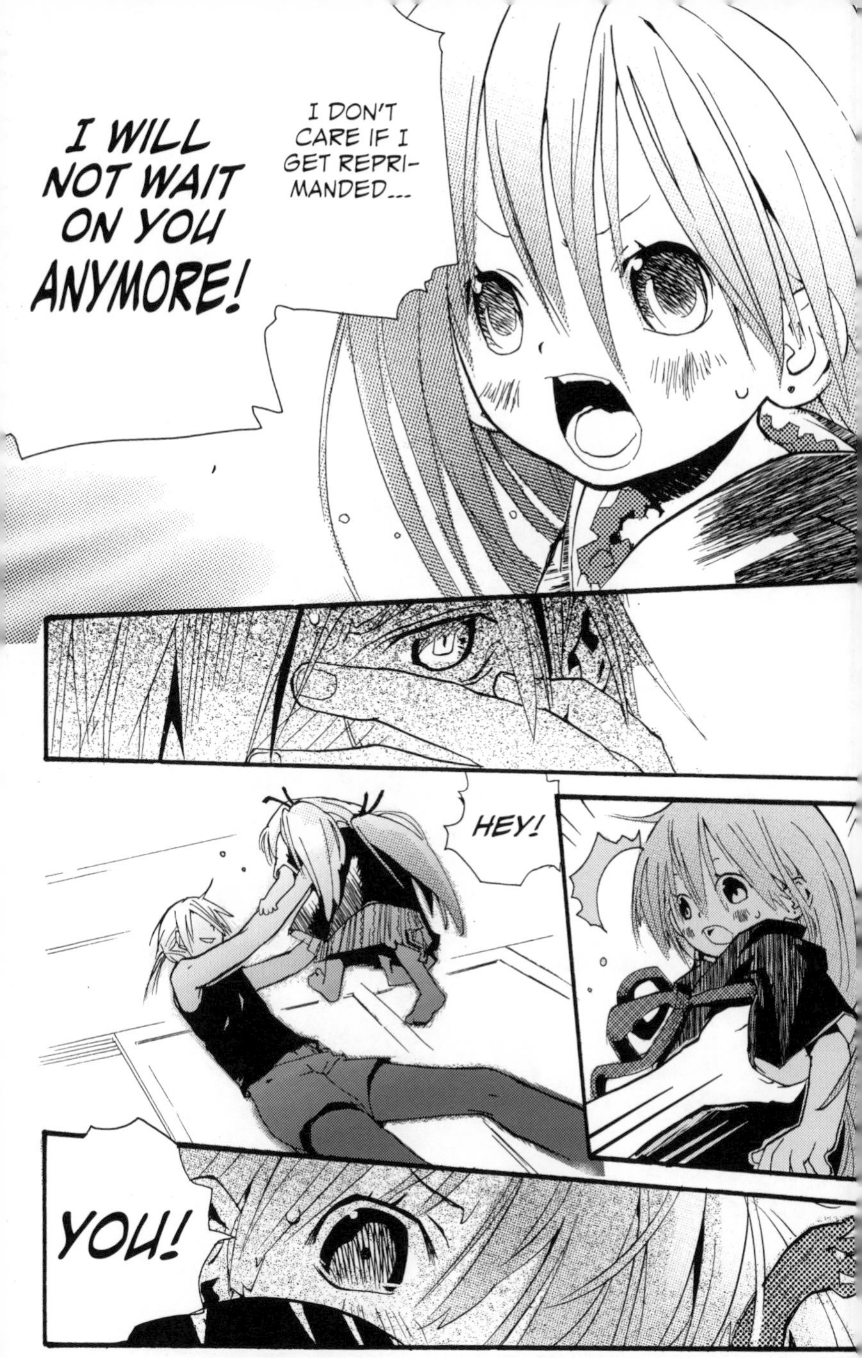
I DON'T CARE IF I GET REPRIMANDED...
I WILL NOT WAIT ON YOU ANYMORE!
HEY!
YOU!

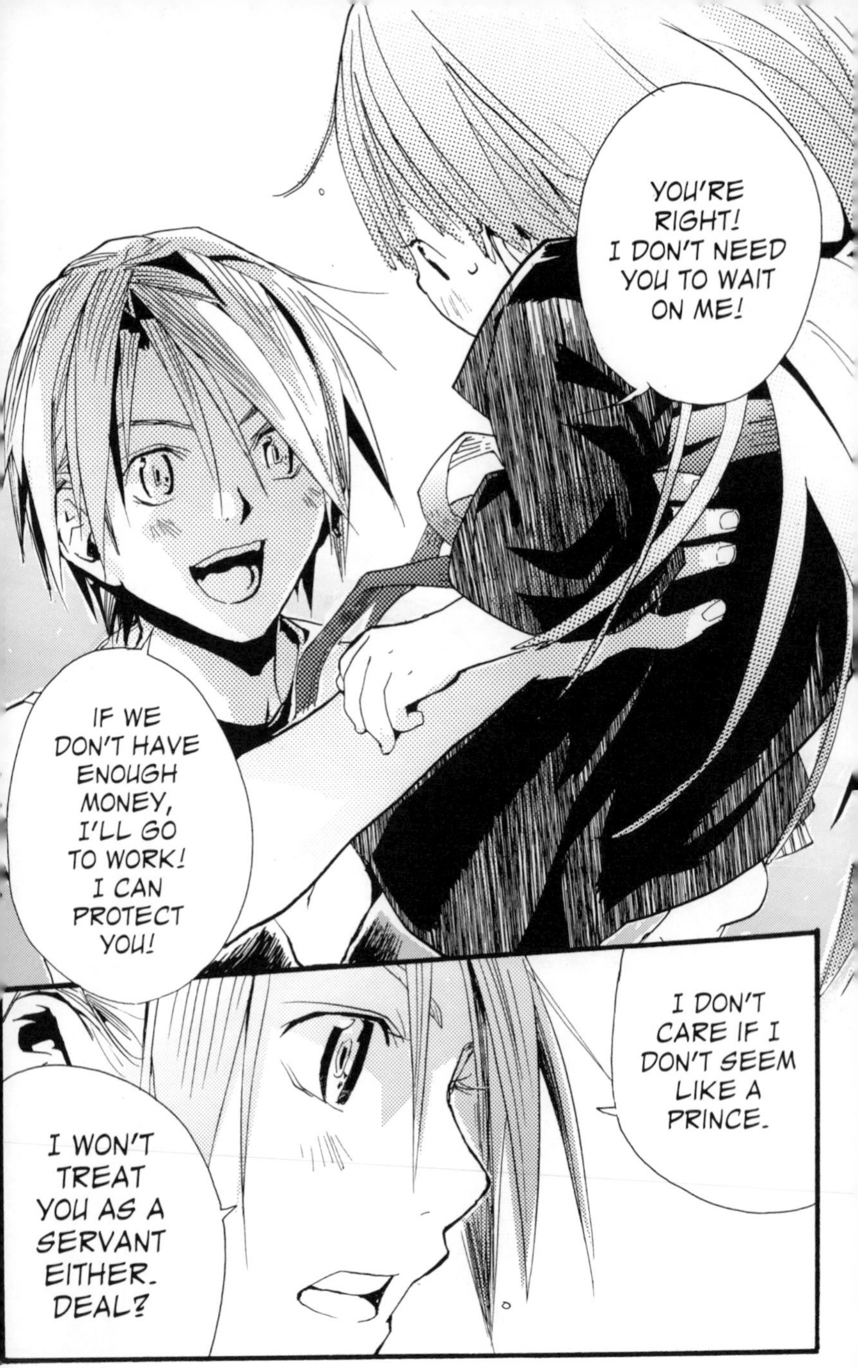
YOU'RE RIGHT! I DON'T NEED YOU TO WAIT ON ME!
IF WE DON'T HAVE ENOUGH MONEY, I'LL GO TO WORK! I CAN PROTECT YOU!
I DON'T CARE IF I DON'T SEEM LIKE A PRINCE.
I WON'T TREAT YOU AS A SERVANT EITHER. DEAL?

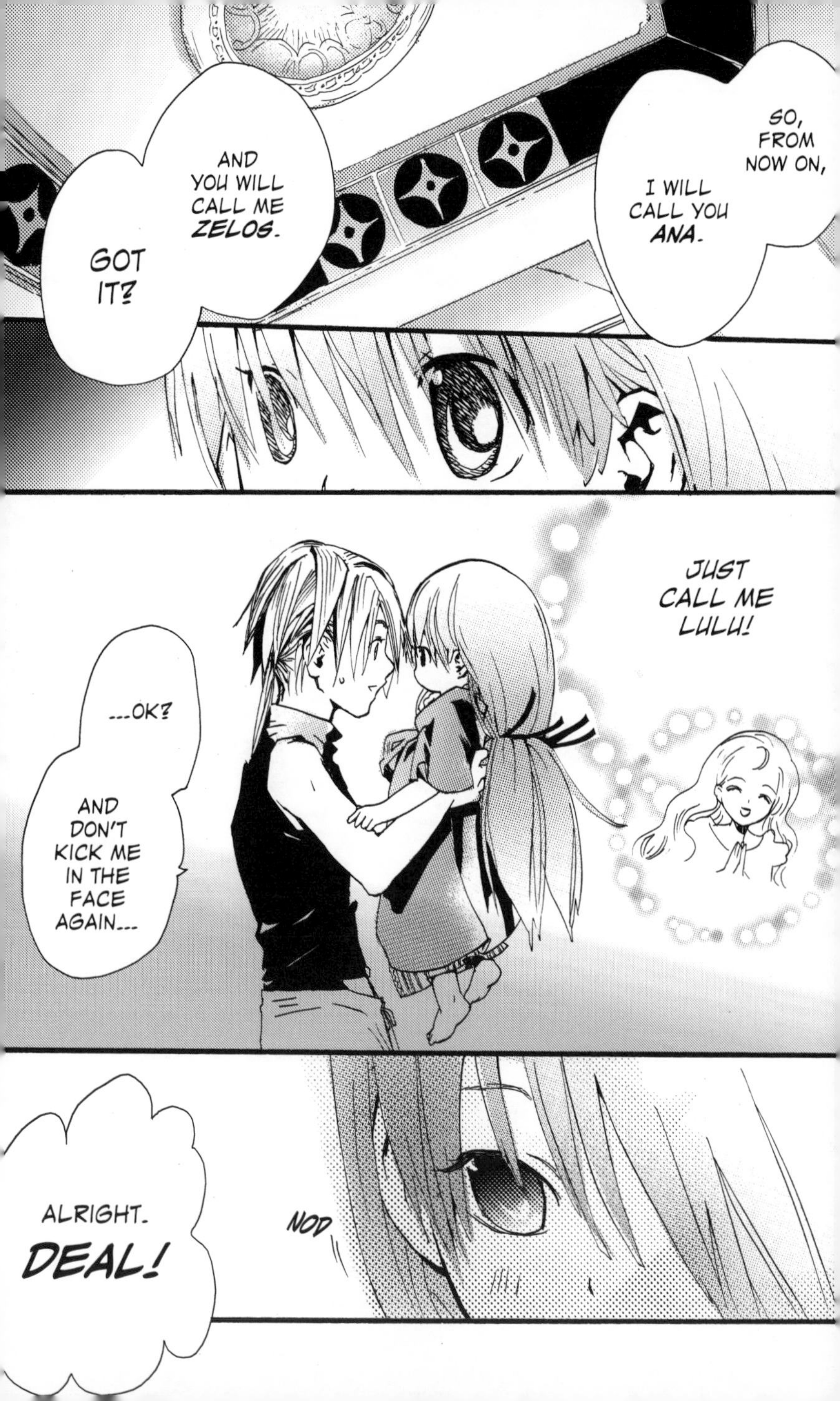

SO, FROM NOW ON, I WILL CALL YOU ANA.
AND YOU WILL CALL ME ZELOS.
GOT IT?
JUST CALL ME LULU!
...OK?
AND DON'T KICK ME IN THE FACE AGAIN...
NOD
ALRIGHT.
DEAL!

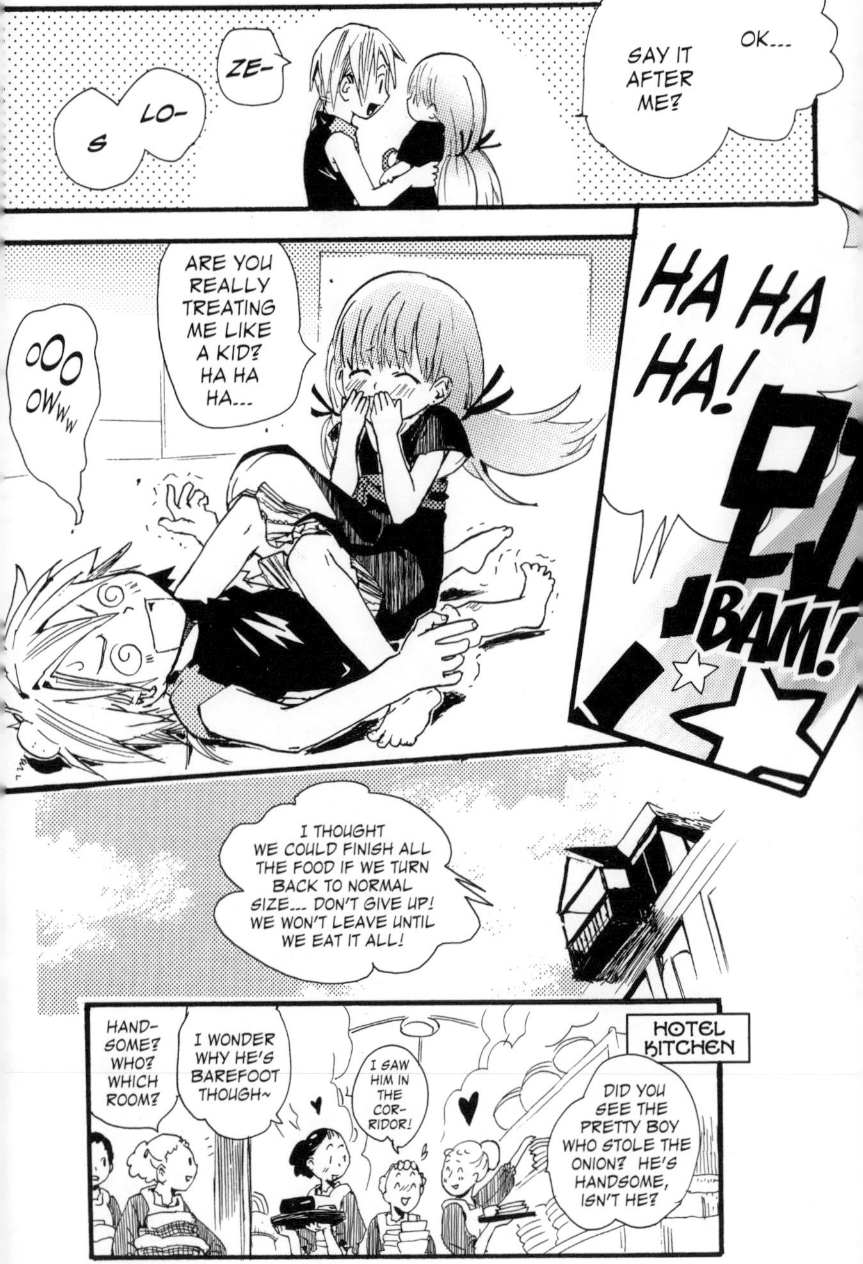
OK...
SAY IT AFTER ME?
ZE-
LO-
S
HA HA HA!
BAM!
ARE YOU REALLY TREATING ME LIKE A KID? HA HA HA...
OOO OWWW
I THOUGHT WE COULD FINISH ALL THE FOOD IF WE TURN BACK TO NORMAL SIZE... DON'T GIVE UP! WE WON'T LEAVE UNTIL WE EAT IT ALL!
HOTEL KITCHEN
DID YOU SEE THE PRETTY BOY WHO STOLE THE ONION? HE'S HANDSOME, ISN'T HE?
I SAW HIM IN THE COR-RIDOR!
I WONDER WHY HE'S BAREFOOT THOUGH~
HAND-SOME? WHO? WHICH ROOM?

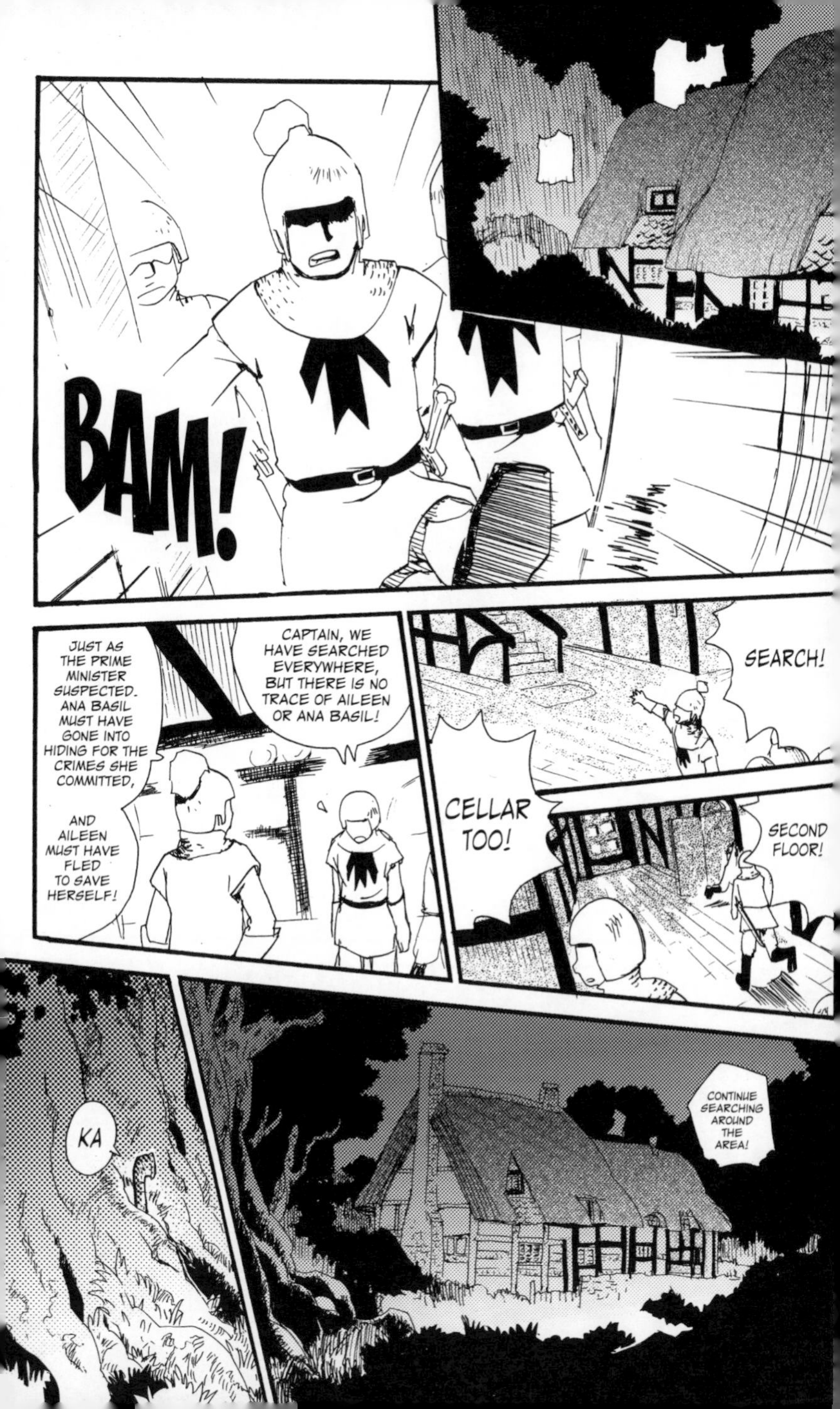
BAM!
SEARCH!
SECOND FLOOR!
CELLAR TOO!
CAPTAIN, WE HAVE SEARCHED EVERYWHERE, BUT THERE IS NO TRACE OF AILEEN OR ANA BASIL!
JUST AS THE PRIME MINISTER SUSPECTED. ANA BASIL MUST HAVE GONE INTO HIDING FOR THE CRIMES SHE COMMITTED,
AND AILEEN MUST HAVE FLED TO SAVE HERSELF!
CONTINUE SEARCHING AROUND THE AREA!
KA

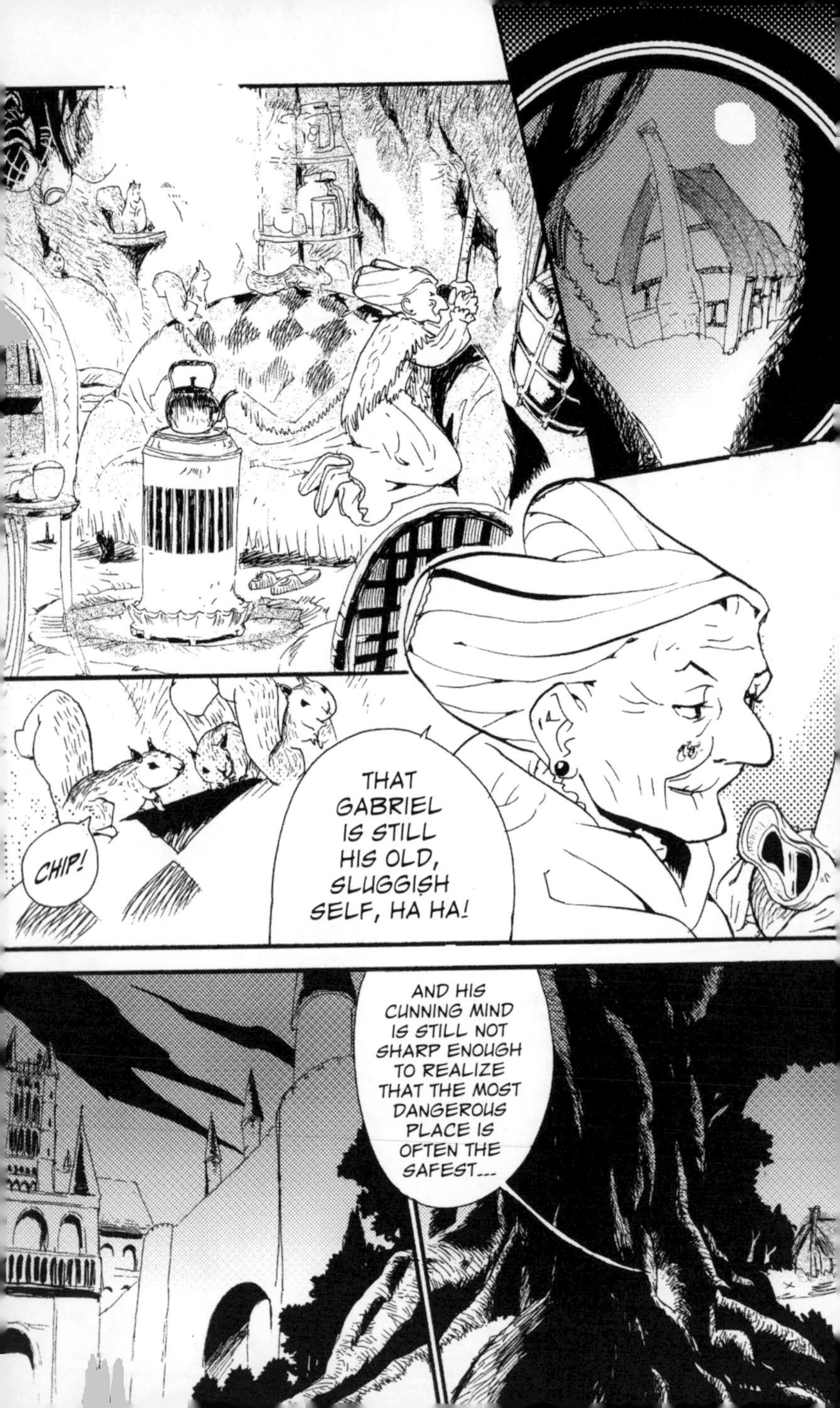
THAT GABRIEL IS STILL HIS OLD, SLUGGISH SELF, HA HA!
CHIP!
AND HIS CUNNING MIND IS STILL NOT SHARP ENOUGH TO REALIZE THAT THE MOST DANGEROUS PLACE IS OFTEN THE SAFEST...

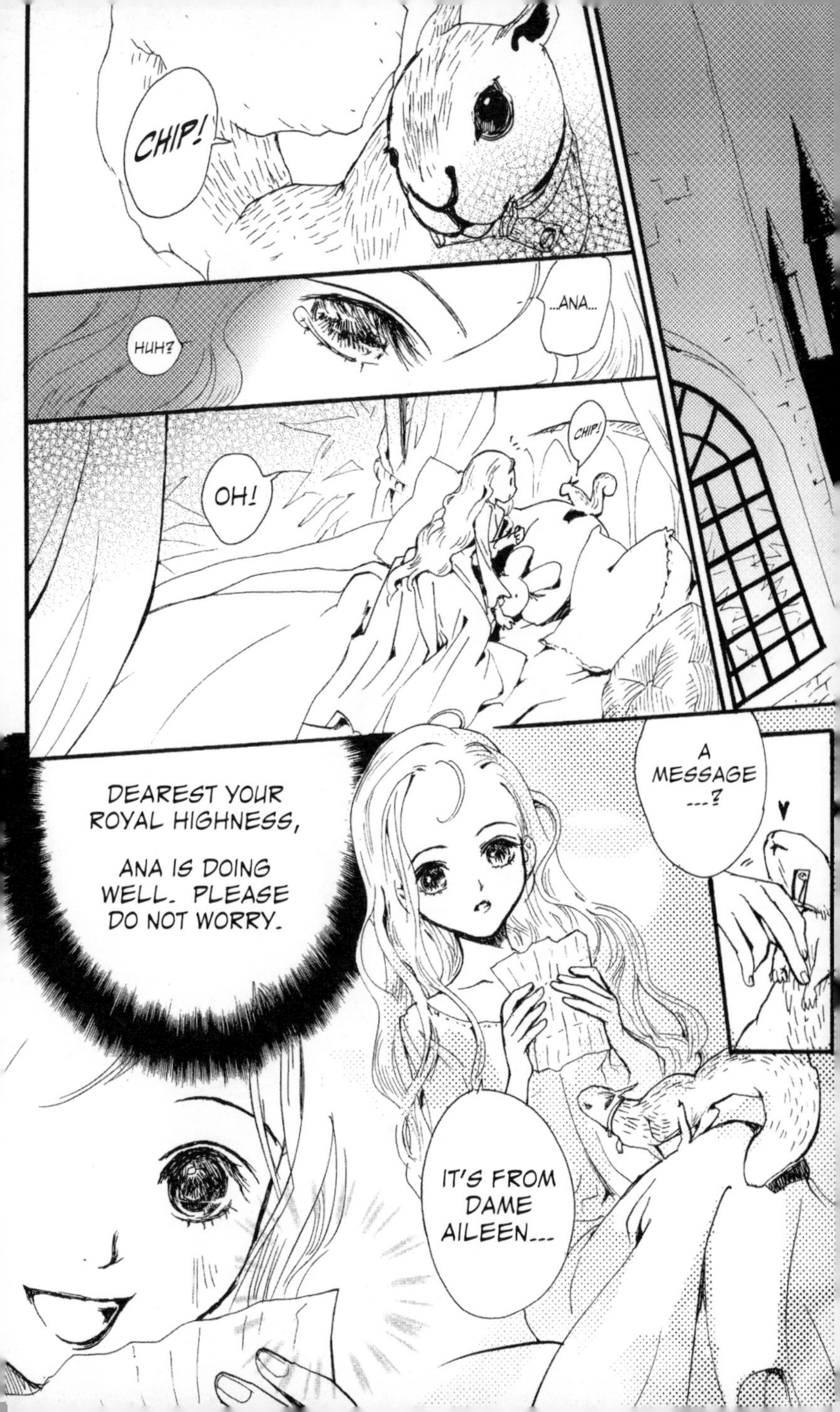
CHIP!
...ANA...
HUH?
CHIP!
OH!
A MESSAGE ---?
IT'S FROM DAME AILEEN---
DEAREST YOUR ROYAL HIGHNESS,
ANA IS DOING WELL. PLEASE DO NOT WORRY.

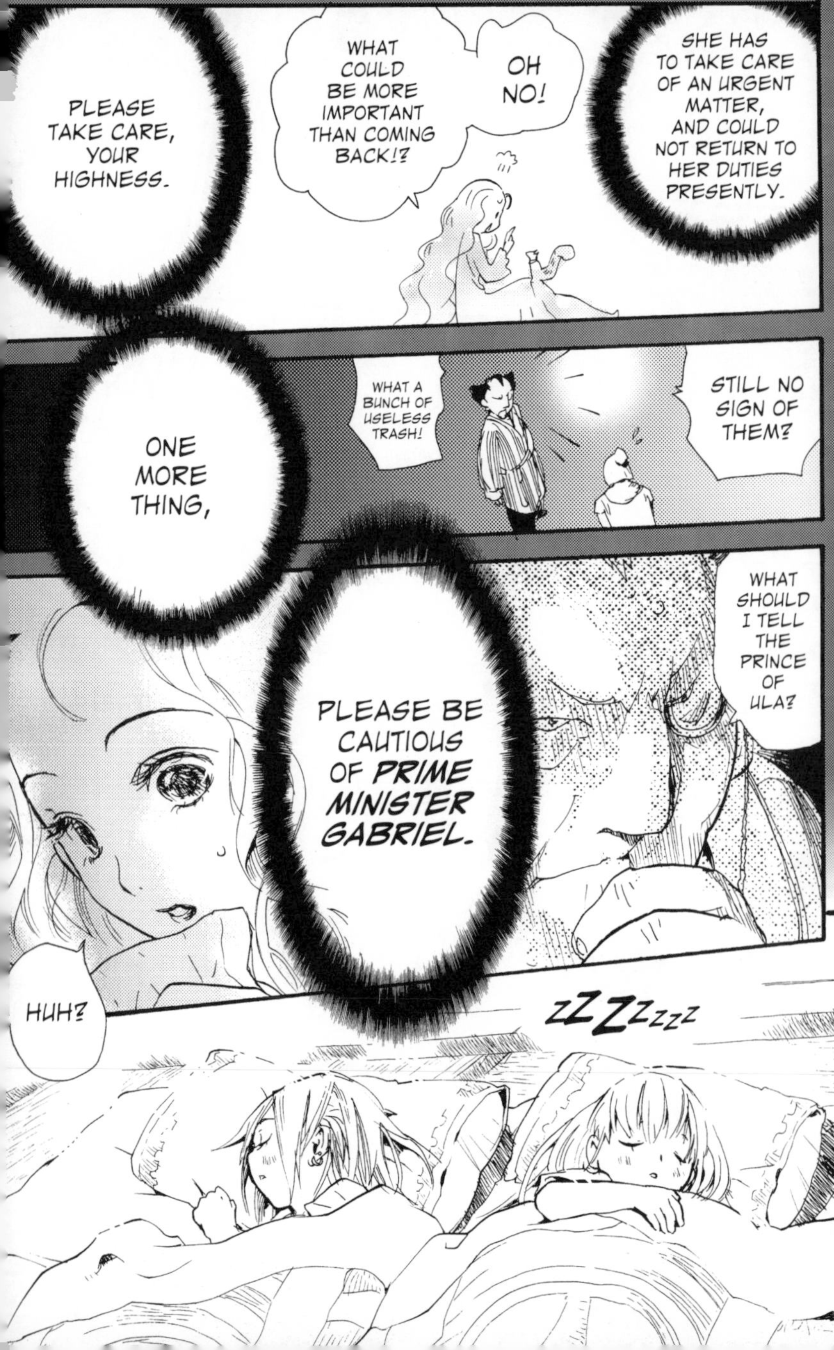
SHE HAS TO TAKE CARE OF AN URGENT MATTER, AND COULD NOT RETURN TO HER DUTIES PRESENTLY.
OH NO!
WHAT COULD BE MORE IMPORTANT THAN COMING BACK!?
PLEASE TAKE CARE, YOUR HIGHNESS.
STILL NO SIGN OF THEM?
WHAT A BUNCH OF USELESS TRASH!
ONE MORE THING,
WHAT SHOULD I TELL THE PRINCE OF ULA?
PLEASE BE CAUTIOUS OF *PRIME MINISTER GABRIEL*.
HUH?
zZZzzzz

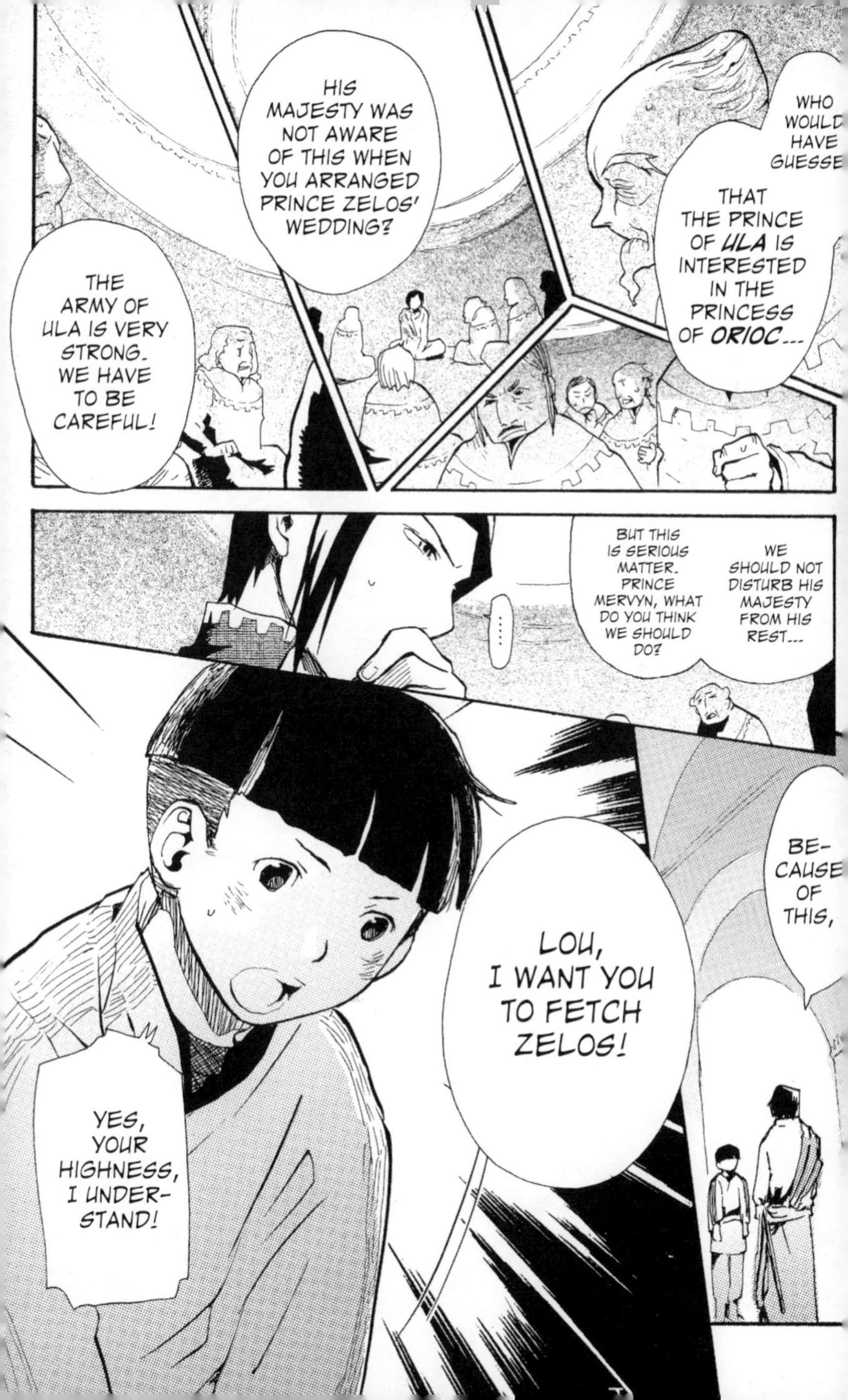

WHO WOULD HAVE GUESSE
THAT THE PRINCE OF ULA IS INTERESTED IN THE PRINCESS OF ORIOC...
HIS MAJESTY WAS NOT AWARE OF THIS WHEN YOU ARRANGED PRINCE ZELOS' WEDDING?
THE ARMY OF ULA IS VERY STRONG. WE HAVE TO BE CAREFUL!
WE SHOULD NOT DISTURB HIS MAJESTY FROM HIS REST...
BUT THIS IS SERIOUS MATTER. PRINCE MERVYN, WHAT DO YOU THINK WE SHOULD DO?
......
BE-CAUSE OF THIS,
LOU, I WANT YOU TO FETCH ZELOS!
YES, YOUR HIGHNESS, I UNDERSTAND!

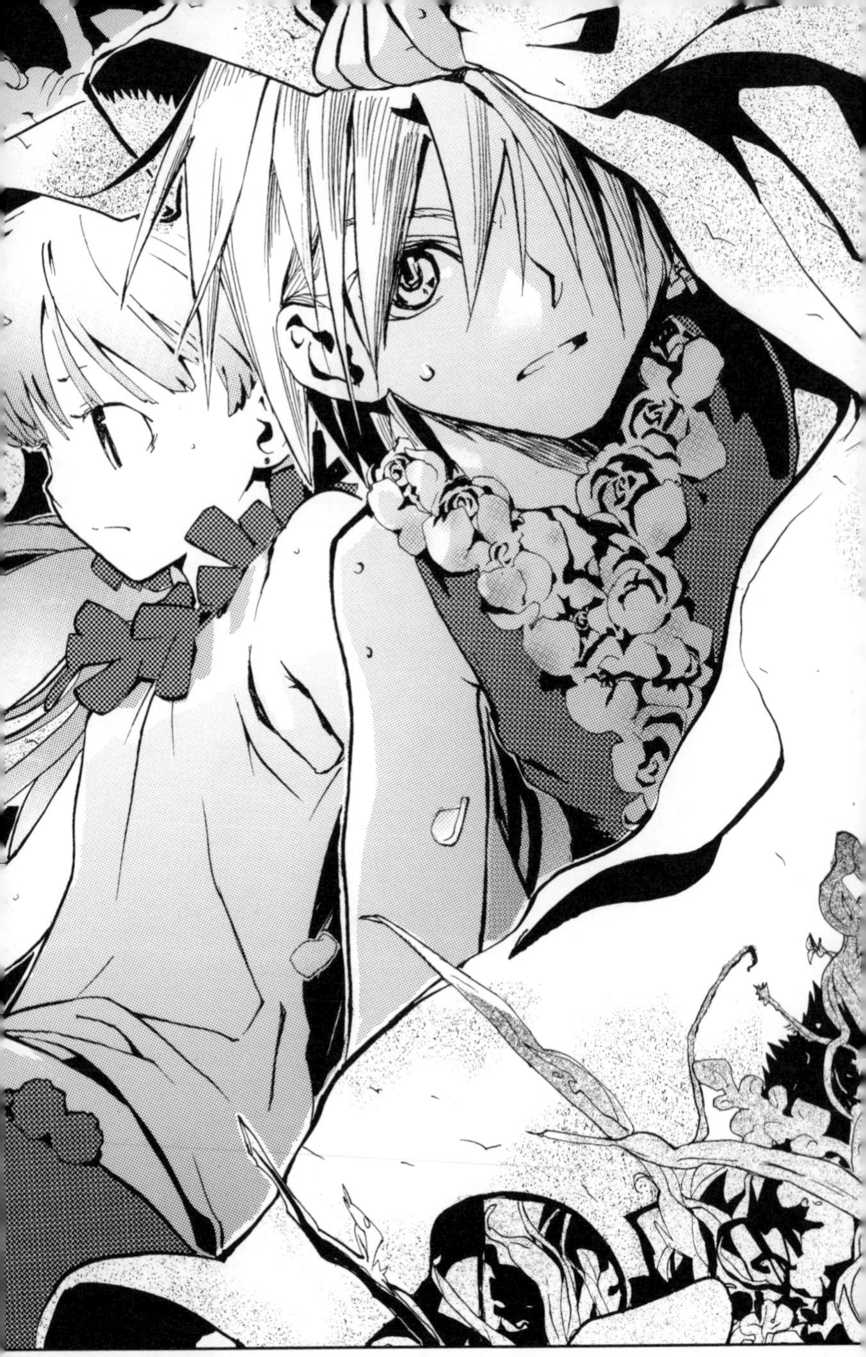

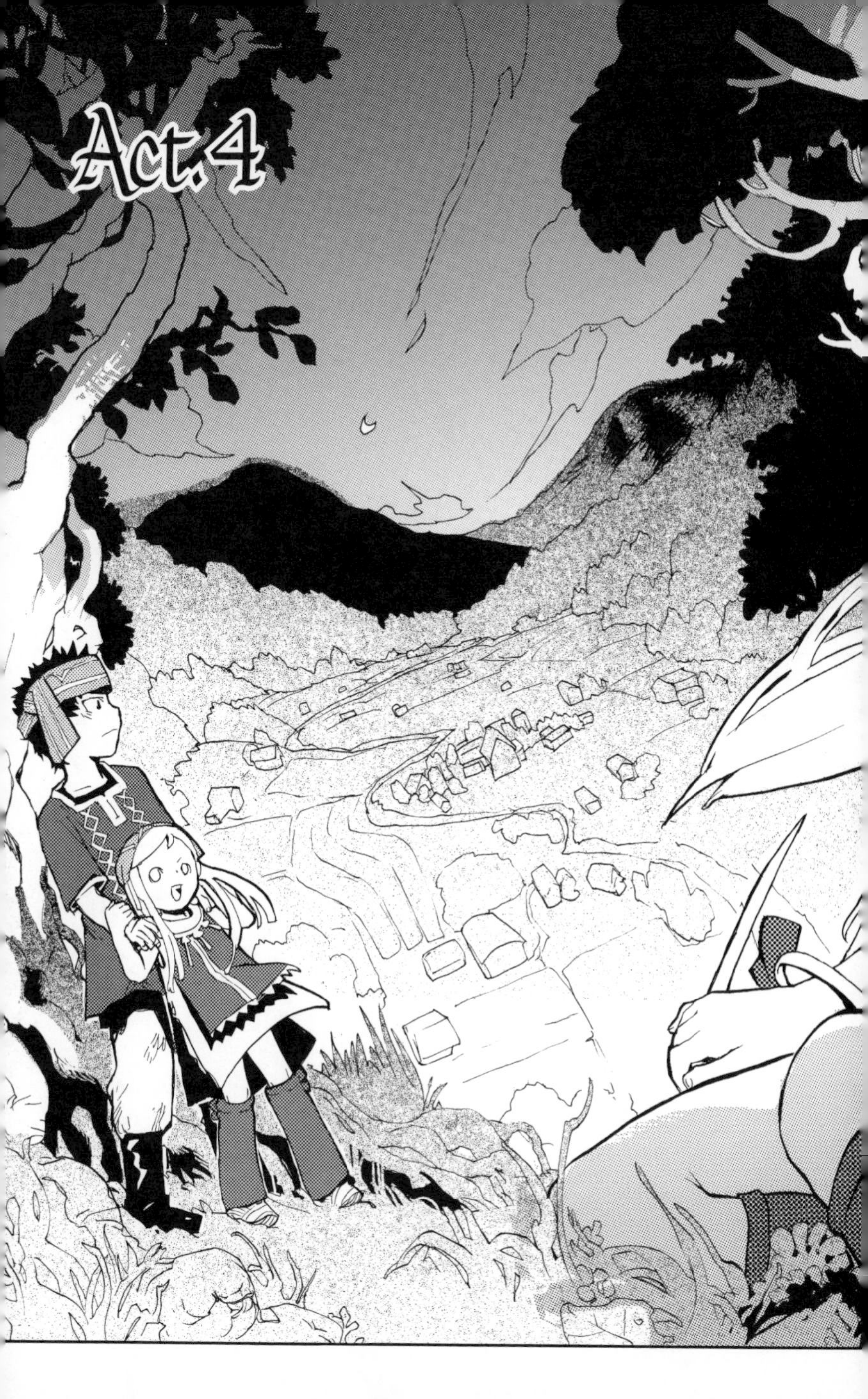
Act. 4

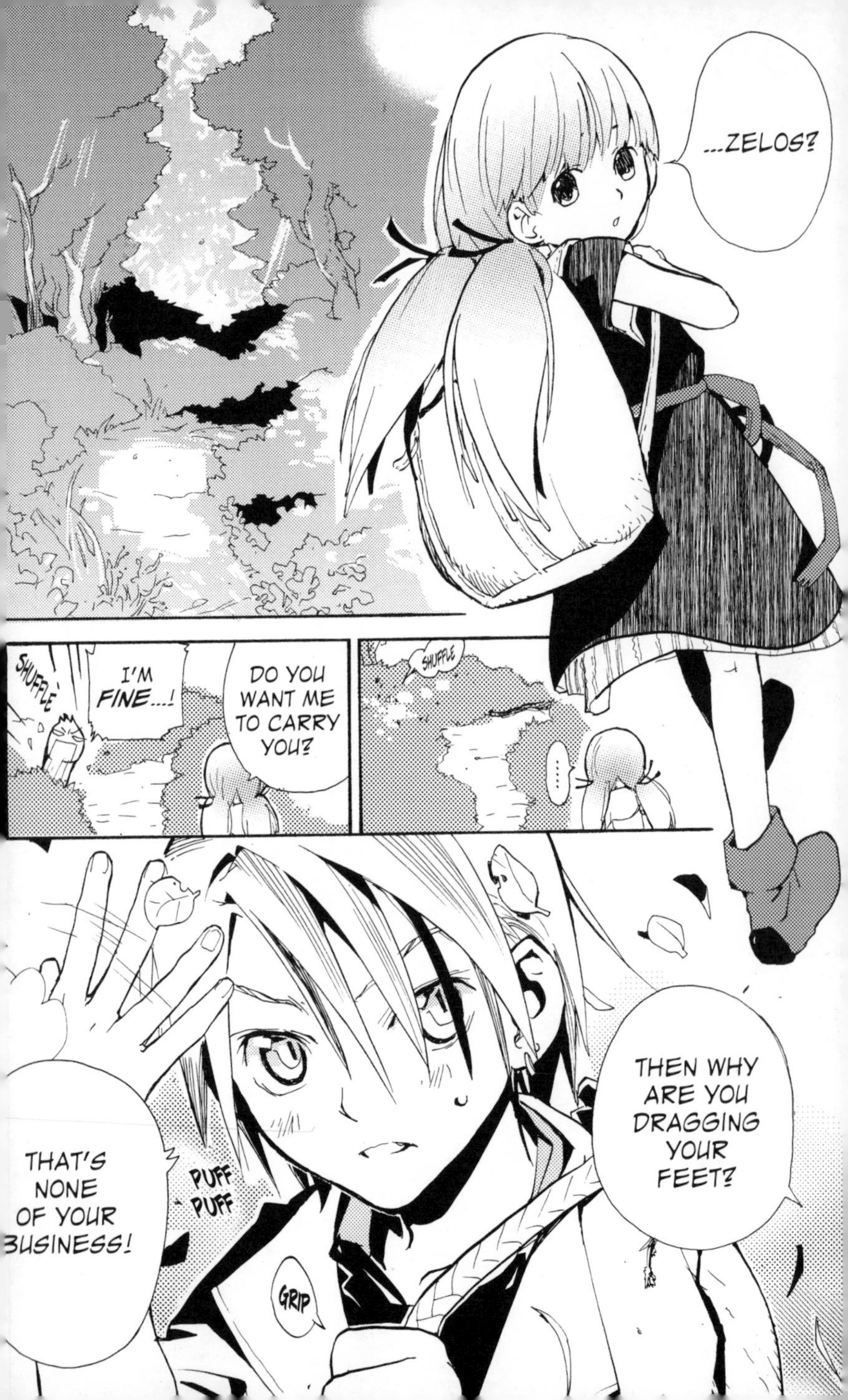
...ZELOS?
SHUFFLE
.....
DO YOU WANT ME TO CARRY YOU?
I'M *FINE*...!
SHUFFLE
THEN WHY ARE YOU DRAGGING YOUR FEET?
PUFF PUFF
GRIP
THAT'S NONE OF YOUR BUSINESS!

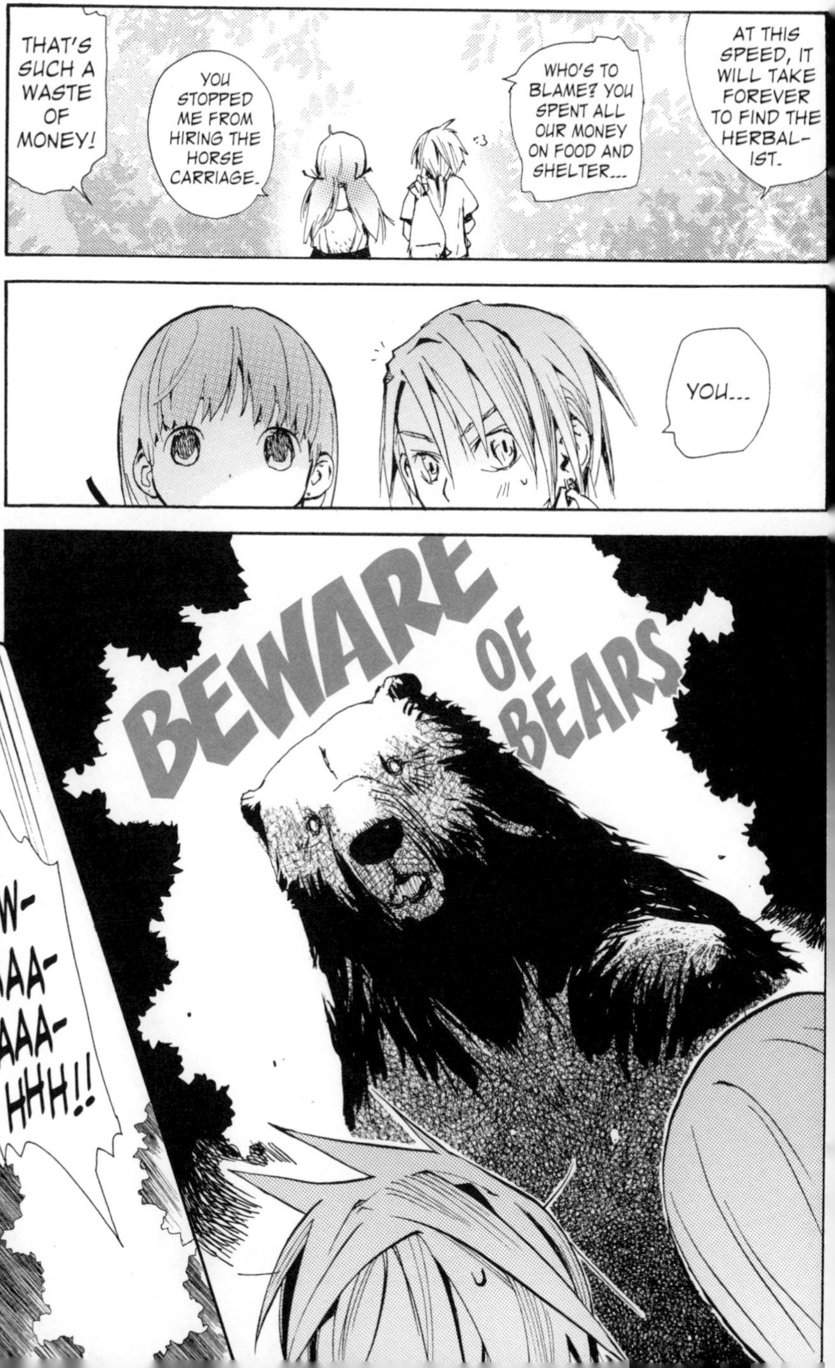
AT THIS SPEED, IT WILL TAKE FOREVER TO FIND THE HERBAL-IST.
WHO'S TO BLAME? YOU SPENT ALL OUR MONEY ON FOOD AND SHELTER...
YOU STOPPED ME FROM HIRING THE HORSE CARRIAGE.
THAT'S SUCH A WASTE OF MONEY!
YOU...
BEWARE OF BEARS
WW-AAA-AAA-HHH!!

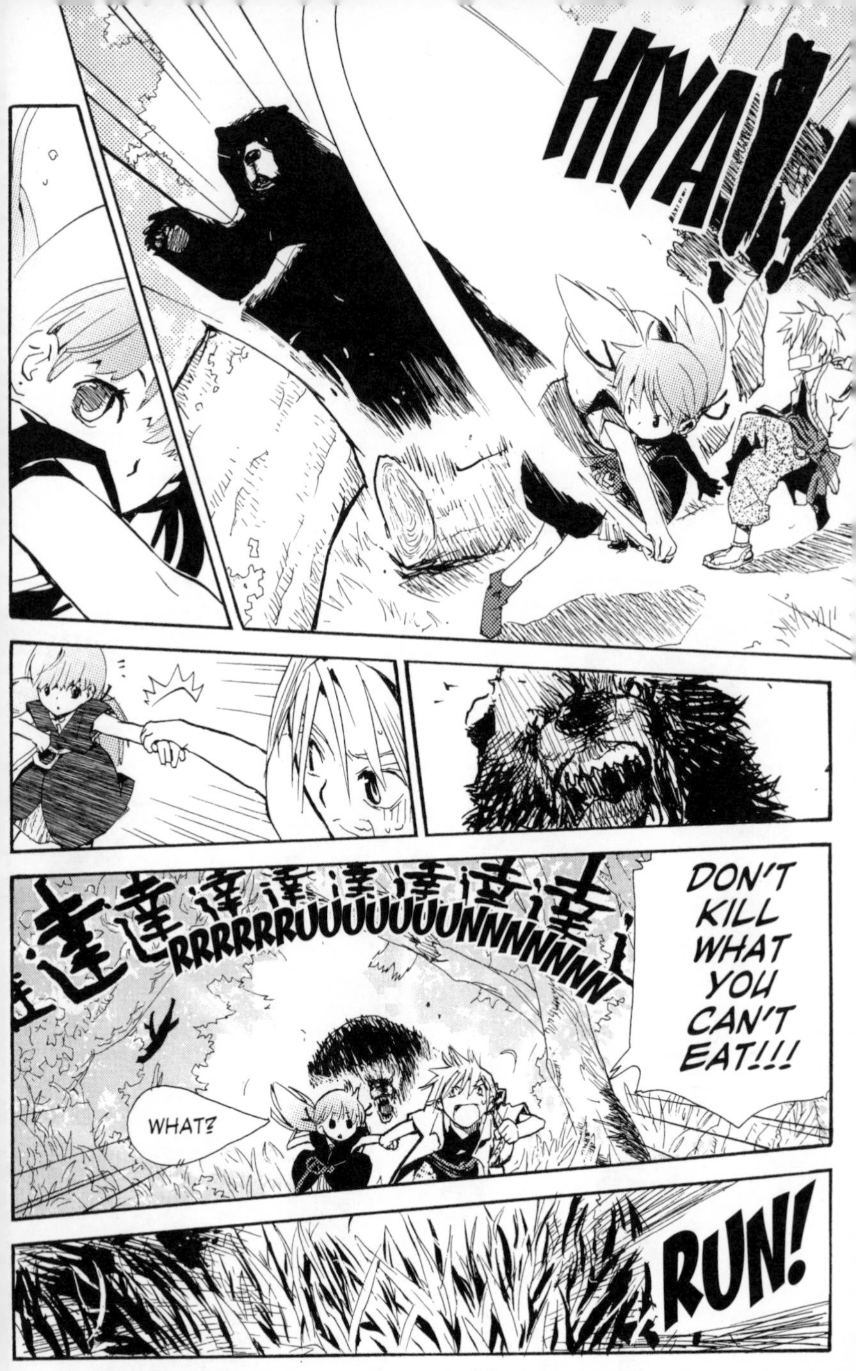
HIYA!!
DON'T KILL WHAT YOU CAN'T EAT!!!
RRRRRRUUUUUUUUNNNNNNNN
WHAT?
RUN!

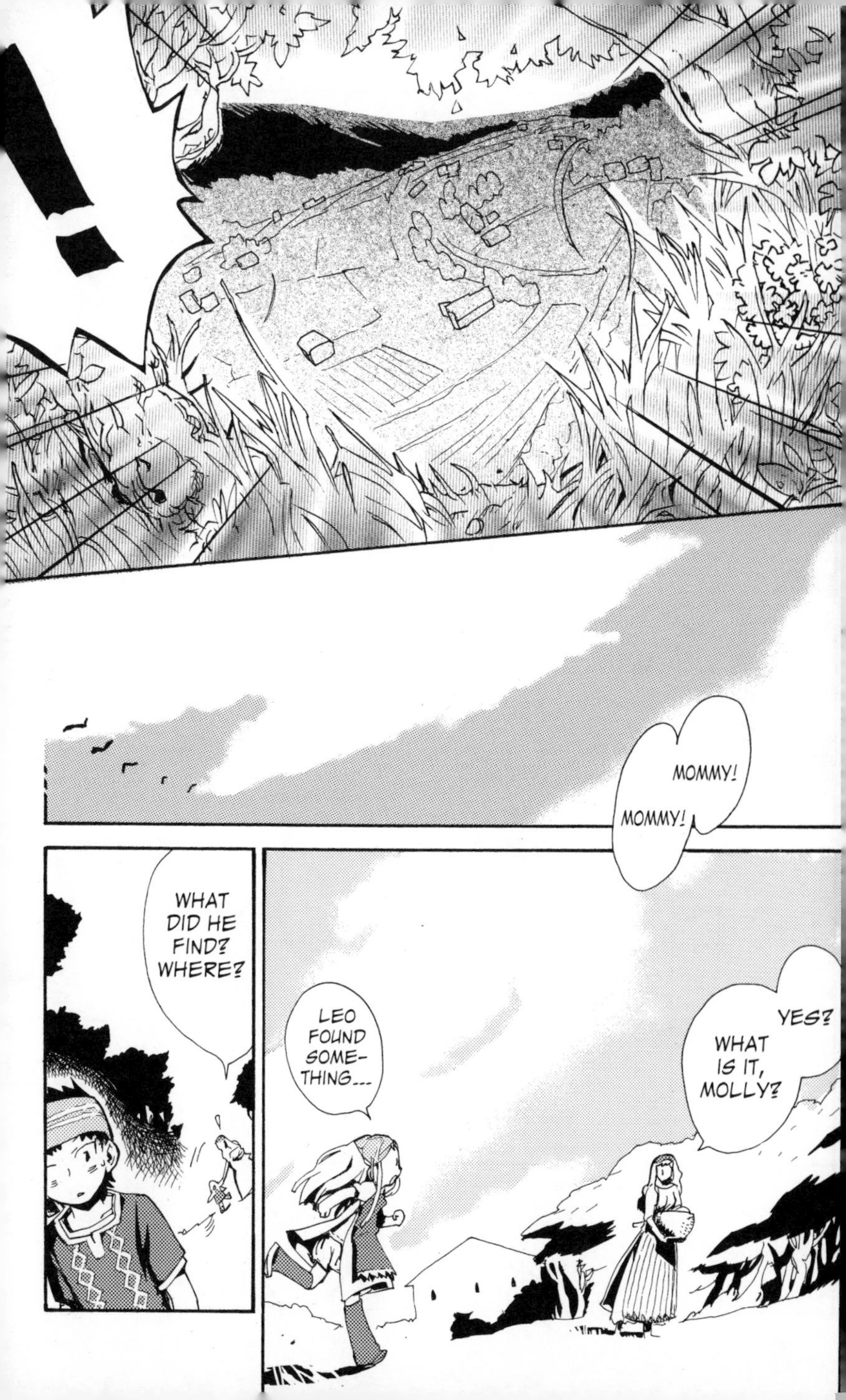
!
MOMMY! MOMMY!
YES? WHAT IS IT, MOLLY?
LEO FOUND SOMETHING...
WHAT DID HE FIND? WHERE?

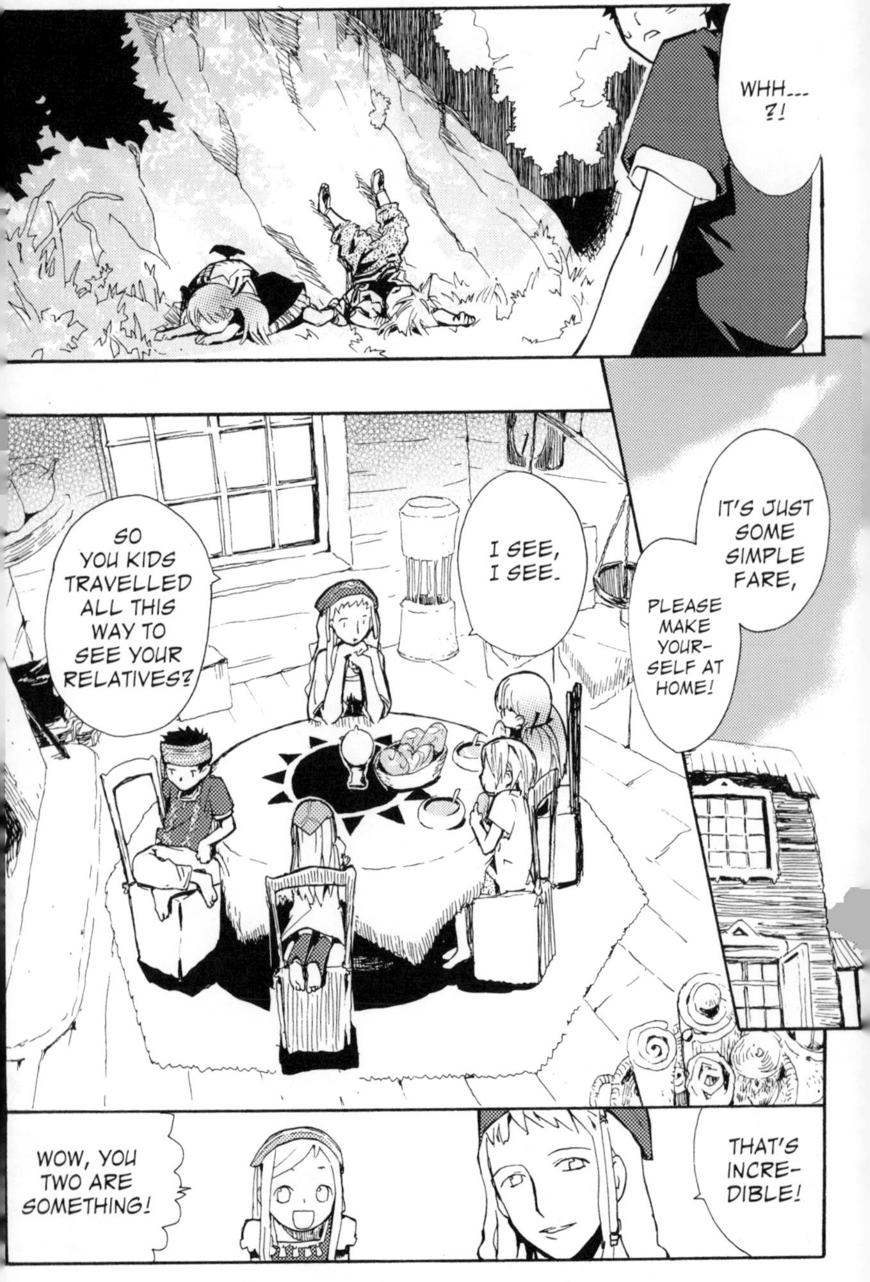
WHH...?!
IT'S JUST SOME SIMPLE FARE,
PLEASE MAKE YOURSELF AT HOME!
I SEE, I SEE.
SO YOU KIDS TRAVELLED ALL THIS WAY TO SEE YOUR RELATIVES?
THAT'S INCREDIBLE!
WOW, YOU TWO ARE SOMETHING!

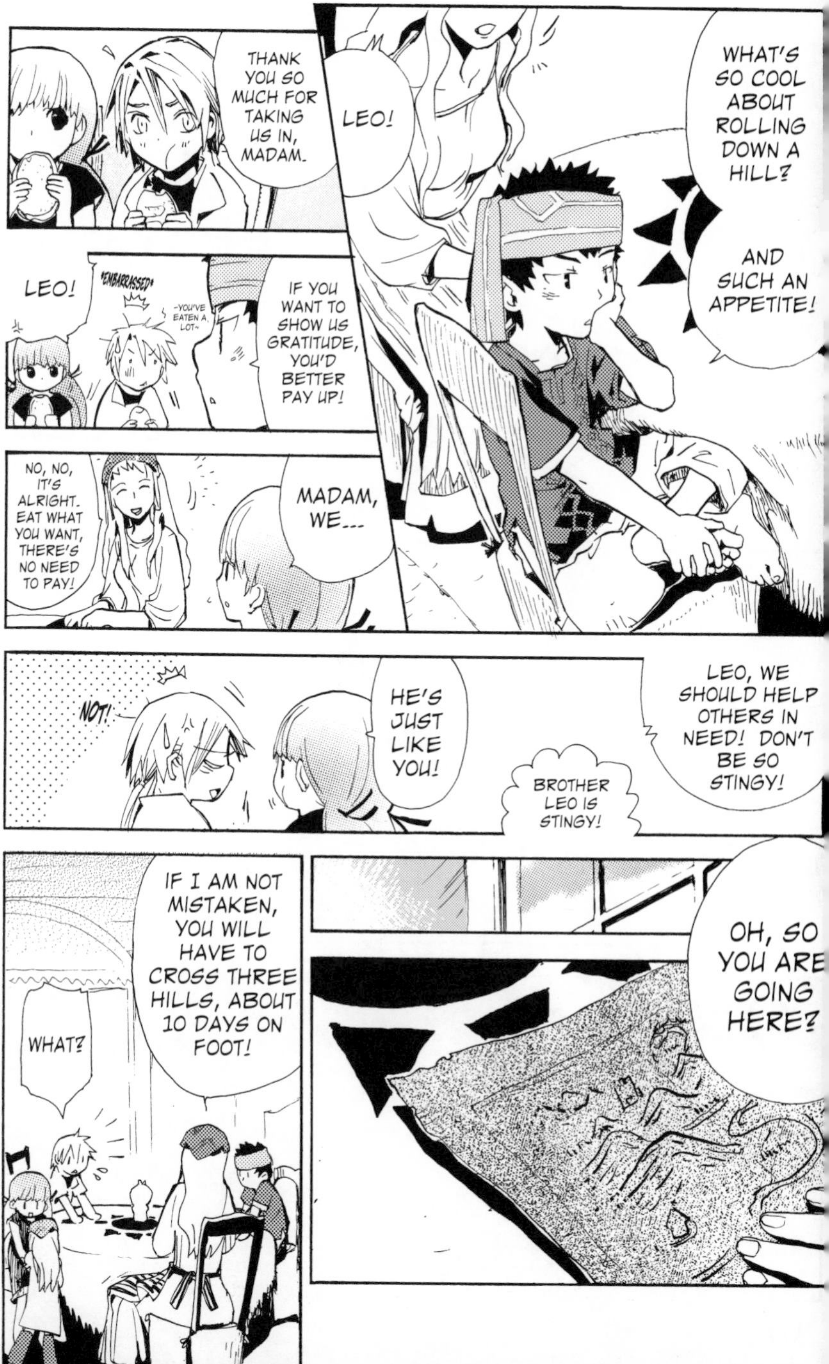
WHAT'S SO COOL ABOUT ROLLING DOWN A HILL?
AND SUCH AN APPETITE!
LEO!
THANK YOU SO MUCH FOR TAKING US IN, MADAM.
IF YOU WANT TO SHOW US GRATITUDE, YOU'D BETTER PAY UP!
-YOU'VE EATEN A LOT-
EMBARRASSED
LEO!
MADAM, WE...
NO, NO, IT'S ALRIGHT. EAT WHAT YOU WANT, THERE'S NO NEED TO PAY!
LEO, WE SHOULD HELP OTHERS IN NEED! DON'T BE SO STINGY!
BROTHER LEO IS STINGY!
HE'S JUST LIKE YOU!
NOT!
OH, SO YOU ARE GOING HERE?
IF I AM NOT MISTAKEN, YOU WILL HAVE TO CROSS THREE HILLS, ABOUT 10 DAYS ON FOOT!
WHAT?

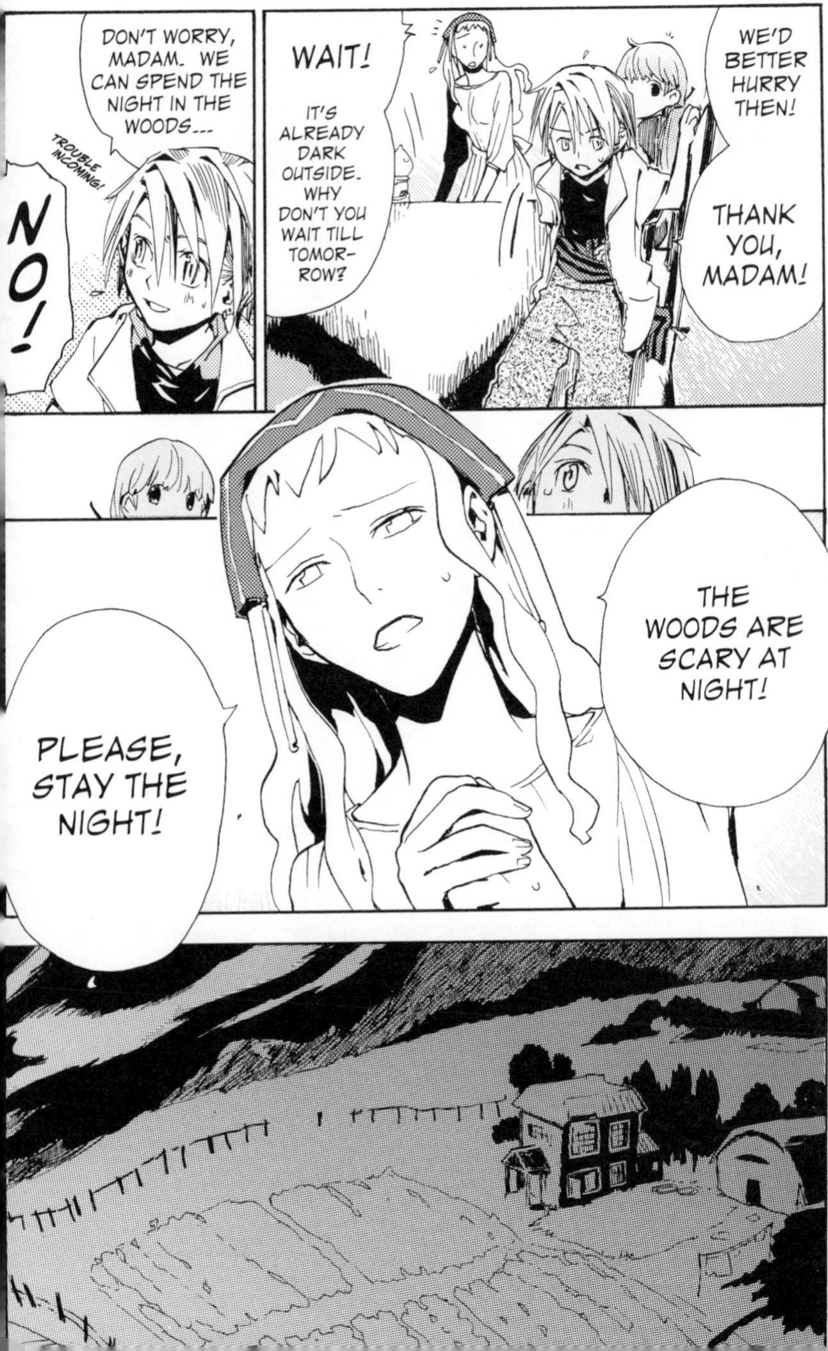
WE'D BETTER HURRY THEN!
THANK YOU, MADAM!
WAIT!
IT'S ALREADY DARK OUTSIDE. WHY DON'T YOU WAIT TILL TOMOR-ROW?
DON'T WORRY, MADAM. WE CAN SPEND THE NIGHT IN THE WOODS...
TROUBLE INCOMING!
NO!
THE WOODS ARE SCARY AT NIGHT!
PLEASE, STAY THE NIGHT!

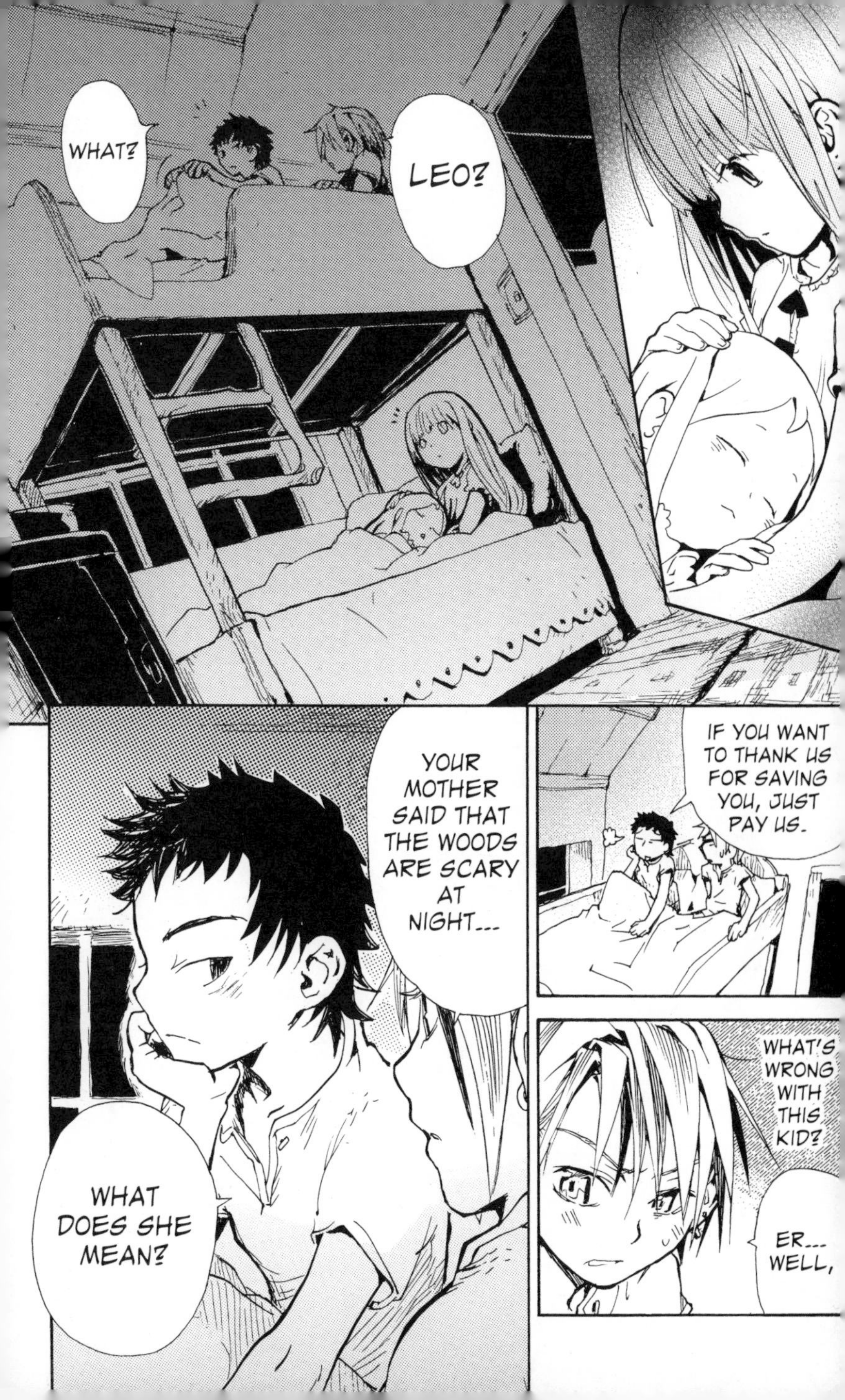
LEO?
WHAT?
IF YOU WANT TO THANK US FOR SAVING YOU, JUST PAY US.
WHAT'S WRONG WITH THIS KID?
ER... WELL,
YOUR MOTHER SAID THAT THE WOODS ARE SCARY AT NIGHT...
WHAT DOES SHE MEAN?

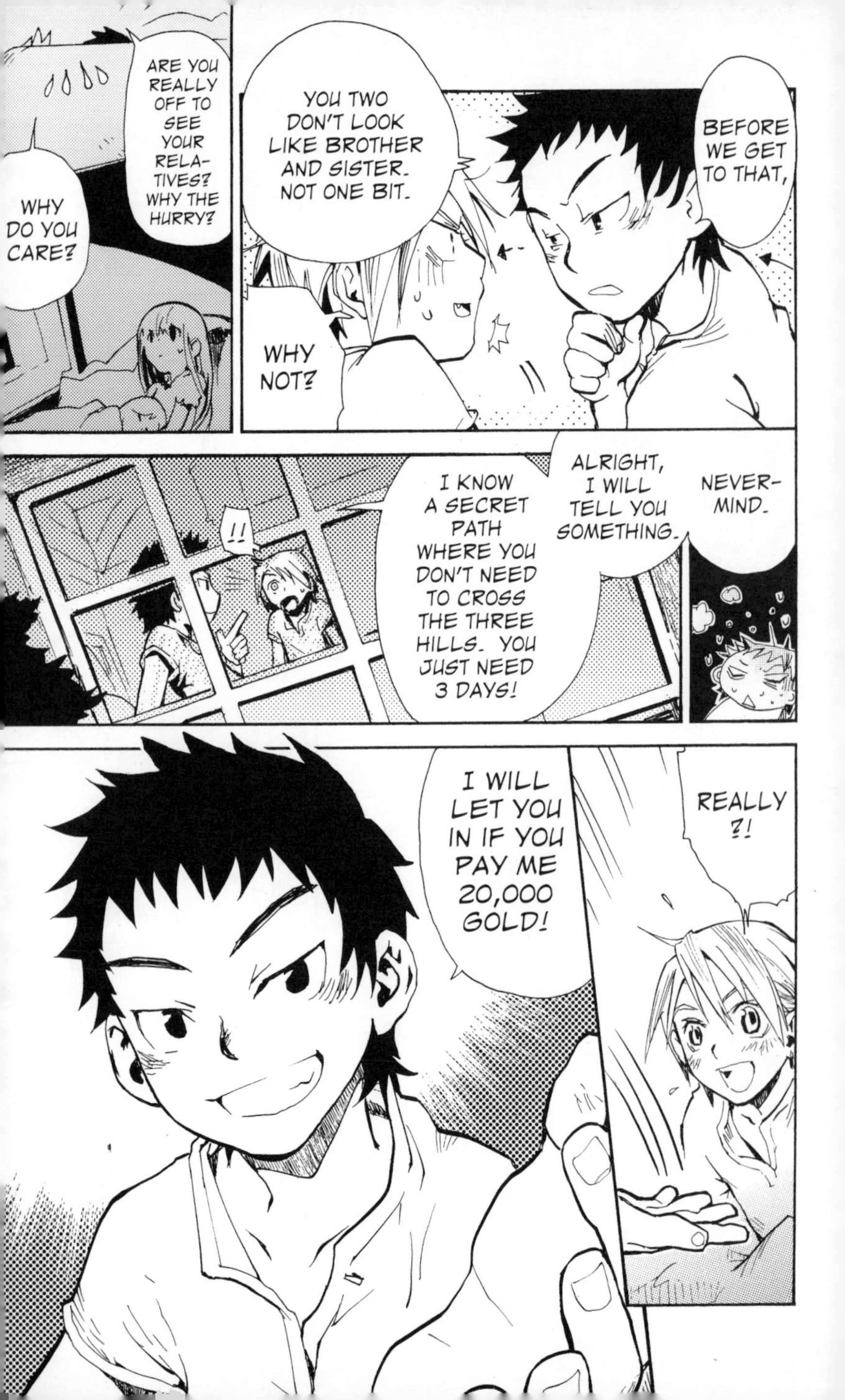
BEFORE WE GET TO THAT,
YOU TWO DON'T LOOK LIKE BROTHER AND SISTER. NOT ONE BIT.
WHY NOT?
ARE YOU REALLY OFF TO SEE YOUR RELA-TIVES? WHY THE HURRY?
WHY DO YOU CARE?
NEVER-MIND.
ALRIGHT, I WILL TELL YOU SOMETHING.
I KNOW A SECRET PATH WHERE YOU DON'T NEED TO CROSS THE THREE HILLS. YOU JUST NEED 3 DAYS!
!!
REALLY ?!
I WILL LET YOU IN IF YOU PAY ME 20,000 GOLD!

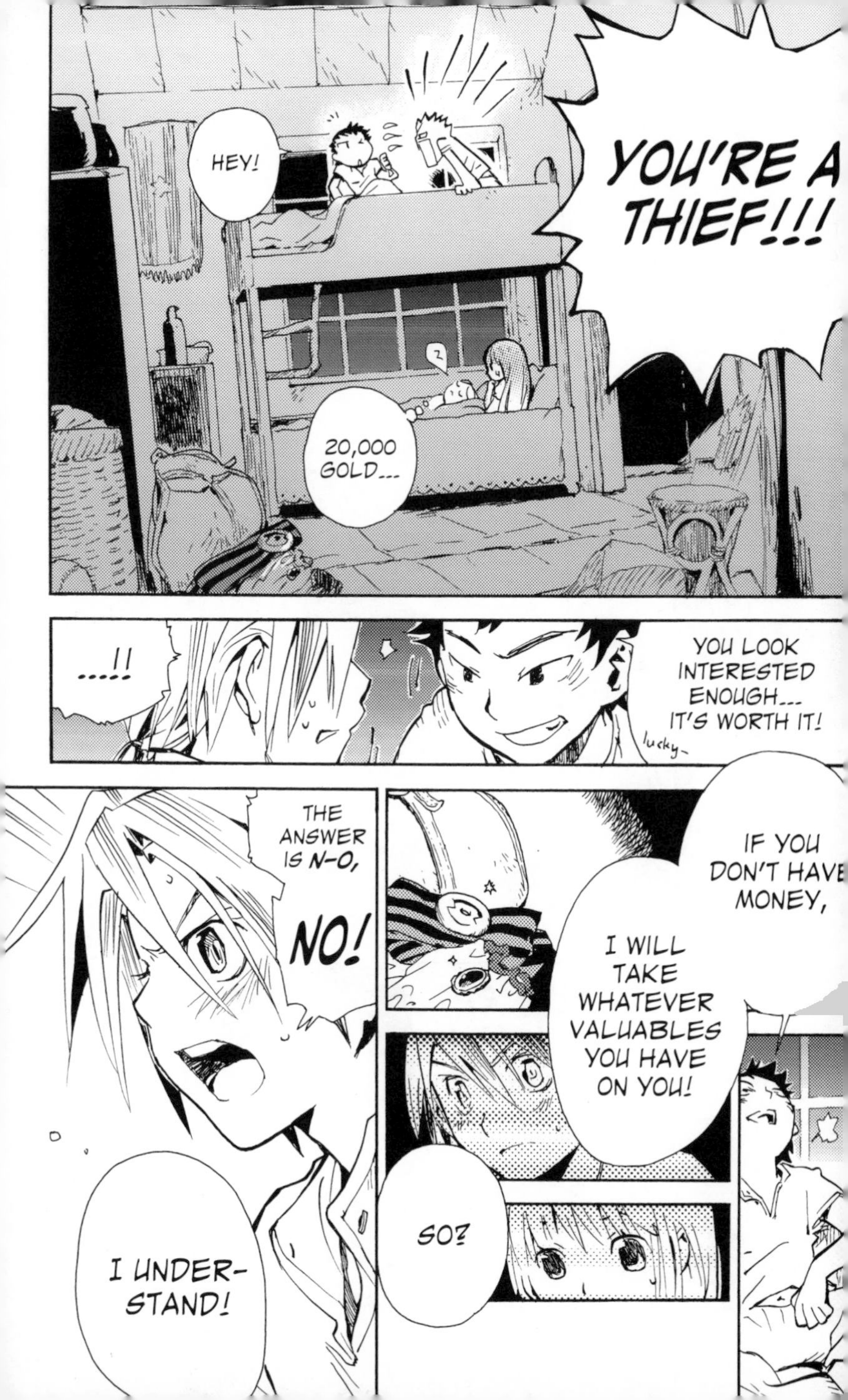
YOU'RE A THIEF!!!
HEY!
20,000 GOLD...
YOU LOOK INTERESTED ENOUGH... IT'S WORTH IT!
lucky~
...!!
IF YOU DON'T HAVE MONEY,
I WILL TAKE WHATEVER VALUABLES YOU HAVE ON YOU!
SO?
THE ANSWER IS N-O,
NO!
I UNDER-STAND!

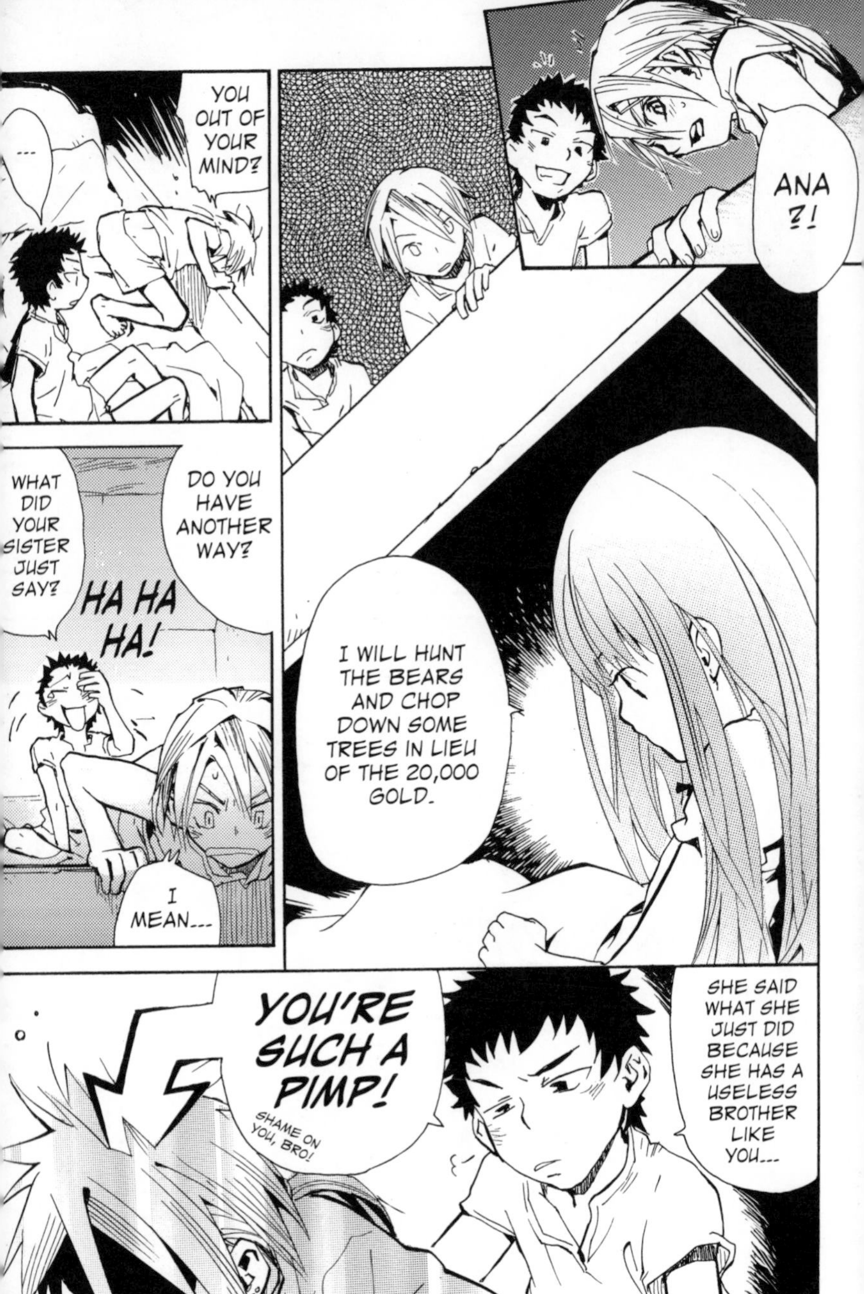
ANA ?!
I WILL HUNT THE BEARS AND CHOP DOWN SOME TREES IN LIEU OF THE 20,000 GOLD.
YOU OUT OF YOUR MIND?
...
DO YOU HAVE ANOTHER WAY?
WHAT DID YOUR SISTER JUST SAY?
HA HA HA!
I MEAN...
SHE SAID WHAT SHE JUST DID BECAUSE SHE HAS A USELESS BROTHER LIKE YOU...
YOU'RE SUCH A PIMP!
SHAME ON YOU, BRO!

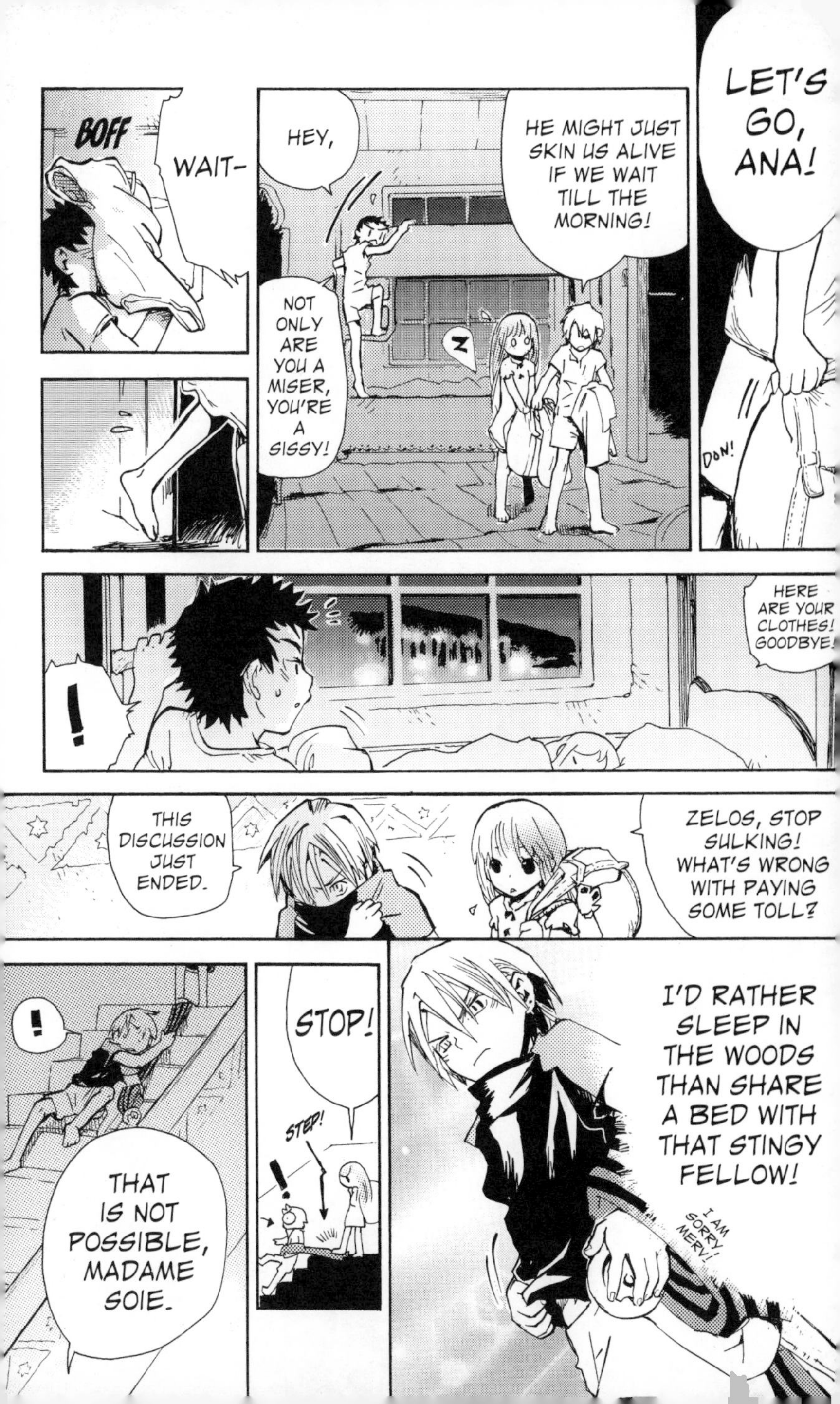
LET'S GO, ANA!
DON!
HE MIGHT JUST SKIN US ALIVE IF WE WAIT TILL THE MORNING!
HEY,
NOT ONLY ARE YOU A MISER, YOU'RE A SISSY!
BOFF
WAIT-
HERE ARE YOUR CLOTHES! GOODBYE!
!
ZELOS, STOP SULKING! WHAT'S WRONG WITH PAYING SOME TOLL?
THIS DISCUSSION JUST ENDED.
I'D RATHER SLEEP IN THE WOODS THAN SHARE A BED WITH THAT STINGY FELLOW!
I AM SORRY MERV!
STOP!
STEP!
!
!
THAT IS NOT POSSIBLE, MADAME SOIE.

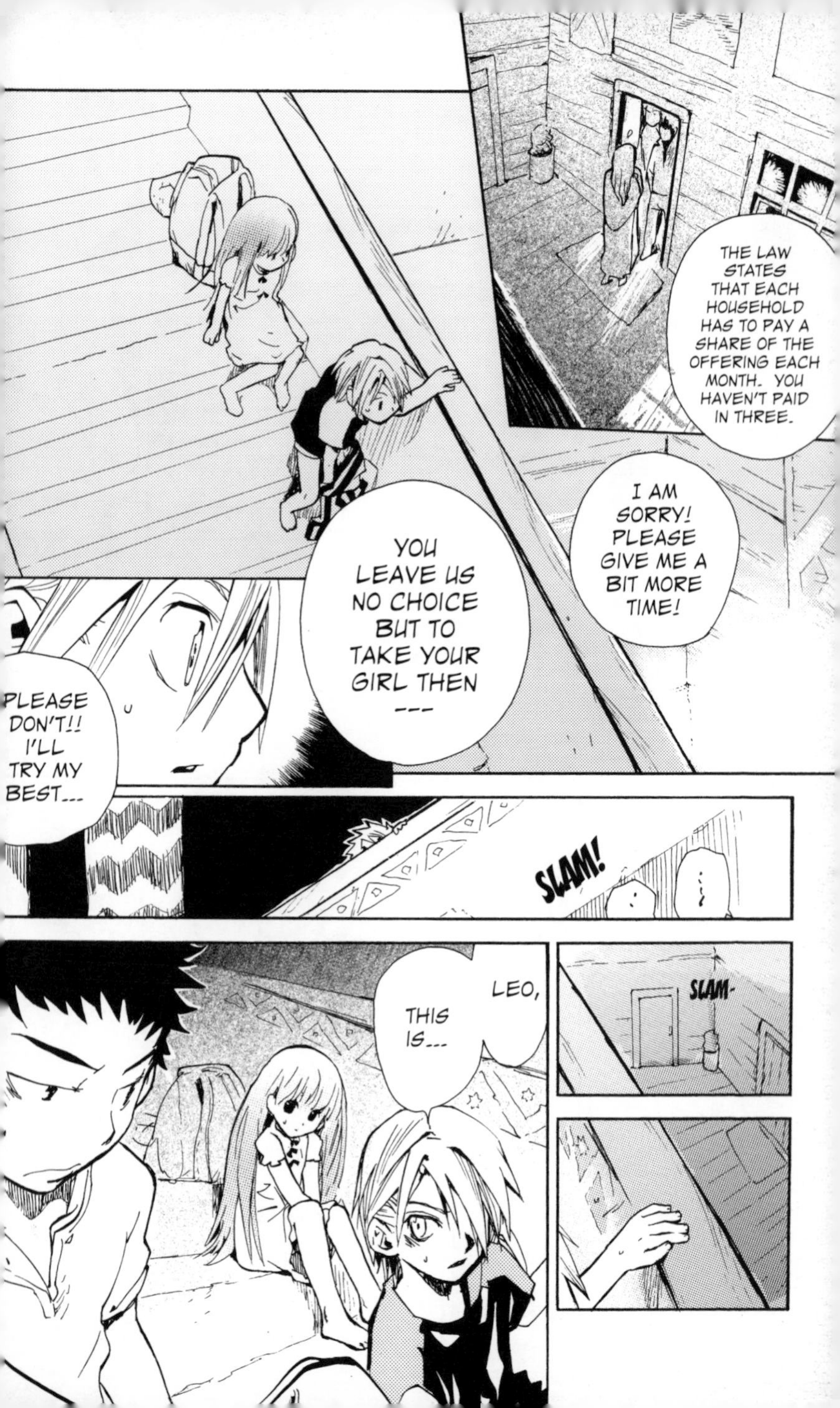
THE LAW STATES THAT EACH HOUSEHOLD HAS TO PAY A SHARE OF THE OFFERING EACH MONTH. YOU HAVEN'T PAID IN THREE.
I AM SORRY! PLEASE GIVE ME A BIT MORE TIME!
YOU LEAVE US NO CHOICE BUT TO TAKE YOUR GIRL THEN ---
PLEASE DON'T!! I'LL TRY MY BEST...
SLAM!
...
SLAM-
LEO, THIS IS...

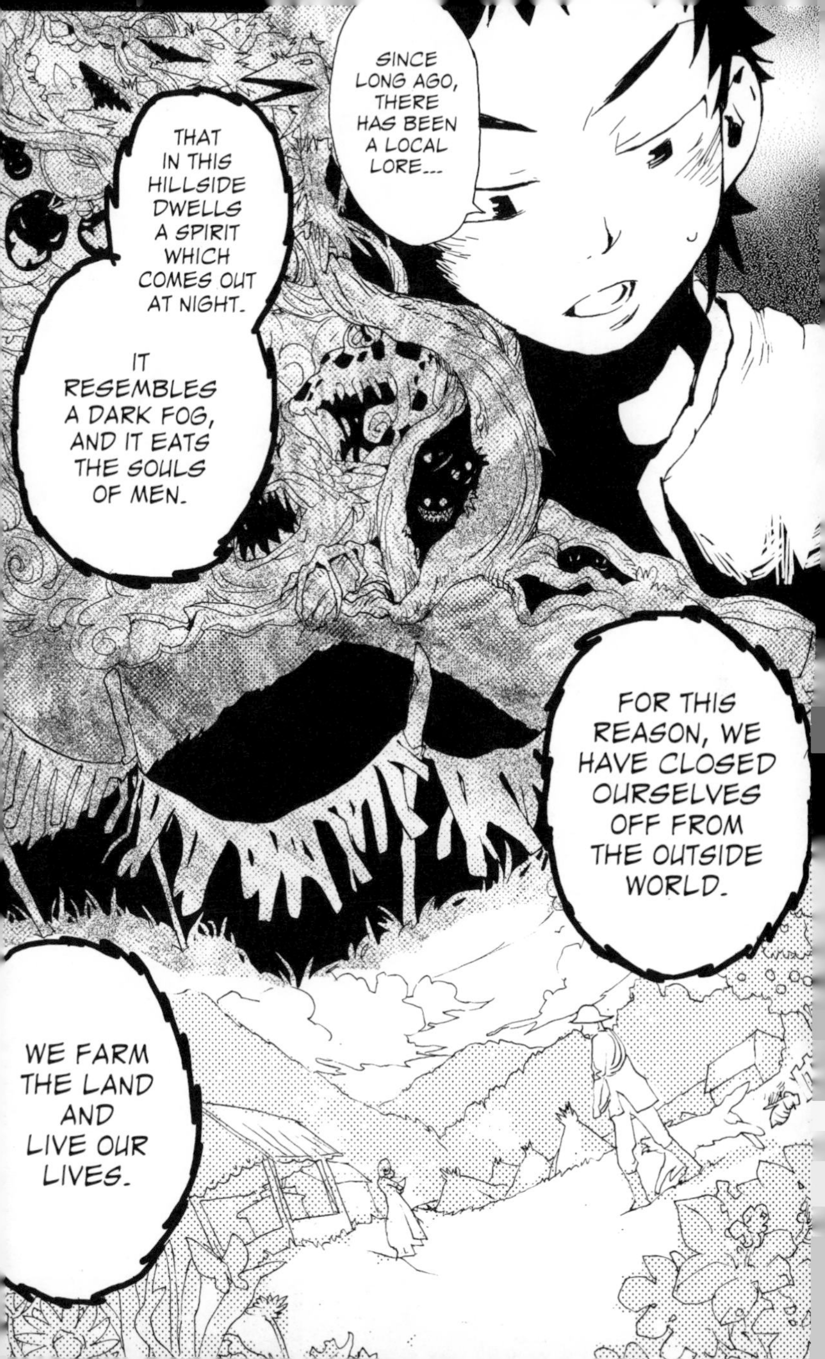
SINCE LONG AGO, THERE HAS BEEN A LOCAL LORE...
THAT IN THIS HILLSIDE DWELLS A SPIRIT WHICH COMES OUT AT NIGHT.
IT RESEMBLES A DARK FOG, AND IT EATS THE SOULS OF MEN.
FOR THIS REASON, WE HAVE CLOSED OURSELVES OFF FROM THE OUTSIDE WORLD.
WE FARM THE LAND AND LIVE OUR LIVES.

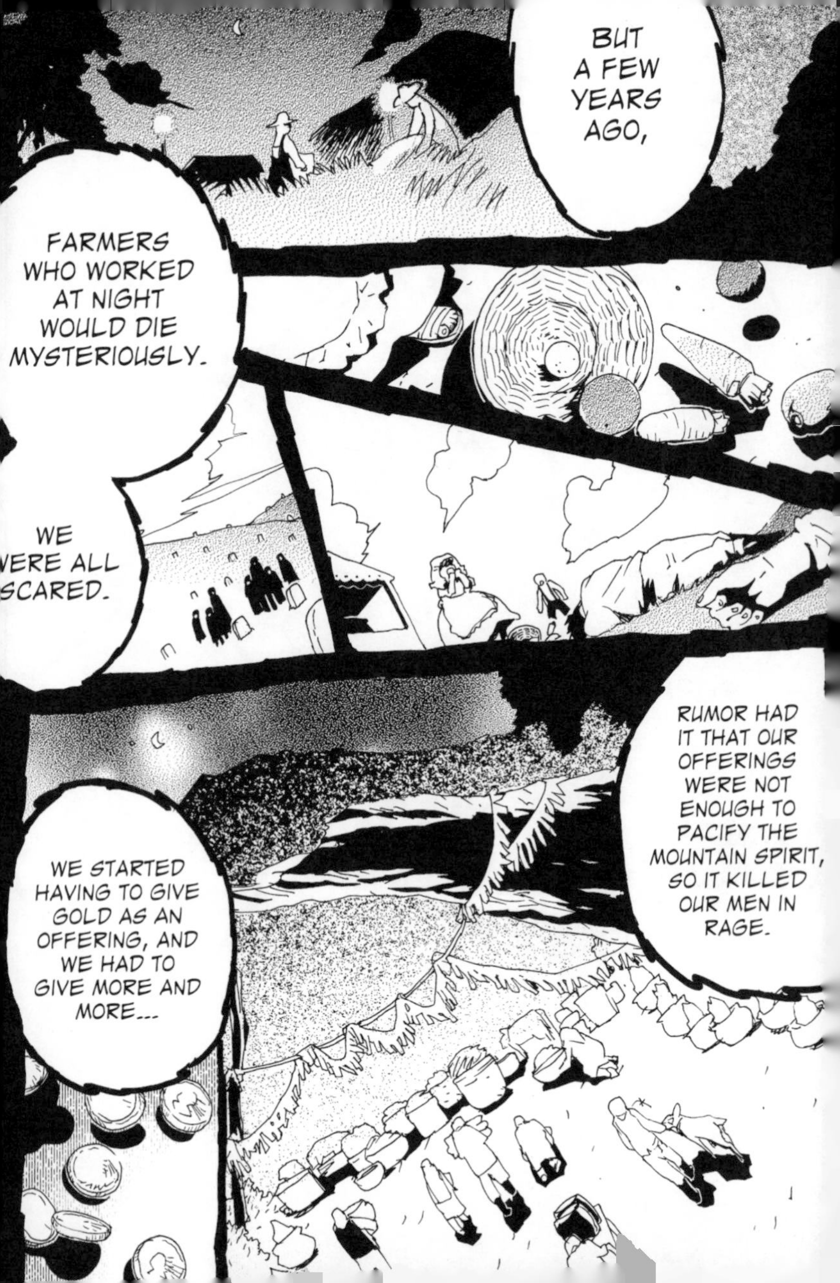
BUT A FEW YEARS AGO,
FARMERS WHO WORKED AT NIGHT WOULD DIE MYSTERIOUSLY.
WE WERE ALL SCARED.
RUMOR HAD IT THAT OUR OFFERINGS WERE NOT ENOUGH TO PACIFY THE MOUNTAIN SPIRIT, SO IT KILLED OUR MEN IN RAGE.
WE STARTED HAVING TO GIVE GOLD AS AN OFFERING, AND WE HAD TO GIVE MORE AND MORE...

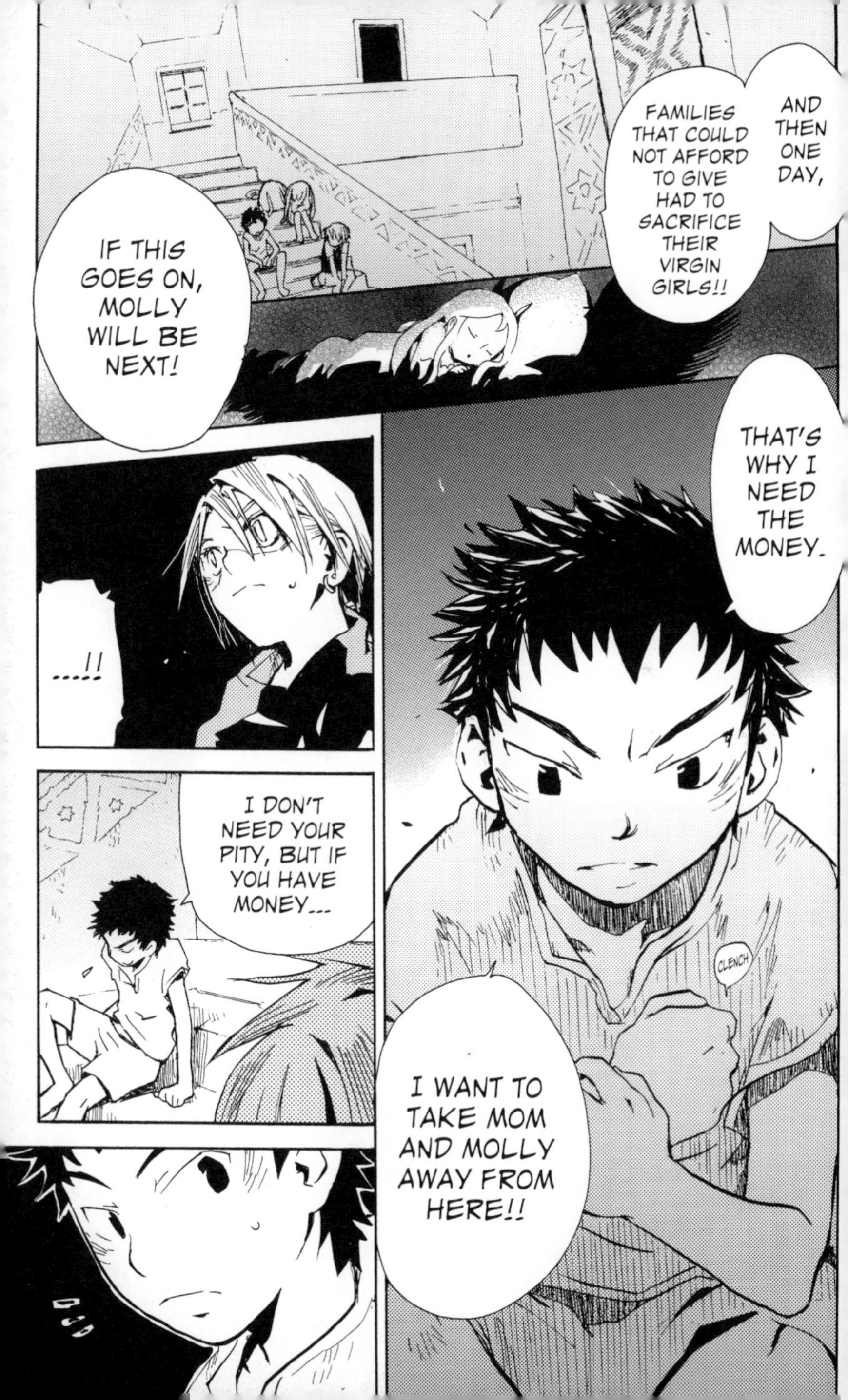
AND THEN ONE DAY,
FAMILIES THAT COULD NOT AFFORD TO GIVE HAD TO SACRIFICE THEIR VIRGIN GIRLS!!
IF THIS GOES ON, MOLLY WILL BE NEXT!
THAT'S WHY I NEED THE MONEY.
CLENCH
I WANT TO TAKE MOM AND MOLLY AWAY FROM HERE!!
...!!
I DON'T NEED YOUR PITY, BUT IF YOU HAVE MONEY...

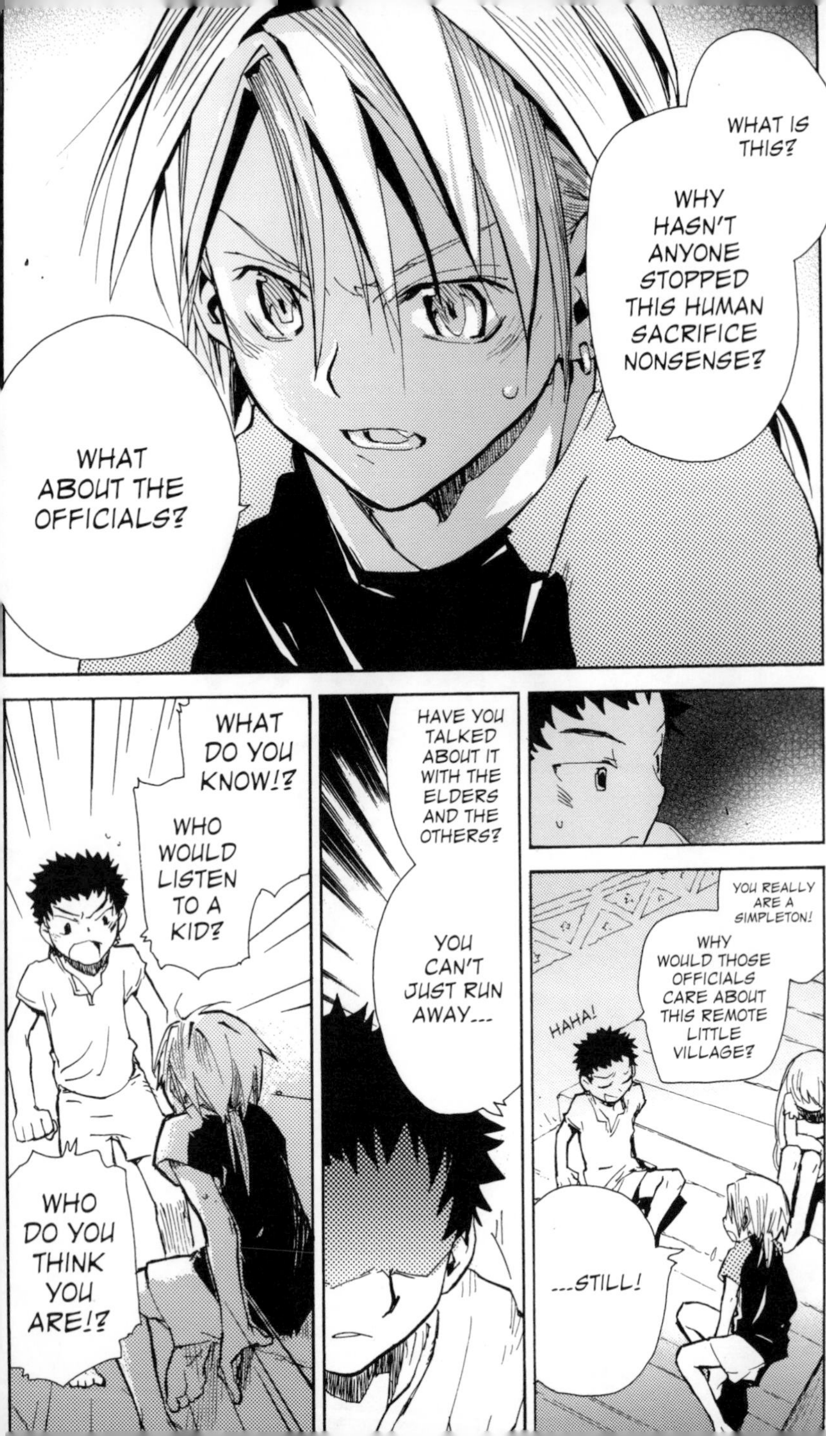
WHAT IS THIS?
WHY HASN'T ANYONE STOPPED THIS HUMAN SACRIFICE NONSENSE?
WHAT ABOUT THE OFFICIALS?
YOU REALLY ARE A SIMPLETON!
HAHA!
WHY WOULD THOSE OFFICIALS CARE ABOUT THIS REMOTE LITTLE VILLAGE?
...STILL!
HAVE YOU TALKED ABOUT IT WITH THE ELDERS AND THE OTHERS?
YOU CAN'T JUST RUN AWAY...
WHAT DO YOU KNOW!?
WHO WOULD LISTEN TO A KID?
WHO DO YOU THINK YOU ARE!?

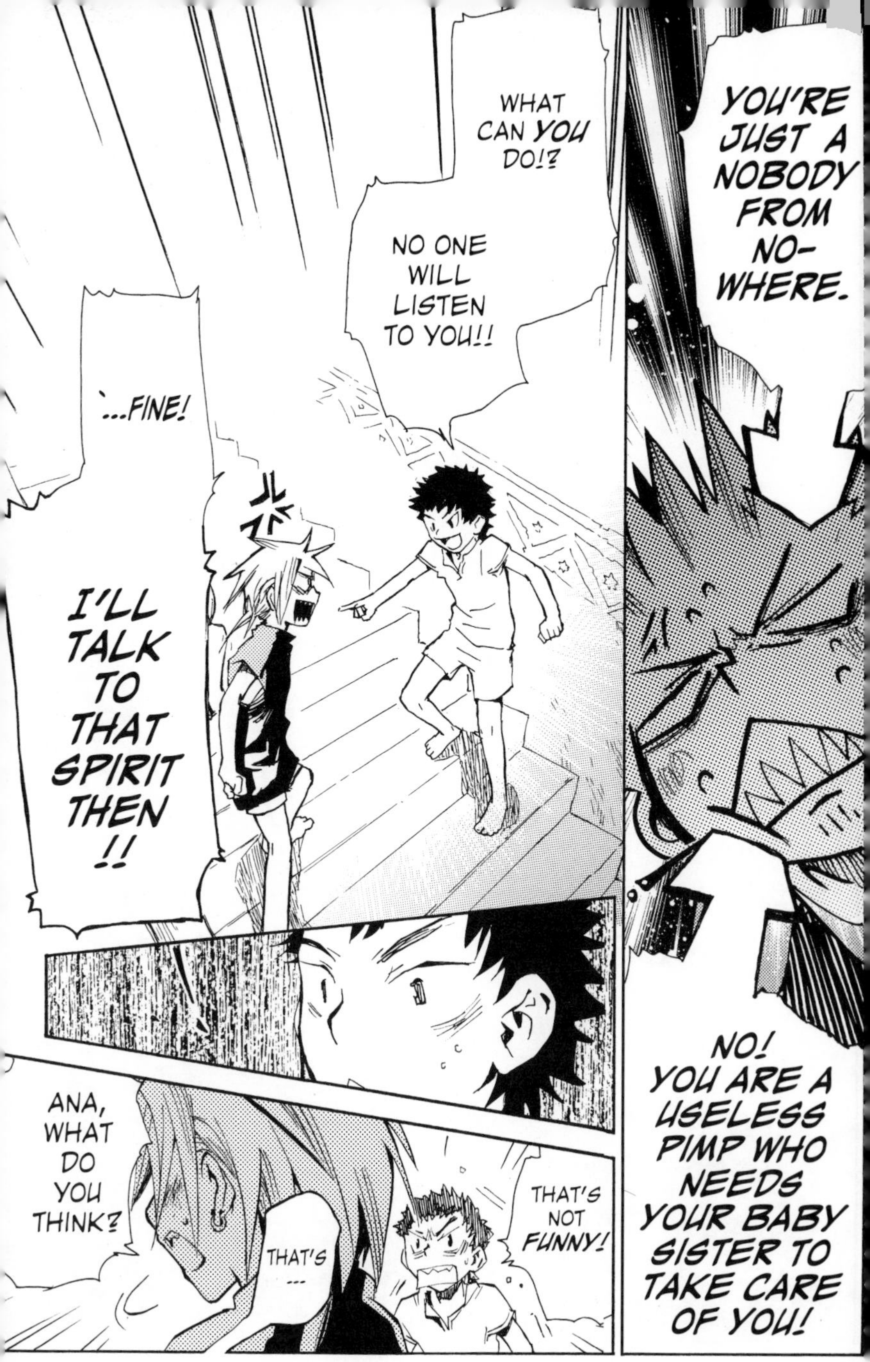
YOU'RE JUST A NOBODY FROM NO-WHERE.
NO! YOU ARE A USELESS PIMP WHO NEEDS YOUR BABY SISTER TO TAKE CARE OF YOU!
WHAT CAN YOU DO!?
NO ONE WILL LISTEN TO YOU!!
...FINE!
I'LL TALK TO THAT SPIRIT THEN!!
ANA, WHAT DO YOU THINK?
THAT'S NOT FUNNY!
THAT'S ---

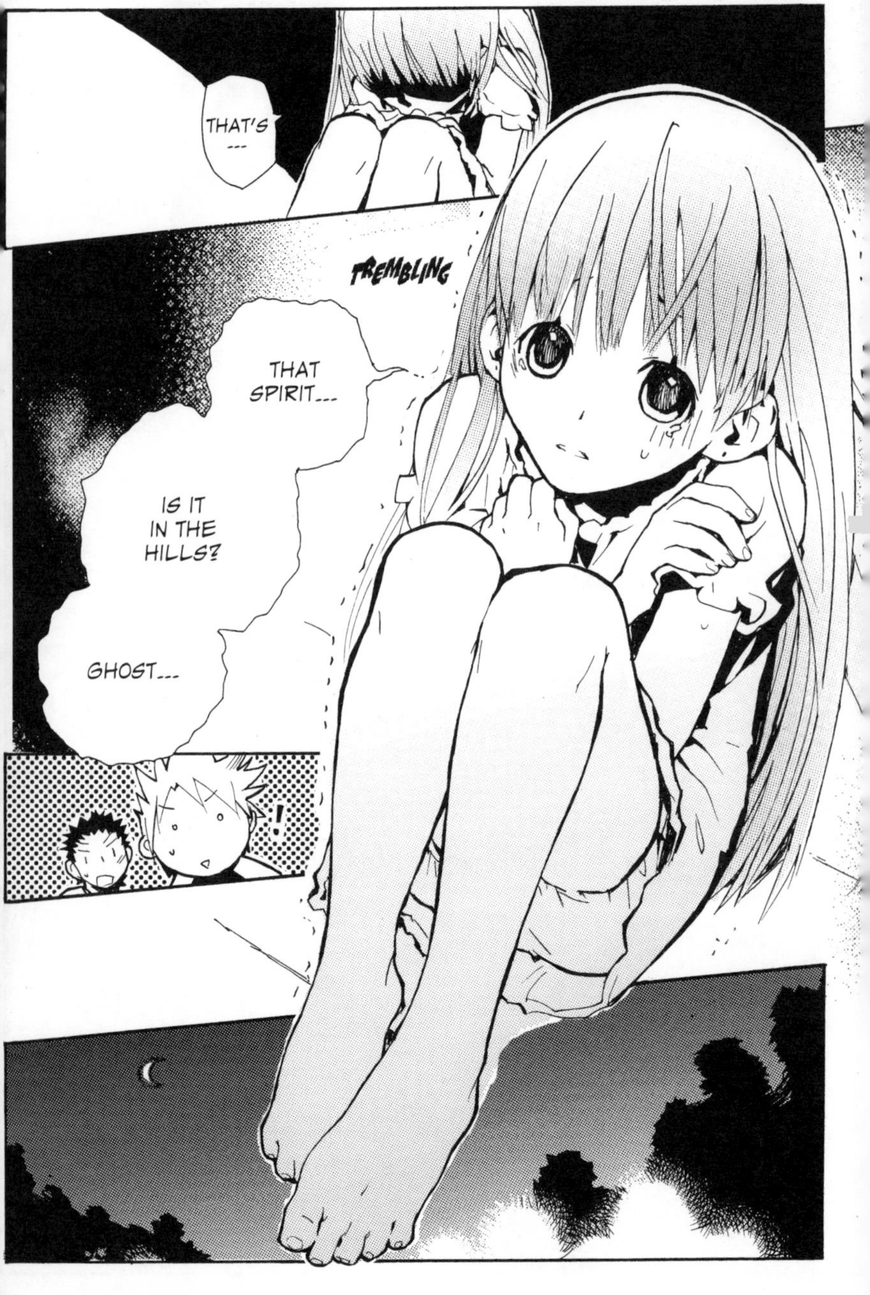
THAT'S ---
TREMBLING
THAT SPIRIT...
IS IT IN THE HILLS?
GHOST...
!

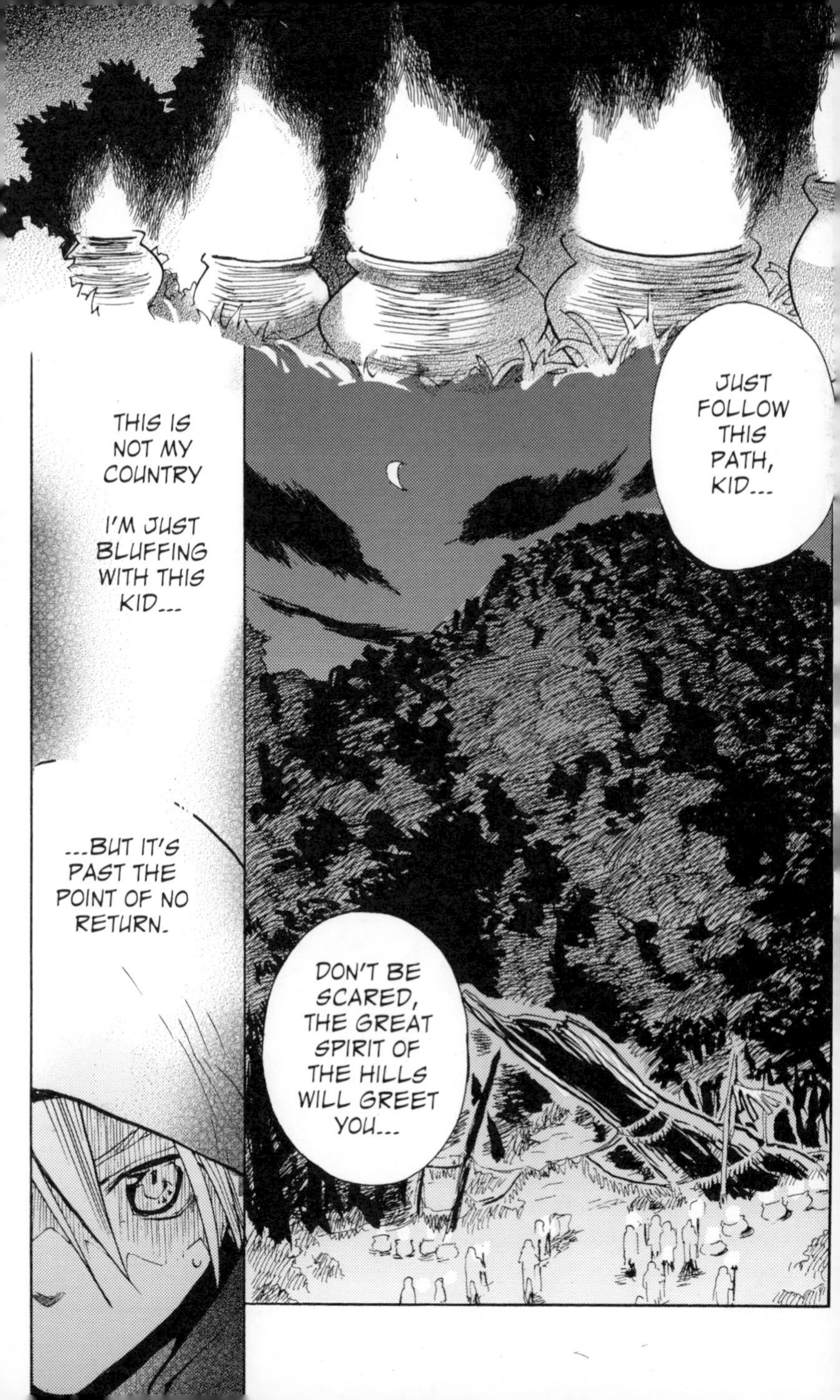
JUST FOLLOW THIS PATH, KID...
DON'T BE SCARED, THE GREAT SPIRIT OF THE HILLS WILL GREET YOU...
THIS IS NOT MY COUNTRY
I'M JUST BLUFFING WITH THIS KID...
...BUT IT'S PAST THE POINT OF NO RETURN.

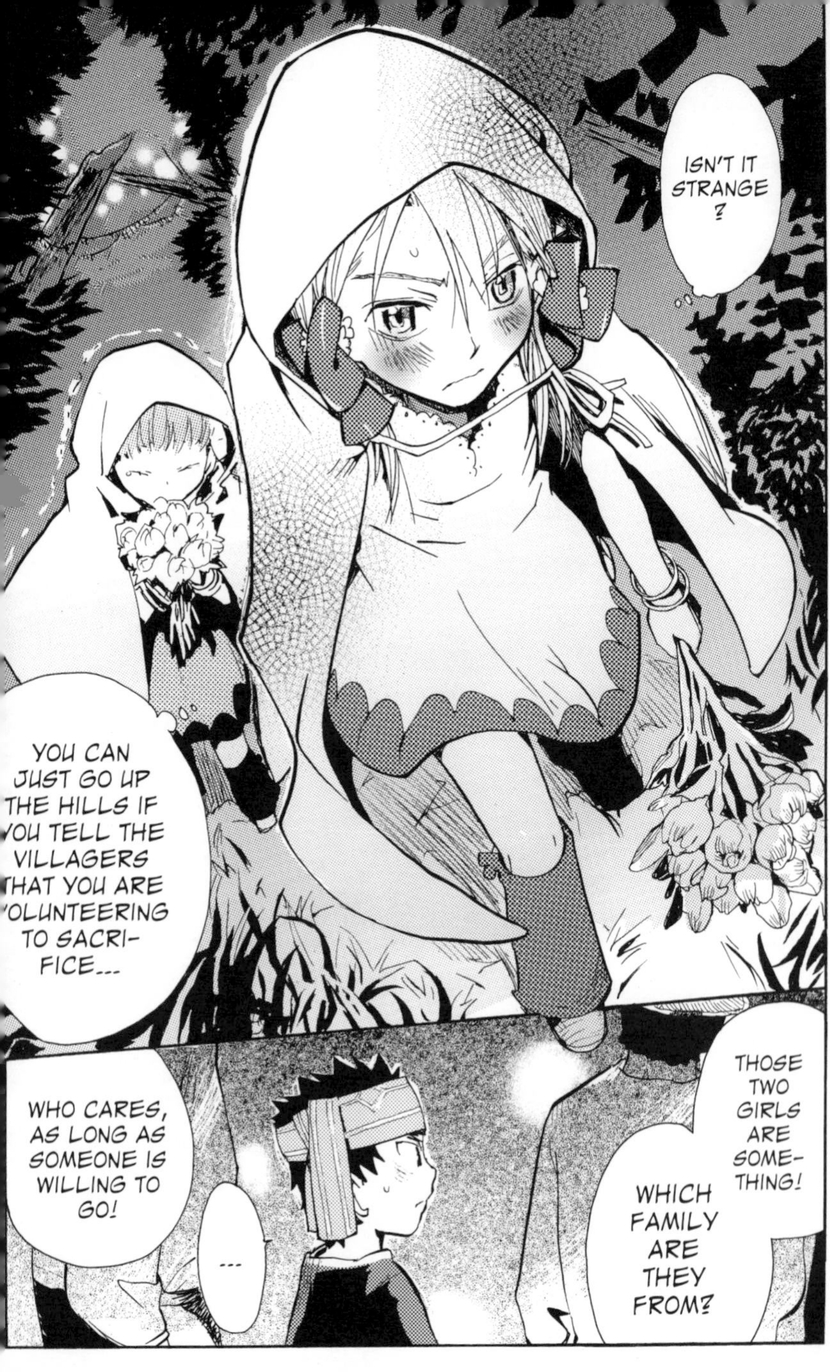
ISN'T IT STRANGE?
YOU CAN JUST GO UP THE HILLS IF YOU TELL THE VILLAGERS THAT YOU ARE VOLUNTEERING TO SACRI-FICE...
THOSE TWO GIRLS ARE SOME-THING!
WHICH FAMILY ARE THEY FROM?
...
WHO CARES, AS LONG AS SOMEONE IS WILLING TO GO!

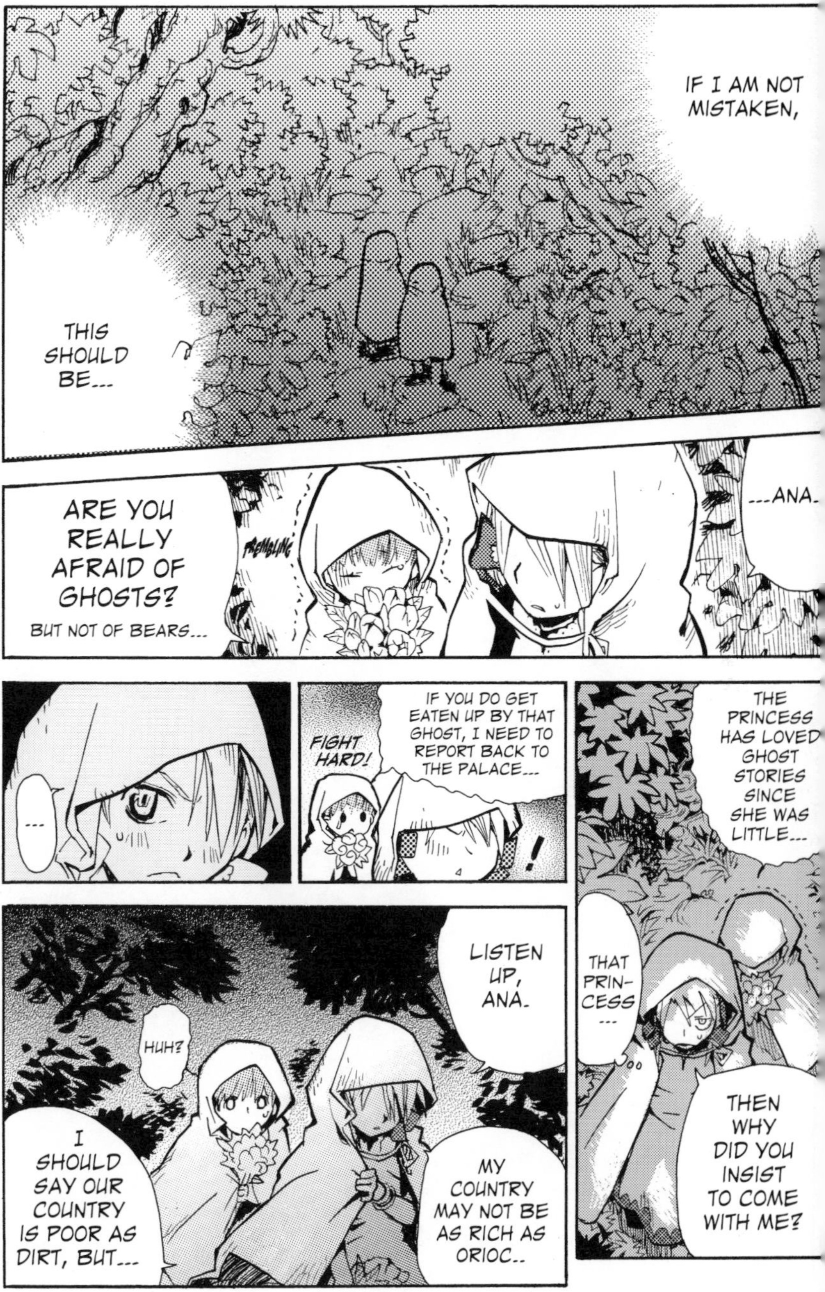
IF I AM NOT MISTAKEN,
THIS SHOULD BE...
...ANA.
TREMBLING
ARE YOU REALLY AFRAID OF GHOSTS?
BUT NOT OF BEARS...
THE PRINCESS HAS LOVED GHOST STORIES SINCE SHE WAS LITTLE...
THAT PRINCESS...
THEN WHY DID YOU INSIST TO COME WITH ME?
IF YOU DO GET EATEN UP BY THAT GHOST, I NEED TO REPORT BACK TO THE PALACE...
FIGHT HARD!
!
...
LISTEN UP, ANA.
HUH?
MY COUNTRY MAY NOT BE AS RICH AS ORIOC..
I SHOULD SAY OUR COUNTRY IS POOR AS DIRT, BUT...

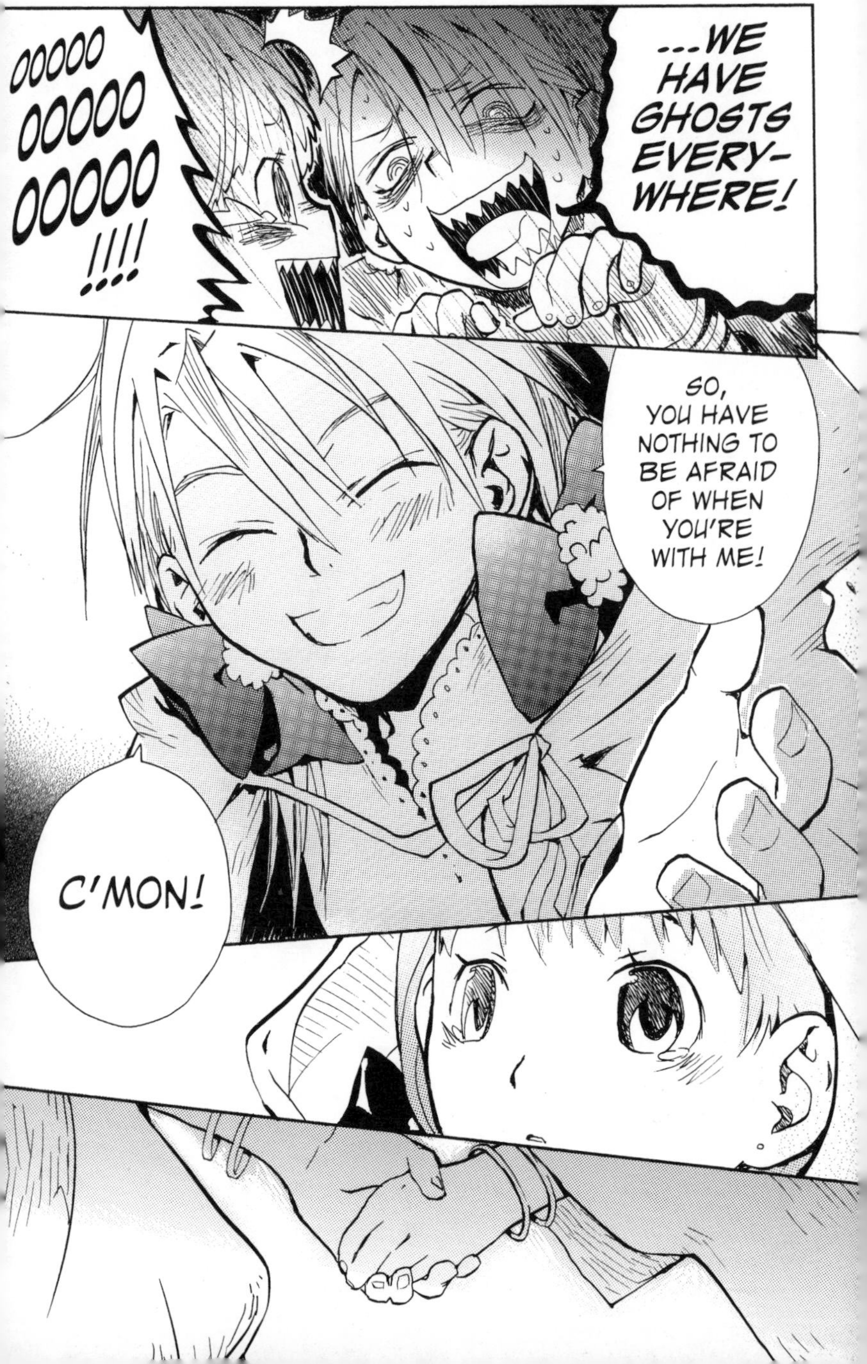
...WE HAVE GHOSTS EVERY-WHERE!
OOOOOOOOOOOOOOO!!!!
SO, YOU HAVE NOTHING TO BE AFRAID OF WHEN YOU'RE WITH ME!
C'MON!

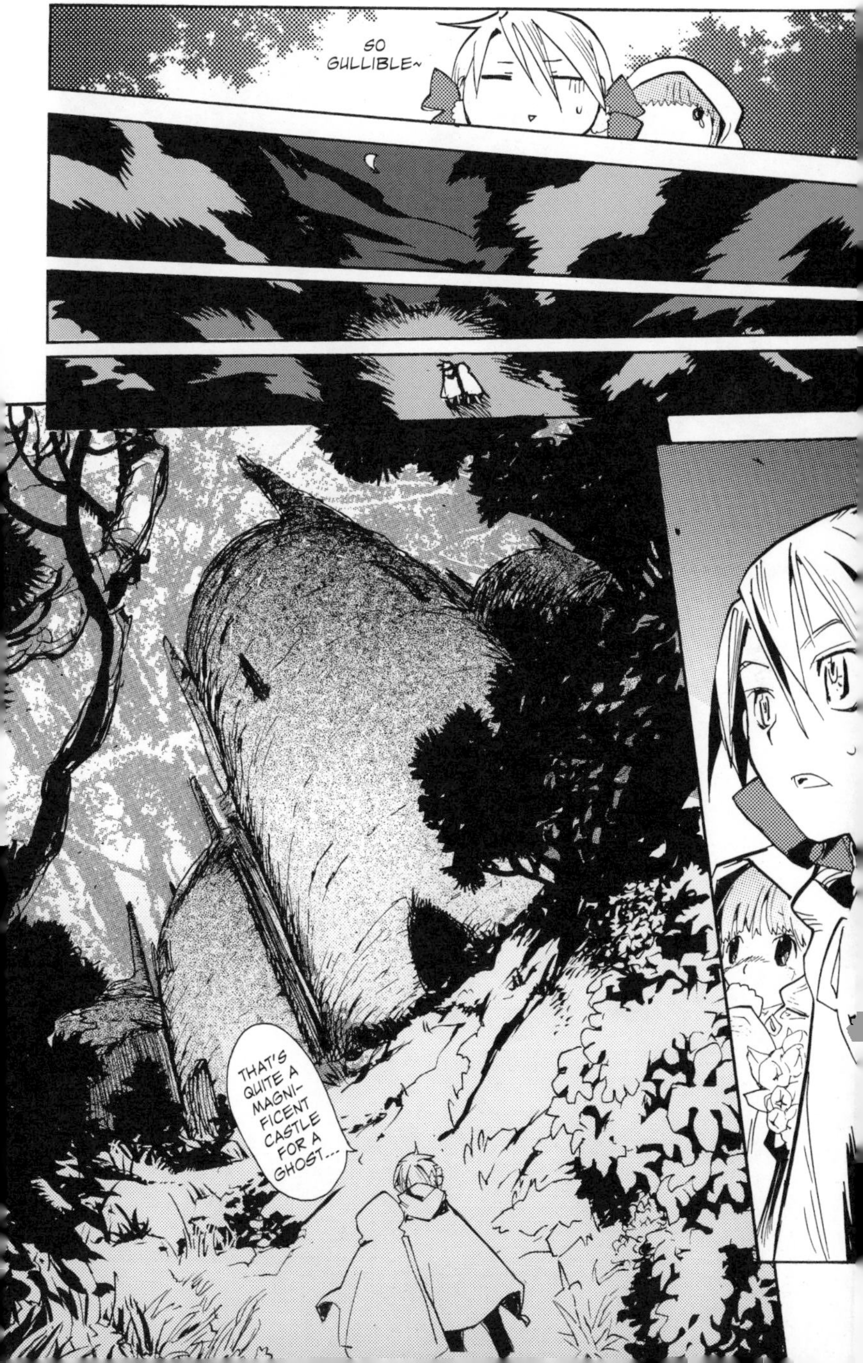
SO GULLIBLE~
THAT'S QUITE A MAGNIFICENT CASTLE FOR A GHOST...

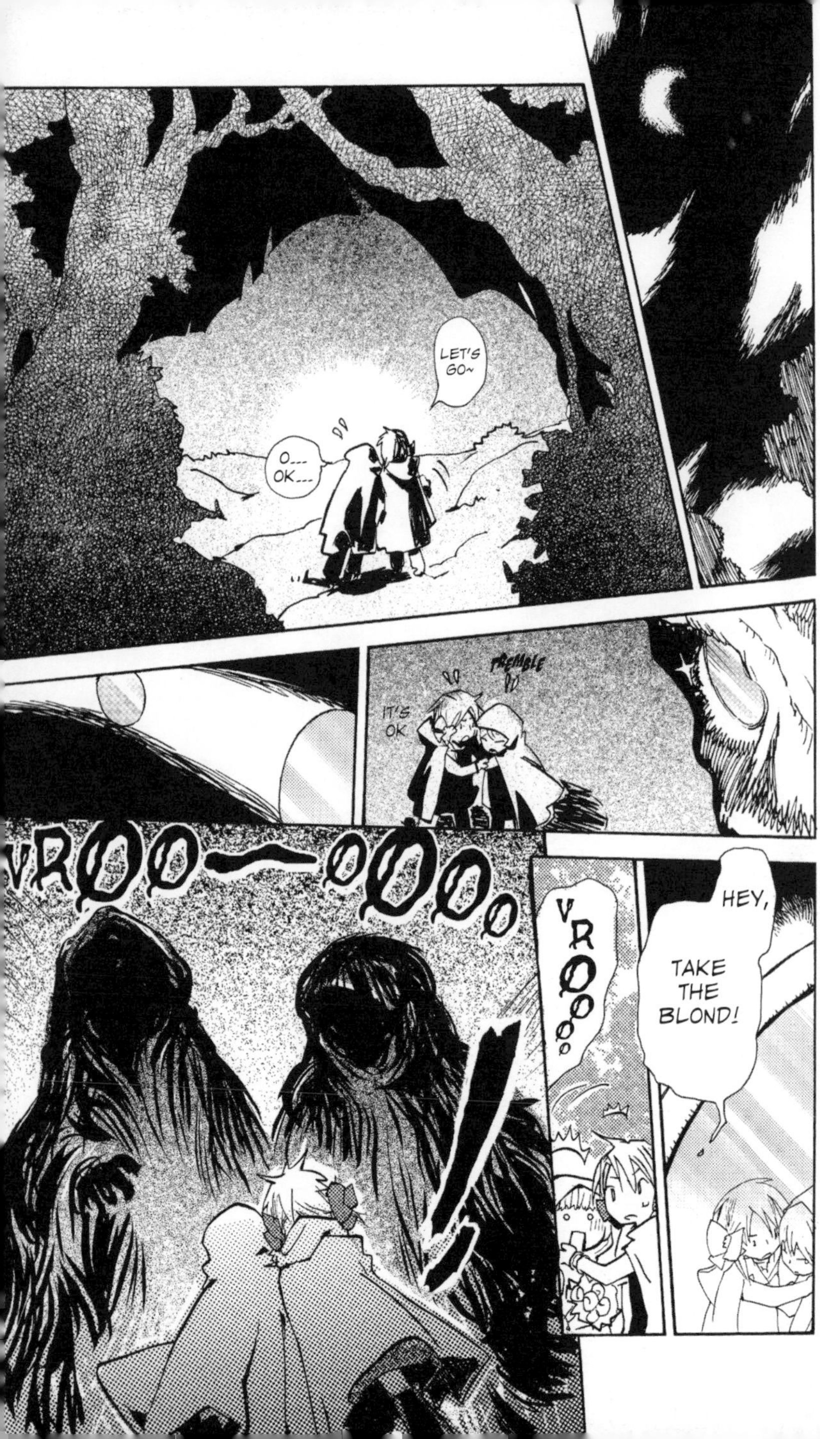
LET'S GO~
O... OK...
TREMBLE
IT'S OK
HEY, TAKE THE BLOND!
VROOOOo
VROO—OOOOo

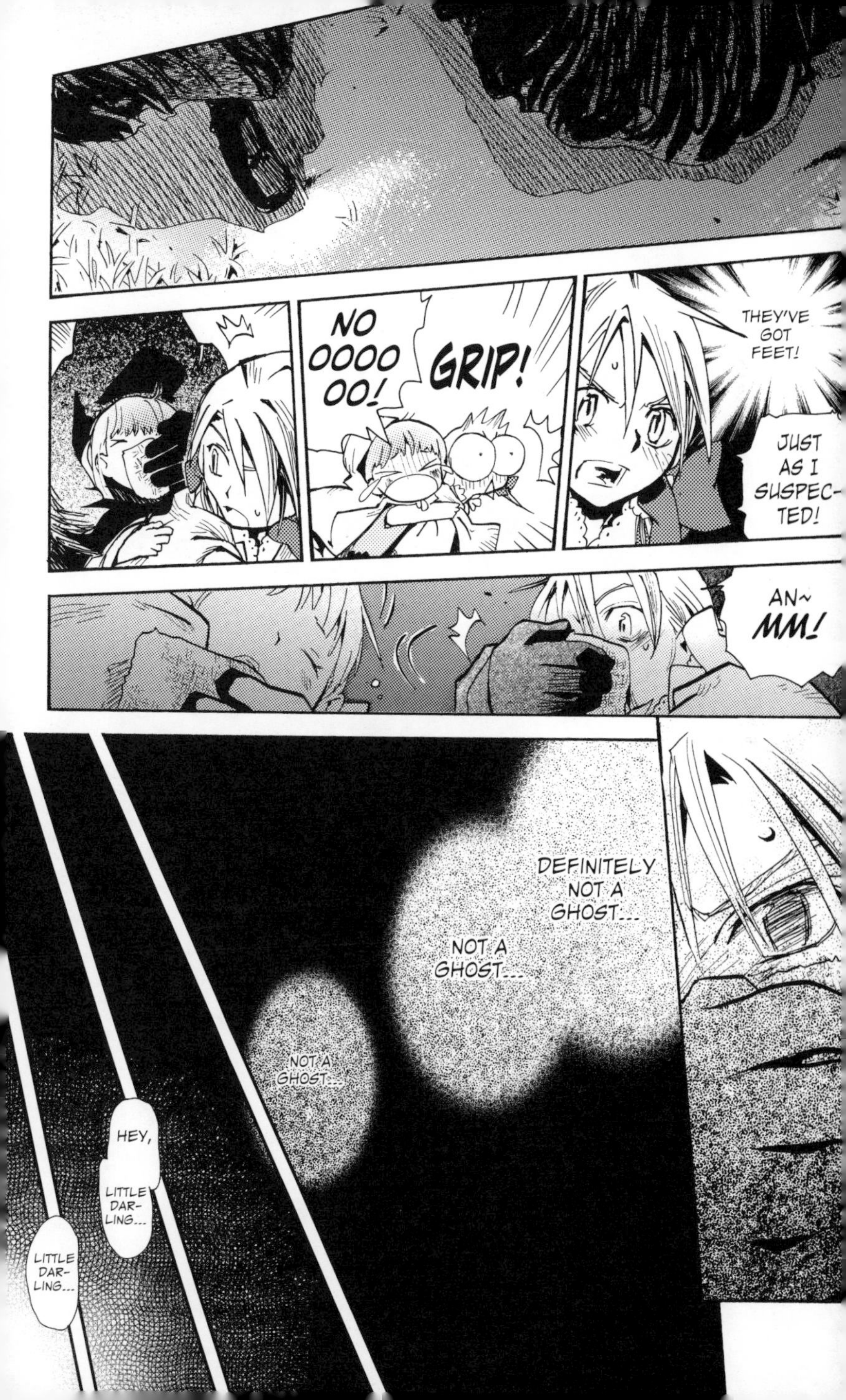
THEY'VE GOT FEET!
JUST AS I SUSPECTED!
GRIP!
NO OOOOOO!
AN~ MM!
DEFINITELY NOT A GHOST...
NOT A GHOST...
NOT A GHOST...
HEY,
LITTLE DARLING...
LITTLE DARLING...

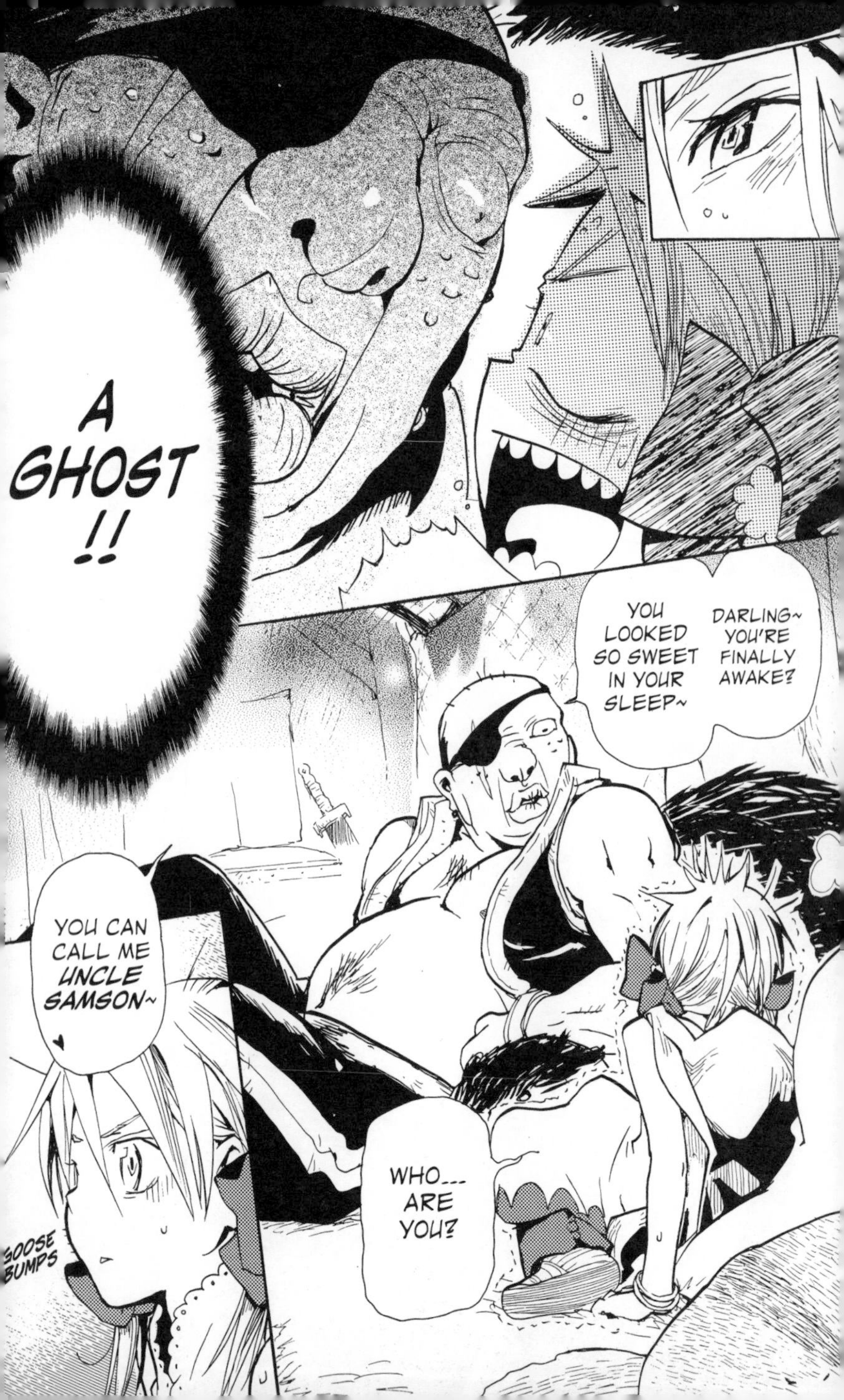
A GHOST !!
DARLING~ YOU'RE FINALLY AWAKE?
YOU LOOKED SO SWEET IN YOUR SLEEP~
WHO... ARE YOU?
YOU CAN CALL ME UNCLE SAMSON~ ♥
GOOSE BUMPS

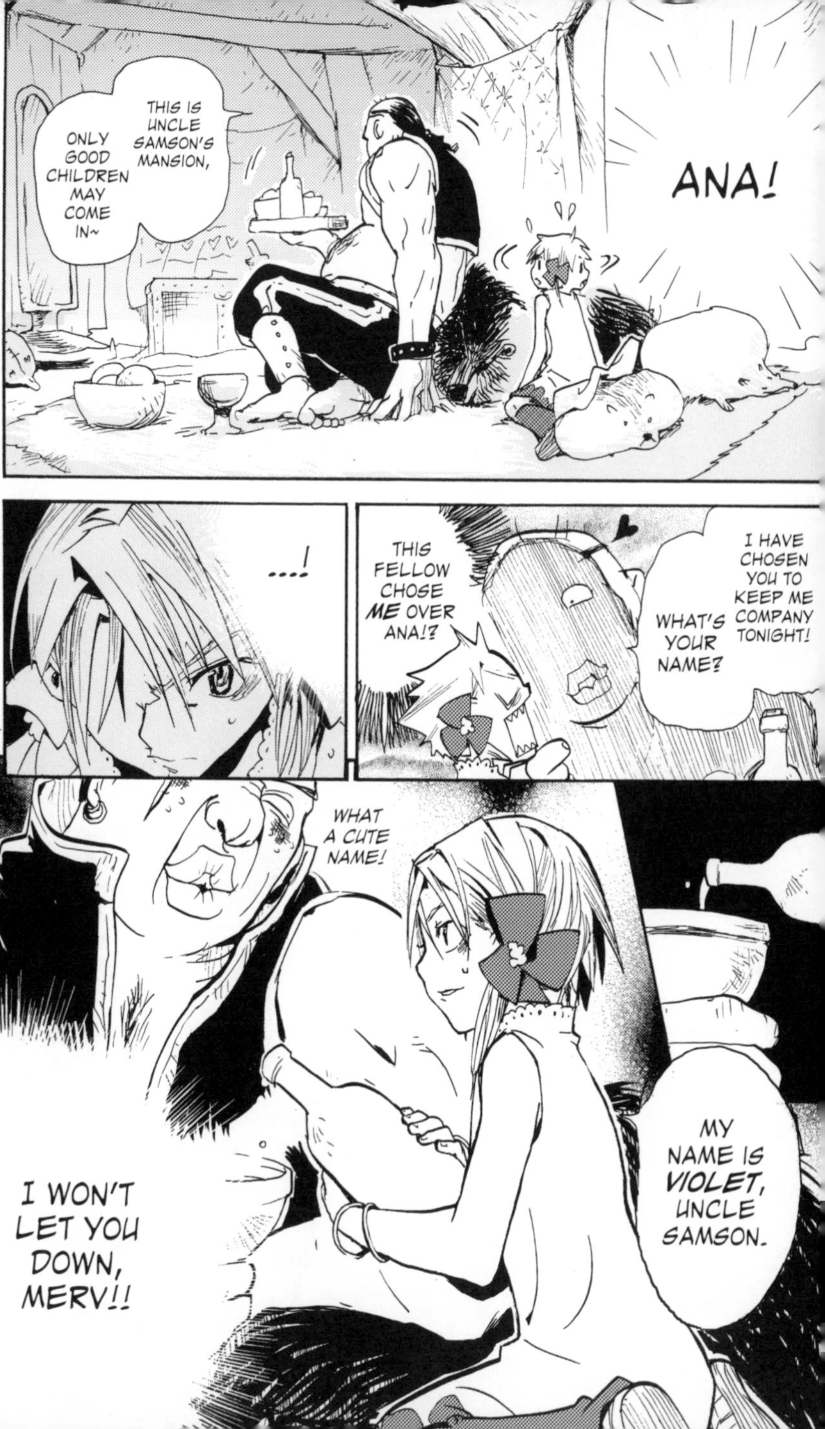
ANA!
THIS IS UNCLE SAMSON'S MANSION, ONLY GOOD CHILDREN MAY COME IN~
I HAVE CHOSEN YOU TO KEEP ME COMPANY TONIGHT! WHAT'S YOUR NAME?
THIS FELLOW CHOSE *ME* OVER ANA!?
...!
MY NAME IS *VIOLET*, UNCLE SAMSON.
WHAT A CUTE NAME!
I WON'T LET YOU DOWN, MERV!!

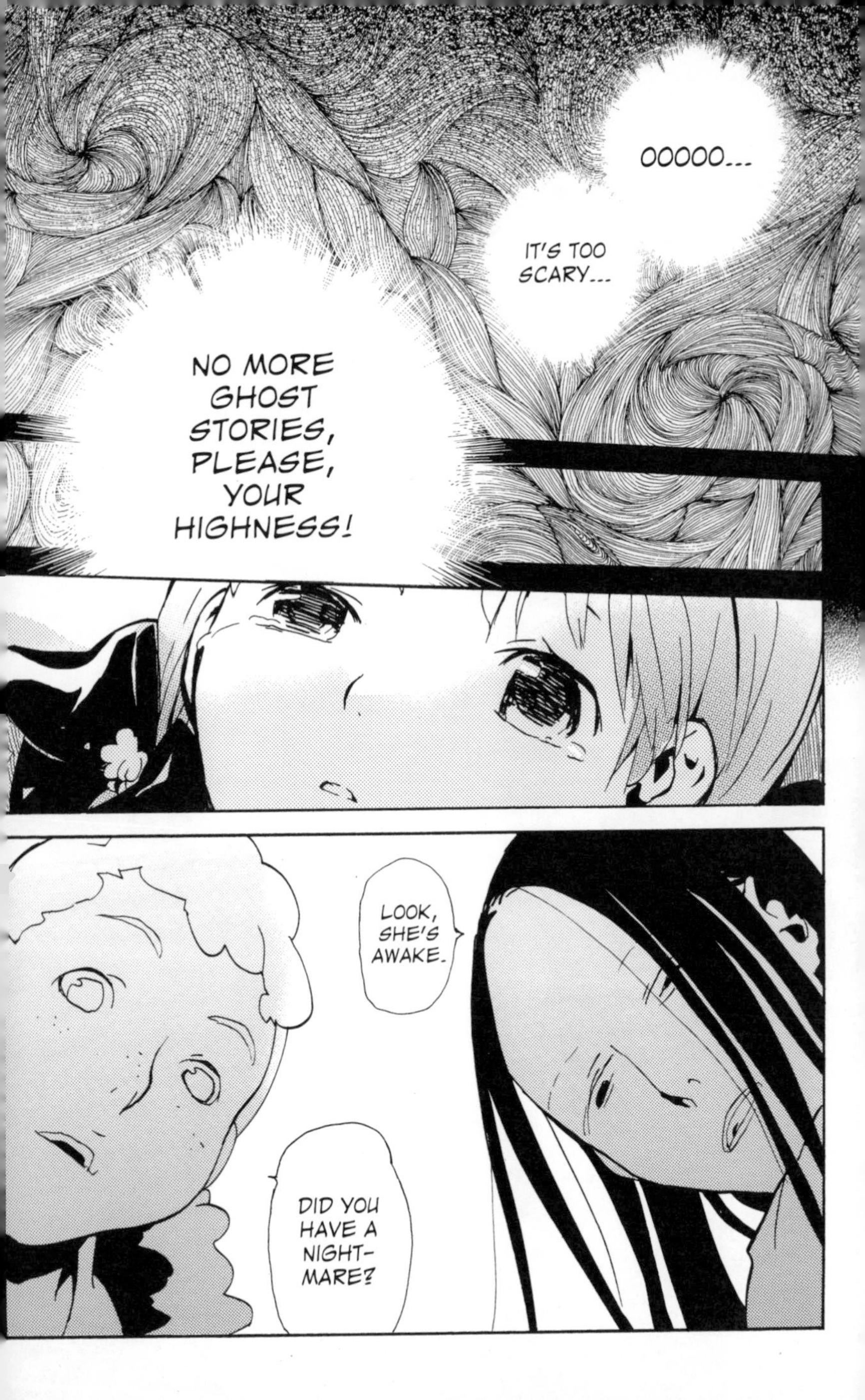
OOOOO...
IT'S TOO SCARY...
NO MORE GHOST STORIES, PLEASE, YOUR HIGHNESS!
LOOK, SHE'S AWAKE.
DID YOU HAVE A NIGHTMARE?

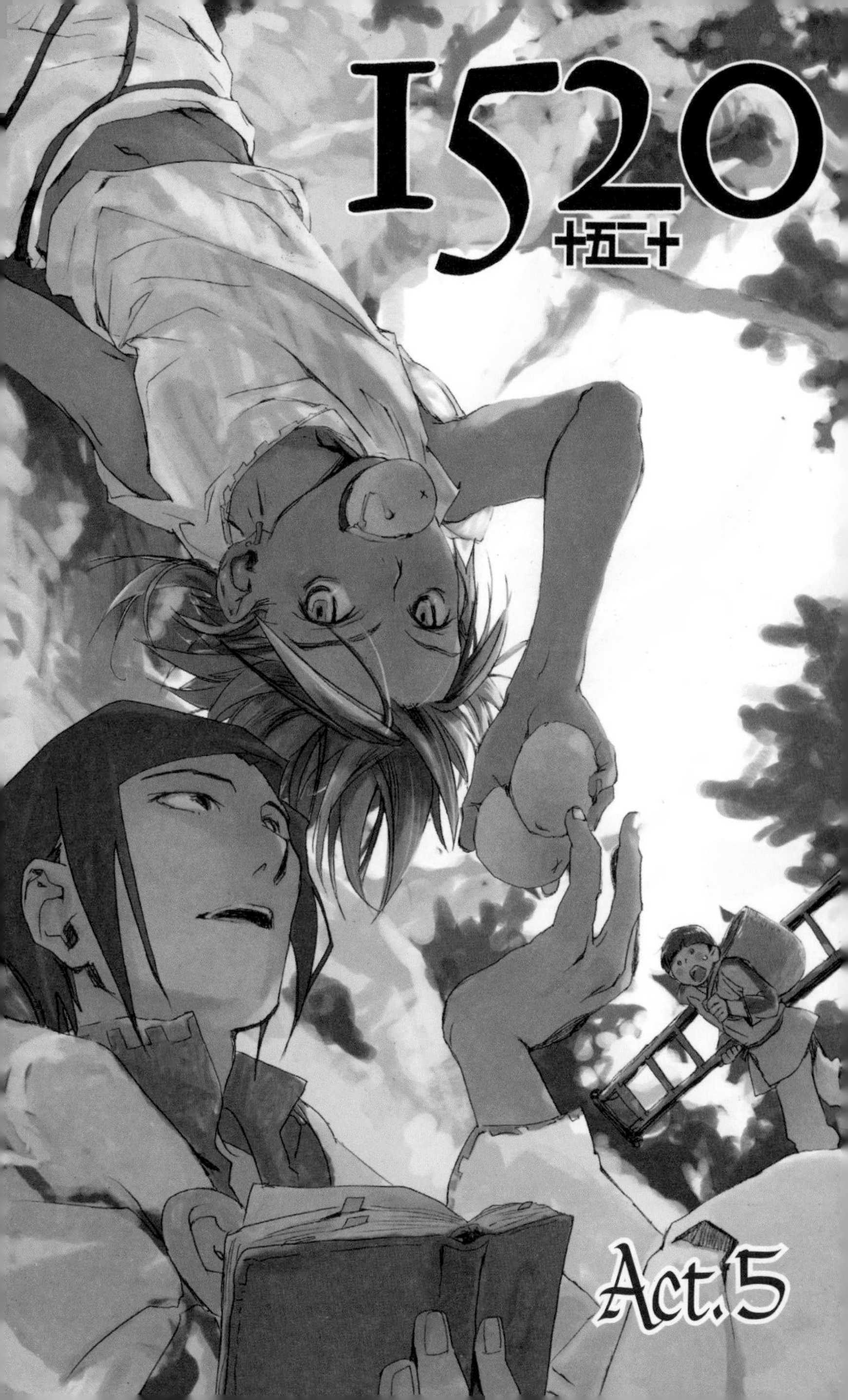
1520
十五二十
Act. 5

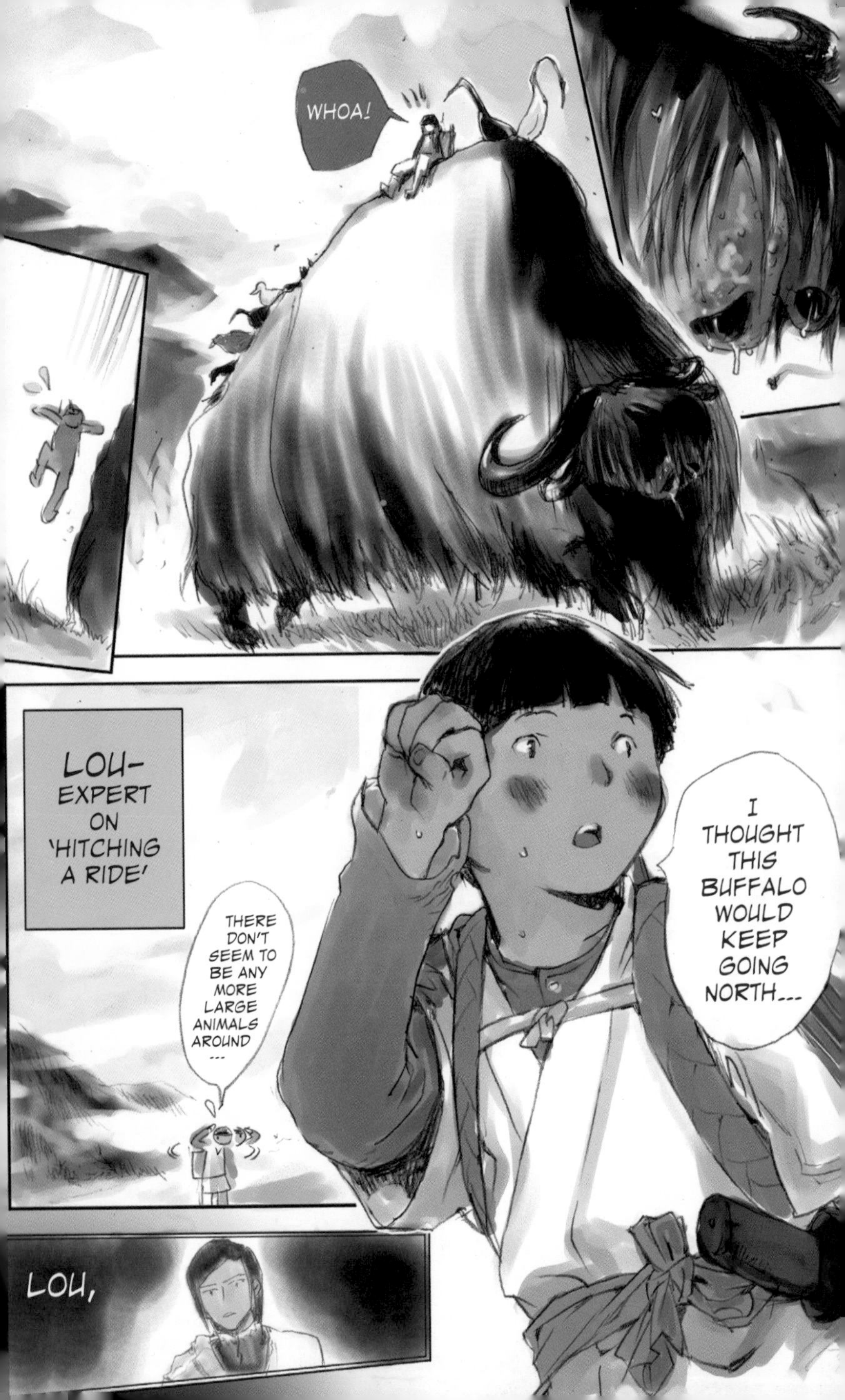
WHOA!
I THOUGHT THIS BUFFALO WOULD KEEP GOING NORTH...
LOU- EXPERT ON 'HITCHING A RIDE'
THERE DON'T SEEM TO BE ANY MORE LARGE ANIMALS AROUND...
LOU,

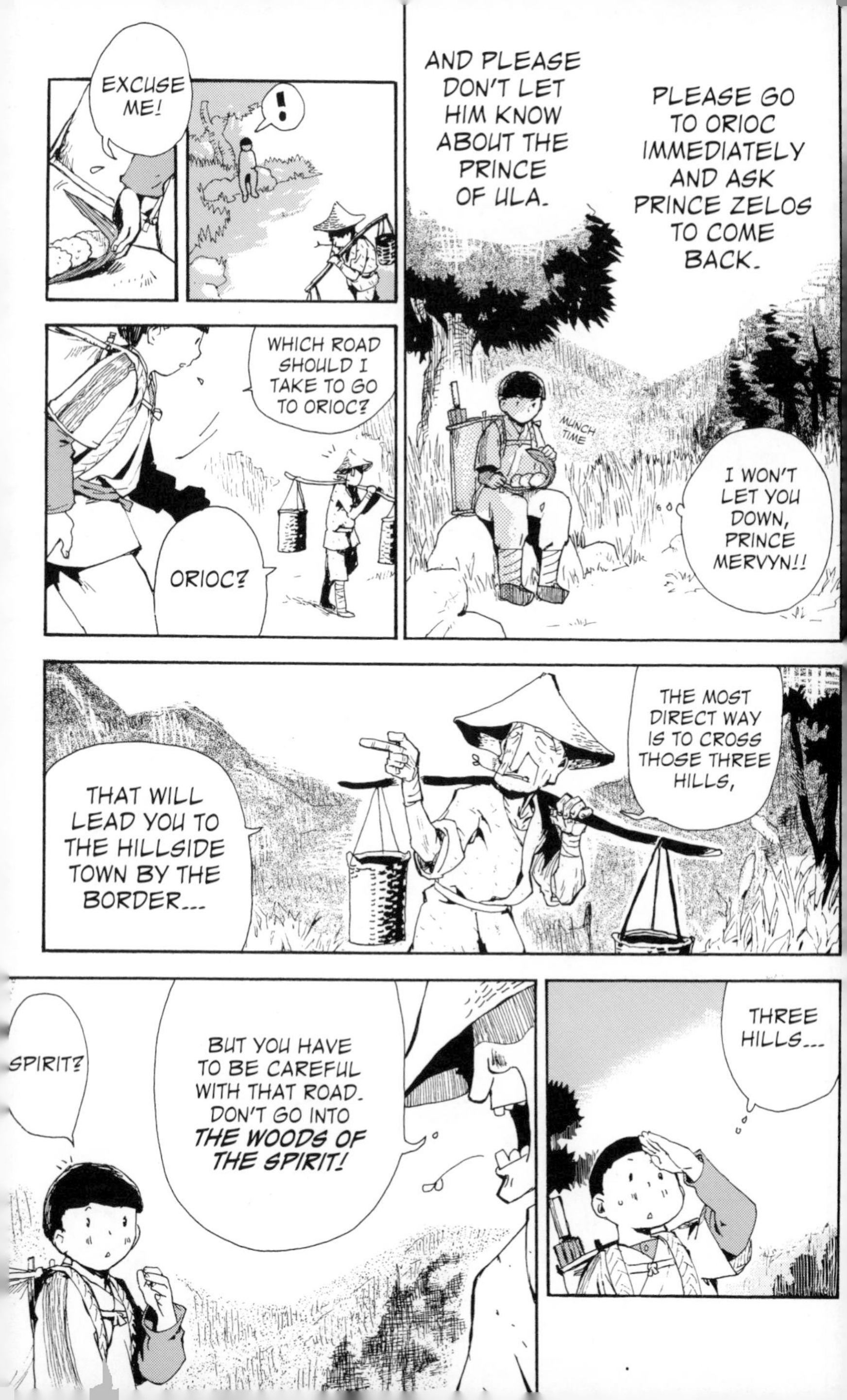
PLEASE GO TO ORIOC IMMEDIATELY AND ASK PRINCE ZELOS TO COME BACK.
AND PLEASE DON'T LET HIM KNOW ABOUT THE PRINCE OF ULA.
MUNCH TIME
I WON'T LET YOU DOWN, PRINCE MERVYN!!
!
EXCUSE ME!
WHICH ROAD SHOULD I TAKE TO GO TO ORIOC?
ORIOC?
THE MOST DIRECT WAY IS TO CROSS THOSE THREE HILLS,
THAT WILL LEAD YOU TO THE HILLSIDE TOWN BY THE BORDER...
THREE HILLS...
BUT YOU HAVE TO BE CAREFUL WITH THAT ROAD. DON'T GO INTO *THE WOODS OF THE SPIRIT!*
SPIRIT?

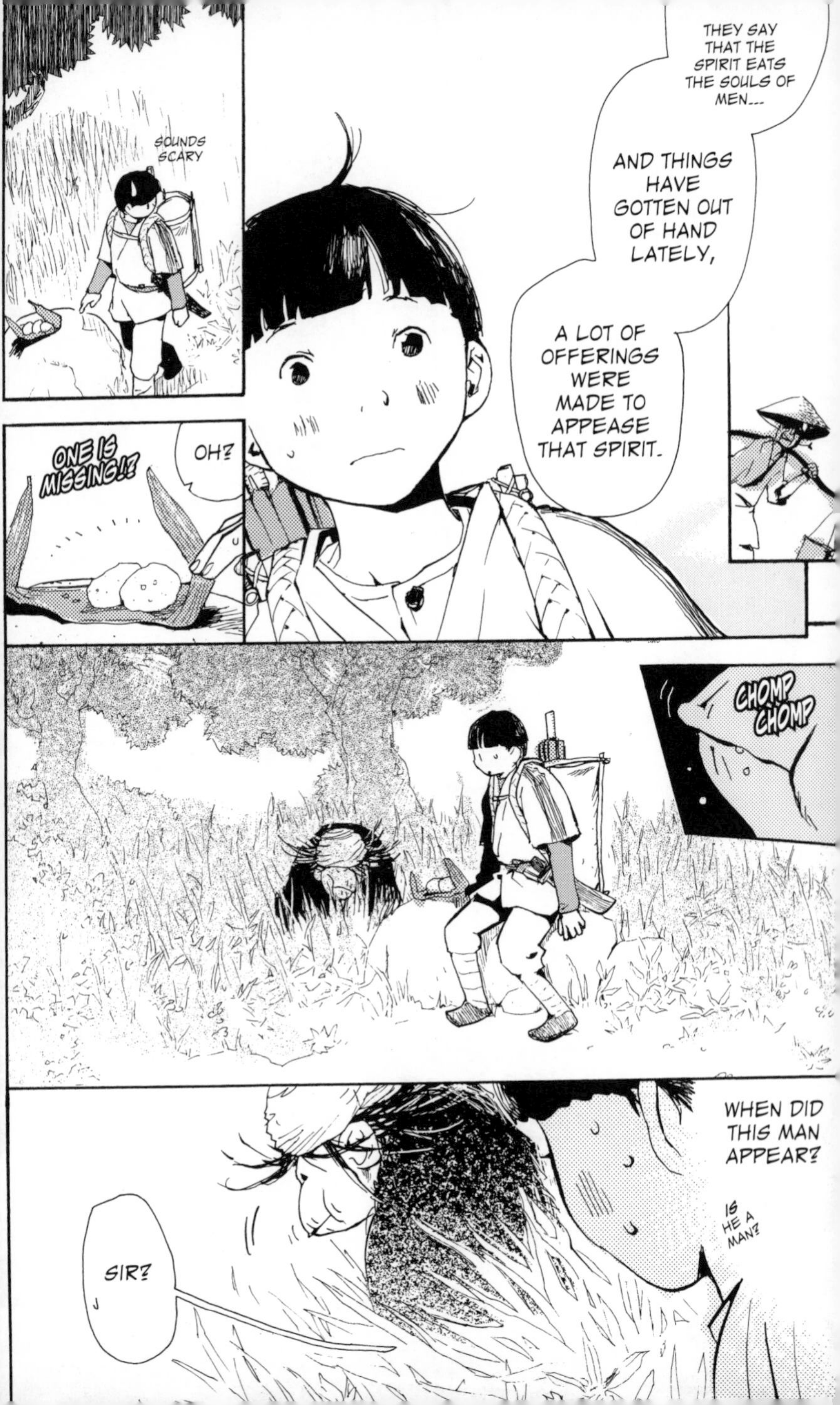
THEY SAY THAT THE SPIRIT EATS THE SOULS OF MEN...
AND THINGS HAVE GOTTEN OUT OF HAND LATELY,
A LOT OF OFFERINGS WERE MADE TO APPEASE THAT SPIRIT.
SOUNDS SCARY
OH?
ONE IS MISSING!?
CHOMP CHOMP
WHEN DID THIS MAN APPEAR?
IS HE A MAN?
SIR?

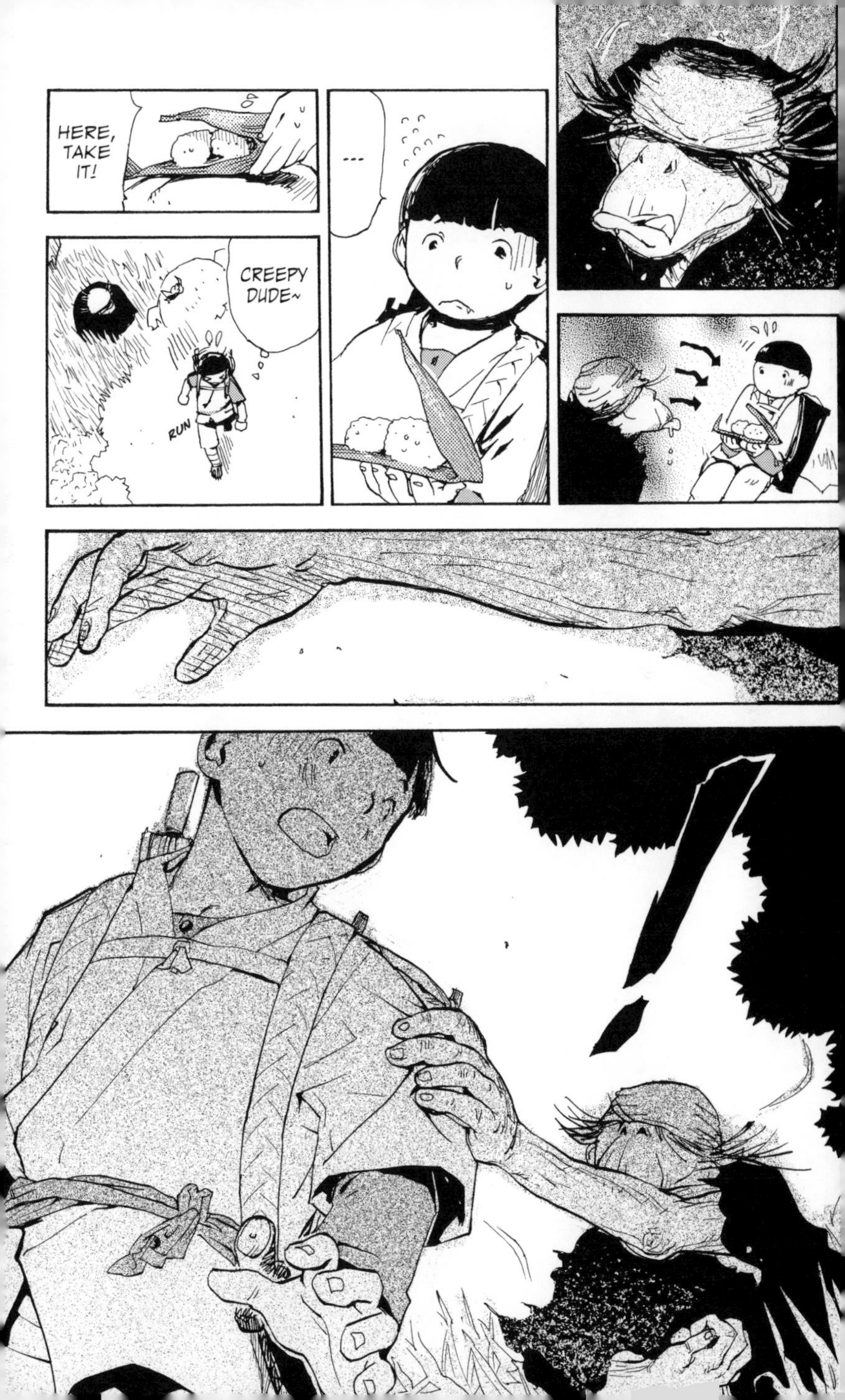
...
HERE, TAKE IT!
CREEPY DUDE~
RUN

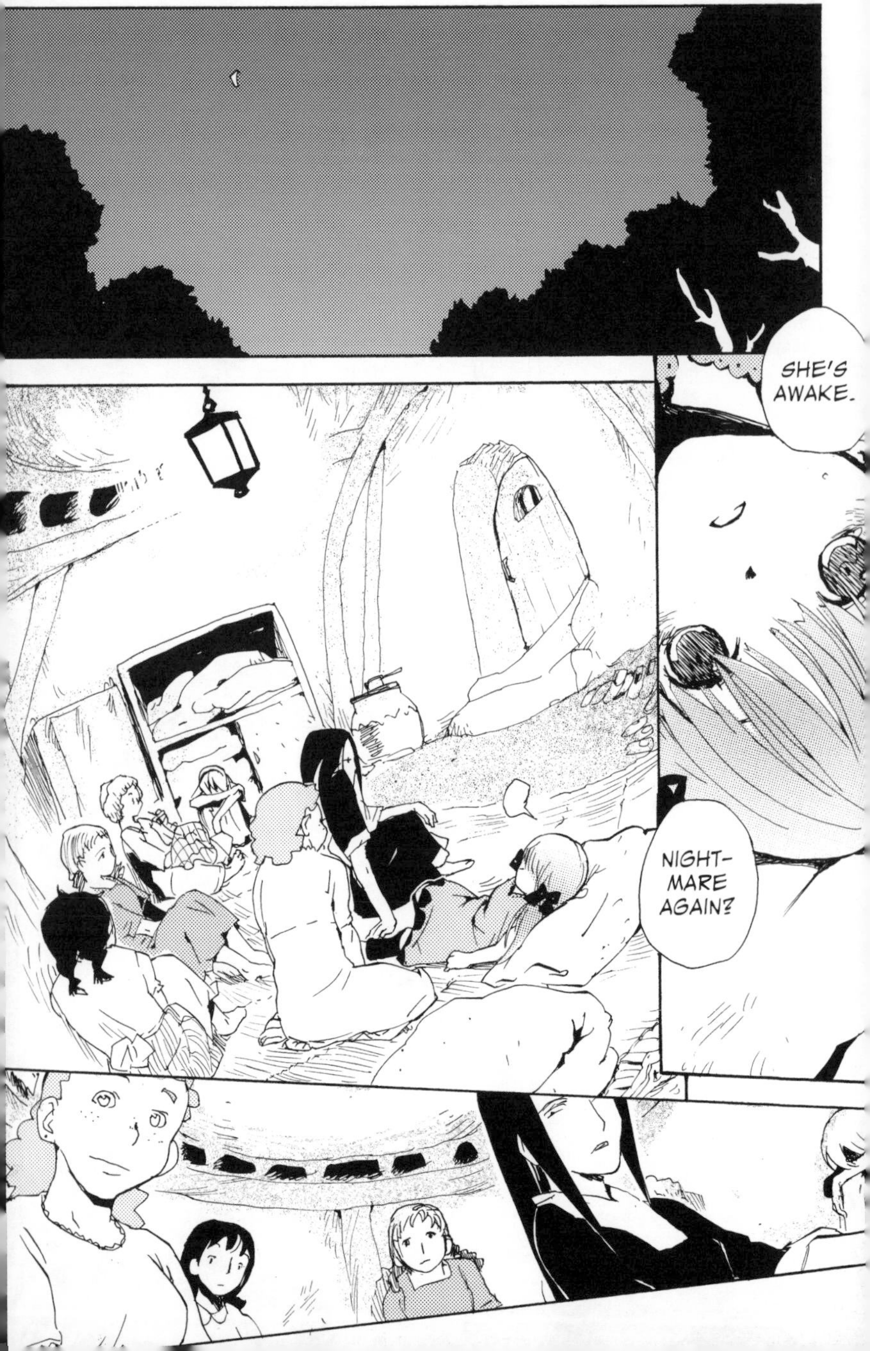
SHE'S AWAKE.
NIGHT-MARE AGAIN?

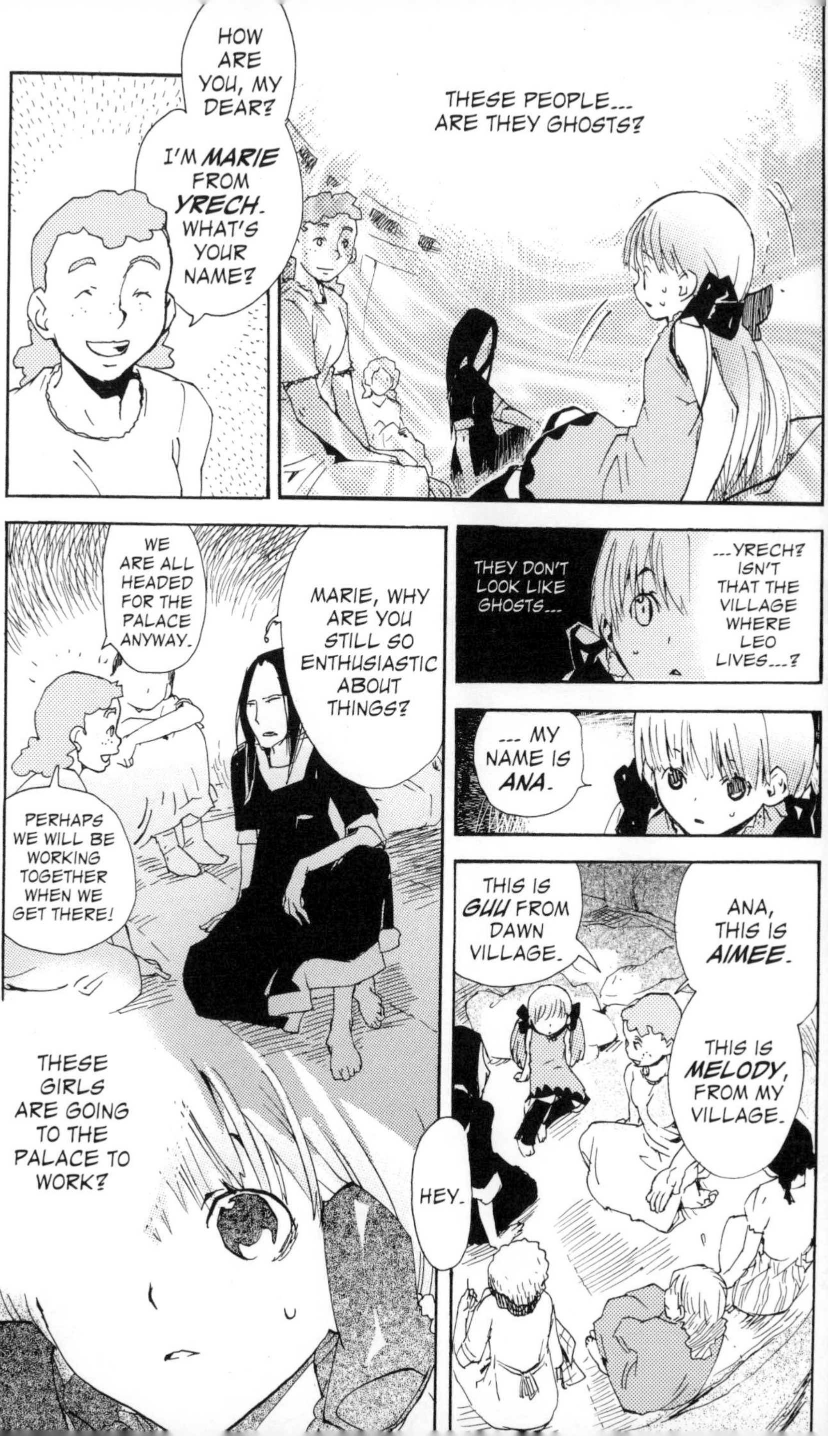
THESE PEOPLE... ARE THEY GHOSTS?
HOW ARE YOU, MY DEAR?
I'M MARIE FROM YRECH. WHAT'S YOUR NAME?
...YRECH? ISN'T THAT THE VILLAGE WHERE LEO LIVES...?
THEY DON'T LOOK LIKE GHOSTS...
... MY NAME IS ANA.
ANA, THIS IS AIMEE.
THIS IS MELODY, FROM MY VILLAGE.
THIS IS GUU FROM DAWN VILLAGE.
HEY.
MARIE, WHY ARE YOU STILL SO ENTHUSIASTIC ABOUT THINGS?
WE ARE ALL HEADED FOR THE PALACE ANYWAY.
PERHAPS WE WILL BE WORKING TOGETHER WHEN WE GET THERE!
THESE GIRLS ARE GOING TO THE PALACE TO WORK?

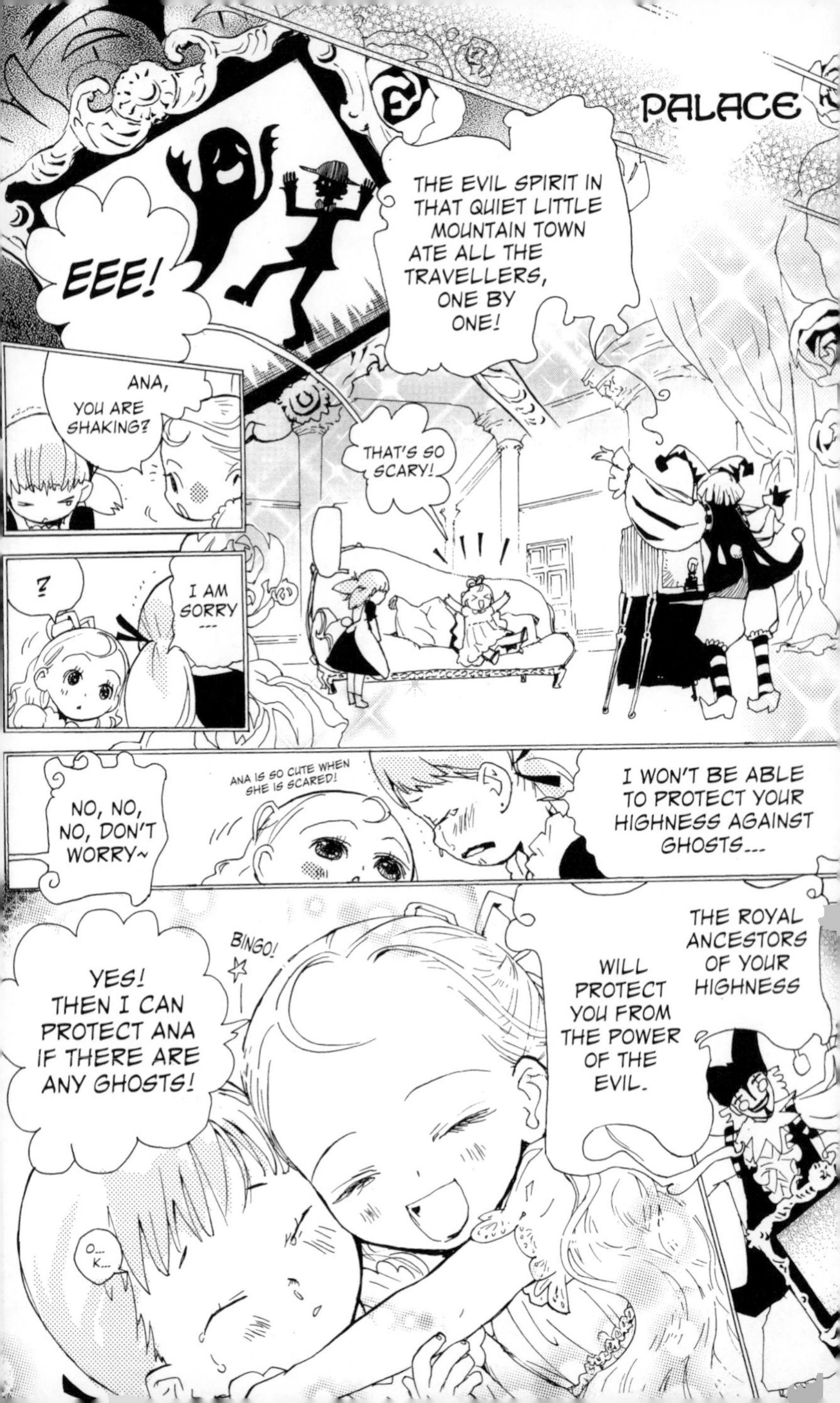
PALACE
THE EVIL SPIRIT IN THAT QUIET LITTLE MOUNTAIN TOWN ATE ALL THE TRAVELLERS, ONE BY ONE!
EEE!
THAT'S SO SCARY!
ANA, YOU ARE SHAKING?
I AM SORRY...
?
I WON'T BE ABLE TO PROTECT YOUR HIGHNESS AGAINST GHOSTS...
ANA IS SO CUTE WHEN SHE IS SCARED!
NO, NO, NO, DON'T WORRY~
THE ROYAL ANCESTORS OF YOUR HIGHNESS
WILL PROTECT YOU FROM THE POWER OF THE EVIL.
BINGO!
YES! THEN I CAN PROTECT ANA IF THERE ARE ANY GHOSTS!
O... K...

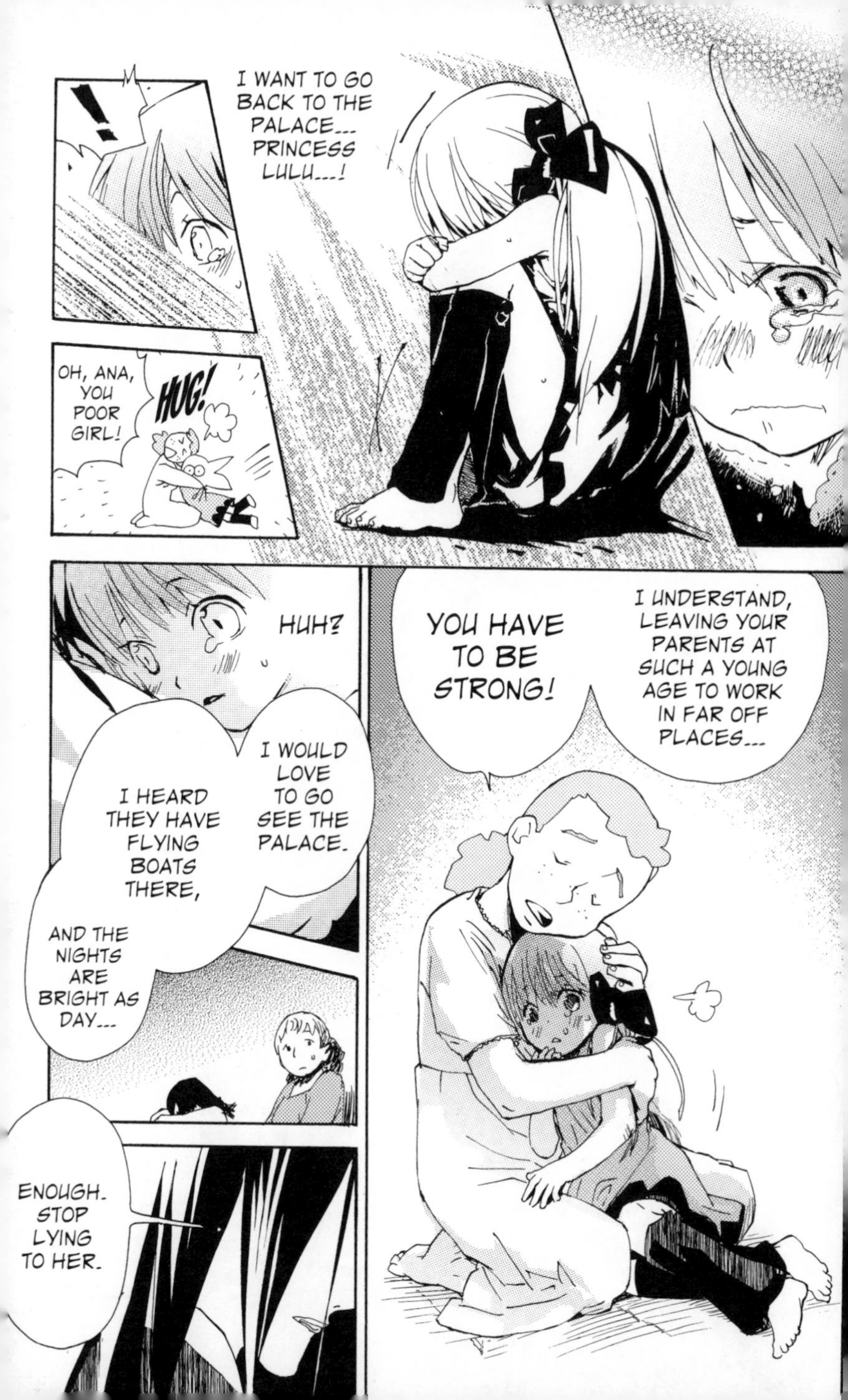
I WANT TO GO BACK TO THE PALACE... PRINCESS LULU...!
!
OH, ANA, YOU POOR GIRL!
HUG!
I UNDERSTAND, LEAVING YOUR PARENTS AT SUCH A YOUNG AGE TO WORK IN FAR OFF PLACES...
YOU HAVE TO BE STRONG!
HUH?
I WOULD LOVE TO GO SEE THE PALACE.
I HEARD THEY HAVE FLYING BOATS THERE,
AND THE NIGHTS ARE BRIGHT AS DAY...
ENOUGH. STOP LYING TO HER.

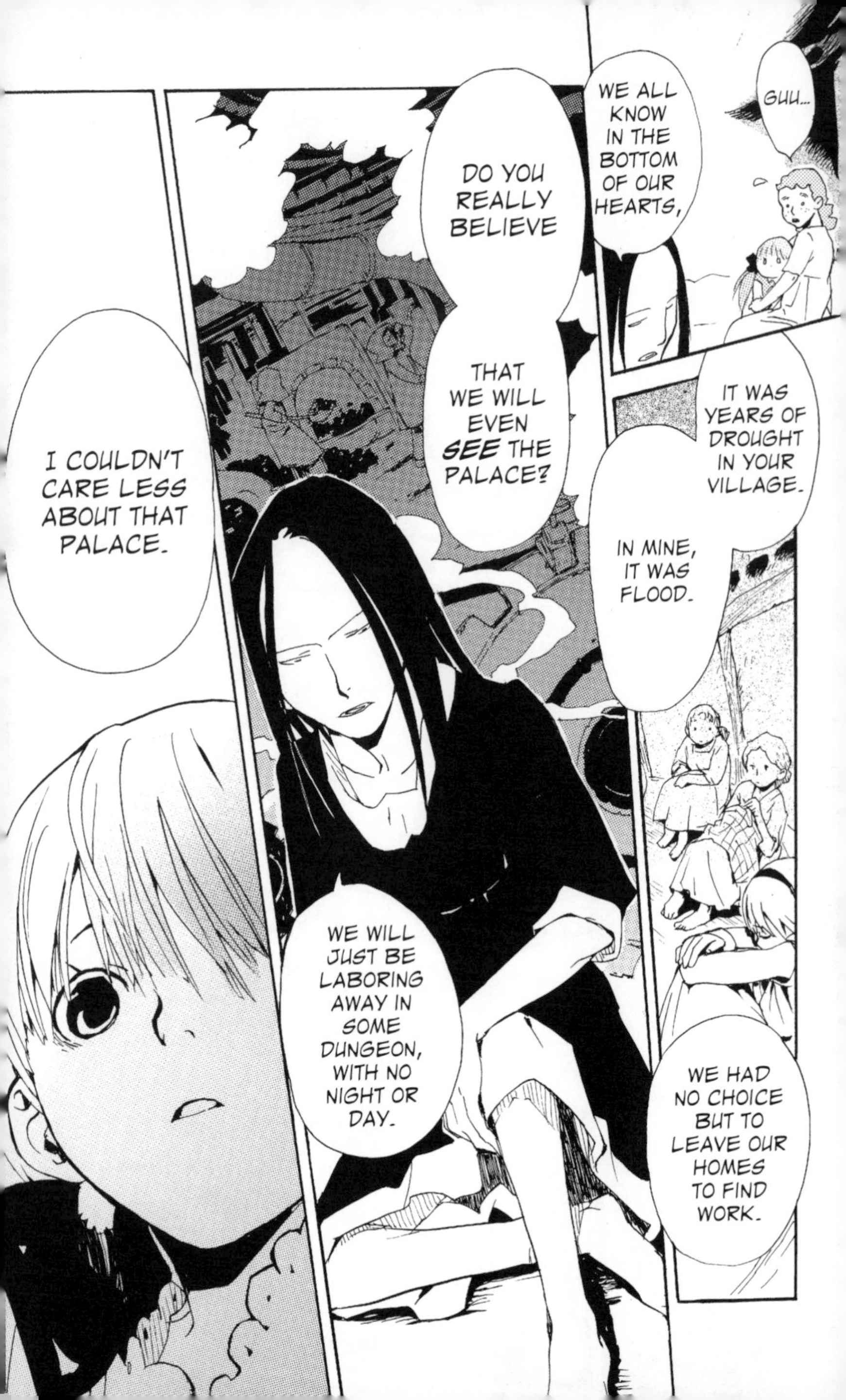
GUU...
WE ALL KNOW IN THE BOTTOM OF OUR HEARTS,
IT WAS YEARS OF DROUGHT IN YOUR VILLAGE.
IN MINE, IT WAS FLOOD.
WE HAD NO CHOICE BUT TO LEAVE OUR HOMES TO FIND WORK.
DO YOU REALLY BELIEVE
THAT WE WILL EVEN *SEE* THE PALACE?
WE WILL JUST BE LABORING AWAY IN SOME DUNGEON, WITH NO NIGHT OR DAY.
I COULDN'T CARE LESS ABOUT THAT PALACE.

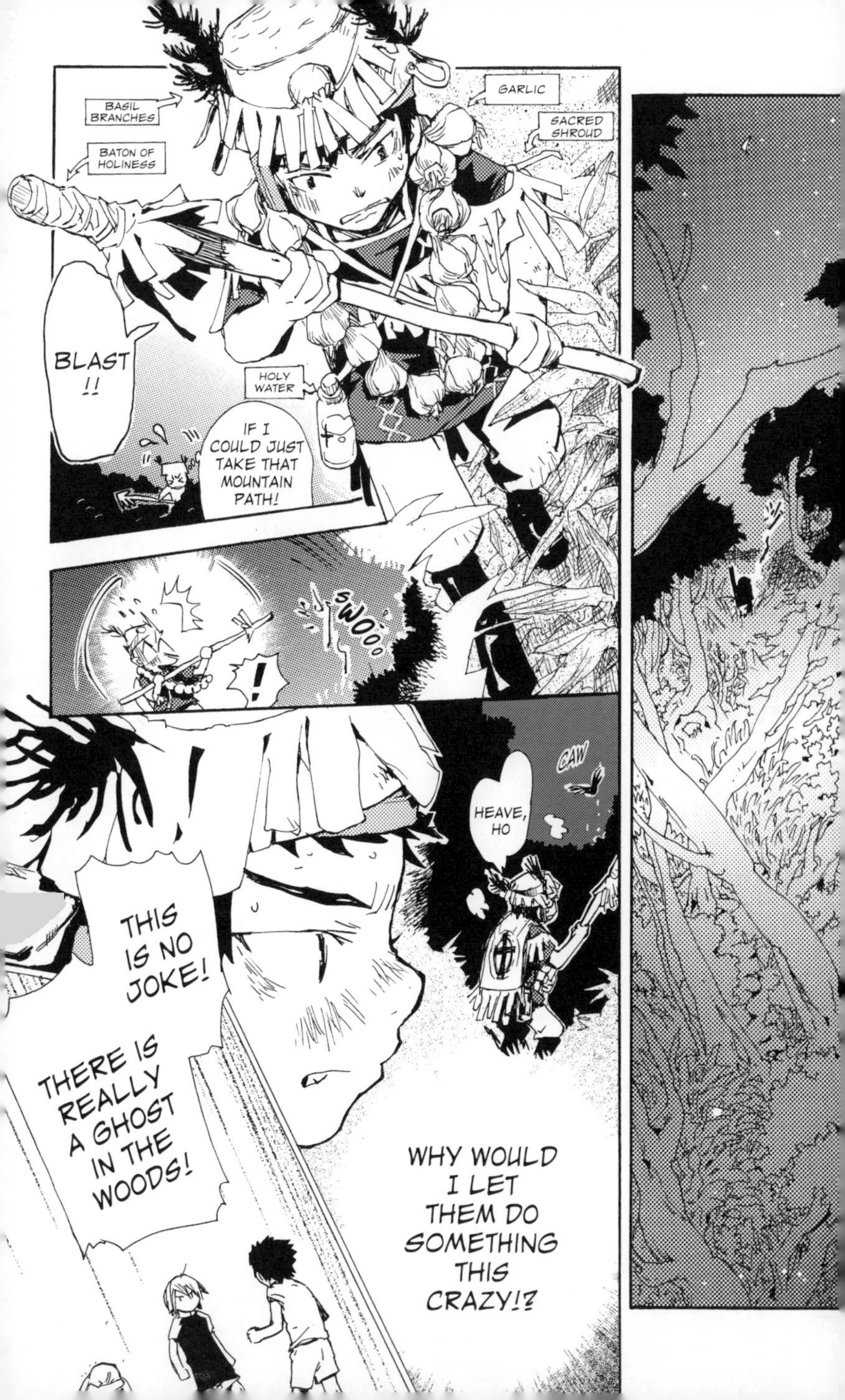

GARLIC
SACRED SHROUD
BASIL BRANCHES
BATON OF HOLINESS
HOLY WATER
BLAST !!
IF I COULD JUST TAKE THAT MOUNTAIN PATH!
SWOOOO
!
CAW
HEAVE, HO
THIS IS NO JOKE!
THERE IS REALLY A GHOST IN THE WOODS!
WHY WOULD I LET THEM DO SOMETHING THIS CRAZY!?

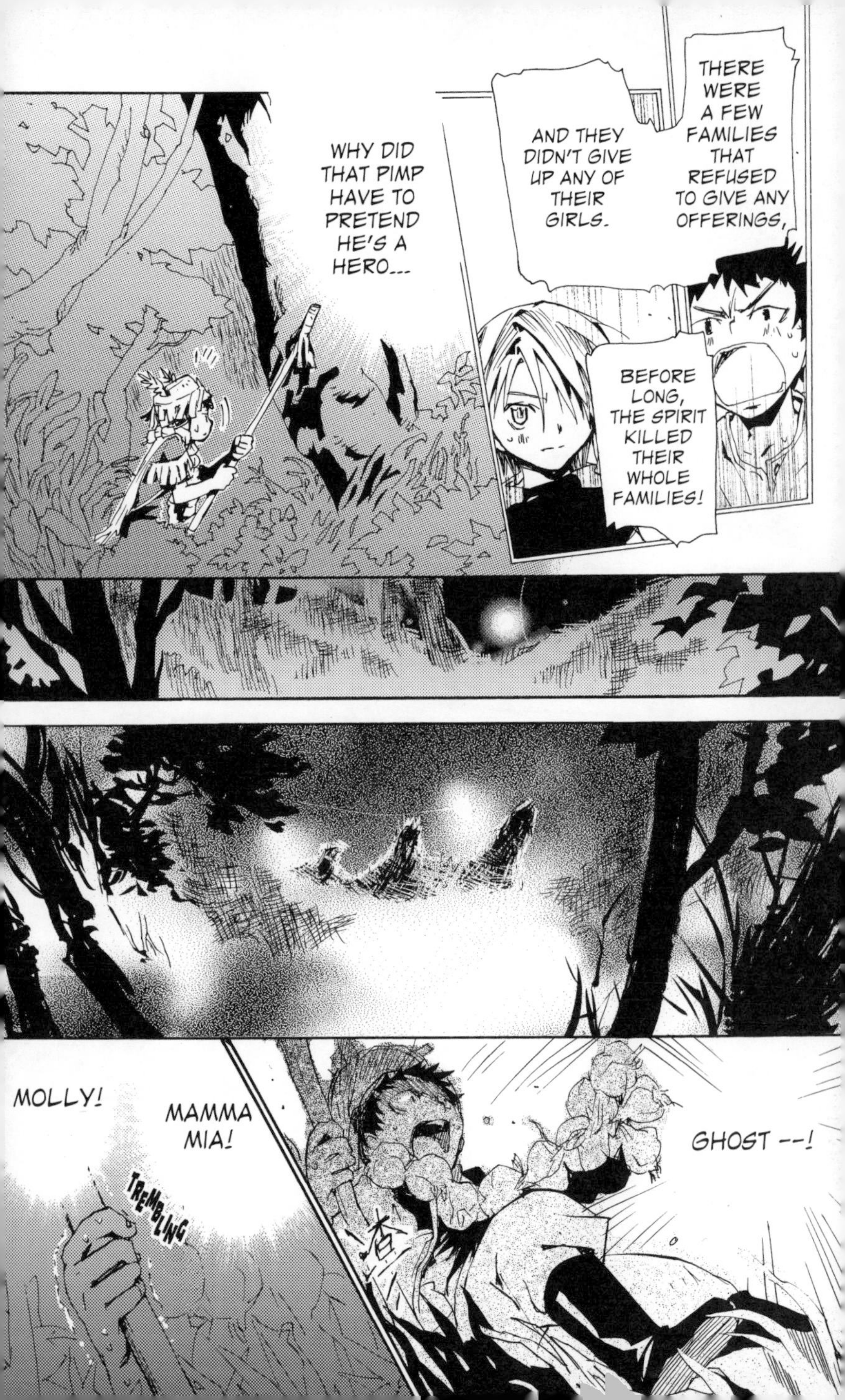
THERE WERE A FEW FAMILIES THAT REFUSED TO GIVE ANY OFFERINGS,
AND THEY DIDN'T GIVE UP ANY OF THEIR GIRLS.
BEFORE LONG, THE SPIRIT KILLED THEIR WHOLE FAMILIES!
WHY DID THAT PIMP HAVE TO PRETEND HE'S A HERO...
GHOST --!
MAMMA MIA!
TREMBLING
MOLLY!

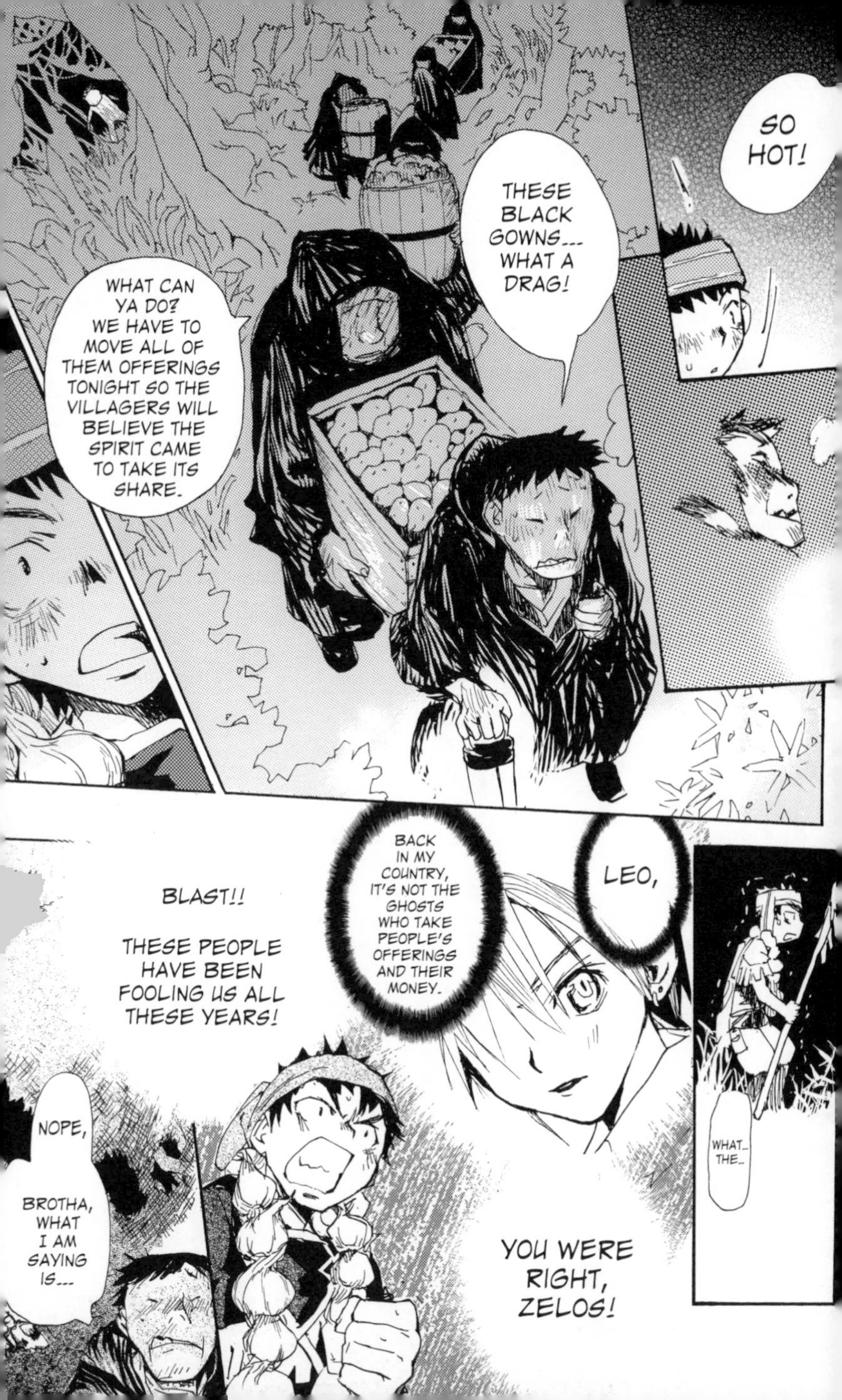
SO HOT!
!
THESE BLACK GOWNS... WHAT A DRAG!
WHAT CAN YA DO? WE HAVE TO MOVE ALL OF THEM OFFERINGS TONIGHT SO THE VILLAGERS WILL BELIEVE THE SPIRIT CAME TO TAKE ITS SHARE.
WHAT... THE...
LEO,
BACK IN MY COUNTRY, IT'S NOT THE GHOSTS WHO TAKE PEOPLE'S OFFERINGS AND THEIR MONEY.
BLAST!!
THESE PEOPLE HAVE BEEN FOOLING US ALL THESE YEARS!
YOU WERE RIGHT, ZELOS!
NOPE,
BROTHA, WHAT I AM SAYING IS...

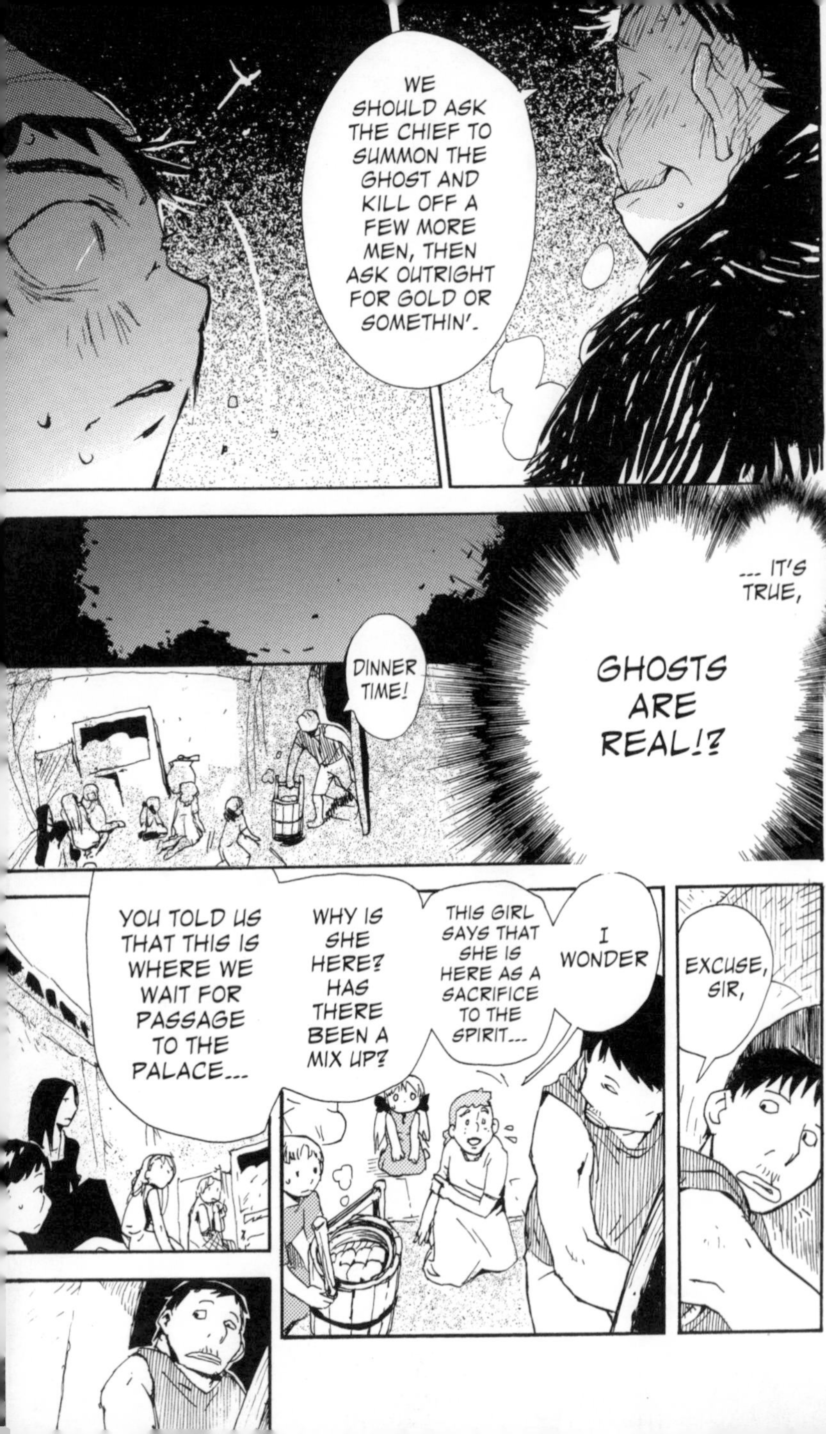
WE SHOULD ASK THE CHIEF TO SUMMON THE GHOST AND KILL OFF A FEW MORE MEN, THEN ASK OUTRIGHT FOR GOLD OR SOMETHIN'.
--- IT'S TRUE,
GHOSTS ARE REAL!?
DINNER TIME!
EXCUSE, SIR,
I WONDER
YOU TOLD US THAT THIS IS WHERE WE WAIT FOR PASSAGE TO THE PALACE---
WHY IS SHE HERE? HAS THERE BEEN A MIX UP?
THIS GIRL SAYS THAT SHE IS HERE AS A SACRIFICE TO THE SPIRIT---

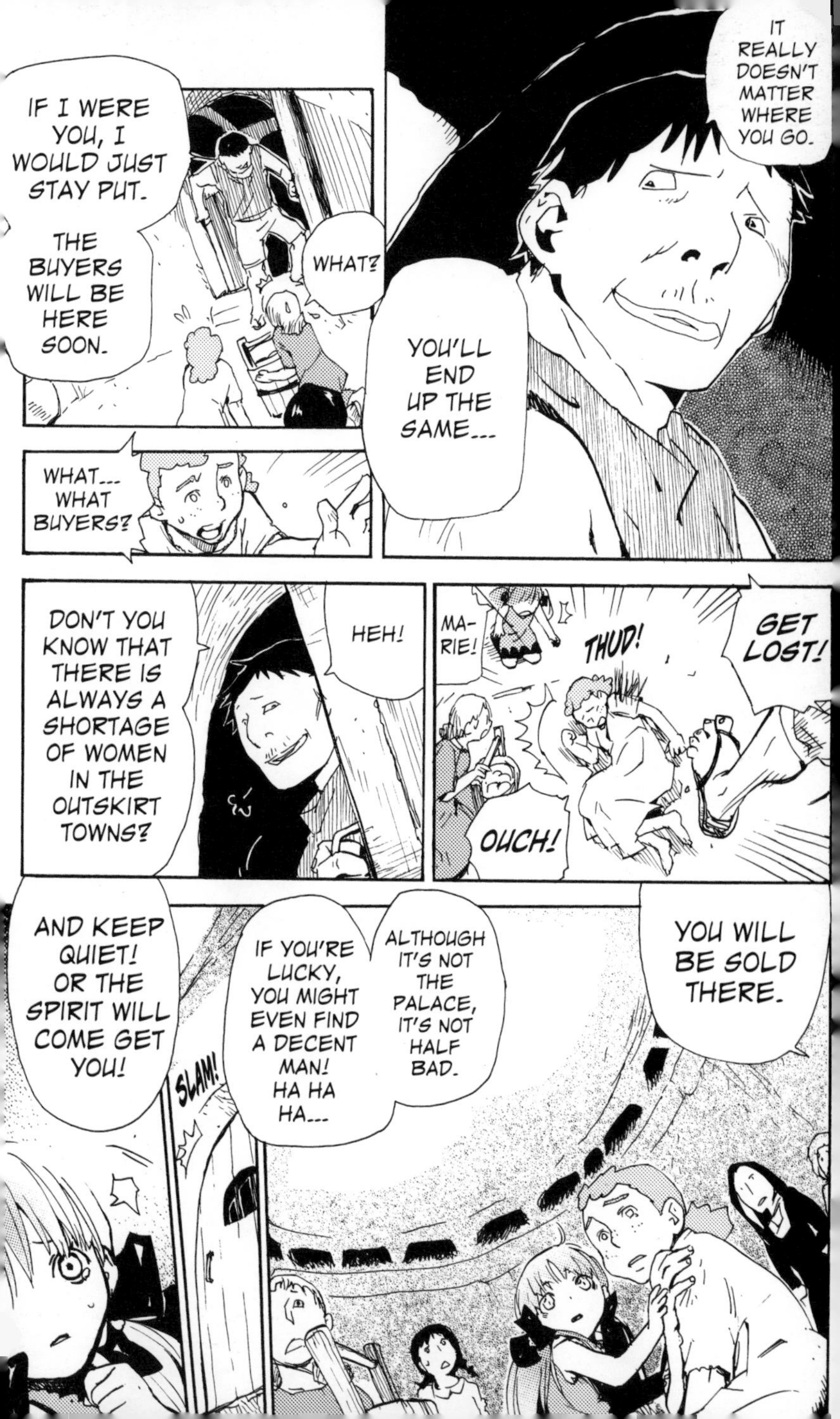
IT REALLY DOESN'T MATTER WHERE YOU GO.
YOU'LL END UP THE SAME...
IF I WERE YOU, I WOULD JUST STAY PUT.
THE BUYERS WILL BE HERE SOON.
WHAT?
WHAT... WHAT BUYERS?
GET LOST!
THUD!
MA-RIE!
OUCH!
HEH!
DON'T YOU KNOW THAT THERE IS ALWAYS A SHORTAGE OF WOMEN IN THE OUTSKIRT TOWNS?
YOU WILL BE SOLD THERE.
ALTHOUGH IT'S NOT THE PALACE, IT'S NOT HALF BAD.
IF YOU'RE LUCKY, YOU MIGHT EVEN FIND A DECENT MAN! HA HA HA...
SLAM!
AND KEEP QUIET! OR THE SPIRIT WILL COME GET YOU!

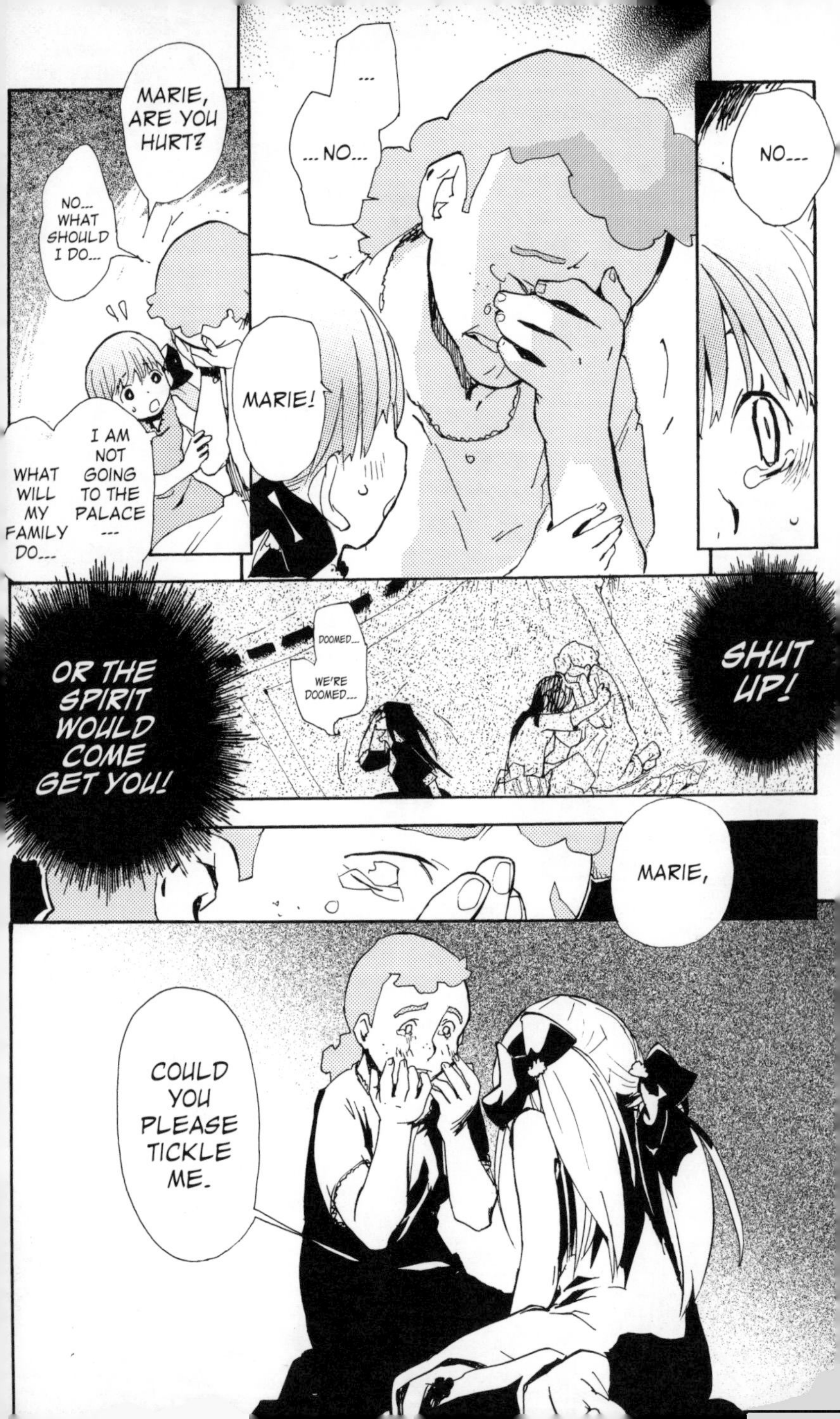
NO...
...
...NO...
MARIE!
MARIE, ARE YOU HURT?
NO... WHAT SHOULD I DO...
I AM NOT GOING TO THE PALACE ---
WHAT WILL MY FAMILY DO...
SHUT UP!
DOOMED...
WE'RE DOOMED...
OR THE SPIRIT WOULD COME GET YOU!
MARIE,
COULD YOU PLEASE TICKLE ME.

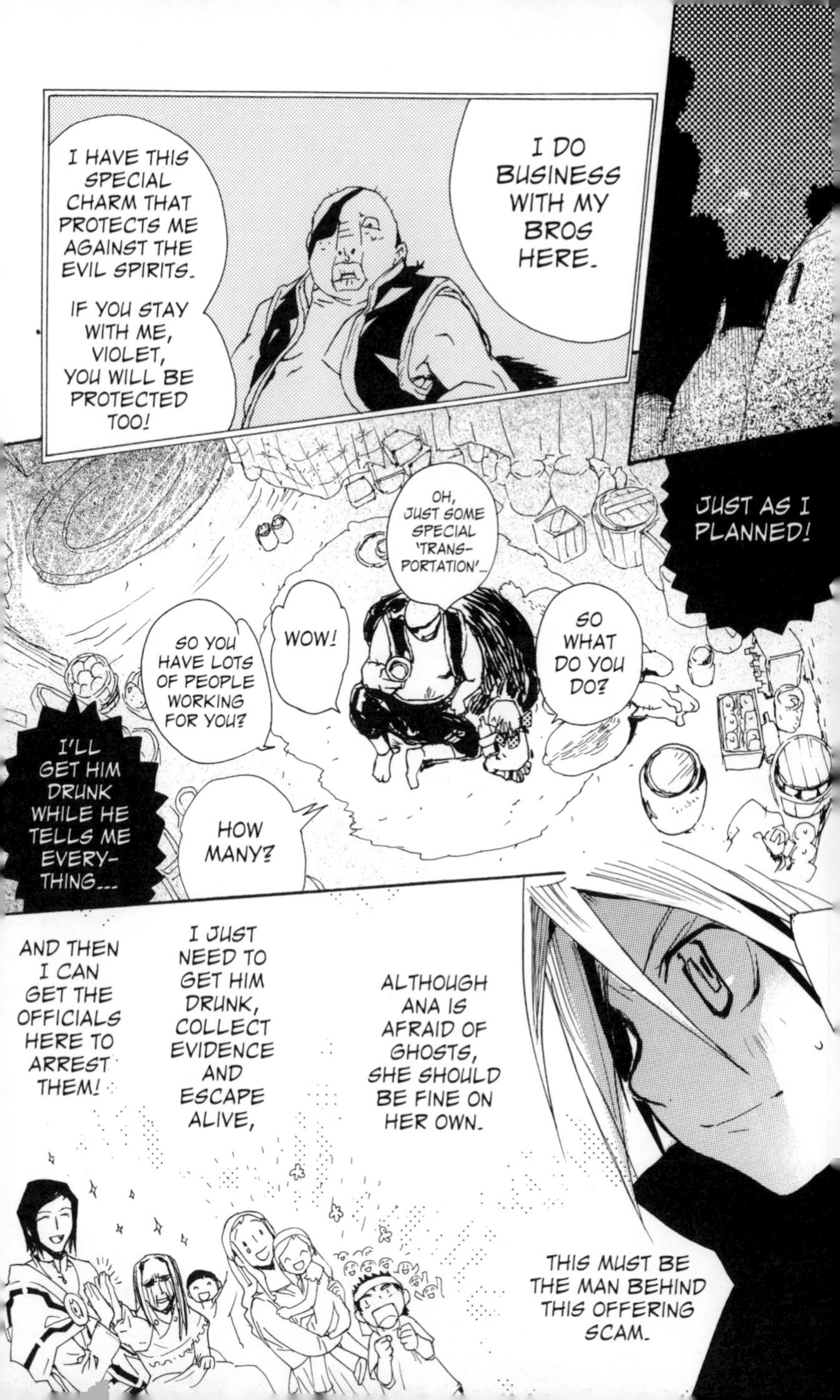
I DO BUSINESS WITH MY BROS HERE.
I HAVE THIS SPECIAL CHARM THAT PROTECTS ME AGAINST THE EVIL SPIRITS.
IF YOU STAY WITH ME, VIOLET, YOU WILL BE PROTECTED TOO!
JUST AS I PLANNED!
OH, JUST SOME SPECIAL 'TRANS-PORTATION'...
SO WHAT DO YOU DO?
WOW!
SO YOU HAVE LOTS OF PEOPLE WORKING FOR YOU?
I'LL GET HIM DRUNK WHILE HE TELLS ME EVERY-THING...
HOW MANY?
THIS MUST BE THE MAN BEHIND THIS OFFERING SCAM.
ALTHOUGH ANA IS AFRAID OF GHOSTS, SHE SHOULD BE FINE ON HER OWN.
I JUST NEED TO GET HIM DRUNK, COLLECT EVIDENCE AND ESCAPE ALIVE,
AND THEN I CAN GET THE OFFICIALS HERE TO ARREST THEM!

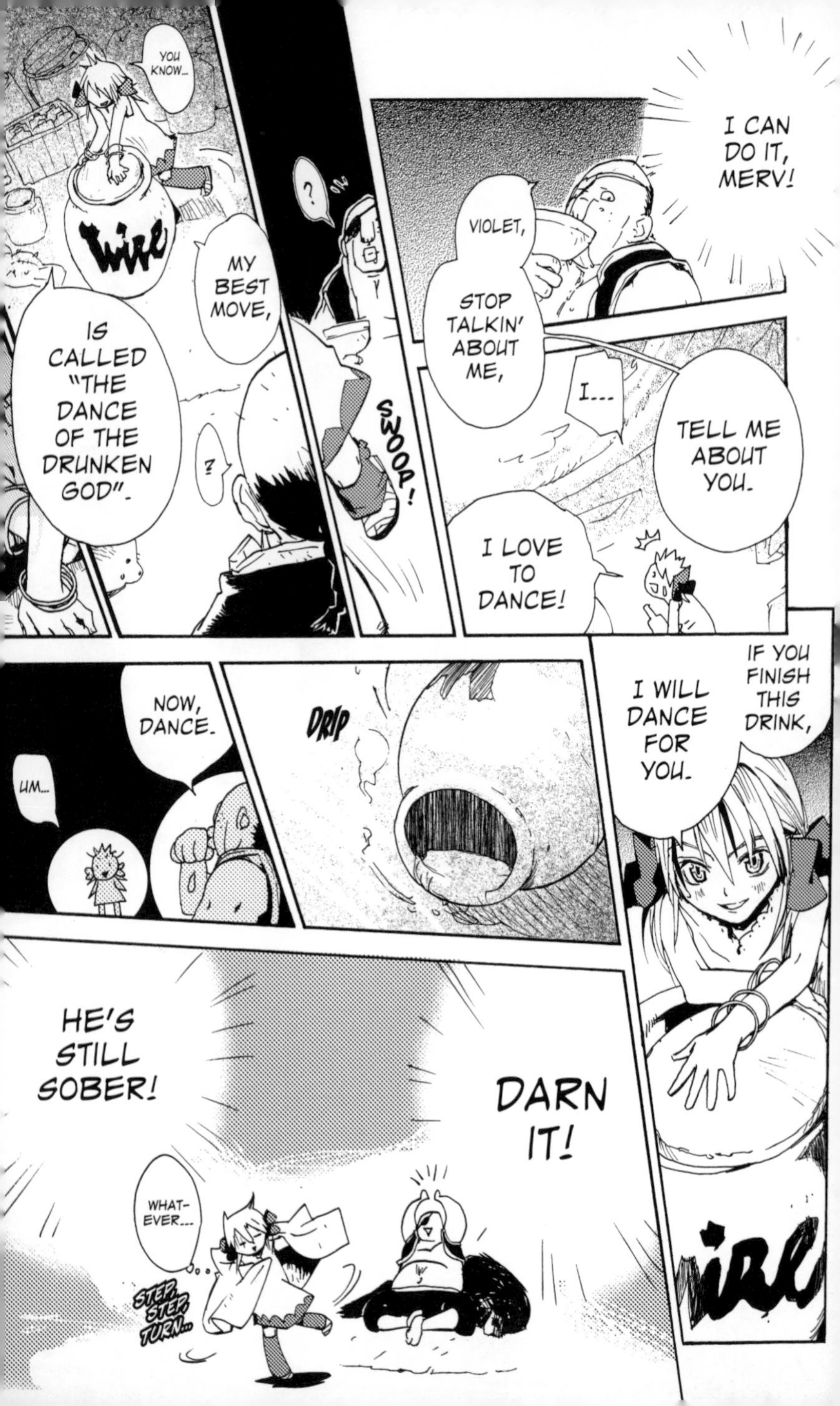
I CAN DO IT, MERV!
VIOLET,
STOP TALKIN' ABOUT ME,
TELL ME ABOUT YOU.
I...
I LOVE TO DANCE!
?
SWOOP!
YOU KNOW...
MY BEST MOVE,
IS CALLED "THE DANCE OF THE DRUNKEN GOD".
?
IF YOU FINISH THIS DRINK,
I WILL DANCE FOR YOU.
DRIP
NOW, DANCE.
UM...
DARN IT!
HE'S STILL SOBER!
WHATEVER...
STEP, STEP, TURN...

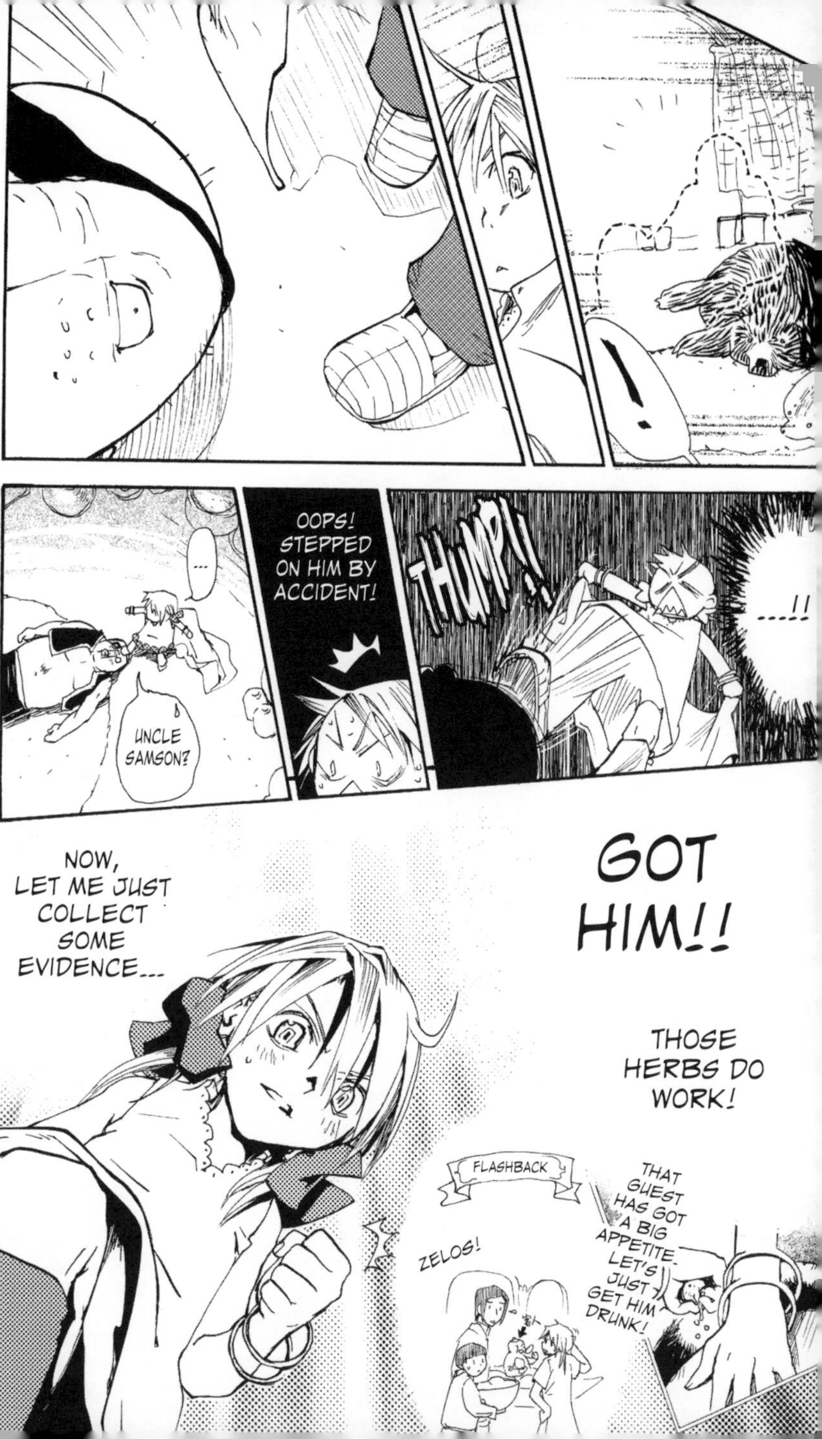
!
...!!
THUMP!!
OOPS! STEPPED ON HIM BY ACCIDENT!
...
UNCLE SAMSON?
GOT HIM!!
NOW, LET ME JUST COLLECT SOME EVIDENCE...
THOSE HERBS DO WORK!
FLASHBACK
THAT GUEST HAS GOT A BIG APPETITE. LET'S JUST GET HIM DRUNK!
ZELOS!

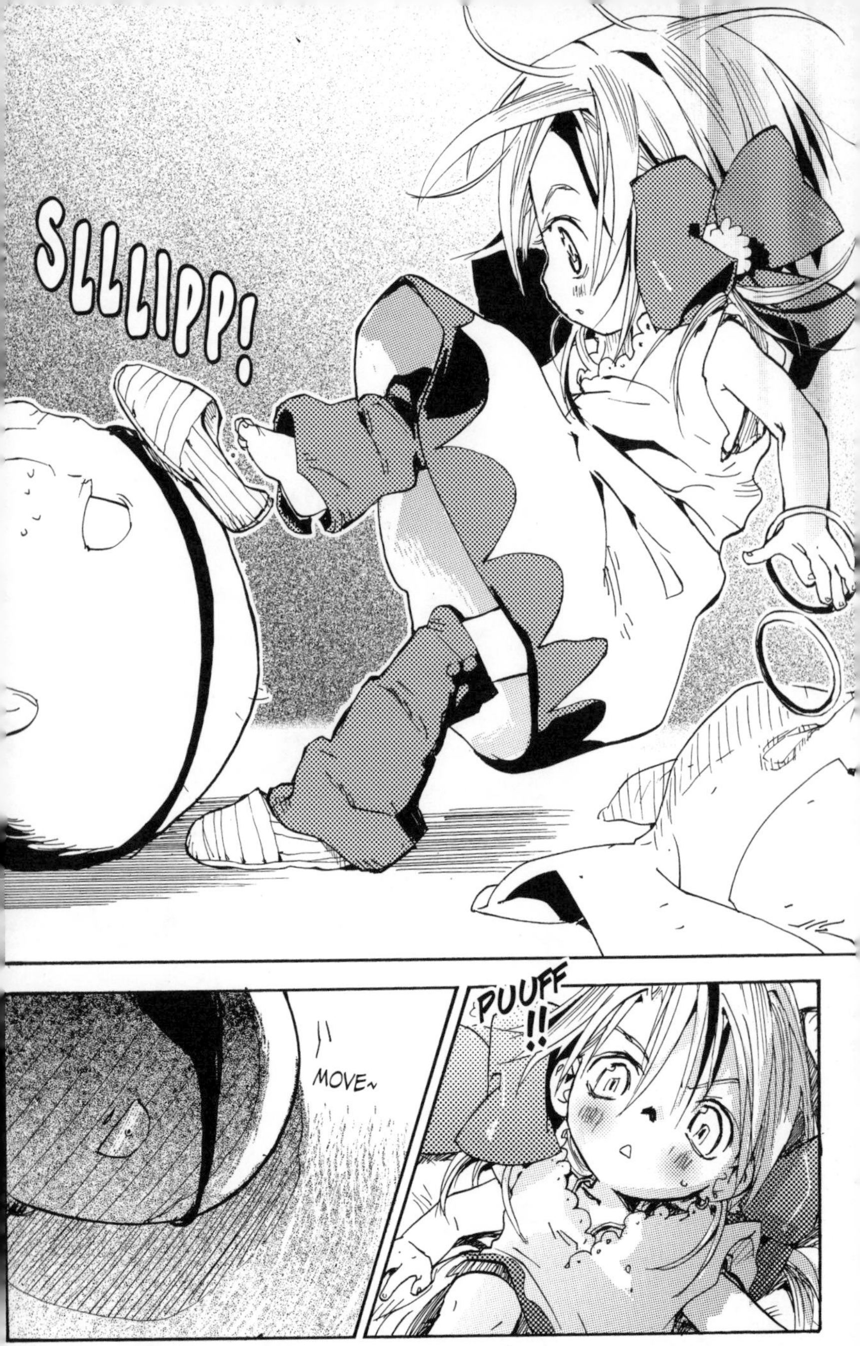
SLLLIPP!
PUUFF!!
MOVE~

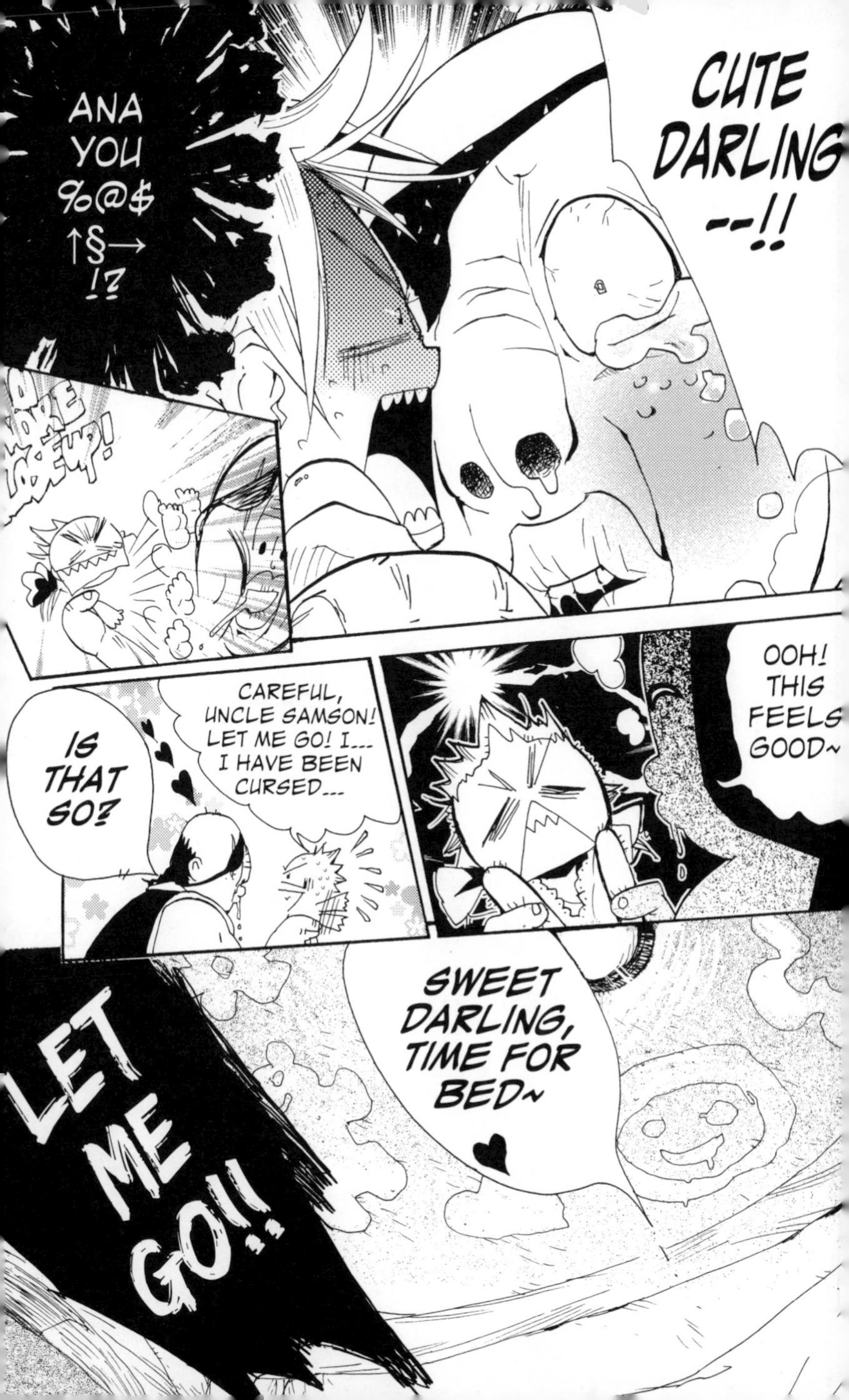
CUTE DARLING --!!
ANA YOU %@$ ↑§→ !?
OOH! THIS FEELS GOOD~
CAREFUL, UNCLE SAMSON! LET ME GO! I... I HAVE BEEN CURSED...
IS THAT SO?
SWEET DARLING, TIME FOR BED~
LET ME GO!!

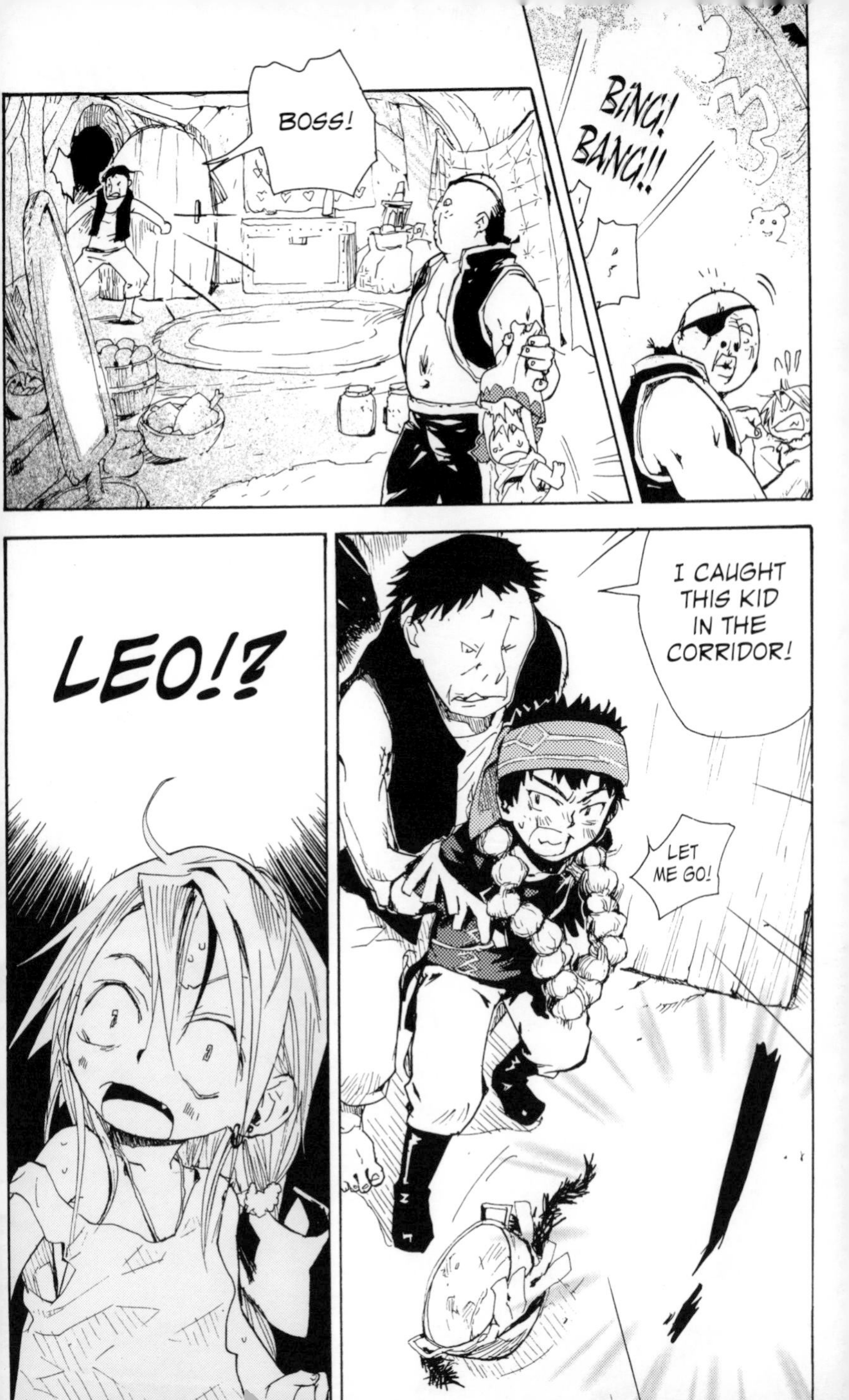
BING!
BANG!!
BOSS!
I CAUGHT THIS KID IN THE CORRIDOR!
LET ME GO!
LEO!?

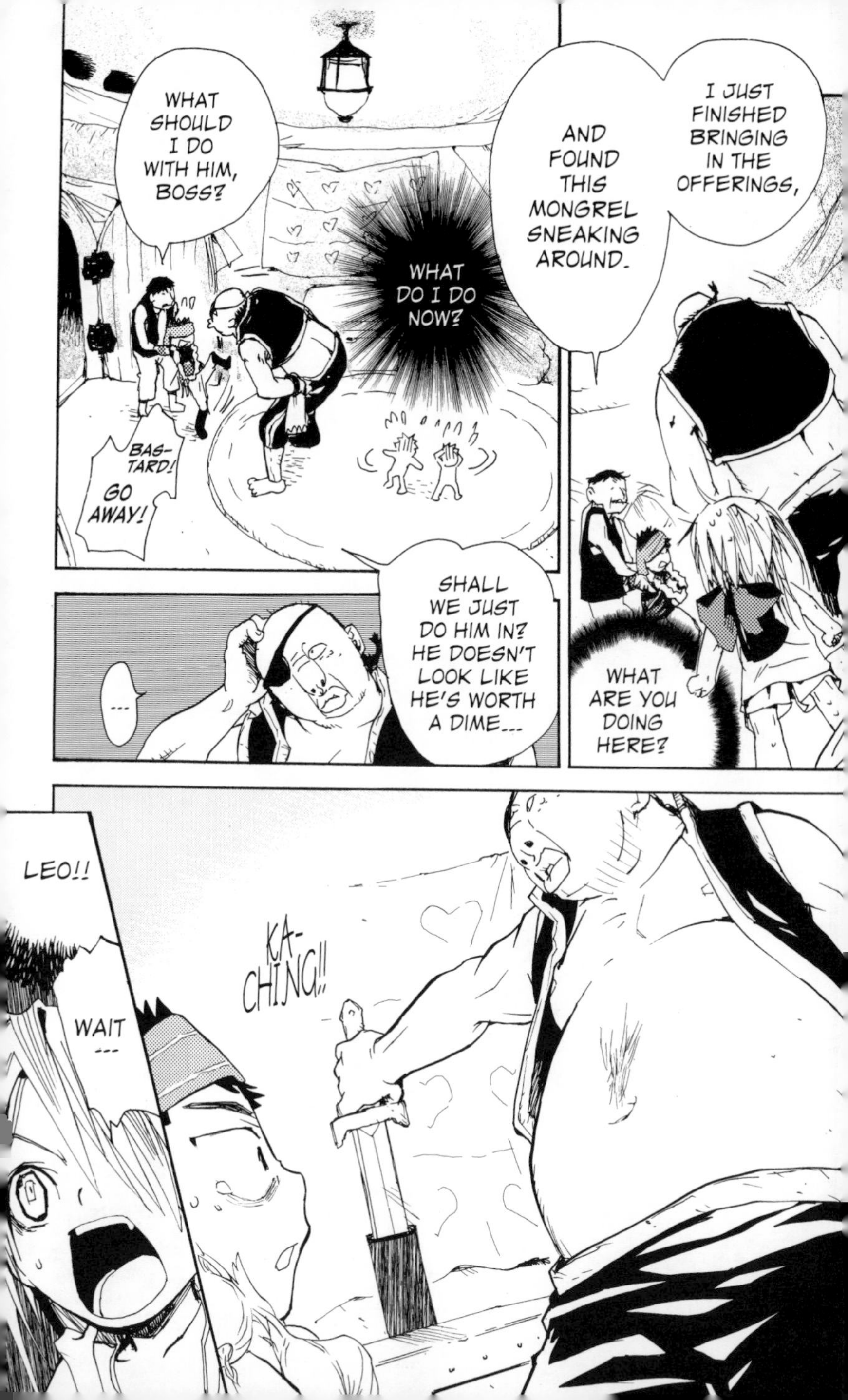
I JUST FINISHED BRINGING IN THE OFFERINGS,
AND FOUND THIS MONGREL SNEAKING AROUND.
WHAT ARE YOU DOING HERE?
WHAT SHOULD I DO WITH HIM, BOSS?
WHAT DO I DO NOW?
BASTARD!
GO AWAY!
SHALL WE JUST DO HIM IN? HE DOESN'T LOOK LIKE HE'S WORTH A DIME...
...
KA-CHING!!
LEO!!
WAIT ---

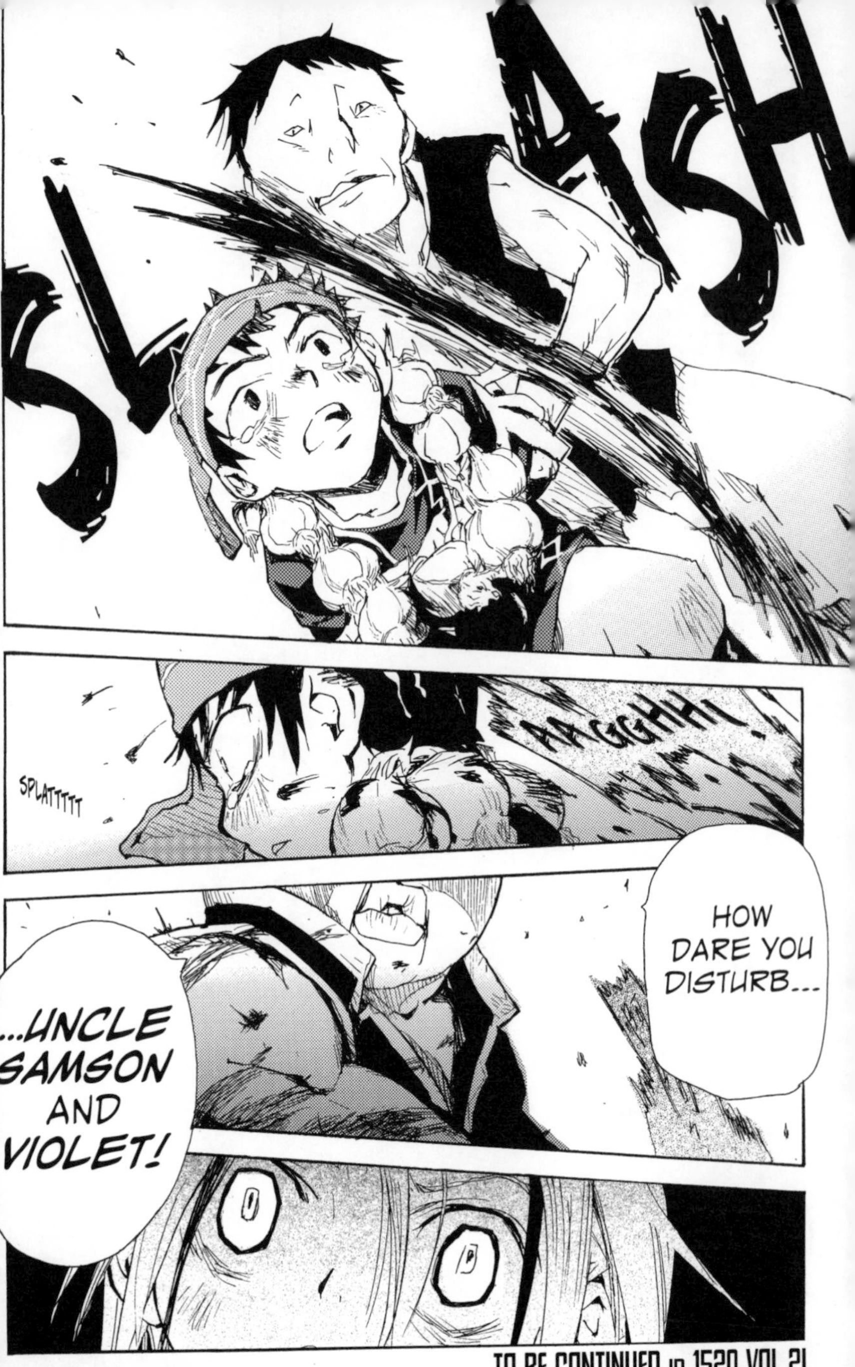
SLASH
AAGGHH!
SPLATTTTT
HOW DARE YOU DISTURB...
...UNCLE SAMSON AND VIOLET!

TO BE CONTINUED in 1520 VOL 2!

POSTSCRIPT

The gist of this story is about the transformation of age and size. It was meant to be a short story, and I am very surprised that it has accumulated into a whole volume.

Perhaps the spark of creativity of this story comes from the observation of little children. I hope I don't get into trouble for staring at them all the time!

(Perhaps I AM crooked.)

There is a three-stage transformation in this story. It wasn't easy to depict the differences. Perhaps it would have been more realistic to draw it like the illustrations below, but realism... is just too bothersome!

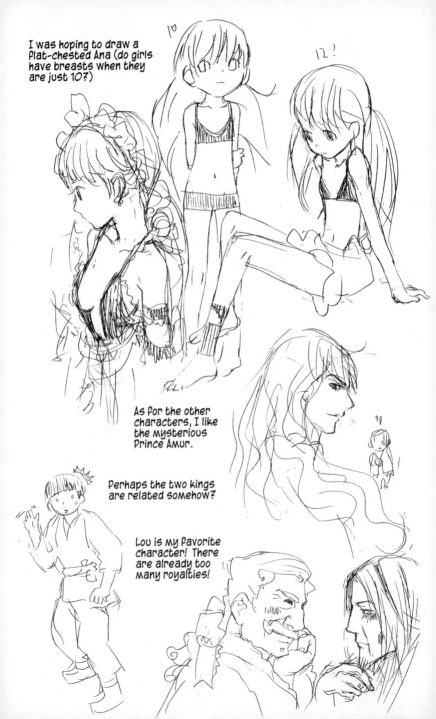

I was hoping to draw a flat-chested Ana (do girls have breasts when they are just 10?)

As for the other characters, I like the mysterious Prince Amur.

Perhaps the two kings are related somehow?

Lou is my favorite character! There are already too many royalties!

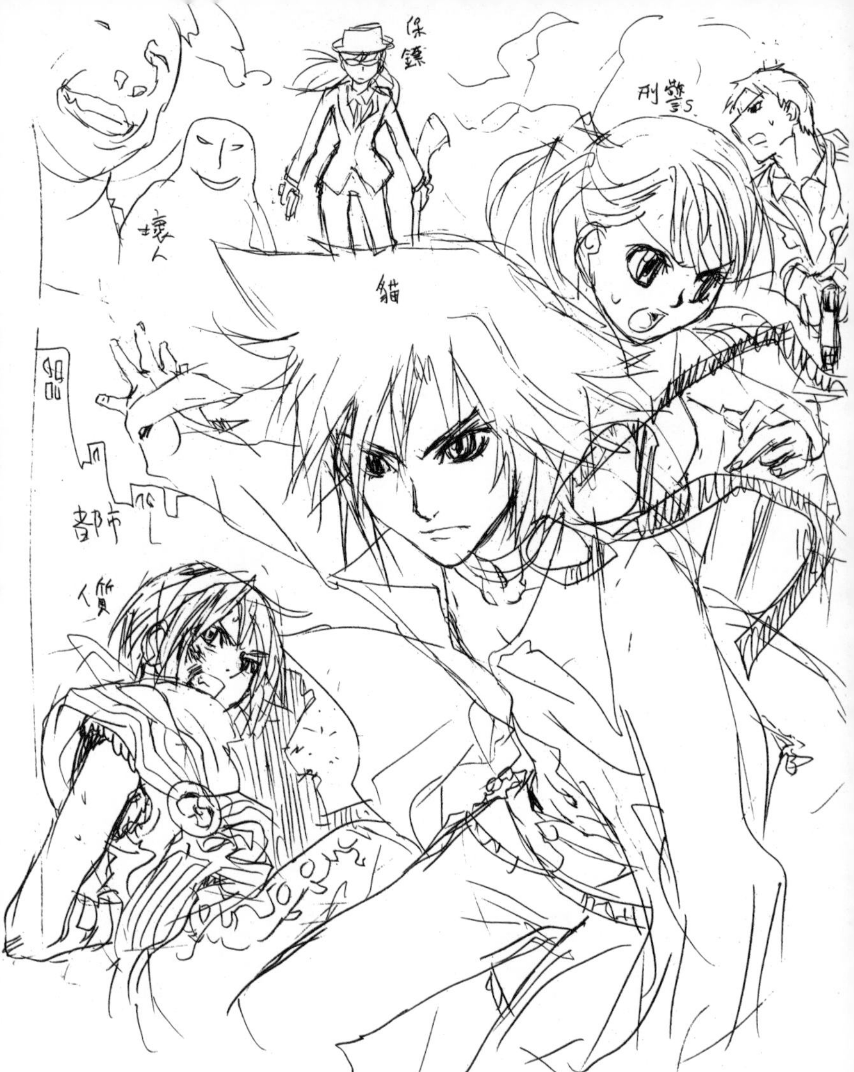
保鏢
刑警s
壞人
貓
都市
人質

If I could do a crossover of *1520* I'd do *Koon the Teenage Feline Detective*. A foreign prince is held ransom, and the Feline Detective must solve all puzzles and catch the villain!

Many thanks to Giffy, Lulu, and our anonymous brother for your tireless assistance, helping me through hell, a.k.a. deadlines. A big thank you to the editor for staying by my side. I count on you in the future!

Thank you, everyone!

KAVIE

NEXT ISSUE!

UDON

THE ADVENTURE
CONTINUES
1520 VOLUME 2,
ON SALE
NOVEMBER 2008!

1520 Vol.2
ISBN: 978-1-897376-06-5

1520 十五二十 Volume ①

Story and Art : KAI

English Translations : Leslie Chulasewok

Lettering: Matt Moylan

UDON STAFF
Chief of Operations: Erik Ko
Project Manager: Jim Zubkavich
Marketing Manger: Matt Moylan

English launguage version produced and published by
UDON Entertainment Corp. P.O. Box 32662, P.O. Village Gate,
Richmond Hill, Ontario, L4X 0A2, Canada.

www.udonentertainment.com

First Printing: August 2008
ISBN-13 : 978-1-897376-05-8   ISBN-10 : 1-897376-05-7
Printed in Canada

! WHOOPS

This is the back of the bo

1520 is a manga series originally published in Hong Kong. Traditional m is read in a 'reversed' format, starting at the right and heading toward left. The story begins where English readers expect to find the last because the spine of the book is on the opposite side.

Preserving the original artwork, we've decided to leave the original for intact. Check the examples below to see how to read the word balloons in proper order.

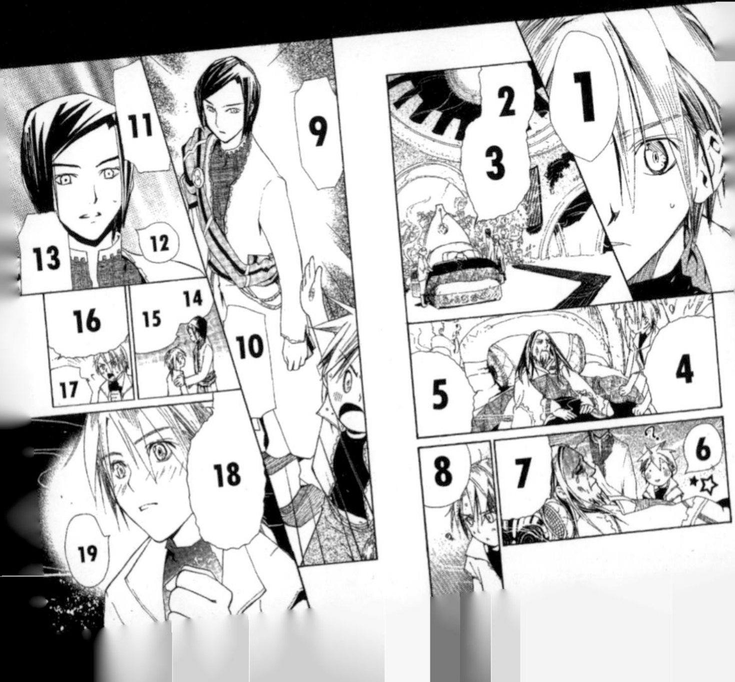
1
2
3
4
5
6
7
8
9
10
11
12
13
14
15
16
17
18
19